THE FARMER IN ENGLAND, 1650–1980

Rural Worlds: Economic, Social and Cultural Histories of Agricultures and Rural Societies

Series Editor: Richard W. Hoyle, University of Reading, UK

We like to forget that agriculture is one of the core human activities. In historic societies most people lived in the countryside: a high, if falling proportion of the population were engaged in the production and processing of foodstuffs. The possession of land was a key form of wealth: it brought not only income from tenants but prestige, access to a rural lifestyle and often political power. Nor could government ever be disinterested in the countryside, whether to maintain urban food supply, as a source of taxation, or to maintain social peace. Increasingly it managed every aspect of the countryside. Agriculture itself and the social relations within the countryside were in constant flux as farmers reacted to new or changing opportunities, and landlords sought to maintain or increase their incomes. Moreover, urban attitudes to the landscape and its inhabitants were constantly shifting.

These questions of competition and change, production, power and perception are the primary themes of the series. It looks at change and competition in the countryside: social relations within it and between urban and rural societies. The series offers a forum for the publication of the best work on all of these issues, straddling the economic, social and cultural, concentrating on the rural history of Britain and Ireland, Europe and its colonial empires, and North America over the past millennium.

Series Advisory Board:
Paul Brassley, University of Exeter, UK
R. Douglas Hurt, Purdue University, USA
Leen Van Molle, KU Leuven, Belgium
Mats Morell, Stockholm University, Sweden
Phillipp Schofield, Aberystwyth University, UK
Nicola Verdon, Sheffield Hallam University, UK
Paul Warde, University of East Anglia, UK

The Farmer in England, 1650–1980

Edited by
RICHARD W. HOYLE
University of Reading, UK

Routledge
Taylor & Francis Group

LONDON AND NEW YORK

First Published 2013 by Ashgate Publisher

Published 2016 by Routledge
2 Park Square, Milton Park, Abingdon, Oxfordshire OX14 4RN
711 Third Avenue, New York, NY 10017, USA

First issued in paperback 2016

Routledge is an imprint of the Taylor & Francis Group, an informa business

British Library Cataloguing in Publication Data
A catalogue record for this book is available from the British Library

The Library of Congress has cataloged the printed edition as follows:
The farmer in England, 1650–1980 / edited by Richard W. Hoyle.
    pages cm. -- (Rural worlds : economic, social, and cultural histories of agricultures and rural societies)
  Includes bibliographical references and index.
  ISBN 978-1-4094-3961-5 (hardcover)
1. Agriculture – England – History. 2. Farmers – England – History. 3.
Farm life – England – History. I. Hoyle, R. W. (Richard W.), editor of compilation.
  S522.G7F37 2013
  635.0942--dc23

2013008983

ISBN 13: 978-1-138-27225-5 (pbk)
ISBN 13: 978-1-4094-3961-5 (hbk)

For Ted Collins

Contents

List of Figures

List of Tables

List of Abbreviations

AgHR	*Agricultural History Review*
BPP	*British Parliamentary Papers*
JRASE	*Journal of the Royal Agricultural Society of England*
ODNB	*Oxford Dictionary of National Biography*
RO	Record Office

List of Abbreviations

List of Contributors

John Broad is currently based at the Cambridge Group where he is writing a book on rural housing, and researching landownership and tenancies from the 1798 Land Tax.

Joyce Burnette is Professor of Economics at Wabash College in Crawfordsville, Indiana, and is author of *Gender, Work and Wages in Industrial Revolution Britain* (2008).

Philip Conford is an authority on the history of the organic food and farming movement in Britain, and a former doctoral student of Ted Collins. His most recent book is *The Development of the Organic Network: Linking People and Themes, 1945–95* (2011).

Hilary Crowe qualified as a chartered accountant and returned to History in mid-career. She now lectures for the Open University and is a director of the University of Cumbria. She also serves, as did Ted Collins, as Treasurer of the British Agricultural History Society.

Peter Dewey's research interests are in nineteenth- and twentieth-century British agrarian history. He is currently working on a history of the international farm machinery industry. Many years ago he was Ted Collins's doctoral student.

Andy Gritt is senior lecturer in history at the University of Central Lancashire. He researches rural history and poverty and welfare in the north-west of England.

Jennifer Holt has long been a student of history. For part of her working life she was an accountant and combines both areas of expertise in the work presented here. She is also the editor of the *Diary of Thomas Fenwick of Burrow Hall and Nunriding, 1774–94* (four vols, 2012–13).

Richard W. Hoyle succeeded Ted Collins as Professor of Rural History at the University of Reading. He is editor of *Agricultural History Review*.

John Martin is Reader in Agrarian History at De Montfort University and has published widely on the transformation of the countryside since 1900. He was the series consultant for the BBC 'Wartime Farm' series (2012). His PhD (of 1992) was supervised by Ted Collins.

Nicola Verdon is Reader in Modern British History at Sheffield Hallam University and has published widely on women, work and the countryside since 1800.

Susanna Wade Martins is an Honorary Research Fellow in the School of History at the University of East Anglia. She has written on agricultural and landscape topics. Her most recent publication is a biography of Thomas William Coke of Holkham, *Coke of Norfolk (1754–1842): A Biography* (2009).

Chapter 1

Introduction: Recovering the Farmer

Richard W. Hoyle[1]

As is the case in every occupation in which a large number of persons are engaged, we find amongst farmers great diversity of character, means and attainments. The farming class includes men of every imaginable description and reputation, from the most honourable and upright down to those who would not hesitate to take every kind of advantage of their neighbours when they could find a safe opportunity of doing so. In it we find also men possessed of very considerable wealth – more than equal, in this respect, to meet any demands likely to be made on them in their circumstances; while we find also men of more moderate means, able only to carry on their businesses profitably, and also men who are much straitened in their circumstances as to be in a state of comparative poverty. In it we also find men possessed of strong natural talents, and of high attainments, fully qualified to carry on their business on enlightened principles; while of course, a large proportion are men of moderate capacity and attainments, sufficient to enable them to conduct their business in the usual routine way; and not an inconsiderable proportion are so ill-informed and unskilful as not to be able to conduct their concerns in such a way as to insure either profit or comfort to themselves, or those with whom they have to deal.

This great variety of character is only what is to be expected in a class of men made up of all grades of society; for here we find retired merchants and tradesmen, with professional men of every description, besides those that have been brought up as cultivators of the soil; and hence we find all kinds of management on different subjects held, according to the views entertained by the respective parties, which are, of course, biased according to the particular training each has had in his earlier pursuits and habits in life.[2]

In writings on agricultural history, farmers are so often the bridesmaid and so rarely the bride.[3] Their role in the capitalist agriculture that emerged in England in the eighteenth-century (and perhaps earlier) is well understood.

---

[1]   I am grateful to Paul Brassley for his comments on an earlier version of this chapter.

[2]   Robert E. Brown, *The Book of the Landed Estate* (Edinburgh, 1869), p. 19. Brown described himself as a factor and estate agent of Wass, Yorkshire.

[3]   My own interest in farmers, and appreciation of their significance, has been fired by two meetings: the first a symposium on farmers arranged by John Beckett and Michael Turner at the Agricultural History Society conference in 1995, and a conference organised by Jeremy Burchardt at

Sometimes they owned the land they farmed, but more usually they rented it from a landlord who used the farmer to distance himself from the day-to-day business of cultivation. The farmer paid a rent – normally fixed for a period of years – and brought his capital and skill to exploit the land. He accepted the risk of farming, both in the sense of variable prices and variable yields. His income could therefore fluctuate widely from year to year, but out of this he had to pay rent, a variety of local rates and his workforce (Figure 1.1).[4]

To a limited degree the tenant farmer could use his landlord as a banker, looking to him for credit in poor years (by deferring rent payments) and perhaps asking him for investment in his farm. But without a farmer, the landlord had no rent, forcing him to either farm the land himself or leave it unexploited. Landlords needed tenants much more than tenants needed landlords: the relationship is, to coin a phrase, asymmetrical. Moreover, with the growing sophistication of farming, the landlord was not simply looking for a tenant with skill, but one with capital on a scale which would allow the farmer to operate the farm at a high level of efficiency to generate a high level of rent, and which would allow him to outride poor years.[5] And in this English farmers, it would be agreed, were spectacularly successful. At its best English agriculture was extremely efficient. The size of the unit of production progressively grew through the eighteenth and nineteenth centuries whilst the tendency of the farmer to become a tenant became more marked. Farmers themselves could live well, at least until the 1870s. Thereafter, farming profits were low, agriculture was depressed and farmers struggled to turn a penny in profit. This long agricultural recession lasted from the 1870s to the outbreak of the Second World War with only a few years of remission: something like it blanketed British farming between the late 1980s and the early years of this century. For a historically short period, from the beginning of the Second World War to the late 1980s, farming was again profitable, and farmers grew profits on a regime of state-fixed prices and government subsidies. By this time a much larger proportion of farmers were not tenants but owner-occupiers.

This is what the textbooks tell us. And yet we know very little about farmers as either a social group or as individuals, and one of the purposes of this introduction is to ask why. It is true that the seventh volume of the *Agrarian History of England and Wales*, edited by Ted Collins and covering the years 1850 to 1914, contains a chapter on the farmer by the late Gordon Mingay alongside ones on landlords and farm labour, and a further discussion by Alun Howkins, but none of the other volumes of the *Agrarian History* covering the

---

the Rural History Centre, University of Reading, in 2001, 'A man outstanding in his field? The social history of farmers.' Regrettably neither meeting was given the permanence of print.

⁴　For evidence of the variation in income, below pp. 92–3, Table 3.6.

⁵　John M. Wilson, in his *Rural Cyclopedia* (4 vols, Edinburgh, 1847–49), II, p. 223, directly connected the amount of rent a tenant could pay with his capital.

Figure 1.1   'The Farmer's Taxed-Cart', from *Punch*, 9 March 1850, p. 94

last half millennium had one, certainly not the volume for the early twentieth century solely authored by Edith Whetham.[6] Indeed, there is still no twentieth-century equivalent to Mingay's chapter anywhere in the literature.[7] Howkins' recent textbook on the *Death of Rural England* paid the farmer little attention, lumping landowners and farmers together in one chapter and devoting the next one to farm workers and domestic servants.[8] And so whilst books on landowners – collectively and singly – proliferate, farmers have yet to find their Boswell – or their F.M.L. Thompson.[9]

The purpose of this book is to focus attention on the farmer. We do not propose a revival of the old approach of eulogising a minority of improving farmers or men of unusual prominence.[10] Instead our farmers are selected for the quality of the records they left behind, so whilst their lives and contribution to progress might be more ordinary, the historian is able to draw their economic and even political life in greater detail. But our hope is, that like the progressive farmer, we will be emulated. We hope to show the potential yields that might be secured by exploiting the farmers' own records and other sources which record their voices.

I

Before proceeding further, we ought to note that the title of this book is, to a degree, an anachronism.[11] Whilst today we understand a farmer to be a person who cultivates land for profit rather than subsistence (so 'farmer' is the

---

[6] Gordon Mingay, 'The Farmer', in E.J.T. Collins (ed.), *The Agrarian History of England and Wales*, VII, *1850–1914* (2 vols, Cambridge, 2000), I, pp. 759–809 and Alun Howkins, ibid., 'Social, Cultural and Domestic Life', II, pp. 1369–86. For an earlier essay along similar lines to Mingay's, see B.A. Holderness, 'The Victorian Farmer', in G.E. Mingay (ed.), *The Victorian Countryside* (2 vols, London, 1981), I, pp. 227–44.

[7] See here the comments in M.E. Turner, J.V. Beckett and B. Afton, *Farm Production in England, 1700–1914* (Oxford, 2001), p. 29 which remain every bit as true as when they were written more than a decade ago.

[8] Alun Howkins, *The Death of Rural England: A Social History of the Countryside since 1900* (2003).

[9] For an earlier period, there is the pioneering work of Mildred Campbell, *The English Yeoman under Elizabeth and the Early Stuarts* (New Haven, 1942, repr. 1960) which continues to read very well. Thompson has written extensively on the aristocracy as landowners throughout a long career, starting with *English Landed Society in the Nineteenth Century* (1963).

[10] Arthur Young, *On the Husbandry of Three Celebrated British Farmers* (London, 1811); James A. Scott Watson and May Elliott Hobbs, *Great Farmers* (1937, 2nd edn, London, 1951); and see also J. Wentworth Day, *The New Yeomen of England* (London, 1952).

[11] This discussion is an expansion of comments made by Turner, Beckett and Afton, *Farm Production*, pp. 30–31.

Table 1.1   Farming occupations in wills proved in the Prerogative Court of Canterbury, 1600–1858

	Farmer		Husbandman		Yeoman		Total
	n	per cent	n	per cent	n	per cent	
1600–09	0	0.00	419	20.16	1659	79.84	2078
1610–19	0	0.00	669	20.54	2588	79.46	3257
1629–29	1	0.03	509	17.41	2414	82.56	2924
1630–39	0	0.00	585	17.65	2730	82.35	3315
1649–49	3	0.08	560	15.83	2975	84.09	3538
1650–59	31	0.16	4118	21.88	14,669	77.95	18818
1660–69	3	0.10	445	14.11	2705	85.79	3153
1670–79	3	0.19	130	8.21	1451	91.60	1584
1680–89	4	0.28	130	9.09	1296	90.63	1430
1690–99	9	0.82	106	9.71	977	89.47	1092
1700–09	9	0.81	68	6.13	1032	93.06	1109
1710–19	22	2.07	64	6.03	976	91.90	1062
1720–29	39	3.05	102	7.97	1139	88.98	1280
1730–39	37	3.44	98	9.11	941	87.45	1076
1740–49	66	6.46	90	8.81	865	84.72	1021
1750–59	113	9.78	91	7.88	951	82.34	1155
1760–69	221	12.62	147	8.40	1383	78.98	1751
1770–79	327	17.04	125	6.51	1467	76.45	1919
1780–89	434	20.99	112	5.42	1522	73.60	2068
1790–99	590	26.62	92	4.15	1534	69.22	2216
1800–09	1039	31.31	114	3.44	2165	65.25	3318
1810–19	1247	35.14	112	3.16	2190	61.71	3549
1820–29	1439	37.82	91	2.39	2275	59.79	3805
1830–39	1687	42.36	70	1.76	2226	55.89	3983
1840–49	2289	51.16	58	1.30	2127	47.54	4474
1850–59	2278	56.77	54	1.35	1681	41.89	4013

Source: Calculated from the online catalogue for TNA, PROB 11. Note that the court acts as a national court during the 1650s, hence the very large number of wills proved. The figures for this decade are not comparable with those from before or after.

opposite to 'peasant'), the usage was less well established in the eighteenth and earlier centuries. The word is a coinage from the verb 'to farm', whose original meaning was to take an asset at rent. It was therefore usual to talk of the farm of lands but also the farm of taxes or the farm of tithes. Early usages of this sort are noted in the *Oxford English Dictionary* from Chaucer onwards. We have William Harrison in the 1560s speaking of 'The yeomen are for the most part farmers to gentlemen' meaning that they were tenants. It was a small step sideways from the farming of any asset to the more specific meaning of 'One who rents land for the purpose of cultivation'. The current definition of farmer as one who 'One who cultivates a farm, whether as tenant or owner; one who "farms" land, or makes agriculture his occupation' is familiar from the late sixteenth century onwards. On the other hand, the people we call farmers were widely referred to as yeomen or husbandmen, both coinages surviving into the nineteenth century. It may be suggested that yeoman was a status designation where farmer was more of an economic designation, and people who were farmers preferred to be called yeoman (or husbandman) on formal occasions. Yeomen may have been regarded as farmers who owned their own land albeit, in some cases, as a copyholder rather than a freeholder. The *Oxford English Dictionary* helpfully quotes William Cobbett on this point in 1821: 'Those only who *rent* ... are, properly speaking, *farmers*. Those who till their *own land* are *yeomen*; and, when I was a boy, it was the common practice to call the former *farmers* and the latter *yeomen-farmers*.' Of course this may have been a pedantic distinction: someone meeting a cultivator of the land in the road could hardly ask about his tenurial status before deciding whether he was a farmer or a yeoman. Increasingly it was simply assumed – from manners and dress – that he was a farmer. Of course, well-off farmers might well expect to be called gentlemen and, of course, plenty of gentlemen farmed.

The way in which the three titles of farmer, husbandman and yeomen continued to be used side by side (and perhaps interchangeably) may be seen from Table 1.1. This gives the relative usage of the terms by persons making wills proved in the Prerogative Court of Canterbury between 1600 and the closure of the court in 1858. The numbers are large, but this is an odd sample because those whose executors sought probate here, rather than at a diocesan court, were probably more prosperous individuals drawn mainly from southern England. In the 1650s the nature of the court changed and it was, for a short period, the national probate court, hence the large number of wills proved in that one decade. The word 'farmer' as an occupational designation was virtually unknown before the Civil War and really only entered common usage after the beginning of the nineteenth century. Husbandman as a descriptor tailed away after the mid seventeenth century but the title was still being used in the early nineteenth by small numbers of testators whilst – surprising to say – there were nearly as many people coming to the court each year in the early nineteenth century being called yeomen as there were before the Civil War. Contemporary usage therefore differs somewhat from the historians', for many of the latter would probably regard the title yeoman as obsolete by the beginning of the eighteenth century, and would see its reappearance late in the century as the name for the militia as being a deliberately anachronistic revival, which conveyed a sense of solidity and patriotic virtue.

There would doubtless always have been a high degree of interchangeability. In 1651 Nathaniel Newbury published *The Yeoman's Prerogative or the Honour of Husbandry: A Sermon Preached to Some and Dedicated to all the Yeomen and Farmers of Kent* but if he meant to imply any distinction between the two, he referred throughout his sermon to the husbandman. An anonymous writer published a volume entitled *The Rational Farmer and Practical Husbandman* in 1745. In 1792 the Rev. John Trusler preached on the *Importance, Utility and Duty of a Farmer's Life*, but he too freely referred to husbandmen. To gauge from the titles of their books, late eighteenth-century agricultural authors saw their audience as being farmers: so the *Farmer's Kalender* by Arthur Young (first edition 1771), Richard Parkinson's *The Experienced Farmer* (1798), William Hogg, *The New and Complete English Farmer* (1798) and so on.

'Farmer', then, is best regarded as an occupational category. Correctly, farmers were people who made their living from rented land and might be distinguished from the more status-based title of yeoman who were, in effect, farmers who owned their land and therefore had a range of political rights.[12] But in economic terms, husbandmen are taken to be smaller farmers and yeomen larger ones. The more successful farmers and yeomen probably assumed the title of gentleman. This matter of nomenclature could doubtless be followed much further, and its nuances unpicked. For the moment we can be clear that the word we use probably only adopted its present usage in the eighteenth and was far from universally adopted in the nineteenth century.

As an occupational designation, the term 'farmer' covers a wide range of individuals. The point is readily made that farmers were not a homogeneous category of people. Robert E. Brown has already been cited on the range and diversity of the farming community. Any discussion has to acknowledge an enormous range in holding size.[13] Size cannot be separated from landscape and economy: superficially enormous farms in upland England such as those

---

[12]   For an attempt of 1796 to define a farmer, see John Broad in Chapter 6 of this volume. Interestingly, this author thought that a farmer needed a weight of rent on his back to stimulate his production.

[13]   The literature on farm size after records become readily available in the mid-nineteenth century is enormous. See, for illustrative specimens, D.B. Grigg, 'Farm Size in England and Wales from Early Victorian Times to the Present', *AgHR* 35 (1987), pp. 179–98; Collins in *Agrarian History* VII (i), pp. 179–89; B. Afton and M. Turner, 'The Size of Agricultural Holdings', in *Agrarian History* VII (ii),

considered subsequently by Hilary Crowe might contain extensive areas of poor grazing, whilst smaller pastoral farms might actually be quite lucrative for their proprietors where they had a ready sale for dairy products.[14] We need to remember that in every generation there were always some farmers whose properties were perhaps too small, who lacked capital to farm them efficiently, and who therefore lived in state of relative poverty: a someone writing as 'Scrutator' in *Baily's Monthly Magazine* in the early 1860s described a 'variety of farmer':

> the man who has sprung from the ranks, that is, one from small beginnings, as a retailer of potatoes, ducks and chickens, or other country commodities, has got on little by little, screwing and half starving himself and his family the while, until his industry and perseverance have been awarded by the purchase of a cow, the taking of a few acres of land – four or five only at first – and has now perchance become the occupier of some forty or fifty, for which he pays a higher rent than any other farmer in the parish – simply because he happens to be the poorest! This is the way of the world. The poorer the individual, the more he must pay for everything. And truly these men do deny themselves almost every comfort in life, to squeeze out the hardly-earned money and it is surprising how they can make up their rent at all and support their families ... Farmers of this class ... if farmers they may be called – although thinly scattered over the grazing districts and midland counties, abound chiefly in Devon and Wales.[15]

Smaller farmers may well have had to have by-employments to supplement their income from farming: a milk round, for instance, ought to be considered a by-employment. This leads us into the whole question of proto-industrialisation where small farmers, often pastoral farmers, have manufacturing employments.[16] At the other extreme, we can identify farmers operating on a very different scale whose role in the farm was limited to supervision and management, employing farm bailiffs as managers.

---

pp. 1836–76; Leigh Shaw-Taylor, 'Family Farms and Capitalist Farms in Mid Nineteenth-Century England', *AgHR* 53 (2005), pp. 158–91.

[14]   M. Winstanley, 'Industrialization and the Small Farm: Family and Household Economy in Nineteenth-Century Lancashire', *Past and Present* 152 (1996), pp. 157–95.

[15]   'Scrutator', 'Farming and Foxhunting', *Baily's Monthly Magazine of Sports and Pastimes*, 1 Nov. 1861, p. 349.

[16]   There is little recent writing on dual economies in English rural societies. For the most recent discussion of this issue, Jan de Vries, *The Industrious Revolution: Consumer Behavior and Household Economy 1650 to the Present* (Cambridge, 2008) esp. ch. 3. Key to the idea of proto-industrialisation is the idea of household income to which all the members of the household contribute, often by exploiting crafts which are not the primary household income, e.g. spinning and weaving on small farms. For women's work of this sort, Verdon, *Rural Women Workers*, ch. 5.

It is possible that 'gentlemen' farmers of this sort were largely a creation of the years of high prices during the Napoleonic wars. With enhanced farming profits, farmers were able to adopt a higher standard of living, symbolised by the parlour and the piano. As we shall see, this brought down on them (or more precisely on their wives) a degree of social criticism if not ridicule. By the 1860s there was a perception that the character of the farmer had changed again. After lamenting the passing of the familiar 'John Bull' style of farmer, 'Scrutator' wrote scathingly of his successor. He was:

> half-trader, half-farmer – who, being pushed forwards, by his friends supplying him with capital sufficient for the undertaking, embarks in the agricultural, as he would in any other business, with a superficial stock of knowledge, acquired by two or three years' sojourn in some farm-house, and a little smattering of chemistry, by which he thinks to eclipse all the old clodhoppers, whose apprenticeship commenced at the plough-tail.[17]

This generation might indeed have put too much of its faith in science and technology, and high inputs to compensate for low prices, and was often ill-equipped to deal with the downturn of the 1870s and 1880s. In turn, they were replaced by lean men, sometimes Scots or northern English who, by their own labour and cutting costs generally were able to make a living when prices were low.[18] Their approach to farming perhaps survived much of the way through to the Second World War.

And there were always those farmers who were the farming equivalents of absentee landowners, placing their farming affairs in the hands of a bailiff and perhaps only coming to the farm for weekends or holidays. As they relied on other sources of income, they were perhaps insulated from some of the rallies and falls in farm income. Dr Dewey's James Mason could perhaps be read in this way: a man of great wealth who saw farming as a hobby, perhaps also as challenge, but who was not a farmer himself.[19] The primary purpose of

---

[17]   'Scrutator', Farming and Fox-hunting', p. 347.

[18]   For a clear perception that the personnel of farming changes, and that one style of farming was replaced by another in the depression after the 1870s, R.J. Olney, *Rural Society and County Government in Nineteenth-Century Lincolnshire* (History of Lincolnshire, 10, Lincoln, 1979), pp. 60–2; E.H. Hunt and S.J. Pam, 'Agricultural Depression in England, 1873–96: Skills Transfer and the "Redeeming Scots"', *AgHR* 59 (2011), pp. 81–100.

[19]   Was Rider Haggard referring to Mason when he retailed the story of 'a rich man who had taken a portion of a poor land, Oxfordshire estate in hand and after a while was heard to declare that he could stand to losing £1,000 a year over farming, but to lose from £5,000 to £10,000 was more than he had bargained for'? H. Rider Haggard, *Rural England, Being an Account of the Agricultural and Social Researches Carried Out in the Years 1901 and 1902* (2 vols, 1906), II, p. 112.

the farm might be to offer a sporting experience rather than rather farming profit.[20]

G.T. Garratt, writing in 1930, formalised the diversity of farmers with a sixfold categorisation: the 'Spare-time farmer' working evenings and holidays on his farm; the 'Part-time farmer'; the 'Family farmer', a 'working farmer mainly dependent on the unpaid labour of his family', the 'Dirty-boot farmer' who employed men; the 'Clean-boot farmer', 'who expects a comfortable standard of living, whose supervision of the farm is of a general and not detailed character, and who spends most of his time managing the business side of his farm' (and who we might call a 'gentlemen farmer'); and the 'hobby farmer' (a 'man of independent means whose main interests in his farm is non-commercial and who delegates the day-to-day management to a bailiff or agent').[21] At least some of this categorisation can be read back into the nineteenth century and perhaps earlier too.

We might also usefully observe that farmers form part of a larger body of people who we might call the farming interest. These are people who are associated with farming in some way and who often depended on its fortunes for their own livelihood. So, we can include within it those providing services to farmers, from the relatively menial – mole and rat catchers, hedgers and ditchers and carriers – through millers, malsters, corn dealers, cattle dealers, manure, fertiliser and feed merchants, agricultural machine makers to the suppliers of professional services – veterinary surgeons, land surveyors, land agents, solicitors – indeed, the whole market town economy. Many of these people saw their interests in the nineteenth century as being aligned with that of the farmers, especially on the question of protection.

Farmers then were never a homogeneous group but differed greatly in scale. Moreover the very personnel of farming may have changed over time as men with new capital and new ideas entered the profession to replace those who were not adept at changing with the times and left, whether voluntarily or involuntarily. All of this needs to be seen in a context of farmers' numbers and farm size: in every generation there were fewer farmers and farms were larger.

II

Given the diversity of character and background identified by Brown, it goes without saying that farmers were not a professional group in the normal sense

---

[20] Hobby farming was a recognised category in the analysis of the National Farm Survey of 1941/2 when 2.6 per cent of occupiers were placed under this heading. *National Farm Survey of England and Wales: A Summary Report* (London, 1946), Table 1.

[21] Taken from Viscount Astor and B. Seebohm Rowntree, *Mixed Farming and Muddled Thinking* (London, 1945), pp. 101–103.

of the word.[22] Even though twentieth-century farmers had a 'union' which defended their interests and offered them professional services, not all farmers were ever members of the National Farmers Union (NFU). A number of independent small farmers and tenants organisations justified their existence by the belief that the NFU did not represent their interests.[23] Farmers shared no common education, nor did they take any qualifying examination to allow them to practice. In fact, the whole question of farmers' education is too large and complicated to be given a full treatment here, but an outline can be given.

There was always a divide between those who believed that farming required a higher level of skill and education than many farmers possessed or that 'learning on the job' could provide, and those who held that the key form of education was hands-on experience. Even so, those who believed in the need for agricultural education often advocated education by apprenticeship rather than education in the college or school room.

English agricultural education began relatively late and was slow to develop.[24] The pioneer college at Cirencester, founded in 1845, remained relatively small even at the end of the century. It did not recruit much within the farming community and there was no guarantee that its alumni would go into farming as opposed to professions like land management. As Brassley has shown, the numbers passing through it were infinitesimally small compared to the size of the farming population.[25] Provision developed quite quickly at the end of the century as the result of a mixture of county council and Board of Agriculture initiatives (some of which, as in Lancashire, were directed at the improvement of standards in cheese- and butter-making and so aimed more at women). By the interwar period a network of county colleges and one or two private (fee-paying) institutions existed in England.

Surveys of the 1970s found that only a minority of farmers had any specific training, and those who did tended to be the larger ones. Newby found that 50 per cent of farmers of 1,000 acres or more had no agricultural training although a quarter had a university degree (not necessarily in agriculture), but of farmers as a whole, three-quarters had no agricultural qualification and only 5.4 per cent

---

[22]   For a discussion of the professional position of farmers, Paul Brassley, 'The Professionalisation of English Agriculture', *Rural Hist.* 16 (2005), pp. 235–51.

[23]   For instance, Philip Lowe et al., *Countryside Conflicts: The Politics of Farming, Forestry and Conservation* (1986), pp. 90–1.

[24]   For a convenient overview of educational provision in agriculture, Paul Brassley, 'Agricultural Education, Training and Advice in the UK, 1850–2000', in N. Vivier (ed.), *The State and Rural Societies: Policy and Education in Europe, 1750–2000* (Turnhout, 2008); also Paul Brassley, 'Agricultural Science and Education', ch. 8 of Collins (ed.), *Agrarian History*, VII (I), pp. 594–649.

[25]   Brassley, 'Professionalisation', p. 244 and see Howkins, *Agrarian History*, VII (II), p. 1372 for a revealing comment from the college about its intake.

were graduates. Admittedly by the end of the century the proportion of farmers with some formal qualification had increased.[26]

Given that farmers were often born to the land and picked up the rudiments of farming at a young age, the education of farmers came very largely from gaining experience on their father's farms, or periods boarding as a farm pupil, or from travelling.[27] In this volume both Broad and Wade Martins show how important travelling and visiting other farms was to farmers, and not only those at the beginning of their careers.[28] In the twentieth-century advice could be secured from feed and fertiliser salesmen, the developing networks of county council and government agricultural advisers as well as the agricultural press (in which we must include the BBC's agricultural provision). We should not equate a lack of college training with any lack of curiosity about developments in farming, or any want of desire to know how farming could be done better. But it may also be true that it was perceived changes in the complexity of farming and increases in its capitalisation which prompted calls for the better education of farmers. In the mid nineteenth century there was a perception that farming had changed and that old-style farmers were no longer equipped to cope in current conditions. To quote Brown again:

> Agriculture has become a very different pursuit from what it was forty or fifty years ago, and we must seek to elevate the educational status of all classes of farmers in order to enable them to meet in some degree the pressure which is now brought to bear on the resources of British agriculture.[29]

---

[26] Brassley, 'Professionalisation', p. 243; Howard Newby, *Green and Pleasant Land? Social Change in Rural England* (London, 1979), pp. 97–8.

[27] Brown recommended that the aspirant farmer should spend three years on three different farms as a pupil, and only then go to agricultural college: *Book of the Landed Estate*, pp. 24–6. Even Henry Stephens saw his *Book of the Farm* as being to support farm pupils' practical learning rather than the sole cup from which the aspirant farmer should drink. Stephens, *The Book of the Farm* (4th edn in 6 vols, revised by James MacDonald, Edinburgh, 1891), I, pp. 1–6 discusses farm pupillage.

[28] For a particularly elaborate account of farm tourism, see Anne Orde (ed.), *Matthew and George Culley: Travel Journals and Letters, 1765–98* (British Academy Records of Social and Economic History, 35, 2002). There are similarities between the (self-)education of a figure like Rex Paterson, described by John Martin below, and a Victorian figure like Henry Stephens. In an autobiographical note published as a preface to his *Book of the Farm*, Stephens (for whom see *ODNB*) described how after a school education in Dundee, he spent three years as a farm pupil at a farm in Berwickshire, undertaking all the tasks on the farm and finally acting as steward in lieu of his master. He then spent 12 months travelling in Europe before returning to take lease on an undeveloped property in Forfarshire. As Conford shows, Stuart employed methods he had had encountered in India in Scotland.

[29] Brown, *Book of the Landed Estate*, p. 29. Elsewhere he comments, 'I have met with many farmers – too many I am sorry to state – who are so far behind the age and who are men of no education, that I could not consistently recommend to any landlord to give them a lease', p. 64.

Part of this was the development of agricultural chemistry. We have already seen 'Scrutator' dismiss a knowledge of chemistry as a substitute for an apprenticeship at the plough. But some understanding of chemistry became an essential:

> When a farm has been reduced by bad management to a low state of productiveness, what is the right manure to apply? In 1864 the merest tyro in farming can answer this question. *Nitrogen for corn – phosphorous for turnips –* are household words. Twenty years ago, what would have been the stereotyped answer? 'The midden is the mither of the meal-kist'.[30]

The Royal Agricultural Society of England took an interest in farmers' education in the years following 1863 finding that other than Cirencester, there was barely any provision for educational instruction in the country at that time.[31] This did not turn into a call for a proliferation of farming colleges although R. Vallentine, writing in the Society's *Journal*, called for the establishment of half a dozen regional colleges to supplement those, like Cirencester, which were already in existence.[32] The need for a practical education kept reasserting itself, Vallentine holding that 'any one intending to become a farmer should learn the practical part upon a farm when sixteen or seventeen'. T.D. Acland, contributing to that debate, likewise acknowledged that some skills could be learnt at school, but others 'are better formed at home or under a trusted relative or friend'.[33] Reviewing the results of a questionnaire he circulated:

> ... there is one point on which all seem agreed, that the most indispensible requisite for a farmer is the understanding of livestock; that this must be acquired young, and in contact with people living by their business and easily accessible for the purpose of obtaining their explanations, This opinion is favourable to the principle of apprenticeship and unfavourable to that of professorial instruction in special agricultural knowledge either at school or college.[34]

---

[30] H.S. Thompson, 'Agricultural Progress and the Royal Agricultural Society', *JRASE* 25 (1864), p. 40.

[31] S.B.L. Druce, 'Summary of the Proceedings of the Royal Agricultural Society of England in Reference to Agricultural Education', *JRASE* 2nd ser. 2 (1866), pp. 209–25; and in the same volume essays by R. Vallentine, Lewis Evans and W.H. Beever on 'Middle Class Education'.

[32] R. Vallentine, 'On Middle-Class Education, Having Reference to the Improvement of the Education of Those Who Depend upon the Cultivation of the Soil for Their Support', *JRASE*, 2nd ser. 2 (1866), p. 3. Of course, there was no discussion of appropriate education for farm women.

[33] T.D. Acland, *Agricultural Education: What It Is and How to Improve It* (1864), p. 28.

[34] Ibid., p. 42.

But the farmer also needed a training in letters: as one of Acland's correspondents wrote:

> Farmers should have all the general intellectual culture they can get at school,
> Besides being farmers they have many social duties to perform, as voters, as jurors,
> as guardians of the poor and members of various local boards[35]

thus making point that the farmer had a social and political role to fulfil. Little resulted from this debate. Half a century later Sir Daniel Hall was still dissatisfied with the education of farmers:

> what the ordinary farmer needs above all is better education: and by this we mean
> not so much additional knowledge of a technical sort, but the more flexible habit
> of mind that comes from reading, the susceptibility of ideas that is acquired from
> acquaintance with a different atmosphere than the one in which he ordinarily
> lives

although he seemed to believe that this would lead the farmer to cooperation. A page later, he dismisses some farmers as simply lacking intelligence ('the low mental calibre of many of the men occupying the land'): it was this that was responsible for 'for most of the deficiencies that can be justly charged against our farming'. Hall though saw great promise in the systems of agricultural education then being established but as we have seen, farmers were slow to take advantage of the training it offered, preferring to learn 'by looking over the hedge'.[36] One wonders how far the adoption by farmers of agricultural education in the second half of the twentieth century was to meet the expectations of landlords and bank managers that their tenants and clients should have some formal education in agriculture as well as enabling farmers to deal with them on equal terms.

Every assessment of the farming community identifies a minority of farmers who were recognised as innovators and a somewhat larger minority who were overcautious, who farmed by rote in trusted and traditional ways, probably eschewing the chance of high profits for a relative certainty of a comfortable livelihood. These men may perhaps be equated with the 'B' farmers of the National Farm Survey of 1941–43 who were securing from their holding between 60 and 80 per cent of its potential output: they formed just about two-fifths of farmers.[37] To do them justice, some may have been farmers who lacked

---

[35] Ibid., p. 43.

[36] Sir A.D. Hall, *A Pilgrimage of British Farming, 1910–1912* (1913), pp. 440–41.

[37] MAFF, *National Farm Survey of England and Wales: A Summary Report* (1946), pp. 52–3: for these people, Charles Rawding, 'The Treatment of "Failing" Farmers in South-West Lancashire

the capital to run their holdings at an optimum level as well as those who were nearing the end of their farming lives.

What has undermined agricultural education and perhaps the professionalisation of farming is the simple truth that farmers become farmers because they have access to land through inheritance (or the promise of inheritance) or by being able to access agricultural networks which operated to their benefit (which in turn implies that that they were drawn from the farming community). A small minority enter farming in each generation because they have the capital – from a previous career, or from legacies – to set themselves up in business. A varying number enter by means of the 'farming ladder' where men start with smallholdings and, by a process of capital accumulation, move to bigger tenancies or enlarge small farms by acquiring additional land. The existence of this mechanism really needs some scrutiny. Earlier we saw 'Scrutator' describe the man who had started off with potatoes and poultry before acquiring a cow and a little land and then a small farm although he also suggested that such men were most commonly found in Devon and Wales. Rider Haggard's account of his travels in *Rural England* in the first years of the twentieth century describes many men who entered farming with capital saved from labouring.[38] The smallholding movement was intended to generate a stock of entrepreneurs who could move up the farming ladder although there is later evidence that few did so.[39] It might be suggested that when the demand for land was flat, landowners were willing to deal with men of this sort, but when the demand for land was high from existing farmers, the new man was squeezed out.

So far as new entrants from other occupations are concerned, we overlook at our peril the ubiquity of basic farming skills in the nineteenth and perhaps even in the early twentieth centuries. Large numbers of people who were not farmers had some knowledge of agriculture from being brought up in the country or working there when young. The basic skills were perhaps as familiar as van driving or operating a cash till are today. A new entrant to farming with money to spend could buy in the skills of a farm bailiff (as Mrs Cresswell did) especially if he didn't intend to be resident on the farm, but to use it as a weekend estate or retirement home. Of course, it was perhaps a big step from this to actually making money.

Ultimately there was nothing to stop anyone calling himself a farmer or practising the trade of farming. Farmers had no need to register with the state.

---

during the Second World War', in Brian Short, Charles Watkins and John Martin (eds), *The Front Line of Freedom: British Farming in the Second World War* (Agricultural History Rev., Supp. Ser. 4, 2006), pp. 179–93.

[38]   Rider Haggard, *Rural England*, to give a few examples from vol. II, pp. 176, 190, 219, 296, 354, 355, 405, 412–13, 451. See also A. Mutch, 'The "Farming Ladder" in North Lancashire, 1840–1914: Myth or Reality', *Northern Hist.* 27 (1991), pp. 162–83.

[39]   Newby, *Green and Pleasant Land*, pp. 96–7.

They did not need to be licensed to keep livestock (although increasingly they had to submit themselves to public health regimes applying to milk and eggs and more recently animal welfare regulations). A training in agriculture may have been an additional asset for those who intended or hoped to farm, but it did not in itself bring access to land except perhaps as a salaried farm manager.[40] There are those who are born to farming, and a smaller number who come to it by a variety of routes.

III

If, in this discussion, we have tried to dispel any notion that farmers were all of a sameness, then we have also tended to discuss them as though they were all male. As Dr Verdon reveals in her chapter, an appreciable number of farmers in the late nineteenth century were women, many of whom had inherited a farm either from a parent or from a husband.

Discussions of the role of women in agriculture have developed rapidly over the past decade, but on occasion different roles have been conflated and it may be helpful to distinguish them.[41] Firstly we have those female farmers who made a choice to pursue farming as a profession and acquire the land needed to do so, either by purchase or tenancy, occasionally by descent or gift. Those who could not draw on either family land or money were probably limited in the types of agriculture they could pursue to poultry-keeping or branches of horticulture. Dr Verdon and others have recently explored how farming became acceptable as a career for middle-class women, and the development of female agricultural education.[42] Secondly, there are those women who took over the running of a farm after the death of a husband or father, and who expected to manage it only until a son came of age. Given that farming is semi-hereditary, even where the farmers had only tenancies at will, there must have been a large number of women who fulfilled this role for a period. The alternative – of leaving the farm – would have implied the disinheritance of the son. In her chapter in this volume considering the career of the Norfolk farmer Louisa Cresswell – a widow and reluctant farmer – Dr Verdon shows how widow-farmers were viewed with some scepticism by estates and many believed that they were given no opportunity to show their ability as a farmer

---

[40]   See Hall, *Pilgrimage*, p. 438 for the lack of opportunities for graduates.

[41]   The key work is Nicola Verdon, *Rural Women Workers in Nineteenth-Century England: Gender, Work and Wages* (Woodbridge, 2002). A study carrying this into the twentieth century would be most desirable.

[42]   Nicola Verdon, 'Business and Pleasure: Middle-Class Women's Work and the Professionalization of Farming in England, 1890–1939', *J. British Studies* 51 (2012), pp. 393–415.

before being eased out.[43] Overcoming initial doubts, Cresswell seems to have been both a successful farmer on the Sandringham estate and to have been accepted as one by her peers. But at key moments she was also dependent on the support of friends and the willingness of her foreman to support her. The Fell household, described by Jennifer Holt, is a variant on this, run by a widowed woman and her daughters. Thirdly, there are the farmer's wives who, we now recognise, often had a defined sphere of responsibility within the farm – poultry, the dairy – as an annex to their responsibilities as the manager of the household. It seems likely though that the work of the farmer's wife on the farm ebbed and flowed over time.[44] Fourth, we have those women who milked, churned butter and made cheese all under the supervision of the farmers' wife. The unmarried female servants amongst them were probably often co-resident with the farm household. Fifth, we have women who were employed – often seasonally – to undertake field work including picking stones, weeding and harvesting.[45]

Each of the five categories, we might suggest, has its own history. The first – women who came into farming as career – are probably distinctively a late nineteenth and twentieth-century phenomenon. The fifth and last category of field workers probably disappear in the third quarter of the nineteenth century as public attitudes hardened against women's field work. The scale of the fourth category – the dairy and cheese maids – depended on the character of the farm: but this area of women's work probably also diminished with the growth of raw milk sales and the disappearance of farmhouse butter and cheese in the early twentieth century.[46]

As we shall see, the increasing separation of the farmer's wife from the daily round of the farm was commented on at widely different times in the late eighteenth and nineteenth century. We may hazard a guess that the active involvement of farmer's wives continued longest where domestic farm production of butter and cheese survived and where a distinctively female craft made a contribution to the income of the farm.[47] We might understand the early

---

[43] *Punch*, 22 Feb. 1845, p. 69, reproduced a report from the *Aylesbury News* of a widow on the Duke of Buckingham's estate being refused permission to remain on the farm, given notice and having the farm let over her head even though the farm had been in the tenant's family for nearly a century and the tenant had invested nearly £400 in underdraining.

[44] Nicola Verdon, "'… subjects deserving of the highest praise": Farmers' Wives and the Farm Economy in England, *c.*1700–1850', *AgHR* 51 (2003), pp. 23–39.

[45] Nicola Verdon, 'The Employment of Women and Children in Agriculture: A Reassessment of Agricultural Gangs in Nineteenth-Century Norfolk', *AgHR* 49 (1999), pp. 41–55.

[46] For the earlier history of women's involvement in dairying, Deborah Valenze, 'The Art of Women and the Business of Men: Women's Work and the Dairy Industry, *c.*1740–1840', *Past and Present* 130 (1991), pp. 142–69.

[47] Verdon, "'… subjects deserving of the highest praise" shows this clearly.

withdrawal of farm women to the parlour and a life of sociability as being more characteristic of grain-growing areas although Gillrays' satirical engraving of 1809 (which we discuss subsequently) is careful to locate Farmer Giles and his wife in a pastoral context. Where there was no butter or cheese to produce, the key question was probably whether the income of the farm household was strong enough to allow the farmer's wife *not* to contribute to the farm's income. Davidoff, however, has suggested that female farmers had largely been excluded from farming by 1850, key farming institutions becoming increasingly male and contemporaries increasingly holding that female farming was incompatible with female claims to gentility. And yet it is not quite clear to which of the first three categories of female activity Davidoff is referring, nor whether her account can be applied universally.[48] Having described the poorer farmer with his grinding poverty, 'Scrutator' went on to stress the importance of his wife to the family enterprise:

> The wives work like slaves, and the veriest trifles by which a halfpenny can be realized are not overlooked; flowers, fruit, vegetables, the produce of the garden as well as that of the poultry-yard, [all] contribute their quota to the stock ... I have often seen their wives and children sitting in open streets on market-days – winter and summer alike – without any protection from the weather, save an old umbrella – with their stock in trade exposed for sale, and little suckling-pigs, wrapped up in old blankets, more carefully defended from rain and cold than themselves.[49]

Depression may have made the work of wives and children even more important to the success of the farm.[50] One would surmise that wives remained key to the economy of the small farm and to the farm in pastoral areas so long as butter and cheese continued to be made in farm dairies, but that where they had disappeared from the fields, they often made something of a return in the last quarter of the nineteenth century.

It seems unlikely that there were many women who embarked on farming as a career before 1850 unless, by chance, they inherited land or a tenancy. Many more became farmers unintentionally and unwillingly, that is that they had to step up from the third category of farmer's wife to the second category of farmer in lieu of a husband with the responsibility for managing the family business until an inheriting son came of age. Estate managers may not have liked this,

---

48   Leonore Davidoff, 'The Role of Gender in the "First Industrial Nation": Farming and the Countryside in England, 1780–1850', in Rosemary Crompton and Michael Mann (eds), *Gender and Stratification* (1986), repr. in Davidoff, *Worlds Between: Historical Perspectives in Gender and Class* (1995).

49   'Scrutator', 'Farming and Fox-Hunting', p. 349.

50   Mutch, '"Farming Ladder"', p. 181 for some comment along these lines.

PUNCH, OR THE LONDON CHARIVARI.—MAY 8, 1929.

THE PAMPERED PESSIMIST.

"THEY RELIEVE ME OF MY RATES, BUT THEY DON'T GIVE ME RAIN. THEY PROMISE TO BUY MY BEEF FOR THE FIGHTING SERVICES, AND THEN THEY TALK ABOUT DISARMAMENT. THERE'S ALWAYS A CATCH SOMEWHERE."

Figure 1.2 'The Pampered Pessimist', from *Punch*, 8 May 1929, p. 507. The farmer seeks solace in a conversation with his bull

but equally where tenants had leases, or where the estate felt some responsibility for tenant families, it could not simply dispossess a farmer's widow. But is it not clear that there were fewer women pitched into this situation in 1850 than 1750, or that those that who were less welcome in the institutions of farming at the end of the period than at the beginning. It is entirely possible that women farmers of this sort were dependent on trusted farm servants to undertake some of the public tasks of the farm such as selling in local markets, but at the same time larger farmers were probably placing more responsibility in the hands of farm bailiffs anyhow and were themselves withdrawing from some of the daily business of the farm. It is certainly not clear that a woman who was farming to protect her son's tenancy in some way lost her gentility: she may well have been the object of sympathy rather than public disapproval, or so the experience of Mrs Cresswell suggests.

IV

Farmers have, at some periods, been seen as the essence of England, whether the beef-eating John Bull character of the eighteenth-century or the saviours of the domestic front during the Second World War. At other times they have attracted a degree of sympathy, often coupled with a keen appreciation that the farmer's lot was not an easy one at moments when economic conditions were running against him.[51] Such is the impression gained from the representation of the farmer in periodicals such as *Punch* (Figure 1.2).

It is often held that farmers had a good war, and their treatment in the 1947 Agriculture Act was both a reward to them as well as a recognition that farming could not simply be allowed to return to the doldrums into which it had been pitched by the 'Great Betrayal' of 1921. Post-war farming was also a strategic, cold war industry. The need for self-sufficiency was plain enough at a time when the country lacked the dollars to buy American wheat and feared that in any renewed war, the import of food might again be disrupted. The logic of running agriculture at a high level brought its own disadvantages. As the recollection of the war years diminished, farmers became criticised for implementing what were, in effect, government policies; doubts arose over the use of pesticides, landscape change notably in the form of hedgerow removal or the extension of arable farming into marginal areas with the aid of government grants, the loss of wildlife habitats that these changes implied, and, the introduction of new and unfamiliar crops. For instance, the British Social Attitudes Survey in 1985 found that 63 per cent of interviewees agreed or agreed strongly with the proposition that 'modern methods of farming have caused damage to the countryside': in 1987 it was 68 per cent. The proposition that 'all things considered, farmers do a good job in looking after the countryside' secured the agreement or strong agreement of 74 or 75 per cent of interviewees.[52] There was a rising conviction

---

[51]   For example, Paul Langford, *Public Life and the Propertied Englishman, 1689–1798* (Oxford, 1991), p. 333 quoting an eighteenth-century ballad.

[52]   Ken Young, 'Interim Report: Rural Prospects', in Roger Jowell et al. (eds), *British Social Attitudes: The Fifth Report* (1988), p. 164.

that farmers were doing very nicely out of the taxpayers' subventions which encouraged overproduction. Farmers' reputation also suffered greatly from the rise of animal welfare issues, whether battery hens (and the belief that their eggs were often infected with salmonella), broiler chickens, cows selectively bred to produce gargantuan amounts of milk or the use of calves for veal. Public distaste on these issues was often marked. Public understanding was much more limited.

Farmers have frequently been the butt of public criticism.[53] Doubts about whether their interests were inevitably aligned with those of society as a whole are very old:

> He prays for rain in harvest, night and day,
> To rot and consume the grain and hay:
> That so he mows and reeks, and stacks that mould,
> At his own price he may translate to gold.
> But if a plenty come, this ravening thief
> Torments and sometimes hangs himself with grief.[54]

Returning from Thirsk market in April 1796, on a day which had seen a fall in grain prices, a woman called out to the farmer William Metcalfe:

> as I went through Sowerby saying I should have a halter provided for me against my return for we farmers would hang ourselves on account of the reducing price of corn etc. I told her if every impertinent person was entitled to a halter, she would not escape.[55]

Attitudes to the farmer could change rapidly. Indeed one might suspect that when food was cheap, he was near invisible, but when food was expensive, the charge of profiteering was all too easy to make. Amongst historians one suspects that a great deal of the antipathy to farmers comes from the fact that they were capitalists and often had capitalist's decisions to take, whether in persisting campaigns to keep down the poor rates or the wages of their labourers, both of which required the maintenance of political hegemony over their villages through the vestry in the eighteenth century and the property franchise between 1832 and 1884, or the suppression of union activities at a later date. It was only in 1884 that a universal male franchise was established in the village, but the farmer's authority was a long time a-dying. The conviction that farmers treated

---

[53]   For earlier comments see Langford, *Public Life*, pp. 372–7.

[54]   John Taylor, 'The Country Yeoman', in *The Works of John Taylor* (1630), p. 12, cited by Campbell, *English Yeoman*, p. 375.

[55]   A.W. Dyson (ed.), *William Metcalfe His Book: The Diary of a North Yorkshire Farmer and Banker, 1786–99* (Leeds, 1931), p. 29. See too the comment of Paul Langford, *Public Life*, p. 331: 'Farmers were assumed to be monopolists who exacerbated the plight of the poor customer.'

Figure 1.3   James Gillray, 'Farmer Giles and his wife shewing off their daughter
Betty to their neighbours, on her return from School' (1809)

Note: The location is Farmer Giles's sitting room. He and his wife stand watching, in fawning
admiration, their daughter Betty playing and singing at the square piano: another younger
woman, perhaps a further daughter, sings with a fan in her hand. Three matrons are sat at the
card table on which are samplers with B. Giles embroidered into them: they are ignoring the
piano playing. A well-dressed young man, either a visitor or a son, sits watching and fidgets:
a rather inept liveried servant is bringing in a decanter and glasses on a silver salver. He has
a basket of perhaps cakes, possibly oysters; some are falling out. Over the piano is a painting
in a frame labelled 'Cheese Farm'. This shows a house with thatch and a modern red brick
house to its right. We are evidently in the red brick house at Cheese Farm whose windows
are concealed by the long curtains in the picture. A woman sits milking a horned cow in
the yard. The sampler on the rear wall carries the subscription, 'Betty Giles aged 16. 1808.
Cheese Hall' so even the name of the farm has been altered to show the rising aspirations of
the Giles family.

Source: BM Satires 11444; 1867,1012.615. © Trustees of the British Museum.

their labourers poorly, underpaid them whilst they worked and then shifted
them to the workhouse when they could no longer earn their living is a very old
one. John Clare's *The Parish* draws the farmers of the parish in a unsympathetic
light: we have little from the farmer's own viewpoint with which to counter
Clare. The growing social distance between employer and employee was
remarked upon (to be condemned) in perhaps every generation.[56] So too was the

---

[56]   For instance, Langford, *Public Life*, pp. 375–6; Davidoff, 'Role of Gender', pp. 199–200.

increasing separation of the farmer's wife from the daily round of the farm. For writers as diverse as Young in the 1790s, William Cobbett in the 1820s, Richard Jeffries in the 1870s and Joseph Arch a little later, the acquisition of a piano was totemic of farmers who lived too well and had acquired airs and graces.[57] Gillray represented this cleaving to the middle classes in a satirical print of 1809 in which Betty Giles, daughter of the preening Farmer and Mrs Giles, is shown accompanying herself at a square piano as she sings the fashionable 'Bluebells of Scotland' (Figure 1.3).

In fact the picture is replete with digs at the farmer's new-claimed status. These were the new tastes, acquired during the prosperous war years, that the Select Committee on Agriculture of 1833 found farmers and their wives were loath to give up in leaner times.[58]

A doggerel poet of Burgh-le-Marsh in Lincolnshire also saw the piano as symbolic of a new style of farmer when he compared the farmer of 1800 with that of 1900:

> Farmer at the plough,
> Wife milking cow,
> Daughter spinning yarn,
> Son threshing in the barn,
> All happy to a charm
> Father gone to see the show,
> Daughter at the pian-o
> Madame gaily dressed in satin
> All the boys learning Latin
> With a mortgage on the farm.[59]

And it has to be said that some farmers did live extremely well, particularly in the era of high farming, and adopted elements of the lifestyle of their landlords, including a taste for hunting and shooting. They were probably

---

[57]   For comments on the reputation of farmers in the late eighteenth century, Langford, *Public Life*, pp. 372–4. For examples of comments about farmers' consumption, David Martin, 'Agriculture and Politics in England, 1815–1939', in J.R. Wordie (ed.), *Agriculture and Politics in England, 1815–1939* (Basingstoke, 2000), p. 130 (who cites Young, Cobbett and Arch); David Eastwood, *Governing Rural England: Tradition and Transformation in Local Government, 1780–1840* (Oxford, 1994), p. 29. Eastwood's, *Government and Community in the English Provinces, 1700–1870* (Basingstoke, 1997), pp. 27–30 and Nicola Verdon's chapter in this volume both cite Jeffries.

[58]   Davidoff cites the diary of a farmer's wife from the south Midlands for 1823 who was playing catch-up with Mrs Giles. The diary covers the period of her house's refurbishment with new fireplaces, carpets and curtains in the parlour, pictures and most significantly, the installation of bell-pushes for servants. The social context was all too overt: the lady diarist now felt she could invite the vicar round for *wine*. Davidoff, 'Role of Gender', p. 200.

[59]   Cited by Olney, *Rural Society*, pp. 60–61.

less well-equipped to cope with the thin years which began in the 1870s.[60] As we saw, not all farmers or their wives shared in the dividend of agricultural prosperity but continued in a routine of selling the products of the garden, of poultry and the dairy in the weekly open market. It is perhaps in the twentieth century that there was less for the farmer's wife to do, but one also suspects that many farmer's wives supported smaller farms through their earnings even in the third quarter of the century.

It is not to be doubted that where farmers employed labour, there were constant tensions between farmers and their employees. Farmers unquestionably wanted to keep their workforces on a tight rein: at different moments both allotments and labourers' unions were viewed with the utmost suspicion as giving labourers a focus independent of the farmer. Poor agricultural profits impacted on labourers as much as they did on landowners and the farmers themselves. The rural sociology of Howard Newby and others on the farm labourer was undertaken in the third quarter of the last century just as a whole category of people disappeared in the face of mechanisation and poisonous questions such as the tied cottage slipped into irrelevance.[61] The picture they drew of the exercise of power in the countryside was far from pretty. But, the fact that the farmer has often been the butt of social criticism is no reason not to study him and for agricultural or rural historians, no justification at all, for it was the farmer that made the whole system of agriculture work.

V

If historians have not always found farmers sympathetic as individuals, they have perhaps also been discouraged by the records at their disposal. It is hard to identify farmers who are well-documented in the round in ways which allow a full picture of their lives and lifestyles to emerge. Too often we see them through the eyes of outsiders, and often critical outsiders.

Without a doubt, farmers made and kept papers; the question is not one of creation but preservation. Take here the large collection of papers amassed by the Preston family of Mearbeck near Settle in Yorkshire.[62] The Prestons were at Mearbeck from at least the late sixteenth century until the death of the last family member in 1976. As a family, they bought up the lands of their neighbours and

---

[60] See *Agrarian History* VII (I), p. 167 for comments that by the 1870s farmers had grown too soft to cope with the downturn in conditions. Olney, *Rural Society*, p. 61, reports Lord Burghley saying in 1879 that farmer's wives and daughters should give up the piano and 'put their shoulders to the wheel'.

[61] Howard Newby, *The Deferential Worker* (London, 1977); Newby et al., *Property, Paternalism and Power: Class and Control in Rural England* (London, 1978).

[62] North Yorkshire RO, ZXC.

retained their title deeds. But despite the size – and promise – of their archive, it contains few accounts and virtually no personal materials that might allow us to sketch the lives and lifestyle of successive generations of the family. Nor does it contain much twentieth-century material, and certainly none dating from after 1945.

Confronted with a collection such as this, one is aware of what else there might have been – and is no longer; what has been selected for preservation and what has been thought to have been of no importance. Almost certainly some farmers kept diaries of differing degrees of fullness but we have few of them. Most wrote and received letters and kept accounts of one sort or another. Again, there are only a few extant. A very few may have written autobiographies and just one or two, especially the pioneering farmers of the later eighteenth and nineteenth century, were the subject of obituaries.[63] In every generation there were farmers who wrote, for their own pleasure, the education of their successors or less often for publication, accounts of their farming practices.[64] The twentieth century saw the development of farming journalism where farmers wrote for the press and a few established reputations as popular writers, amongst them the Wiltshire farmer and tenant to the Earl of Pembroke, A.G. Street (1892–1966).[65] By the end of the century, farming autobiography had become almost a minor genre in its own right, but this lies outside the range of this book.[66]

VI

Of all the sources, diaries are the most charming and accessible – many having now been printed – although they vary enormously in detail, from the briefest and most laconic notes made in almanacs to carefully considered (and probably

---

[63]   A particularly full example – albeit not from England – is C. Hope, *George Hope of Fenton Barns: A Sketch of his Life Compiled by His Daughter* (Edinburgh, 1881) which quotes copiously from family correspondence.

[64]   The best and most familiar example is the farming book of Henry Best (d.1645). The edition by D.M. Woodward, *The Farming and Memorandum Books of Henry Best of Elmswell, 1642* (British Academy Records of Social and Economic History, new ser. 8, London, 1984) is to be preferred over the older edition in the Surtees Society. See also the posthumous *Observations in Husbandry by Edward Lisle, Late of Crux-Easton in Hampshire* (2 vols, London, 1757, repr. 1970). Lisle was a gentleman and JP: he died in 1722 (p.v). Much of his book seems to be based on a collation of memoranda or diary entries made over many years: he cites individual conversations as well as observations arising from his own farming.

[65]   For Street, see *ODNB*. His autobiographical *Farmer's Glory* (1932) launched a career as a novelist, newspaper columnist and broadcaster.

[66]   For autobiographies, see for an example of the genre the volumes of autobiography by Michael F. Twist: *Hallowed Acres* (Ipswich, 1996), *The Spacious Days* (Preston, 1992) and *Glory Days* (Preston, 2001).

retrospectively written-up) prose.[67] Amongst the last we might draw attention to a lost diary, that of Richard Hayes of Cobham, Kent, which, if we had the whole, would probably be counted amongst the finest eighteenth-century diaries. Other than the expected details of village life, Hayes offers us accounts of the condition of the London corn markets seen from Kent and the practical problems of hop growing. But his diary also describes the leisure activities of the farmer, including his shooting and is an important witness to early cricket. In 1764 he and his brother made a cross-Channel sailing to Calais from where they went to see Dunkirk.[68] Amongst other farming diaries available in print we might notice the Lancashire farmer and nonconformist clergyman Peter Walkden, most of whose diary is lost, but a single extant volume of which was printed some years ago.[69] There is also the diary of a farmer's wife, Mary Hardy of Letheringsett in Norfolk, 1773–1809.[70] The authenticity of the diary of a second farmer's wife, that of Ann Hughes, for 1796–97, has been a matter of some debate.[71] One of the most important eighteenth-century diaries, that of Richard Bulkeley of Brynddu, in Llanfechell, Anglesey (1691–1760), remains unpublished but is available online. The surviving two volumes cover the years 1734–43 and 1747–60. Bulkeley perhaps ought to be disallowed as a farmer: as a landowner and quondam JP, he perhaps came from the social strata above the farmer. Nonetheless, his diary is replete with discussion of his farming and observations on the state of the market.[72]

---

[67]   For an example of a diary written in printed volumes, in a laconic style, see N. Verdon, 'The Diaries and Miscellaneous Papers of Thomas Doubleday of Gosberton, Lincolnshire, 1812–1833', *Rural History Today* 1 (2001), pp. 6–7. Adam Smyth has recently shown how common diaries kept in almanacs were: *Autobiography in Early Modern England* (Cambridge, 2010), ch. 1.

[68]   Ralph Arnold, *A Yeoman of Kent: An Account of Richard Hayes (1725–1790) and of the Village of Cobham in Which He Lived and Farmed* (London, 1949).

[69]   Chipping Local History Society, *The Diary of the Reverend Peter Walkden for 1733–34* (Otley, 2000); R.W. Hoyle, 'Farmer, Nonconformist Minister and Diarist: The World of Peter Walkden of Thornley in Lancashire, 1733–34', *Northern Hist.* 48 (2011), pp. 271–94.

[70]   B. Cozens-Hardy (ed.), *Mary Hardy's Diary* (Norfolk Rec. Soc. 37, 1968).

[71]   Anne Hughes, *The Diary of a Farmer's Wife, 1796–1797* (London, 1980, Penguin edn, Harmondsworth, 1981). The 'diary' was published in instalments in *Farmers Weekly* in 1937 and the columns were gathered together as a book in 1964. This has been reprinted in a number of occasions, including by Penguin in 1981 when a number of reviewers denounced it as a fake or hoax publication. A subsequent Penguin edition of 1992 gathered together what could then be discovered about the dairy from which the *Farmers Weekly* columns were drawn, the original having never been seen. A research group with a website continues to investigate the question of whether there really was a diary and if so, what happened to it (www.annehughesdiary.co.uk). They suggest that it did exist, but was given or lent to an American soldier in 1944. It is clear though that the printed diary is not in any straightforward fashion a transcript of a lost original. What impresses me is its vagueness about both people and places and the faux-dialect. That and the persistent failure to identify a historical Anne Hughes leads me to the conclusion that it is more likely to be poorly executed fiction of the 1930s than a diary of the 1790s.

[72]   For the diary see http://bulkeleydiaries.bangor.ac.uk//index.html.

A good diary gives the texture of relationships in rural society as well as a sense of the daily round like no other source. The studies which employ diaries in this volume show that all too well, Dr Wade-Martin's diaries giving a real sense of what it was to be a farmer on the Holkham estate whilst the slightly earlier diary of John Carrington, discussed by John Broad, shows the retired farmer in his leisure. Both make important contributions to our knowledge of social distance, Wade Martins to the level of contract between a tenant farmer and his landlord, Broad to the way in which a farmer and former overseer of the poor might seek out and enjoy the company of his contemporaries on whom fortune had not smiled. Farmers' autobiographies are rare before the twentieth century. Broad considers an eighteenth-century autobiography in his chapter, written by a clergyman farmer, John Mastin, who kept a foot in both camps. Louisa Cresswell wrote her memoirs from her involuntary retirement in Texas having been a tenant farmer on the Prince of Wales' Sandringham estate. Her purpose was plainly revenge; the picture she drew of the prince and the management of his shooting estate was designed not to be flattering. Here Verdon reads the autobiography against the grain, using it not as an account of the troubles of a farmer on a sporting estate, but as evidence of the ease with which a lady farmer could make her way in Norfolk farming society and manage a farm in the dying days of High Farming. That she ended up in arrears to the estate may be as much a reflection of conditions – both generally and locally – as her competence as a farmer.

VII

The most familiar and perhaps most numerous record left by farmers is the farm account. As long ago as 1965 Eric Jones and Ted Collins published an article in the *Journal of the Society of Archivists* urging county record offices to seek out farm accounts and add them to their collections, whether the originals or copies.[73] At Reading this was taken seriously, and a large collection was amassed in the 1960s and 1970s which has occasionally been added to since. Supplemented by accounts held in county record offices and other repositories, this collection formed the basis of the Turner, Beckett and Afton volume on farm productivity and the continuing work of Joyce Burnette, an instalment of which appears in this volume.[74]

---

[73]   E.L. Jones and E.J.T. Collins, 'The Collection and Analysis of Farm Record Books', *J. Society of Archivists* 3 (1965), pp. 86–9.

[74]   Turner, Beckett and Afton, *Farm Production*; Joyce Burnette, 'The Wages and Employment of Female Day-Labourers in English Agriculture, 1740–1850', *EcHR* 57 (2004), pp. 664–90; 'Child Day-Labourers in Agriculture: Evidence from Farm Accounts, 1740–1850', *EcHR*, forthcoming.

When considered in total, farm accounts form an enormous body of material; and yet they have never quite fulfilled the promise that Jones and Collins saw in them. Neither Jones nor Collins made much use of them in their own research,[75] and the pioneers came in the next generation, including Hueckel on the profitability of farming in the Napoleonic wars and Celia Miller in her studies of female employment on mid nineteenth-century Gloucestershire farms.[76]

Where farmers chose not to keep accounts, they perhaps did so deliberately. They were surely aware of the general layout of accounts, especially if they had served as a parish officer or on a vestry. Keeping accounts was a matter of self-discipline, but also self-knowledge: it was not only an aptitude but also an attitude. Writers on agriculture from Arthur Young onwards urged farmers to keep accounts.[77] Young outlined the way to do so in a prefatory note to his *Farmers' Kalender* of 1771. The farmer should 'keep a ledger, or account for every article in the farm ... the farmer should in this book directly, without the intervention of a waste book or a journal, enter all his expenses'. But he also envisaged that the farmer should do this field by field so that he could determine the profitability of individual rotations, and so his overheads needed to divided and allocated. Whilst he saw this as a simple method, his readers may not have been convinced. In the expanded edition of the *Kalendar* published in 1804, he added some comments about the desirability of keeping accounts under October. 'The most plain and simple method used is that of entering all payments on one side of a book and all receipts on the other and balancing when the transactions of the year are ended, and this method gives a tolerable idea of the single object of profit and loss.' He then provided fuller details of how to keep accounts in an appendix.[78] Sinclair in his *Code of Agriculture* (2nd edn, 1818) noted that gentleman farmers habitually kept accounts, but 'the accounts of a farmer, occupying even a large estate, and consequently employing a great capital, are seldom deemed of sufficient importance to merit a share of attention equal to that bestowed by a tradesman

---

[75]   Collins and others were surely right to spot the potential of farm accounts, but their full exploitation had to wait to the advent of cheap and powerful computing, and spreadsheet packages such as Excel.

[76]   Glenn Hueckal, 'English Farming Profits during the Napoleonic Wars, 1793–1815', in *Explorations in Economic History* 13 (1976), pp. 331–45; Celia Miller, 'The Hidden Workforce: Female Field Workers in Gloucestershire, 1870–1901', *Southern Hist.*, 6 (1984), pp. 139–55; ead. (ed.), *The Account Books of Thomas Smith, Ireley Farm, Hales, Gloucestershire, 1865–71* (Record Section of the Bristol and Gloucestershire Record Soc., 13, 1985).

[77]   The fullest discussion of farm accounts is Turner, Beckett and Afton, *Farm Production*, ch. 2, and the important – if iconoclastic – paper by R.A. Bryer (which uses only one set of manuscript accounts), 'The Genesis of the Capitalist Farmer: Towards a Marxist Accounting History of the Origins of the English Agricultural Revolution', *Critical Perspectives on Accounting* 17 (2006), pp. 367–97.

[78]   Arthur Young, *The Farmers Calender* (new edn, London, 1804), pp. 489, 533–48.

on a concern of not one twentieth part of the value'. Having explained why the keeping of accounts was so important, and the advantages they brought, Sinclair also outlined a method for keeping them in an appendix.[79] To give a third example, John M. Wilson in his *Rural Cyclopedia* (1847–49), having noted at length that farmers often didn't keep accounts argued that:

> The occupier of a small or simple farm needs only a cash-book for noting all receipts and payments; a ledger for recording all transactions of sale and purchase, of profit and loss; and an inventory-book for keeping a list of all implements, livestock, produce, manures and other matters in which capital is invested and for entering a seriatim valuation of them at the end of the year. Even the most extensive farmer, entangled in all the possible multitudinous affairs of the mixed husbandry, needs only a cash-book, a day-book, a ledger and an inventory book, – or, at the utmost, two additional or separate books for the record of labour and of produce, and if he have never seen any of the special systems of farm book-keeping which have been recommended, he may readily render the common method of book-keeping by double entry, which is taught in all the commercial and parochial schools, available for all the purposes of his accounts. Farm book-keeping, in spite of all the mystery and magniloquence and illusion which have been thrown upon the subject, requires no greater modification of the ordinary book-keeping of the schools than are required by the book-keeping of many factories and mercantile establishments.[80]

Other examples can be offered of writers who both complained that fewer farmers kept accounts than should, and who offered model accounts for farmers to follow.[81]

Even in the last years of the nineteenth century and the beginning of the twentieth, commentators on agriculture could still hold that many farmers did not keep accounts. It was a matter of comment in the Royal Commissions which punctuated the depression of the 1880s and 1890s.[82] It continued to appear in the didactic literature, so *Beeton's Field, farm and garden* of 1895:

---

[79]   Sir John Sinclair, *The Code of Agriculture* (2nd edn, London, 1819), pp. 66–8, 538–46.

[80]   Wilson, *Rural Cyclopedia*, II, p. 226.

[81]   Stephens, *Book of the Farm*, VI, pp. 507–23. For another outline of how accounts should be kept and the books needed to do so, John Coleman (Professor of Agriculture at Cirencester), 'Farm Accounts', *JRASE* 19 (1858), pp. 122–43. A few accounts were also printed as specimens for farmers to follow, for instance William Bailey Jun., *British Agriculture as Illustrated by the Accounts of a Mid-Lothian Farm, Embracing the Expense of Cultivation and Returns of Produce for a Series of Years* (Edinburgh, 1857), apparently printed by a 'chemical manure manufacturer'.

[82]   Turner, Beckett and Afton, *Farm Production*, p. 50. Bryer has an interesting critique of their reading of this; 'Genesis of the Capitalist Farmer', p. 391.

The habit of keeping accurate accounts amongst farmers is, unfortunately, very much neglected and is so often the occasion of very unsettled farm practice, the chief obstacle to proper book-keeping being the want of a sufficiently simple method. No tradesman or business man of any pretension to ability would even dream of being able to manage his affairs without a proper system of book-keeping.[83]

Or we have Hall, writing on the eve of the First World War:

many of the big farms are excellently managed, but it all depends on one man's instinct and memory: for very often he keeps no books beyond a cash record, sometimes he lets his bank pass-book serve even for that, whilst his dealings are jotted down on the backs of envelopes and the like.[84]

In 1924 C.S. Orwin could complain that 'The backwardness of farmers in book-keeping is proverbial.'[85] At the end of the 1970s Howard Newby could characterise small farmers as those for whom 'administrative duties are confined to wet days and other slack periods: the accounts, traditionally, are kept behind the clock on the living-room mantelpiece'.[86]

It was the conviction that farmers lacked key information about their activities that allowed outsiders to assume that the answer to depression was better accounting, as in the example of James Mason considered by Peter Dewey later in this volume. Rex Patterson based his enterprise on detailed accounting, including milk recording, where the productivity of individual animals was monitored. But the oft-repeated opinion of the agricultural writers poses twin conundrums. We believe that farmers in the eighteenth century, and certainly in the nineteenth, were agrarian capitalists, but how could they be without accounts and so without the means to maximise profit?[87] And if the reports that farmers did not keep accounts are correct, what are the documents that we have and which survive in large numbers? Part of the answer to this question has to come by refining what we mean by accounts.

Beckett, Turner and Afton identified three types of accounting documents, farm account books, labour records and farm memoranda books. The first, the accounts, might be kept journal style, chronologically, with expenditure on the left hand page and income on the right. A farmer dealing in livestock

---

[83] S.O. Beeton, *Beeton's Field, Farm and Garden* (London, 1895), p. 363.

[84] Hall, *Pilgrimage*, p. 438.

[85] C.S. Orwin, *Farm Accounts* (2nd edn, Cambridge, 1924), p. 2. He made similar points about the lack of farmer's accounts in *Speed the Plough* (1942), p. 43.

[86] Newby, *Green and Pleasant Land?*, p. 102.

[87] An issue which lies at the heart of Bryer's paper.

might enter the purchase of livestock on the left and their sale on the right. These pages might be totalled; a yearly total might also be inserted giving a sense of whether income exceeded expenditure over the year. In the present volume, this is the sort of account exploited by Andrew Gritt in his study of the Lancashire farmer Richard Latham (although for Latham we only have his expenditure accounts, and these are a mixture of farm and household expenditures). The account might be more elaborately kept with transactions on a single individual or a single aspect of the business placed on facing pages. Other farmers attempted to adopt some form of double-entry booking to suit their needs. The account discussed by Jennifer Holt in her contribution to this book, maintained by Sarah Fell of Swarthmore, could be interpreted as a journal or day book from which transactions would be transferred into another book maintained on double-entry book-keeping lines, each account having its own page.

Examples of well-kept accounts can be found which predate Young's *Farmers Calendar*. The accounts for Chancellor's Farm at West Harptree in the Somerset Mendips for 1766–67 are arranged as separate accounts for areas of the farm as follows:

Sheep accounts
cattle accounts
Horse accounts
pig accounts
Oats and wheat sold
butter and cheese sales and butter used in the house [one account]
Housekeeping accounts
General accounts, 'payments of what it is usual for a tenant to pay' [mostly labour]
Totals
Costs of rebuilding a lime kiln
Cost of lime.

The accounts shows signs of having been used as a check on costs as where a comparison is made between the per capita costs of the household at Chancellor's farm and another farm.[88] But this also gives the game away; these are accounts kept by a farm bailiff, responsible to a landlord.[89] This gives us the first reason

---

[88]   Thelma Munckton (ed.), *Chancellors Farm Accounts, 1766–1767* (Weston-super-Mare, 1994), p. 33.

[89]   A number of authors have noted that a high proportion of the extant accounts are actually bailiff's rather than farmer's accounts, Turner, Beckett and Afton, *Farm Productivity*, p. 45; Bryer, 'Genesis', p. 388. For recommendations on how the accounts of home farms should be kept, T. Bowick, 'On the Management of a Home Farm', *JRASE* 23 (1862), pp. 260–66.

why accounts were made: that the accountants were in a subordinate position and responsible as a bailiff to the farm's owner.

The second form of records identified by Beckett, Turner and Afton are labour books containing a daily or weekly record of who worked, for how many days and at what rate, often also specifying the nature of the task undertaken. As they have cautioned, these books often only deal with daily wage labour and not the costs of annually hired servants or gangs brought in to undertake a specific task (ditching or hedging for instance). In the Chancellor's Farm books, this material is simply included under the general accounts: otherwise we would expect the totals from a labour or wage book to be transferred into the general accounts.

The third and final form of records identified by Beckett, Turner and Afton are the miscellaneous category of memoranda books, amongst them farm diaries, cropping and field books, granary and winnowing books (an example of which is used by Hoyle in his essay in this volume) and daybooks, often small pocket books in which the farmer noted contracts he had entered into. Some farmers also maintained commonplace books in which they noted facts and figures about their farming activities and their observations of the world at large. This category ought to be divided between those records which are really subsidiary accounts (like granary and willowing books) and those whose purpose is not to underpin accounts but to act as aide memoir. As an example of this, the recently published 'account books' of Richard Wigglesworth of Conistone in Upper Wharfedale, 1683–1719 contain memoranda of parish business, including an agreement for the upkeep of the church, notes of bequests for the poor and township accounts as well as recipes for medicines for both animal and human, notes of leases made, servants hired, money lent and borrowed, wages earned and paid and the inevitable list of cows bulled. They include the expenditure incurred at Wigglesworth's mother-in-law's funeral, money given to his father-in-law in his retirement and the cost of building Wigglesworth's house. The confusion in which the book was kept was not aided by it being used again years after Wigglesworth's death by his son.[90] Another example would be the early eighteenth-century 'account book' of Clement Taylor of Finsthwaite in the southern Lake District, 1712–53. This contains a variety of accounts, rarely kept systematically, and the volume feels more like a collection of financial memoranda than accounts as they might normally be construed.[91] The memoranda book of Mary Bacon (1743–1818) of Aylesford Farm near Basingstoke contains some accounts but also

[90] Peter Leach (ed.), *The Account Books of Richard Wigglesworth of Conistone and His Sons, 1683–1719* (Northallerton, 2012).

[91] Janet D. Martin (ed.), *The Account Book of Clement Taylor of Finsthwaite, 1712–53* (Record Society of Lancashire and Cheshire, 135, 1997).

memoranda about the weather, extracts from newspapers, recipes, spiritual writings and a list of her books.[92]

Now it may be suggested that all at times, most if not all farmers kept some sort of notebook if only in which to note when money was due or had been paid.[93] There were a whole range of other dates which the farmer needed to record: the days on which servants had been hired (and their terms), the dates on which bonds and other payments were due to be made, prosaically but crucially, the date on which cows were put to the bull. One imagines that no farmer was without his pocket notebook. Much of what it contained was material from which accounts might in the end be drawn, but they were not accounts in themselves. The point is not that farmers didn't have records, but that many of them were not sufficiently structured to pass muster as accounts.[94]

From the beginning of the nineteenth century, the farmer who was unsure how to organise his accounts could buy printed account books which contained instructions as to how they should be filled in.[95] One such is *Baxter's Highly Approved Farmer's account book, in four parts, on an entirely new plan*, the sixteenth edition of which was published by the Lewis firm of J. Baxter in 1819, and advertised some years later as 'the most simple of any system of accounts available'. This gave the farmer a volume of ruled sheets under four headings: a 'workpeoples' book', a second section for corn, hay seeds and the like, a third section for livestock, both these sections arranged on double-entry book lines with parallel pages, and then a ledger and cash book. The final section was accompanied by instructions as to how to calculate the profit or loss of a farm in a given year. It also advocated using its pages for keeping a profit and loss account at the level of the individual field and the publisher offered to refer the reader to farmers who used his book to that end.[96] Wilson's *Rural Cyclopaedia* (1847–49) recommended the systems of farm book-keeping by Munro (1821)[97]

---

[92]   Ruth Facer, *Mary Bacon's Worlds: A Farmer's Wife in Eighteenth-Century Hampshire* (Newbury, 2010).

[93]   For another example of an untidy and apparently unsystematic memorandum book with additional pages and receipts pinned in, Smythe, *Autobiography*, pp. 38–9.

[94]   One aspect of this is the frequency with which accounts are encountered which are not added up. Richard Latham's expenditures are an example of this: he inserted a total line after each year but only calculated a total in the years up to 1735, when he stopped. L. Weatherill (ed.), *The Account Book of Richard Latham, 1724–1767* (British Academy Records of Social and Economic Hist., new ser., 15 (1990), *passim*. It is possible that the totals were to be found in another book, now lost.

[95]   For a discussion of printed account books, see Turner, Beckett and Afton, *Farm Productivity*, pp. 39–40.

[96]   There is an unused volume in the Perkins' Library at Southampton University Library.

[97]   Innes Munro, *A Guide to Farm Book-Keeping, Founded upon Actual Practice and upon New and Concise Principles, Suited to Farmers of Every Description* (Edinburgh, 1821).

and Trotter (1825),[98] and a third, the *British Farmer's Account Book*, published nearer his time.[99]

Bespoke printed account books for farmers remained available until well into the twentieth century. A flyer produced by the Maidstone firm of Young and Cooper (with a perforated order slip) in the 1920s advertised *The Kentish Farm Labour Account Book* (5s. 6d.), the *Kentish Farmer's Account Book* (in two page sizes at 7s. 6d. and 10s. 6d.) and the *Kentish Farmers Account Book of Receipts and Payments* (5s.).[100] How these printed books developed over time remains to be examined, but they gave the farmer who wanted to use them a structure in which he could first record, and then cast his accounts.

The question then becomes one of when an account is an account and when it falls short. The key criteria may be how an account treats the capital the farmer has invested in the farm. At the most elementary level it is possible for a simple account to total up income and expenditure to come to a figure for profit and loss. This is fine so long as rent is viewed as a proportion of the turnover of the enterprise (as is often the case in the late eighteenth century). But in the nineteenth the profitability of the farm was predicated in terms of not turnover so much as return on capital. For Arthur Young, as early as 1804:

> if a farmer does not make 10 per cent on his capital, he must either have a bad farm or bad management, or the times must be unfavourable. He ought to make some 12 to 15 per cent. Some farmers make more when corn is at a fair price.[101]

It is possible to trace the view that the purpose of the accounts was to show the return on capital right through to Orwin's comments in his *Farm Accounts*.

A simple income/expenditure account did not show the rate of return. Furthermore, it might conceal the real position of a farm. Let us suppose that a farm is losing money. A tenant farmer might secure some respite by only part-paying his rent, or by selling animals and not replacing them. The farmer himself may have known that what appeared to a superficially happy situation had only been achieved by liquidating capital or incurring debts, but income/expenditure accounts would not, in themselves, show that.

---

[98]   Alexander Trotter, *A Method of Farm Book-Keeping, Exemplified by the Form and Accounts Practiced by the Author* (Edinburgh, 1825).

[99]   The earliest of these known to COPAC is of 1841. Cambridge University Library also has a printed blank account book by one J.M. Davey, land surveyor, *The Kentish Farmer and Grazier's Journal, Being a Simple but Complete Account Book for the Whole Year, Particularly Adapted to the Customs of the Counties of Kent and Sussex* ... (Canterbury, 1834).

[100]   Author's collections.

[101]   Young, *Farmers Kalender*, p. 483. Bryer discusses a set of accounts from a Shropshire farmer of 1744 and 1745 who was going most of the way to making these calculations: 'Genesis of Capitalist Farming', pp. 383–6.

An account which had regard for the capital invested (so a balance sheet rather than a trading account) would start with an inventory of the farm's capital assets at the opening of the account, and would close with a similar inventory. It would add credits and debts outstanding at the beginning and end of the year. It would therefore be plain at the end of the year whether an apparent surplus on the income/expenditure account was actually generated by a capital loss. And knowing the capital invested at the beginning of the year, and being able to see whether it had been added to by the end of the year, the farmer was in a position where he could tell whether he was growing or diminishing his capital, and could work out the rate of return he was getting on it. This rate of return came to be regarded as the key indicator of success or failure. Of course, it was possible to employ different definitions of capital. At the least it might be a simple costed inventory of grain in the barn, animals and implements. At a higher level of sophistication, the inventory value of implements might be depreciated year on year. But capital could also embrace the less tangible assets but which came to be subsumed under the head of tenant's improvements: fences and other improvements made by the tenant, marl and manure in the soil, fruit trees planted.

The idea of keeping accounts which traced the year-on-year accumulation of capital was known in the seventeenth century and quite possibly earlier. Ralph Josselin did it, as did the Lancaster merchant William Stout.[102] Given that making annual calculations of capital was plainly good practice, one wonders why so few appear to have done it. And here one might suggest that more did than we realise. What tends to survive are cash accounts rather than the capital accounts: we know about the turnover of farms but much less about the wealth of farmers. The idea that the farmer should keep several books concurrently for his accounts is inherent in the advice literature, but the result of this is that we may only see one stage of the accounting process. That a farmer kept income and expenditure accounts does not preclude other more summary accounts in which income and expenditure was weighed and placed in a larger context of capital movements. This is a problem which applies to landowners generally: we know about rents and household expenditure, but rarely about cash at the bank (or money under the bed). Hence the apparently full accounts of the farming Brown family of Aldbourne (Wilts.) show transfers to and from Brown's deposit account, but we never have a note of how much was in that account.[103] What remains are indeed farm accounts,

---

[102]   See the full discussion of Josselin's income in Alan Macfarlane, *The Family Life of Ralph Josselin: A Seventeenth-Century Clergyman* (Cambridge, 1970), ch. 3. For Smout, see my forthcoming discussion: the autobiography is J.D. Marshall (ed.), *The Autobiography of William Stout of Lancaster, 1665–1752* (Manchester, 1967).

[103]   For these accounts, see Turner, Beckett and Afton, *Farm Production*, pp. 36–7.

and what we might consider to be capital or deposit accounts are lost. It is so often the case.

It is therefore very difficult to see farmers' enterprises in the round even where good records of the farming enterprise survive. In essence, the best records are those where everything was kept in a single book. The greater the elaboration of the records, the more likely it is that some part of the whole is lost. Books containing details of personal wealth might also have been the most sensitive and increasingly prone to being destroyed by the owners themselves or their heirs especially as fears of an intrusive Inland Revenue grew. The records of the farm itself – of animals bought and sold, labourers hired – were more anodyne and liable to be retained.

It has to be conceded that many farmers never really advanced beyond income and expenditure accounts of the simplest sort, but that it is also quite rare for us to be able to see the whole range of records kept by farmers. And it has to be said that even if farmers did keep thorough accounts, it does not follow that they could deduce anything very meaningful about the profit or loss of their farm, or the efficiency of their farming from their accounts, especially if they incorporated their household costs into their expenditure so that lime and labour sits alongside tea, flour and jam, the costs of clothes and the children's schooling.[104] This problem is compounded by the fact that expenditure was often paid on tradesmen's bills so the entry in the accounts is merely for the settlement of the bill. We do not know whether it was for household provisions or for the farm (although identifying the supplier may well give a clue). The truth is that farm accounts for private farms (as opposed to home farms) are often personal accounts in which private and business income and expenditure are hopelessly mixed. So whilst accounts could be of some sophistication, and serve a useful role in enabling the farmer to understand how well he was doing, it also seems likely that the immediate purpose of accounts was not so much a measure of expenditure but a note that a particular account had been settled by a payment or a receipt. The key indicator of success or failure remained the cash balance at the bank, and how readily the farmer could pay his landlord on rent days.

One does not have to accept the full force of Bryer's comment that only accountants can understand farm accounts, nor has one to have perfect accounts to draw useful material from them. It is the case that so far we have barely scratched the surface in understanding what farmers hoped to achieve by keeping accounts or how the accounts they kept reflect their understanding of

---

[104] This is the case with the Brown of Aldbourne accounts. A leaflet advising farmers on completing an income tax form of 1903 specifically warned that household expenditure was not to be included in farm expenditure. Board of Agriculture and Fisheries leaflet 26, 'Farmers and the Income Tax'.

their business, preferring to exploit them, as several authors in this book do, for the evidence they contain of farming practices.

VIII

What we lack for the nineteenth century is farmers' correspondence. The Culley brothers' detailed, gossiping and hectoring letters to the bailiff on their Durham farm are exceptional.[105] In many cases we have a farmer's letters to their landlord or his agent and on a couple of occasions they have been used to describe the lives of prominent tenants,[106] but correspondence of this sort can only ever give a one-dimensional view of the farmer. Family letters are scarce indeed, but where we might find them are in the records of colonial settlers receiving letters from home. For more public correspondence we need to search local newspapers for evidence of the farmer in his public guises, whether as letter writer on agrarian matters or as speaker at public meetings.

What we will not find before the First World War is much contact between the farmer and the state. Without a doubt farmers always tried to influence the state through petitioning and lobbying, often by societies which claimed to speak on the farmers' behalf and to know his mind. There were rare occasions when the state became involved in the farmer's sphere, notably in outbreaks of cattle disease (there was no farm-level regulation of the corn market in our period). The close direction of farming in the second half of the First World War and again after 1939 was therefore something quite new for the farmer and produced a distinctive genre of literature, the letter from the farmer to the local agents of state pleading for the amendment of the directions he laboured under. In a sense this was the moment when the British farmer came of age and found themselves having to structure their operations not around covenants in leases but according to priorities set in Westminster and transmitted step by step to the local communities by the County War Executives. Hilary Crowe exploits exceptional survivals to draw this world in detail in her contribution to this volume whilst others have shown how much there is to be gleaned from the newspapers of the war years.[107]

---

[105] Anne Orde (ed.), *Matthew and George Culley: Farming Letters, 1798–1804* (Surtees Soc., 210, 2006). See also J.H. Bettey (ed.), 'George Boswell's Letters, 1787–1805', in *Farming in Dorset* (Dorset Rec. Soc., 13, 1993), pp. 117–68 for letters from a Dorset correspondent of the Culleys.

[106] Louisa Cresswell, Mary Mackie, *The Prince's Thorn: Edward VII and the Lady Farmer of Sandringham* (Cambridge, 2008) and for General William Fitzroy, a tenant of T.W. Coke's at Holkham, Mary-Anne Garry in *An Uncommon Tenant, Fitzroy and Holkham, 1808–1837* (Dereham, 1996).

[107] Hilary Crowe, 'Murmurs of Discontent': The Upland Response to the Plough Campaign, 1916–18', below pp. 263–93.; Bonnie White, 'Feeding the War Effort: Agricultural Experiences in First World War Devon, 1914–17', *AgHR* 58 (2010), pp. 95–112.

Writing the history of the twentieth-century farmer may prove to be more difficult than writing that of his nineteenth-century forebears. With the slow decline of the landed estate and the rise of the owner-occupying farmer, there is much less to be discovered in the estate records. Farmers had to be responsible for keeping their own records, and for the most part they did have not had their eyes fixed on posterity. It would not be possible for John Martin to describe the career of Rex Paterson or Philip Conford, Robert Stuart in any detail without their own papers, but these are rare survivals. We do have some assets. There is, for instance, the possibility of exploiting the mass of fictional, semi-fictional and autobiographical accounts of farming. In some locations a lot of oral history material has been gathered. There is a full farming and local press to exploit, to which some farmers were vocal and articulate contributors. Particularly for the period before 1939, we have a moderate number of farm accounts in public archives (although more would be welcome). Richard Tranter has recently published a paper drawing on a number of west Berkshire farm accounts to show how those farms positioned themselves in the poor years of the 1930s.[108] One suspects that increasingly small numbers survive from after the war. Certainly few are in archives and one imagines that only small numbers survive in farm lofts and outbuildings, or in the bottom drawer of the farm office's filing cabinet. What may be a substitute are the records of the Farm Management Survey (which continues as the Farm Business Survey), both the annual reports to government but also the individual farm returns where these survive.[109] The latter are in effect farm accounts constructed to a standard template. Here Hilary Crowe has been doing pioneering work on the re-analysis of the accounts for the Westward in Westmorland using software which could be applied elsewhere.[110] Meanwhile, Michael Winter and a group at Exeter have been re-analysing the south-western farm accounts and, by being able to put names to otherwise anonymised returns, have been able to use the accounts as prompts to discuss farm decision-making with older (often retired) farmers. Some material which one would hope to survive is, however, almost certainly lost. Hampshire has apparently retained the records of its interwar county advisory officers' dealings with individual farmers, but the client records of the post-war government advisory services seem to have been entirely destroyed although one hopes that some may yet turn up. Given the importance of ADAS and its predecessors as the means by which government implemented its policies, this is, at the very least, disappointing.

---

[108]   R.B. Tranter, 'Agricultural Adjustment on the Berkshire Downs during the Recession of 1921–38', *AgHR* 60 (2012), pp. 214–40.

[109]   For the FMS, Richard Moore-Colyer, *Farming in Wales, 1936–2011: 75 Years of the Farm Business Survey* (Talybont, 2011); Paul Brassley, David Harvey, Matt Lobley and Michael Winter, 'Accounting for Agriculture: The Origins of the Farm Management Survey', *AgHR* 61 (2013), pp. 135–53.

[110]   Hilary Crowe, 'A Wasteful Use of the Nation's Resources': Farm Subsidy in the Uplands, 1947–70' (forthcoming).

A number of historians, following the lead of Brian Short, have exploited the wartime materials.[111] In this volume Martin shows how much rich material there is on the dealings of one exceptional farmer – Rex Paterson – in the minutes of the Hampshire County Agricultural Executive Committee but also how necessary Paterson's own papers are to allow a full story to emerge. In general terms it seems likely that the government records dealing with questions of policy have been retained whilst those dealing with individual farmers have been destroyed. In this way, the management of modern records has not altogether served the historian well. Perhaps these comments will have some of the galvanising effect of Jones and Collin's pioneering articles of nearly half a century ago. We cannot rely on fortuitous survival but need to act now to preserve what we, and future historians, might wish to have to study.

IX

The chapters in this volume are all, to a greater or lesser extent, based on chance survivals – of accounts, of diaries or memoirs, a cache of wartime correspondence of a sort normally destroyed, in the case of Paterson and Stuart personal archives. Whilst much more can be done with this sort of material, it does bring the disadvantage that it tends to lead to a certain atomisation of the farming community. There is an alternative approach which we need to consider. Discussion of well-documented individuals gets us so far, and only so far. We also need to have some strategy for considering the much larger number of farmers who are never more than names in rentals and directories. There are sources which can used to construct something of their lives in the nineteenth century. The first is the census which allows us to reach individuals, chart the expansion and contraction of their families, establish their mobility,[112] the acreage they farmed and the numbers they employed. Then, second, there are local newspapers – increasingly digitised – which may allow us to put some flesh on the bones of the census. Finally there are wills – accessible if not properly in the public domain – which may give some evidence for wealth and the disposition of wealth.

---

[111] B. Short, C. Watkins, W. Foot and P. Kinsman, *The National Farm Survey 1941–1943: State Surveillance and the Countryside in England and Wales in the Second World War* (Wallingford, 2000); Janet Waymark, 'The War Agricultural Executive Committee in Dorset: State-Directed Farming or the Preservation of the Landed Estate' and Brian Short, 'The Dispossession of Farmers in England and Wales during and after the Second World War' both in Short et al. (eds), *Frontline of Freedom*.

[112] See here the important paper by David Stead which argues from logic rather than any hard data about farmer's mobility: 'The Mobility of English Tenant Farmers, *c*.1700–1850', in *AgHR* 51 (2003), pp. 173–89.

We need to see farmers not only as individuals but as businesses extending over generations, engaging in both life-cycles of capital accumulation and then distribution but also larger arcs of capital accumulation and decline. It may be suggested, for instance, that in eastern England, the high prices of the Napoleonic wars offered unparalleled opportunities for capital accumulation. It was this which allowed the emergence of the furnishings-rich Farmer Giles and his wife. There then followed an extended post-war period in which the possibilities of accumulation were very limited indeed, and tenants found themselves paying their rent out of capital. At the same time both landlords and tenants recoiled from the making of leases, farmers not wishing to be committed to levels of rent that they could not meet and landlords to missing out of any future bonanza in agricultural profits. An unintended victim of this may well have been the farmer's widow. A landlord whose tenant held by lease could do little about his widow taking over the farm whilst the lease ran, at least until she fell into arrears, whilst a widow whose husband held at will was entirely at the mercy of her landlord as to whether or not he was willing to allow her to keep on the farm. The emergence of tenant right as a species of property that farmers had in land which was not theirs may also be seen as both a reaction to the lack of leases but also the growing sophistication of farming.[113] The mid Victorian years of high farming allowed a new prosperity to arise amongst farmers, but the early 1880s, as depression set in, established farmers were again living off capital and some were withdrawing from farming to try and harbour what they had. The impression from both the Holkham estates discussed by Dr Wade Martins and the Wold farming community described by Dr Olney is that farming was dynastic, both in the sense that generation succeeded generation but also that farmers intermarried, sometimes over quite long distances. By the end of the century the weaker, or perhaps less adaptable, farming families had left the business.[114] As a Suffolk correspondent of Rider Haggard's said: 'The old type of farmers is gone, either dead or pauperised. His capital is gone also'.[115]

Here the records of the bankruptcy courts, often reported in the county newspapers in lurid detail, have a contribution to make. The new men coming into farming, some of them already farmers in northern England and Scotland, had lower expectations than the old and expected their wives to be equally active in the management of the farm and their children to work as labourers. Some landlords found that they drove a hard bargain and were disinterested in the

---

[113]   I have written further about the emergence of tenant right in the sense of compensation for farmers' improvements in my *Tenure in Tawney's Century* (forthcoming).

[114]   S. Wade Martins, *A Great Estate at Work: The Holkham Estate and Its Inhabitants in the Nineteenth Century* (Cambridge 1980), ch. 4 gives helpful figures for the turnover of tenants on the Holkham estate; Olney, *Rural Society*, pp. 58–62.

[115]   Rider Haggard, *Rural England*, II, p. 411.

old paternalist approach of landlords to tenants.[116] By about 1910 the worst of the depression was past and it becomes an interesting counterfactual as to how agriculture might have developed had war not broken out. As it happened, hopes that it would continue to run at a high level were dashed by the 'Great Betrayal' of 1921. But by this time the great estates were dissolving. Tenants who reluctantly bought but who were able to navigate the 1920s and 1930s had, by the 1950s and 1960s, a valuable asset in their land (which they could use to underpin their farming activities) and every incentive to accumulate more when the possibility arose.

There is so much we don't know, both about farmers as individuals, charting a course from year to year in waters which were often choppy, or farmers as a community coping with generation-long episodes of depression in agriculture or taking advantage of moments of agricultural prosperity. If these essays convince others of the importance of the farmer, and persuade some to answer his neglect, then our purpose will have been served.

X

Finally, we offer this book as a gift to E.J.T. Collins, universally known as Ted, albeit more than a decade after his retirement but at a time when he still has projects to bring to fruition and continues to cast an eye over the profession and its doings. Ted has been a constant presence in agricultural history (doubtless his favoured name for the profession) for over 40 years. As a number of contributors have noted, he was amongst the first to spot the potential of farm accounts. His most public contribution came as editor of the gigantean volume VII of the *Agrarian History of England and Wales* published in 2000. Like so many others of his generation, much of his best work is locked within those brown covers and green boards and for that reason has attracted less attention than it might otherwise have done. As Director of the conjoined Institute of Agricultural History and Museum of English Rural Life from 1980 (latterly the Rural History Centre) in the University of Reading, he not only kept the national centre for agricultural and rural history alive – no mean feat which involved him holding his ground against more than one unsympathetic vice chancellor – but also did much of the ground work which ultimately saw the Centre move – after his retirement – to new premises. He masterminded the first bid to the Heritage Lottery Fund and to his credit kept the project alive when that failed. It is a matter of enduring sadness to him that the Museum of English Rural Life (as the Centre is now configured) makes so little contribution to the study of

---

[116] Olney, *Rural Society*, 58–62, Hunt and Pam, 'Agricultural Depression'. See also the anecdote told by Rider Haggard of a Scots tenant taking over a farm in Suffolk, *Rural England*, II, p. 99.

his discipline. Ted has also been a stalwart of the Agricultural History Society, serving from 1979 to 1997 as its treasurer (a notably prudent treasurer too) and from 1998 to 2001 as its president. Most of the contributors to this book have known Ted in some way – as a supervisor or colleague or fellow participant in the conferences of the British Agricultural History Society – and if not personally, then as a beneficiary of the collections which he helped establish at Reading and long presided over. There is nothing in this book about some of Ted's preoccupations – not a mention of edge tools for instance – and he will enjoy some chapters more than others, but it is dedicated to Ted with the affection and gratitude of fellow workers, treading paths he has also trod.

Figure 1.4   E.J.T. (Ted) Collins. Photograph courtesy of Peter Dewey

Chapter 2

A New View of the Fells: Sarah Fell of Swarthmoor and her Cashbook

Jennifer S. Holt

The Fells of Swarthmoor Hall in Lancashire over the Sands have attracted a great deal of attention from historians as one of the founding families of Quakerism. Margaret Fell (1614–1702), the widow of Thomas Fell (1600–1658), married George Fox in 1669.[1] The account books discussed here were kept by Thomas and Margaret's daughter Sarah (1642–1714). Because of the Quaker association, they were first deemed worthy of preservation and then printed as long ago as 1920.[2] On this occasion our interest is not with the Fells' Quakerism but as representative examples of the northern yeomanry who acquired gentry status in the seventeenth century through their access to the universities and the practice of the law. The keeper of the accounts, Sarah Fell, was the fourth of the daughters of Thomas and Margaret Fell. She is normally discussed in the light cast by her stepfather Fox; by definition, much of this writing is hagiographical.[3] Here we exploit the accounts to cast light on the lives of Margaret Fell and her daughters as landowners and farmers in Furness in the 1670s.

I

In her preface to *Margaret Fell, Mother of Quakerism*, Isabel Ross states:

---

[1]   Swarthmoor is the modern spelling but it has, in the past, been interchangeable with 'Swarthmore.' Much of the overview of the family given here draws upon the entry for Margaret Fell in *ODNB*. In all cases, the year has been taken to start on 1 Jan. but the dates are otherwise unaltered. The Lancashire acre given here should be multiplied by 1.6 to give statute acres. Entries in the cashbook are given by date only.

[2]   The cash books are now in the keeping of Library of the Society of Friends, Euston Road, London and are printed in Norman Penney, *The Household Account Book of Sarah Fell of Swarthmoor Hall* (Cambridge, 1920). The whole of Penney's text may now be found at http://www.archive.org/details/householdaccount00fell. Historians owe a real debt of gratitude to Penney for transcribing all the extant text and adding extensive supporting notes.

[3]   An early text, to which many later writers refer and which may be taken to be typical of the genre, is Maria Webb, *The Fells of Swarthmoor and Their Friends* (Philadelphia, 2nd edn, 1896).

Swarthmoor Hall was exceptional in that it received letters and visitors from all parts of the British Isles, from the continent of Europe and from across the Atlantic. At that time, Furness otherwise was part of England to and from which travellers were few.[4]

Some of the evidence for this statement was taken from the cashbook kept by Margaret's daughter, Sarah, which Ross describes as 'unique for a manor house of north Lancashire in the seventeenth century'. However what is truly unique about Sarah Fell's cashbook is its survival when similar records kept by men and women of similar standing were destroyed long ago.[5] As to the isolation of Furness; seventeenth-century records demonstrate that people of much lower social status than the Fell family could travel significant distances across the British Isles. Nor was travel to and from Europe and the Americas as rare as might be assumed. On a more regular basis, ordinary people visited markets and fairs over a wide area. After all, it was they (and not their gentry employers) who normally took livestock and other goods to markets and fairs held across the north-west. All the Fell estates were close to the sea and crossing the Sands of Morecambe Bay was the usual way of reaching areas to the south and east. The family were also well placed to take advantage of the economic opportunities proffered by the Irish Sea and coastal trades and the extant accounts show that these were readily seized.[6]

II

Before considering the surviving records left by Sarah Fell, we need to know something of the Fell family. Thomas Fell (Sarah's father) was born in 1600 and entered Gray's Inn in 1623 when he was named as son and heir of George Fell of Ulverston, gentleman. In 1631, Ulverston contained two wealthy men called George Fell, the elder of whom can now be identified as the father of Thomas. His will has recently been identified and an internal reference dates it to the six months or so before 2 February 1638/9; Fell was dead by 1641.[7] In addition

---

[4]　　Isabel Ross, *Margaret Fell, Mother of Quakerism* (London, 1949), p. vi.

[5]　　Sarah Fell's cashbook was one of two seventeenth-century women's records discussed in Judith Spicksley, 'Two seventeenth-century female "accountants": Joyce Jeffreys and Sarah Fell', *Bull. British Society for the History of Mathematics* 6 (2005), pp. 1–8.

[6]　　The growth of the coastal trade around the Irish Sea in the first part of the seventeenth century, followed by its expansion to continental Europe and the Americas, is discussed in A.B. Appleby, *Famine in Tudor and Stuart England* (Liverpool, 1978), ch. 11.

[7]　　Both George Fells compounded for refusing knighthoods. *VCH Lancashire*, VIII, p. 354, n. 89. I am very grateful to the members of the Swarthmoor Hall History Group for informing me that the will of George Fell had been identified; it may be found at Lancashire Archives (hereafter LA), WRW/F/1681.

to his only son, Thomas, George Fell mentioned a number of sons-in-law, grandchildren and an unmarried daughter, Alice. Thomas Fell combined a good legal mind and a fairly radical political stance; he had a successful career and was appointed a parliamentary sequestrator in 1642. In 1646 Fell was returned to Parliament as one of the members for Lancaster; the other was Sir Robert Bindloss of Borwick Hall. By 1651 he was an assize judge in north Wales and Cheshire and later served as Chancellor of the Duchy of Lancaster. Fell made his will in September 1658 and left £10 to Lord Bradshaw (the regicide) to buy a ring which indicates more than just a professional relationship.[8] In 1632 Fell had married Margaret Askew, the elder of the two daughters of John Askew of Marsh Grange gentleman.[9] This was an entirely suitable marriage for it added the Askew lands at Marsh Grange to the growing Fell estates. Furthermore, it brought Margaret's considerable intelligence, education and determination to bear on her husband's affairs during his necessary absences whilst he pursued his legal career. Sarah Fell was in her thirties at the time she was maintaining the cashbook. She was to marry William Meade in 1681. Their only known child, Nathaniel, was born in 1684 but died without issue in 1760.

When Thomas Fell died in 1658 his wife was already heavily influenced by the teachings of George Fox. During his life, Fell had been able to offer some protection to these early Quakers but subsequently (and especially after the Restoration) Fox and Margaret Fell were to suffer both imprisonment and the confiscation of their property. In early 1664 Fox and Fell were arrested for holding Quaker assemblies at Swarthmoor. At their trial at Lancaster in March 1664 they were required to swear an oath of allegiance to the crown which their Quaker beliefs did not permit. The judge handed down a sentence of Praemunire by which Fell's estates were forfeit to the crown and she could be held in prison indefinitely.[10] Her son, George, petitioned Charles II for a grant of the forfeited estates and this was given to him in January 1665. Margaret Fell remained in prison until June 1668. In 1669, she and Fox (using the conventions of the Society of Friends) asked permission of the Bristol Meeting to marry.[11] This was granted and the marriage took place there on 27 October 1669. Margaret's daughters also seem to have been happy with the acquisition of a stepfather. George Fell was very much against it but whether this opposition arose from an

---

8   The entries for both men are adjacent in the list of Duchy of Lancaster office holders and show that they served together over a number years. Robert Somerville, *Office Holders in the Duchy and County Palatine of Lancaster from 1603* (Chichester, 1972), p. 2.

9   Frances, the younger Askew daughter, had married Matthew Richardson by 1634.

10   Praemunire has a complex history dating back to the fourteenth century but in the seventeenth century it was used to penalise those who (like the Quakers) felt that oaths should be sworn only to God.

11   Although she took her second husband's name, writers normally continue to refer to her as Margaret Fell and that convention has been used here.

oedipal response, a dislike of Fox and his religious views, or fears for the security of the Fell inheritance we cannot now know.[12]

During the period covered by the cashbook Margaret Fell left Swarthmoor to greet Fox at Bristol on his return from America in June 1673. In December of that year Fox was arrested and imprisoned at Worcester until February 1675; during much of this period his health was extremely poor. Both Margaret Fell and Dr Thomas Lower (her son-in-law) spent long periods with Fox during his imprisonment; on his release, he travelled to Swarthmoor where the couple remained together until March 1677. Fox was away from Swarthmoor for the rest of the period under discussion but Margaret Fell remained there until May 1681.

By the time of the cashbooks, Sarah's brother George had died, leaving a widow (Sister Fell) and two children (Isabel and Charles). Margaret Fell junior (born *c.*1633) was married to John Rous and they lived at Mile End outside London with their young children. Bridget was born about 1635 and had married one John Draper of Co. Durham in 1662. She died in the following year and it appears that her share of the sisters' inheritance passed to Sarah and Mary Fell. Isabel, the third sister (1639–1674) was married to William Yeamans of Bristol. Her surviving son features frequently in the cashbook for he appears to have lived with his grandmother and aunts at Swarthmoor. Mary Fell (1646–1720) was married to Dr Thomas Lower; the couple and their many children appear in the cashbooks. The three remaining sisters (Sarah, Susannah and Rachel) were all still unmarried and living at Swarthmoor. The house at Swarthmoor was much altered by Emma Abrahams at the end of the nineteenth century; it is thought that the house Sarah Fell lived in was very similar to Shuttleworth Hall which (externally) is little changed by the centuries. Swarthmoor paid on 13 hearths in the Hearth Tax placing it in the upper echelons of gentry houses in north Lancashire and Westmorland.[13]

III

The financial records upon which this chapter is based were dispersed from Swarthmoor in the later eighteenth century. They were noticed being used by a Lancaster grocer to wrap goods in and rescued for their Quaker interest. This chapter is based on the transcript of the accounts published by Norman Penney in 1920, itself an act of Quaker hagiography. They are usually referred to as 'household account books' but this is misleading and it is preferable to call them cashbooks for they record all the sums passing through Sarah Fell's hands,

---

[12] George Fell may well have feared a second action of Praemunire.

[13] For a photograph of the house see VCH *Lancashire*, VIII, opp. p. 356 and for Shuttleworth Hall, VII, p. 10. The Hearth Tax returns for Westmorland (which is comparable with Furness) show that only 58 houses within the county had more than 5 hearths. Colin Phillips et al. (eds), *Westmorland Hearth Tax Michaelmas 1670 and Surveys 1674–5* (British Record Society Hearth Tax Series 19, 2008), p. 94.

including those she received on behalf of others.[14] As financial records the cashbooks are both fascinating and frustrating. Fascinating because they include references to just about every financial activity available to a gentry family in late seventeeth-century England, frustrating because they do not provide a complete picture of any one of the many trading or agrarian activities in which the family was involved. For instance, whilst the carriage of goods from Lancaster, Kirkby Lonsdale and Newcastle upon Tyne is recorded, the actual purchases were made by others and so the cost and precise nature of the goods is not known.[15] Furthermore, due in part to the complexities of land tenure in this part of north-west England (which are compounded by the various transactions between the Fell siblings and the effects of the imprisonments of Margaret Fell), it has proved impossible to identify fully the nature and extent of the landholdings referred to in Fell's cashbook. The main Fell holding of Swarthmoor appears to have been a free tenancy held from the Prestons of the Manor of Furness but other lands had been purchased and added to the original estate. For instance, in 1650, Thomas Fell bought former Furness Abbey lands lying in Dalton in Furness to which were attached the right to feed 300 milk cows on Sandes Marsh.[16] Lands within Ulverston, held of the manor of Osmotherley, were released to little Charles Fell by all his aunts in 1678 but the route by which they came into their hands is unclear. Marsh Grange, on the other hand, was a tenant right holding and so theoretically remained the property of Margaret Fell during her marriages and widowhoods.[17] Whilst Margaret Fell was imprisoned in Lancaster Castle between 1664 and 1668, George Fell obtained a grant of his mother's forfeited estates.[18] George Fell died during his mother's second period of imprisonment at Lancaster (April 1670 to April 1671). On her release from prison, the king granted her paternal estates at Marsh Grange to her youngest daughters Susannah and Rachel. Ross states that in the following month Sarah Fell bought out the share of Marsh Grange held by the executors of her late brother for £1250.[19] This represented two-thirds of the estate and carried a customary rent

---

[14]   The fundamental difference between a cashbook (a list of cash received and disbursed) and accounts is that, in the latter, balances are drawn and profits/losses calculated. At no time in these records are balances drawn in that way; instead there is the constant reiteration of the accounts to which the cash relates.

[15]   There are also entries such as the 6d. cost of making a container to send clapbread to London, 3 June 1678.

[16]   These lands cost £274 5s. 4d. We should assume that Fell also acquired others lands. Cumbria RO (Kendal), WD RAD/T 19.

[17]   One of the key features of tenant right was that, in the absence of a surviving son (or his issue) the estate went to the eldest daughter and did not pass into her husband's hands on marriage. If a wife died without issue then her tenant right estates went to her own next of kin.

[18]   VCH *Lancashire*, VIII, p. 354.

[19]   As Sarah Fell paid interest on bonds which are designated 'Marsh Grange account', it is possible that these relate to mortgages connected with this purchase. Ross, *Margaret Fell*, pp. 224–7. Cashbook

of £4 16s. 4d. It is said that George Fell's widow, Hannah, continued to live at Marsh Grange until 1676 when Thomas Lower bought it.[20] Furthermore, other lands were leased or rented by the year. Disentangling which lands are being described in the cashbook is often difficult.

The nature of many of the transactions referred to in the cash book is also often hard to ascertain. There are indications of which family member a transaction relates to but not, necessarily, why it does so. The bulk of the cashbook entries relate to Margaret Fell, with 'Marsh Grange' and 'ours/we sisters' almost equalling them in number. In addition, entries refer to 'sisters Susannah and Rachel', 'my account', 'Sister Fell', 'father' (George Fox) and members of the Lower family. Sarah also acted as agent for Henry Coward of Lancaster, Thomas Curwen of London, various Quaker Meetings as well as many of her neighbours, in addition to her own business interests in Force Forge, the sales of iron ore and the partnership she had with Joseph Sharpe.[21] In all, 33 accounts are referred to in the cashbooks. To this complexity may be added the two coastal voyages to Bristol and to Cornwall that the family undertook in 1674 and 1677 which we discuss below. One further problem limits our ability to exploit this resource. As we noted, prior to its rescue the pages of the book were being used as wrapping paper. Consequently, the accounts are incomplete with sheets removed at the beginning and the end; furthermore sheets and half-sheets were torn out of the middle.[22] The effects of these depredations are shown in Tables 2.1 and 2.2 where the gaps indicate total loss and the months in roman type are to a greater or lesser extent lost. The only year for which full coverage remains is 1674 which lies within longer runs from 27 December 1673 to 15 June 1675 for income and 15 December 1673 to 3 June 1675 for expenditure. The net result is that we have, at best, partial entries for all the September entries between November 1673 and August 1678. On the other hand, full April entries exist for all years 1674 to 1678 inclusive. Clearly, when faced with the level of fragmentation shown in Tables 2.1 and 2.2 it becomes much more difficult to generalise about (for instance) yearly patterns of activity.[23]

---

entries for 5 Feb., 23 Apr., 30 Apr., 7 May, 10 May, 15 Dec., 17 Dec. 1674.

[20]   His entry fine of £9 12s. 8d. was recorded as being paid to the Bailiff of the Liberties on 2 Aug. 1677. There are some contradictions in this account of the Fell holdings which can be attributed to a combination of missing documents and faulty readings by others.

[21]   Many of these partnerships fall outside the present chapter. The best introduction to Force Forge and the Fell interests is B.G. Awty, 'Force Forge in the seventeenth century', *Trans. Cumberland and Westmorland Antiquarian and Archaeological Society (CWAAS)* 77 (1977), pp. 97–112.

[22]   It is not always clear from Penney's transcription that this is the case. Only careful examination of his text revealed small but significant gaps.

[23]   The extensive writings on George Fox and the Fells often serve to confuse matters further. Gaps in the data have normally been overlooked so that absence of evidence has been served up as evidence of absence.

Table 2.1   Number of income entries per month
(complete months in bold)

	1673	1674	1675	1676	1677	1678	Average[a]
Jan.		**38**	**35**	8	**10**	**18**	25
Feb.		**32**	**50**	2	**25**	23	33
Mar.		**17**	**31**	**31**	**40**	17	30
Apr.		**30**	**53**	**22**	**29**	**25**	32
May		**37**	**62**	**29**	**29**	21	39
June		**44**	30	**35**	**21**	26	33
July		**77**		**60**	17		69
Aug.		**64**		**35**	16	21	50
Sept.		**33**		**30**	9		32
Oct.	10	**57**		**21**	13		39
Nov.	12	**26**	18	**26**	**20**		24
Dec.	30	**31**	**21**	13	**19**		21

Note: [a] Average for complete months only.

Table 2.2   Number of expenditure entries per month
(complete months in bold)

	1673	1674	1675	1676	1677	1678	Average[a]
Jan.		**100**	**88**	11	**85**	**75**	87
Feb.		**97**	**88**	49	**99**	93	95
Mar.		**74**	**71**	**112**	**112**	71	92
Apr.		**113**	**97**	**89**	**89**	**74**	92
May		**128**	**112**	**82**	**100**	72	106
June		**120**	28	**86**	**74**	46	93
July		**171**		**104**	39	23	138
Aug.		**144**		**62**	76	9	94
Sept.	14	**63**		**91**	3		77
Oct.	108	**131**	11	**101**	99		116
Nov.	112	**69**	**90**	**93**	**89**		85
Dec.	29	**92**	**68**	**81**	**59**		75

Note: [a] Average for complete months only.

In order to get maximum benefit out of the undoubted riches that remain it was decided to discuss farming practice as though only one estate was involved. After all, the problems and opportunities available to Margaret Fell were the same as those presented to 'we sisters' or 'Brother Lower'. It was also decided at an early stage that when making generalisations, only data from complete months would be used. In order to avoid constant repetition of the factual basis for generalisations, the reader is directed towards Tables 2.1 and 2.2 which give the number of entries shown in the extant cashbook.

Consideration of Tables 2.1 and 2.2 show that there was a general increase in the number of entries for both income and expenditure during the spring and summer months, with a peak in July. The number of entries then fall away. A second peak appears in November and the numbers then return to their lower levels in the winter months. This simplicity is misleading for the complexity of Fell's transactions and the huge range in the cash amounts mean that no one month was necessarily busier, or carried more responsibilities for her, than any other. The range of activities with which Sarah Fell was involved included feeding the household, farming the family's lands and maximising agrarian and industrial production. The sums of money handled by Fell ran from fractions of a penny to hundreds of pounds and related to transactions with all sections of the local community and correspondents across the British Isles, Europe and America. Her actual cash in hand also fluctuated but it is noticeable that when the figure got too high, the excess was spent whereas, when the figure dropped, the number of expenditure items also fell. This is logical enough, but may indicate that others were paying for items in place of Sarah Fell. When the cashbook starts in 1674 Fell had a running total of about £30 and little was spent. The year 1675 started low but at the end of January she received £120 and this was used to clear a bond of £100. In 1676 there were running totals of about £20 until December when it moved to around £100 but this fell back again to around £30. In July the cash in hand rose to £120 but had dropped again by September. Autumn 1677 saw a rise which continued into the next year when Fell maintained the higher level of around £70. In February 1678 Fell received £350 which was quickly reduced to £120 and then fell back to around £30. What we cannot tell from this is whether she received funds in order to be able to pay others or whether the receipt stimulated the payment.

What rapidly becomes clear is that this is a most meticulous accounting of the cash passing through Fell's hands. Careful reading shows that a significant proportion of the entries are part payments of larger sums for which we cannot see payment of the balance.[24] With such a high proportion of the entries

---

[24] These take many forms, of which the carriage paid without the sale of goods, the balance for a sale or purchase paid for but no record of the deposit are probably the most common.

reflecting only part of a transaction it must be that other family members were also undertaking transactions on behalf of others.[25]

After such a comprehensive critique, the question may be asked, do the cashbooks really have any value? To which the answer is a resounding 'yes'. Several aspects of the cashbooks give them real value and not least the comprehensive notes which are attached to many of the items, irrespective of monetary value. Fell was carrying a lot of cash on behalf of other people and she could not afford to get confused as to how much, to whom and for what reason the amounts were received or paid. One example must stand for all: '22 March 1674: To money received of Math: Gardner (per Willm Hathornthwait) for 4 bushels of old malt sold to Fra: Washingtons wife of Dalton, of ours at Marshgrange 19s. 6d.' Internal evidence suggests that she made notes in transit and these were copied into the cashbook at the first convenient moment.[26] We may reasonably ask why Fell undertook this huge burden? The most probable reason is that, as the eldest unmarried daughter, it was her role to act as her mother's right hand. Having said that, many of those for whom Fell acted as agent must have known and trusted her understanding of business and competence to deal with the often complex matters which consumed her time.[27]

Although only 1674 provides a full series of entries, those for other years can still be used to generate price series or indicate the seasonality of activities. Furthermore, using the whole dataset allows us to discover not just what people bought but how they obtained goods or undertook activities. Bearing in mind that only actions which generated cash transactions are given, even a single transaction can be used as a picklock to enter this world.

IV

The Fells practiced both arable and pastoral farming but we have more evidence for the former.[28] As might be expected, oats provided the most sales, whether

---

[25]   A useful parallel are the 1737 and 1739 accounts of the 'True Love', a vessel trading out of Lancaster. A share formed part of the inheritance of Ann Fenwick, née Benison, and the captain's accounts for her share are extant in the papers of the Hornby Roman Catholic Mission which she founded. LA, RCHy 2/5/26 and 27.

[26]   It seems very likely that the cashbook was kept safely at home and the neatness of its appearance does contrast with the often scribbled notes made by others in their cashbooks which were clearly aide-mémoires rather than a full explanation. Certainly we can find examples elsewhere of servants submitting claims on scraps of paper but the final sum appearing in the housekeeper's cashbook as though she had paid it direct.

[27]   There were some benefits for Sarah Fell as Thomas Curwen of London, glover, sent her a present of gloves – although she did have to pay 2d. carriage: 16 Mar. 1677.

[28]   The approach taken to this extensive data series needs to be described so that context of the following discussions is clear. All the grain sales were extracted and the price in shillings per bushel

calculated by volume (480 bushels) or value (£92), with wheat in second place by value (£72).[29] The recorded sales show that malt was the usual way of maximising the income from the bigg crop (a type of barley) with the added value coming through the use of their kiln on Petty's Tenement.[30] In terms of both volume and value, rye comes fourth and, although it only appears in the 1675 entries, it is, nonetheless, a useful place to start our examination of grain sales. At least eight bushels of Marsh Grange rye was sold between January and June with the number of sales rising from one in each of the first four months of the year to five in both May and June, with the price rising from 16s. per bushel to 17s. per bushel in the latter two months. There is no obvious reason why only Marsh Grange should produce rye for sale or why it had not done so in earlier or succeeding years.

If we now turn to the quantities and prices of malt, then an even more useful picture emerges which is shown in Figure 2.1. All the recorded malt sales are shown (apart from one for 6d. in October 1676) and, as with the rye sales given above, will be discussed further in the context of the total grain sales and the management of resources.

Before turning to the main grains, passing reference must be made to the two trading enterprises undertaken by the Fells in 1674 and 1677. The 'Bristol Voyage' occurred between April and July 1674 when bigg, wheat and oats were shipped southwards.[31] Grain surplus to the voyage (mainly wheat but some bigg too) was sold by Sarah Fell: the last recorded sale took place in January 1675. The 1677 voyage was referred to interchangeably as the 'Cornwall' or 'Oat Voyage'; the oats shipped on that voyage were purchased from as far afield as Manchester. No sales of oats were recorded in the cashbook between October 1676 and February 1678 and this is assumed to be a side effect of the 'Oat Voyage'. The sales of oats are shown in Figure 2.1 and demonstrate a generally similar trend to that for malt.

Wheat has been left until last as any discussion of its price is much more complicated. For the other grains, the only categories are 'old' or 'new'. In the case of wheat we have the additional grades of 'Marsh Grange', 'March' and 'left over from Bristol Voyage' and these gave rise to noticeable differences in price with the last consistently fetching a higher price. The higher value of wheat generated more sales

---

calculated. The actual values and volumes were then totalled by month to give a starting point of a number (n) of sales relating to volume (bushels) sold for price (shillings). Each month's data was then considered and a 'typical' price identified. In many cases, most or all the prices were the same. In cases where number of transactions was such (less than four per month) and/or there were a range of prices, the preference was given to those sales which were stated to be 'sold at market' or related to larger volumes.

[29]   All totals are minima.

[30]   This was part of the Marsh Grange estate.

[31]   Isabel Fell married into the Yeamans family who were merchants of Bristol. The oats were shipped as grain, groats and meal – see the discussion of the voyage below.

but typically these were for smaller volumes with the lowest being a half hoop (that is, $^1/_{32}$ of a bushel). Virtually all the wheat sales were of one bushel or less. Of the three sales of two bushels of wheat, one was for 'Bristol Voyage' wheat whilst both the others featured amongst a series of grain sales to 'old Kilner wife of Ulverstone'.[32] The comparative prices are nicely displayed in a sale of February 1675 when 'old Kilner wife' paid 16s. for one bushel of rye, 15s. 9d. for one bushel of March wheat and 25s. for one and a quarter bushels of Marsh Grange wheat. In the same month, Swarthmoor wheat was selling at 24s. the bushel.[33]

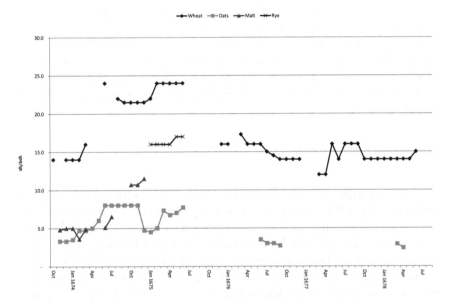

Figure 2.1   Grain prices from Sarah Fells' cashbook

All the grain data discussed above have been used to produce Figure 2.1. There are severe problems in interpreting this chart partly because the sales data are fragmentary but also because we are looking at receipts of cash and not the date of sale. In a general way, the rises and falls in the price of one grain were replicated by the others. The seasonal variation can be identified with (typically) an increase in price as supplies ran low prior to the next harvest. There appears to be a general price rise at the end of 1673 which continued

---

[32]   Penney took this lady to be the one who gave her name to 'Kilner's Wife House' which featured in late seventeenth-century documents. No further information has come to light. Penney, *Household Account Book*, p. 517.

[33]   It should also be noted that the volume of each bushel varied according to the grain type.

into 1674. No clear pattern emerges for 1675 beyond the general point that all grains appear to remain high but in the second quarter of 1676 prices fell and by the end of 1677 the price of wheat seemed to be fairly stable.

The little evidence we have for the purchase of grain does support the sale figures. These are all related to seed corn purchases, the prices of which were generally a little higher than those given for grain sales. In May 1674, 21 bushels of seed oats cost 6.94s. per bushel. Two years later, two bushels were paid for in February 1676 at 4.25s. per bushel but three months later this had fallen slightly and ten bushels cost 4.15s. per bushel. In August 1677, ten bushels cost 2.15s. and in November of that year, eight bushels cost 2.19s. per bushel. The price had risen noticeably by April 1678 when 3.07s. per bushel was paid for five bushels. Similarly, March wheat seed bought in March 1675 cost 18s. per bushel and in the following March this had fallen to 13.33s. per bushel. In October 1676, one bushel of wheat cost 12.5s. whilst two pecks to be sown in 'Angsley' (see below) cost 13s. per bushel. In March 1678, the seed for the March wheat sowing cost 14.93s. per bushel.

V

Whilst the pattern of activities for most livestock is very unclear, that for cattle, though still fragmentary, has fewer portions of the accounts which are completely missing. Bullocks were bought as draught animals but also for the fatstock trade. The bulls owned by Margaret Fell were also a year-round resource for her neighbours though the main time for bulling cows ran between July and September as Figure 2.2 shows. The milk produced by the cows was used to manufacturer butter and cheese for the household and for sale. Surplus stock bred by the Fells also went to market. The recorded purchases and sales show very different patterns. The fairs at which purchases were made spread in a circle from Ravenglass (to the north-west), Ambleside and Hawkshead (to the north), Kirkby Lonsdale (to the east) and Preston (to the south). In contrast, sales were made at fairs which (in general) occurred closer to home. Locations included Dalton in Furness but the bulk of the sales were at Kirkby Lonsdale, Milnthorpe, Hornby and Lancaster. None of the latter lay to the north of Swarthmoor. Logically the Fells would buy from the north and sell to the south (where the demand was greater) and it is interesting to note that this was not the case. Though family members did go through Lancaster and Preston on their journeys, there is nothing to suggest that they went to these fairs and bought or sold for themselves; the indications are that this was delegated to trusted servants. There are other cattle transactions as, for instance, when Margaret Fell exchanged a heifer for a milk cow and paid

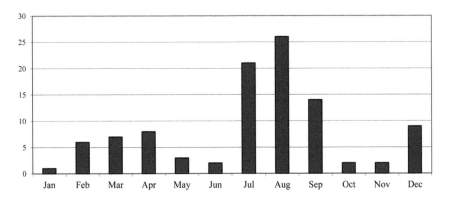

Figure 2.2   Cows bulled in 1674 by date of payment

William Danson £1 7s. 6d. in recognition of the difference in values.[34] In May 1674, she paid £1 4s. for a barrel of Irish beef.[35]

Nor did the Fell womenfolk sell their own butter and cheese at market. The implication of the cashbook entries is that Ellin Pollard ran the Marsh Grange dairy and acted as factor for the sales of both butter and cheese from Swarthmoor and Marsh Grange although Ann Geldart's name also occurs in this context in the early months of 1674 and 1676.[36] The number of cheeses sold is a sufficiently large that we could think of the dairy as a commercial operation rather than one which sold the goods surplus to family needs. The sale of 51 cheeses is recorded in 1674 and 54 in the part-year 1675. There are significantly lower figures for later years. Given the noticeable concentration of bulling dates shown in Figure 2.2, it comes as no surprise to find that the number of cheese and butter sales rose in March and had returned to a low background level by July. However, this may partly be a function of the dataset (see Tables 2.1 and 2.2). Many of the sales combine both cheese with butter or egg sales or do not give the quantities sold. Where a unit price for cheeses could be identified the relevant figures were extracted and are given in Figures 2.3 and 2.4:

---

[34]   27 May 1674.

[35]   30 May 1674.

[36]   The term factor is used deliberately to indicate that both Pollard and Geldart were purchasing butter and cheese but there is no indication of the ultimate destination of these goods. The largest single purchase was for 19 cheeses bought by Pollard on 23 Oct. 1674. In only one case is it stated that the cheeses (four of Margaret Fell's) were sold at market, 7 Apr. 1677.

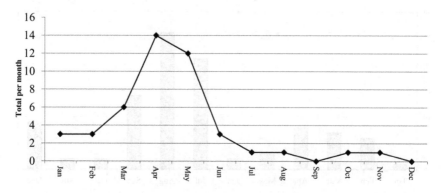

Figure 2.3   Sales of cheeses, totalled by month of sale

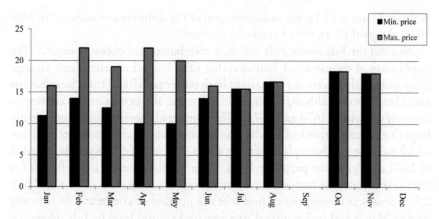

Figure 2.4   Sales of cheeses, price range for each month

Despite the limitations of the figures it was felt important to show the number of cheeses sold where the unit price could be identified.[37] Figure 2.4 shows the maxima and minima of these unit prices. The significant figures are those for the months with the greatest sales where there are marked differences. It is known that spring sales included 'old cheese' and one cheese sold to Pollard on 12 November 1675 for 1s. 6d. was noted 'of 1674 making'. A significant sale of 20 cheeses and 'a piece' was made to Pollard on 16 March 1675 for £1 7s. 9d. which would give a unit price of around 1s. 4d.[38] These two examples suggest that older cheese did not, necessarily, fall significantly in value. This leaves two more possibilities for the price differential: cheeses varied in size or some were

---

[37]   The sales figures represent the number of cheeses, not the number of sales which is much lower.

[38]   The assumption here is that the cheese loft was being cleared ready for the new season's produce.

more adversely affected by mould. No data can be found regarding the size of cheeses. We do, however, have one clue as to the price per pound. In 1677 Sarah Fell had to organise the funeral of her uncle Matthew Richardson; on 22 August she bought 30¾ lbs. of cheese from the wife of Gawen Kirkham at a cost of 5s. which comes to a little more than 1.95d./lb.[39] Although the general pattern of cheese sales was maintained, the proceeds from the sale of butter dwindled to virtually nothing after April 1675. Just one sale of ewe butter was recorded.[40]

Furness was a horse-breeding area and certainly mares with young and the loan of stallions are mentioned in Fell's cash book. However, most information is gained through the cashbook's recipes for horse medicine, mainly for the scab for which the cures included tobacco and 'a pound of brimstone for quicksilver'. In May 1674, four oxen and several horses were blooded by John Fell, smith; this procedure may have been repeated in November and the following April but whether to the same or different horses is unclear.[41] But, the sporadic treatment of horses for scab, sore backs or non-specific illnesses is far outweighed by the healthcare costs for sheep.

Substantial amounts of butter and sheep suet (both used for salves) and tobacco (for sheep washes) were bought at intervals; to the cost of these goods must be added the labour for salving or dipping. The flock sizes are not known but we can use tangential evidence to give a minimum number. If we take J.D. Marshall's estimate of 2lbs of wool per adult fleece, then Margaret Fell (whose clip in 1678 was at least 26 stone) had around 200 sheep whilst the Marsh Grange flock (21 stone) was about 150.[42]

With one exception, there are no records of sheep being purchased.[43] There is, however, plentiful evidence of killing sheep for the table, for market or the selling of animals for the fatstock trade. In May 1675 the hogs were sent to Milnthorpe Fair where the 14 from Swarthmoor fetched 5s. each, but the 15 from Marsh Grange only 4s.[44] In June of that year, Sarah Fell sold nine lambs

---

[39]   Given the circumstances we might expect this to be the best available for the family's reputation would be damaged by cheeseparing. Gawen Kirkham was a mariner – see below – his wife appears to have run an inn at Dalton in Furness.

[40]   This is the only mention of ewe butter: 16 Dec. 1675.

[41]   It is noticeable that different smiths are employed for different purposes and the implication is that there was specialisation. However, a gentry family, such as the Fells, would spread their business across the neighbourhood.

[42]   It is possible that the grazing for 300 cattle on Sandes Marsh referred to above was used for sheep. There is no evidence either way. Marshall built his calculation upon the statement by Hutchinson (in 1794) that 'seven fleeces [from Millom sheep] make a stone in weight'. J.D. Marshall, 'Domestic economy of Lakeland yeoman', *CWAAS* 73 (1973), pp. 192–3.

[43]   One fat sheep costing 7s. 6d. was bought in Apr. 1676 'when William Penn was here'.

[44]   Hogs are sheep before their first clipping: 1 May 1675.

at 3s. 8d. each.[45] In 1676, the hogs were again sold at Milnthorpe Fair when the 20 from Swarthmoor and the 20 from Marsh Grange both fetched 4s. 11d each.[46] In May 1677, Edward Braithwaite incurred costs of 5s. 4d. when he took some of Margaret Fell's sheep to Milnthorpe Fair, but they did not sell. Thirty of her hogs were subsequently taken to Kirkby Lonsdale and sold for 3s. 5d. each. This low sum is in marked contrast with the 4s. 6d. each for the seven hogs and lambs from Swarthmoor sold privately to Jos. Sharpe.[47] The lack of hog sales in 1674 is very odd especially since seven cattle were sold at Milnthorpe Fair that year. Possible explanations include a sale elsewhere and/or the cash was collected by another family member.[48] It is noticeable that both animals and grain from Marsh Grange tended to fetch lower prices than those owned by Margaret Fell which presumably came from the Swarthmoor lands.

Fatstock sales usually took place in December. In 1674 five sheep (four fat wethers and one ewe) were sold to William Danson with the wethers fetchings 8s. each and the ewe only 5s.[49] In December 1675 Ja. Cooper paid £3 15s. for the fat stock he had sold on the sisters' behalf. The following December six fat Swarthmoor sheep were sold for 7.25s. each and, in January 1678 the money was received for three fat Swarthmoor sheep sold for 8s. each. Between August and October 1674 three sheep were killed and their meat sold at market. There is no record of similar sales in other years and so gives rise to another anomaly in 1674 to add to the apparent lack of bulk sales of hogs in May.[50]

The demands of the Swarthmoor livestock were greater than the Fell lands could support and Margaret Fell rented additional grazing and meadowland. These lay in a broad strip running from Plumpton (to the north-east of Swarthmoor) southwards to Gleaston. Margaret Fell had an arrangement over several years to rent Gleaston Milldam Meadow from James Kendall, the customary tenant there, who held Gleaston Castle, the Mill and adjacent lands. The three-acre meadow cost her £4 per annum to which must be added the barn she rented to hold hay at a cost of 5s. per annum. Kendall's family benefited

---

[45]   These came from Roanhead and are assumed to relate in some way to the substantial amount of money owed her by Matthew Richardson: 8 June 1675.

[46]   1 May 1676.

[47]   However, Sharpe was closely concerned with the Fells in a number of projects so it could be argued that this was not 'at arms' length'.

[48]   One other possibility was that they formed part of the lading on the Bristol voyage – this is discussed below.

[49]   The price differential is only partly accounted for by the ewe not being 'fat'. Typical prices at this time in Lonsdale consistently give tups the lowest price per head, ewes 1s. more and wethers a further shilling so that the sliding scale went 5s., 6s., 7s. 10 Dec. 1674. Danson failed to pay on time and was taken to court; he finally paid all the moneys on 7 Apr. 1675.

[50]   It is possible to suggest that the absence of hog sales might be connected to the Bristol voyage. Shipping the hogs to, say, Liverpool as part of a complex coastal operation would be typical of that kind of trading.

further from the arrangement as his wife was paid for feeding the haymakers (in 1674, this was three days' table for two mowers) whilst his children were paid for leading hay and, in April 1678, his son was paid 1s. for 'watering the meadow' – a reference to a practice not generally recorded in Lancashire. In addition to the continuing rental of the Gleaston land, Margaret Fell also rented six acres of meadow in Plumpton for £2 10s. This involved similar costs for housing the hay and 1s. 8d. for two locks and keys to set upon the barn doors. Margaret Fell must have been particularly short of fodder in the spring of 1674 for in March and May she purchased a total of 70 stones of hay at an average price of 4d. in March, falling to 3½d. in May. The only other time that hay was bought in that manner came in 1676 when April saw a purchase of 'two carfuls' at a cost of 5s. 6d. with a second purchase in May costing 4s. 10¼d.

In contrast, in April 1675, Margaret Fell sold 13 stone of hay for 2s. Neither sales nor purchases of hay were recorded in 1677 and 1678. The horses needed for Force Forge placed yet another demand upon the Fell's grazing and it may be for that reason the family apparently sought to improve their hay crop by buying 'clover grass seeds' on 23 March 1676; this was followed, two months later, by the purchase of 'hayseeds' on the Marsh Grange account.[51] In October of the same year, Margaret Fell rented grazing at Rownhead (near Dalton in Furness) for £3 5s. and four oxen grasses at Sandscale at a cost of £1 8s. 6d. This increase in resources might have been made in order to expand hay production which would explain the absence of hay purchases after 1676.

VI

The Fells were involved in a whole range of activities in order to enable their agrarian business to survive; some were long-term but others were of a much more sporadic nature. Some animals were kept but not, apparently, bred by the Fells. With the amount of dairying undertaken at Swarthmoor and Marsh Grange we would expect pigs to figure fairly largely but the references are sparse. In 1675 'dust' was bought on three occasions from two different millers to feed swine: two bushels cost 1s. 4d; one bushel, three pecks cost 1s. 2d. and one bushel, one peck cost 10d. The pigs themselves were bought in twos or threes at fairly regular intervals for prices ranging between 2s. and 3s. 7d. each and appear only to have been for the household: there is no sign they (or their bacon) were sold.

Bees were kept by both Margaret Fell and the Lowers at Marsh Grange with new hives bought in late spring/early summer of 1676 and 1677 at a cost of between 2½d. and 3½d. The household made frequent purchases of fish with

---

[51]   The costs of the seeds are not recorded but the carriage of clover seed from Lancaster was 10d. whilst the hay seed was 9d. These indicate a substantial amount of seed: 23 Mar., 4 May 1676.

herring and salmon being most common. Red herrings came via Lancaster and the highly valued char from the Lakes, whilst the adjacent Sands provided crabs, cockles and the occasional wild duck. It is assumed that domesticated ducks were kept in-house for the only purchases recorded were in February and August 1676; on each occasion only 1s. was spent but that bought two ducks in February and five in August.[52] Whilst ducks were rarely mentioned, there were autumn purchases of geese which were presumably for the Christmas table. Eight geese were fetched by Geo. Millerson in 1673 whilst a total of 28 geese were bought in the following year at prices between 7d. and 8½d. apiece. In September 1676 a total of 17 were bought at 7d. each.

Capons were bought by Margaret Fell but we can assume these were in addition to those bred in the Swarthmoor chicken yard.[53] The evidence for the chicken yard is tangential since it rests on the purchase of cocks at 5d. each in April and May 1676. There was a constant stream of purchases of chickens and eggs, but the former includes pullets bought in October and December of 1676 at 4d. and 4½d. compared to the 2d. per chicken paid almost irrespective of the time of year. Clearly the demands of the household's table outstripped in-house production and this is presumed to be the reason for the irregular purchase of fairly substantial numbers of chickens.[54] In contrast, four turkey cocks were sold at Lancaster in March 1675 for a total of 7s. 4d. Some had also been sold in the previous March at Lancaster market.[55]

Enough apples were grown at Swarthmoor for the occasional small parcel to be sold at market. On at least one occasion, apples were bought for cider making.[56] Hops were brought from Lancaster each winter but only the carriage costs are recorded. Fresh fruit was often bought in very small quantities with strawberries, cherries and pears all appearing upon occasion; the contexts would suggest that Sarah Fell or her sisters were at market and treated themselves. Oranges were sent from London as a present whilst dried fruit (raisins, currants and prunes) make fairly regular appearances on the carrier's cart from Lancaster.

---

[52]   It is possible that the February purchase related to wild duck.

[53]   Contemporary evidence would indicate that livestock gelding was a specialised trade. Richard Lowis was normally employed by the Fells and was paid 2s. 6d for gelding two colts and a bull at Marsh Grange in March 1676.

[54]   1676: Apr. – 13 chickens cost 2s. 2d., Sept. – 14 cost 2s. 9d., Dec. – 10 cost 1s. 8d. 1677: Apr. – 21 cost 3s., June – 12 cost 1s. 9d. 1678: June – 18 cost 2s. 8½d. These are in addition to many purchases of one or two chickens: in 1677 a total of 107 chickens were bought.

[55]   By 1592, the Shuttleworths of Gawthorpe regularly bought turkey cocks and hens of local provenance. John Harland (ed.), *The House and Farm Accounts of the Shuttleworths of Gawthorpe Hall* (4 vols, Chetham Society, old ser., 35, 41, 43, 46, 1856–58), I, pp. 72, 73, 187, 197, 214 and later references.

[56]   Sixteen bushels of apples were bought from Thomas Pearson in Oct. 1676 at a cost of £2 9s. There are other references to cider in north Lancashire around this time in inventories whilst local production is demonstrated by the inventory of Thomas Whitehead of Kirkby Lonsdale (1686) who had 'a presse and a myle for syder' worth 10s. LA, WRW/L/1686.

Rabbits only appear in the cashbook when their skins were sold – mainly to a Kendal hatter. The entries relating to venison and wildfowl (woodcock, snipe, partridge and pigeons) indicate that these were gifts to the family. That was also the case with the two barrels of oysters for which carriage was paid from Lancaster in June 1678.

When it comes to vegetables, however, the evidence becomes a lot clearer although still, in general, irregular. In April 1674, 1s. was paid for three hoops of setting potatoes with similar purchases in March 1676, April 1677 and May 1678. In the autumn of 1673 and 1674 hoops of potatoes were bought but we may presume these were for the table. Beans and peas for seed were annual purchases in March with white seed peas bought in March/April of 1674 and 1675. 'Garden seeds' were bought in all years with payments recorded for turnip seed in August 1674 and June 1677, leek seeds and carrot seeds in the same year and purslane seed in 1678 whilst turnip seed was bought for Swarthmoor in August 1673 and for Sister Lower in June 1677.[57] Both cabbage seed and plants were annual purchases in the spring. Cabbages appear again in sales of young plants in June at Ulverston market and then at the kitchen door from November into the following spring. Over this period the unit price dropped from 2d. or more to about 1d. The sales of peas and beans appear in each year. The high price of beans at 4s. 9d. per peck in July 1674 (compared to 4s. per peck for peas in the same month) presumably indicates that these were for the table.[58] The occasional parcel of onions was also sent to market. Other seeds such as mustard, fenugreek and aniseed are mentioned but the contexts indicate that these were purchased for medicinal use.

A range of other foods were bought at market or at the kitchen door, some of them on a seasonal basis. November and December of each year saw the purchase of numbers of neats' tongues and it may be that these were preserved for winter eating: the typical price was 4d. each. Whilst only five were recorded as bought in 1673, the number rose to 20 in 1676 and 26 in 1677. Alongside these, sides or quarters of beef were also bought at the beginning of November and were also (presumably) for salting.

An important byproduct of livestock keeping was the manure. The dungheap was highly valued by farmers and is one of the items specifically mentioned in inventories albeit, often with the poultry, peats or 'odd timbers' with which it shared a space. In the case of the Fell family, the manure produced by their farming was largely invisible beyond the costs of leading it to the fields and spreading it. Peggy/Margaret Dodgson was paid most often for muck-spreading

---

[57] On 12 Apr. 1677 Sister Lower bought French beans from Lancaster which, given the timing, may have been young plants.

[58] This could indicate they were not field (broad) beans at all but runner beans.

but three different men were each paid once for this task.[59] On the other hand, there is good evidence for the purchase of manure. In all years, Margaret Fell bought manure at costs ranging from a few pence to 10s. or more. Most purchases were made between 1 November and the end of May. The occasional payment also appeared during the summer months but these could be delayed payments for winter purchases. In 1674 there were 13 purchases (total cost 40s. 10½d.) followed by 18 in 1675 (61s.), 5 in 1676 (10s. 6d.) 17 in 1677 (31s. 10d.) and 21 in 1678 (51s. 10½d.). The context of the purchases was not always given but in those cases where it was, then it was generally linked to boosting fertility in order to grow wheat. However, bigg (barley) was manured once in 1674 and twice in spring 1678 in connection with the improvement of 'Dodgson Wife Close' prior to the spring sowing of this newly rented land. On earlier occasions, Margaret Fell had purchased manure to improve newly rented ground: in 1675 for 'Angsley' and in 1676 for 'Round Leva Heades'. In the autumn of 1677, Fell bought more manure for 'Angsley' with wheat as the crop. In 1678, unit costs were 2½d. for a double coop/cowp full.[60]

The impression throughout the cashbook is that fixed costs were kept to a minimum and beyond the core of household servants, labour was only hired as and when it was needed. Certainly, a substantial number of the local population appear as temporary labour for a wide range of the annual tasks. It is these temporary staff who are easier to identify as they received their day's pay for specific tasks. A man's day-rate was 3d. for sheep washing, dipping or 'topping lambs' and 4d. for hedging or walling; 4d. was also the tailor's rate for making sacks. In May 1674, Thomas Greaves was paid for ploughing 6½ acres. It took eight days and Greaves supplied the horse; he was paid 7s. 6d. In the previous month, three boys had been paid 3s. 9d. for 30 days harrowing which worked out at 1½d. per day although 'Miles Hunter wife lad' was only paid 3d. for three days at the same task. It was traditional to give workers their dinner so that must be factored in. Whilst tradesmen such as wallers supplied their own tools (but not materials), items such as hedging mittens were a regular expense costing about 8d. per pair: they could be repaired for 1½d. Rakes cost 1½d. or 2d. whilst sickles cost 7d. or 11d. and scythes 2s. 6d. Peat spades, however, cost 1s. whilst a curry comb was 4d. Swills cost around 2½d. or 4d. (presumably dependent upon size) but a fish basket was only 2d. In December 1674, 6½d. was spent on powder and shot 'to keep crows off the wheat' but only 3d. was spent for shot for the same purpose in November 1676. Most of these items were bought locally but occasionally we see the cost of carriage from Lancaster for garden shears, spades or scythes; in these cases, the goods were paid for by someone other than

---

[59]   It may be that Margaret Dodgson was the owner of 'Dodgson Wife Close'. It has not proved possible to identify the lands discussed in this section.

[60]   This is not, unfortunately, as straightforward as it seems: in two instances both double and single cowps are mentioned and the latter is quoted at 2d.

Sarah Fell. In November 1677, Margaret Fell paid for 20lbs. of hemp to make rope. The raw materials cost 3s. 9½d. and the roper was paid 9d. to convert the fibre into a whole range of products: six pairs of traces, eight halters, two pairs of hair carropes, a little cord for the jack and a cow tie.[61]

Of the textiles produced through the Fell's own agrarian activity, wool was the crop with the highest value, lambs' wool being sold at 6d. per pound in June 1674 to James Bancroft, hatter of Lancaster. In May 1678, Margaret Fell sold 26 stone of wool at 5s. per stone but the Marsh Grange wool clip of 21 stone only fetched 4s. 6d. per stone. Both sales were made to Edward Daniell of Leeds. Small parcels of wool were also sold to local women, typically the same women who were paid to spin the family's wool for blanket yarn. The sale of the higher value wool clip – and to the merchants of Leeds and Bradford – is typical of north Lancashire and forms a clear contrast with plant-derived textiles which were much more likely to be processed at home.[62] The nature of textile plants is that they must be retted in order to extract the fibre. The transport costs of bulky products meant that processing would be done as close as possible to the source. Consequently a very high proportion of households possessed the basic equipment of heckles and so forth needed to remove the waste outer material. There was clearly a fairly active market in the unspun fibre but, where possible, households also did the spinning in order to add value and make a greater profit on their crop. This broad principle also applied at Swarthmoor.[63] However, as Swarthmoor was a very large house of 13 hearths with a household to match, we might expect the domestic and agrarian needs for hemp and flax-based products to swallow up the whole of the Fells' production.[64] There were however, other aspects of textile production where the Fells demonstrate wider roles than those of processor and consumer. In March 1674 Margaret Fox sold two pecks and one hoop of linseed for 7s. 4d. followed by the sale of one hoop in April for 10d.[65] In the following March she sold 1½ hoops for 2s. 7½d. and two pecks for 5s. 8d. However, in March 1676 she bought one peck for 2s. In April 1677 sister Lower bought two hoops for 7d. but in March 1678 'we sisters' sold one peck two hoops for 1s. 0½d. whilst Margaret Fox bought three hoops for 1s. 6d.

---

[61]   Jacks were made of iron and formed part of the kitchen equipment.

[62]   Further discussion may be found in J.S. Holt, 'Hornby town and the textiles of Melling Parish in the early modern period', *Trans. Lancashire and Cheshire Antiquarian Society* 101 (2005), pp. 39–70.

[63]   The textiles of Swarthmoor Hall, as manifested in the cashbooks, are the subject of a paper by Barbara Pidcock which does not always recognise the limitations of the data: 'The spinners and weavers of Swarthmoor Hall, Ulverston, in the late seventeenth century', *CWAAS* 95 (1995), pp. 153–67.

[64]   Whilst flax normally produced the finer yarns for underclothing and bedding, hemp tended to be the source of rope, netting and the wide range of containers for grain, flour and other agrarian produce for which we now use plastic products.

[65]   There were four hoops to the peck and four pecks to the bushel. Grain, peas and beans were all sold by these measures, though occasionally a half-hoop is mentioned: 30 Mar. 1674.

We would expect these springtime sales of linseed to be for sowing but linseeds are tiny and two pecks would provide enough seed for a very large area. The inference must be that Fells were acting as middlemen in at least some of these transactions.[66]

VII

Most goods arriving or leaving Swarthmoor were from or bound for local markets and fairs. Goods also arrived from London, Europe (via Newcastle upon Tyne) and Ireland. Whilst the number of such transits may be unusually high due to the family's Quaker links, there was nothing particularly unexpected about the sources. The Fells were well placed to benefit from the coastal trade. They are known to have organised two voyages, to Bristol in 1674 followed by one to Cornwall in 1677 (the 'Oat Voyage'). Although the main export from Furness appears to have been grain, if we had the voyage accounts (to which the cashbooks refer), we might be forced to revise this view. In both cases, family members were available to organise handling of the cargoes at their destinations. Isabel Fell had married William Yeamans, a member of an active Bristol merchant family, whilst Mary Fell was married to Thomas Lower of Tremeer. In fact we do not know the precise destination of the Oat Voyage, but it was also referred to as a voyage to 'Cornwall' and Tremeer lies to the east of Padstow which was a significant harbour with a market. Furthermore, we are told that slate was shipped on the return leg and the Delabole Slate Quarry lies a short distance to the east of Tremeer.[67] The only facts we have come from Sarah Fell's efforts in organising the ship and its cargo, its loading and securing the customs clearance though other entries do allow us to make some further assumptions.[68]

The ship owner for the Bristol or 'Corn voyage' of 1674 is not known but the master was Richard Hodgson who could be the man named as the master of the 'Supply of Lancaster' in 1683–85.[69] In order to buy the grain, a total of £75 was borrowed by the Fells upon bond for one year: at least £95 14s. 4d. is known to have been expended on the purchases. Unfortunately, we have prices without

---

[66]   The cash book shows Margaret Fox buying linseed oil in Apr. 1677 to rub on a horse's back so it seems unlikely that the family were using it for culinary purposes especially since 'sallet oil' was a fairly regular purchase.

[67]   If this assumption is correct, then this is the earliest known reference to the shipping of Delabole Slate into the north-west of England.

[68]   Grateful thanks go to Dr Margaret Robinson for her help in identifying the masters and owners of the two ships hired by the Fells. The discussion which follows draws very heavily upon her research but the interpretations are the author's.

[69]   Although Hodgson was normally associated with a very localised coastal trade in wines and tobacco.

volumes and vice versa so that all we can say is the wheat purchases cost at least £60. The bigg, of which at least 46 bushels was purchased, cost at least £14 11s. We have no values for oats but at least 30 bushels were bought. Thomas Clegg was paid 2s. 7d. for drying 31 bushels of oats for groats and these may be the oats that were shipped. In any event, Mathew Fell, tailor, was paid 8d. for making four bags from coarse harden to hold them.[70] Similarly, (oat)meal was shipped in two hogsheads which cost 7s. to purchase.[71] The bulk of the wheat appears to have come through Lancaster merchants but the oats and bigg apparently came from closer to home, with references to bigg being moved from 'the Mannor' to Rampside. Much of the bigg and oats purchased was supplied by Walney farmers so loading probably also took place at Rampside with its deep-water access. A caveat must be entered here for, as usual, we cannot be certain that all the purchases went through Sarah Fell's hands and we know that they had partners in this venture. The Fells did not carry the whole of the risk of the Bristol voyage, which was split into at least 12 shares, one of which was held by their 'servant' Joseph Sharpe and a second by Ja. Lancaster.[72] When the ship sailed in April 1674, at least two bushels of bigg and nine of wheat were left over and sold by Sarah Fell over the next few months. This was presumably only the family's share as Sharpe was paid 8d. on 31 May 1674 for 'expence at Walney when the wheat was divided that left from Bristol voyage'; the location would support the idea that the main loading took place at or near Rampside. It has not proved possible to identify the return cargo but it probably included glass bottles for there are other references to these being shipped from Bristol.

For the 'Oat voyage' in 1677, we have fewer details of the grain shipped (though 60 bushels of oats were carted from Manchester at a cost of 6s. 6d.) but we have far more detail about its organisation and the return cargo. The shipowner was Gawen Kirkham of Dalton who was paid £53 for the 'freight of his vessel', the 'Blessing of Peel'.[73] Originally, it had been intended to rent a Whitehaven vessel. Warehouse space was rented at Grange over Sands so the vessel could have been partly loaded by tender from there.[74] However, iron was brought from Penny Bridge for loading at Barrow in Furness so part of the

---

[70] In fact, 20 yards of this hempen cloth was bought at a cost of 7¾d. per yard but only part of this was used for the bags: 12 Mar. 1674.

[71] The nails for them were supplied by the blacksmith: 28 Mar. 1674.

[72] Both Sharpe and Lancaster were Friends and appear frequently in the cashbook in positions of trust. The identity of the owners of the other shares is not known.

[73] Kirkham was registered as master of the 'Blessing of Wyre' in 1667 and the 'Blessing of Peel' in 1679 the ship's identification is based on those dates. His destinations included all parts of the Irish Sea and even to Oporto and Bordeaux.

[74] However, William Hathornthwait, who provided some of the grain and who probably lived at Sunbrick, was paid 4d. on 4 Apr. following for 'some poles of wood to set up in the loading of oats ... May 1677' which might indicate the use of much more temporary structures for loading.

products of Force Forge must have been included. The ship appears to have left in late May or early June but was certainly back by the end of July with a mixed cargo that included 'slabs of tin', slate and wine.[75] In contrast with the Bristol voyage, the Cornwall voyage appears to have been funded by complex transactions which included at least one bill between Henry Herle of Cornwall and Edward Herle esq. of Wigan.[76]

VIII

Sarah Fell was a remarkable woman but was not by any means unique. The reason we have heard of her derives from her position within the Society of Friends which led to her cashbook being (partly) preserved. She is representative of many other women who were equally skilled and, when the opportunity arose, demonstrated considerable ability. One important point, which is partially concealed by the nature of the cashbook entries, is that by no means all the transactions were instigated by Sarah Fell and her role was often limited to being the cashier for others. Realistically, no one person could have been in charge of all the activities which generated these items of income and expenditure. Furthermore, Sarah Fell was a young woman of education and wealth, her role as daughter, sister or friend was to supervise those effecting orders rather than (as it were) to take the sheep to market herself.[77]

The one occasion on which we know that Fell was the initiator and acting for herself is in relation to her uncle, Matthew Richardson of Roanhead in Dalton in Furness esquire (1616–77). Richardson, educated at Queen's College, Oxford and Gray's Inn, married Frances Askew of Marsh Grange in 1649. By the 1670s he had built up a substantial legal practice across Furness and beyond but he also owed Sarah Fell £200 upon bond and when it fell due, he was unable to pay. In February 1675, Fell arranged a sale of Richardson's 'goods' in connection with which she paid 2d. to the 'caller' and 1s. to Richard Rawlinson for acting as clerk at the sale.[78] The sale did not, however, clear the debt, of which the bond may only have been part. In August 1677 Richardson died leaving a widow who was incapable of acting as his administrator: consequently, as principal creditor, Fell

---

[75]   There are no expenditure entries from 16 June to 29 July 1677 which could serve to throw further light on this.

[76]   This is based on the total of £480 received by Fell, of which £30 came via Henry Coward of Lancaster for 'corn and iron sold' in Cornwall: 25 July, 30 Dec. 1677, 17 Feb. 1678.

[77]   It is clear that, when Fell did go to market, she was not always alone for she recorded payments for refreshment for others. Equally, we may expect those others to pay upon occasion so that visits could become invisible in the record.

[78]   At that time and place, 'goods' probably indicates livestock.

was appointed instead.[79] There is not space to discuss her actions here but she farmed his lands until the debts due to her were cleared.[80] This episode largely lies outside this discussion but it does allow us to see her effectiveness in action.[81]

The Fells were a wealthy family with links across England. They were typical of their class, time and location in having enough land to allow diversification and a willingness to try different crops, as their potatoes and turnips demonstrate. The land they farmed was held by both freehold and customary tenure. Additional arable and meadow was rented as needed, but they also let lands to others. Local tradesmen were employed to improve output as when Myles Fell of Mountbarrow was paid to graft trees at Swarthmoor and Marsh Grange.[82] Thomas Lawson, a noted herbalist who lived at Rampside, was paid 10s. for coming to Swarthmoor and instructing Dr Lower and 'sisters in the knowledge of herbs'.[83] All possibilities for productive use of these varied lands were exploited, with grain, livestock, vegetables, wool and textile plants produced for sale.[84] However, there was no blind determination to be self-sufficient where it did not make economic sense and the opportunities presented by a range of markets and fairs – both local and regional – were seized as appropriate. On those occasions when value could sensibly be added to goods by processing them, then this was done. The natural resources of Furness were exploited via partnerships which (inter alia) traded in grain, iron ore, smelted iron and mined coal. The Fells' involvement in the coastal trade appears to have been a continuing one. Their web of kin, friends and co-religionists was used to provide capital for the business needs of a national network. So comprehensive was their credit network that we can describe Sarah Fell as a country banker: she collected small sums to lend for larger enterprises and redeemed larger loans which permitted the funding of

[79]   The situation is in fact more complex than this since Richardson left sons who clearly inherited considerable wealth but that may have been protected by their parents' marriage settlement. Will of Thomas Richardson. Esq., of Roanhead, LA, WRW/F/1717.

[80]   Less Fell appear to be of an avaricious nature through the actions described here, the reader should be assured that she undertook all the funeral arrangements deemed proper for the time, the full details of which may be found in the cashbook.

[81]   It also allows us to record the fact that her uncle was farming to halves with his tenant and that Fell completed the agreement. Farming to halves was fairly widespread in the area although it is rare for the full picture to appear. Jennifer S. Holt, 'Farming to Halves in the north-west of England', paper given at the Rural History 2010 Conference, University of Sussex, Sept. 2010.

[82]   Myles Fell also sold geese besides undertaking more general farm tasks as a day-worker, 2 Apr. 1674.

[83]   5 July 1674.

[84]   This contrasts with Beckett's assessment of the Lowther family of nearby Holker for the period up to 1750: 'There is little evidence of progressive farming and the few surviving leases do not suggest that the tenants were invoked to use imaginative agricultural practices.' J.V. Beckett, 'The Lowthers at Holker: Marriage, inheritance and debt in the fortunes of an eighteenth-century landowning family', *Trans. Historic Society of Lancashire and Cheshire* 127 (1978), pp. 47–64.

smaller transactions. For, make no mistake, without detracting for a moment from their religious devotion and commitment to living the godly life, the Fells were capitalists to the core with an entrepreneurial eye for new opportunities.

Chapter 3

Why Was There No Crisis in England in the 1690s?

Richard W. Hoyle[1]

One of the preoccupations of English historians – and I use the adjective English advisedly – is demonstrating that in whatever area of endeavour, England was first and its precocious development was emulated by its European neighbours. This approach is as true in social and economic history as it is in political history. It is an aspect of the former with which we engage on this occasion. England made an early escape from the curse of famine – certainly half a century before Scotland, perhaps a whole century before France and most of two centuries before Ireland. Other than the human pain and suffering involved in moments of severe food shortage, the eradication of crisis mortality and stabilisation of death rates plainly has larger implications. Moreover, the disappearance of famine is often viewed as indicating a moment in the development of the state. Understanding why famine disappeared is therefore an important task for the economic historian.

In any account of the disappearance of famine from England, the 1690s has a particular part to play. There was, it is well known, severe famine in both Scotland and northern France. Indeed, Scottish historians have recently been arguing that the severity of the 'Seven ill years' has been, if anything, understated.[2] There is some evidence for excess dearth mortality in upland Wales during the decade, but England did not suffer any significant level of excess mortality in these years.[3] There had certainly been regionally important famines in 1586–87, 1595–97 and 1622–24. Hindle has recently argued for famine conditions in the

---

[1]   The first version of this chapter was written at the invitation of Gérard Beaur for a meeting he convened at Ca'Tron, Treviso, on 'A Critical Re-Examination of Demographic and Economic Crisis in Western Europe from the Middle Ages to the Early Twentieth Century', 4–6 July 2009. I am grateful to Paul Brassley for his continued interest in Crakanthorp and to Philip Saunders of the Cambridge RO for information about the Crakanthorp archive.

[2]   K. Cullen, C.A. Whatley and M. Young, 'King William's Ill Years: New Evidence on the Impact of Scarcity and Harvest Failure during the Crisis of the 1690s on Tayside', *Scottish Historical Rev.* 85 (2006), 250–76; Karen J. Cullen, *Famine in Scotland: The 'Ill Years' of the 1690s* (Edinburgh, 2010).

[3]   On Wales, see David Jenkins, 'The Demography of Late Stuart Montgomeryshire, *c.*1660–1720', *Montgomery Collections* 78 (1990), pp. 85–91.

late 1640s which both contributed to, and have been masked by, the political turmoil of those years.[4] But there was no repeat of these conditions in the 1690s. The difficulty then is one of employing an understanding of what happened to explain what did not happen. In doing this we will traverse ground covered by Andrew B. Appleby in a seminal article of 1978, in the course of which we will have to cast doubt on some of his ideas which have been taken as received truths by economic historians over the past two or three decades.[5]

Any discussion of these issues is strangely intractable. Thanks to the work of Bruce Campbell, we now have data on harvest yields for the two centuries before the mid fifteenth century based on the accounts of manorial demesnes. There is nothing equivalent for the early modern period, nor will there ever be. The medievalists' secret weapon is the manorial demesne and its standardised account which allows a whole range of financial and agricultural data to be established. With the disappearance of demesne farming in the fifteenth century, both the reason for the keeping of accounts but also the understanding of how accounts should be kept was lost. Early modern accounts, where they survive for agricultural enterprises, are much more irregular in their contents and format. They reflect the preferences of the landowner rather than any understood body of accounting conventions. Whilst accounts are relatively common, useful accounts are few and far between and it is this which forces the historian to use accounts which are far from ideal, which lack the rigour and clarity of the medieval accounts. This is the case with the present chapter which perseveres with accounts which might not attract the historians' attention should better data be available. But it is not, and 22 years of consecutive accounts – albeit of a rather odd character – is not to be gainsaid.[6]

The data which is most readily available to early modernists is price data. The problems with the available series – based as they are on purchases made by institutions largely in southern England – is well known. For the later seventeenth century we have – for a short but useful period – the market prices collected by John Houghton and published in his weekly *Collection for [the] improvement of husbandry and trade*.[7] There is no simple linear relationship between supply and

---

    4   S. Hindle, 'Dearth and the English Revolution: The Harvest Crisis of 1647–50', in S. Hindle and J. Humphries (eds), *Feeding the Masses* (supplement to *Economic History Review*, 61, 2008), pp. 64–98.

    5   A.B. Appleby, 'Grain Prices and Subsistence Crises in England and France, 1590–1740', *Journal of Economic History*, 39 (1979), pp. 865–87. This article was also influential in some of the essays in Appleby's memorial volume, J. Walter and R. Schofield (eds), *Famine, Disease and the Social Order in Early Modern Society* (Cambridge, 1989).

    6   The hope that tithe data might give historians an alternative means of accessing productivity has never come to pass: tithes were generally leased in this period and accounts are few and far between.

    7   John Houghton, *A Collection for the Improvement of Husbandry and Trade* (1692–1703). I have used the 1727 reprint, itself reprinted in facs. in 1969. For an introduction to Houghton, Natasha Glaisyer, 'Readers, Correspondents and Communities: John Houghton's *A Collection for Improvement*

prices especially at a period when the first tentative steps towards price support (through subsidised exports) were being made. Nonetheless, after a discussion of famine, it is with the price data that we start before reviewing the evidence of accounts from Cambridgeshire which, like many seventeenth-century accounts, are utterly *sui-generis*.

I

The first task, though, is to explain what famines are. For the layman, this may seem simple enough. Famines are periods when people go hungry and even die because of a failure of food supply. Common sense, though, is not enough and here there are a number of points we need to note. First and foremost, in a historical context observable famine is an extreme phenomenon. Normally we see it as a heightened number of deaths in parish registers, sometimes followed by a delayed reduction in the number of births. But we know from modern observation that famine operates by forcing people onto the road in the search of food and work. In the same way as a burial register can never record the full scale of epidemic disease because it neither acknowledges those who were ill, but recovered, and those who fled to die elsewhere, mortality data alone cannot describe the full extent of famine. Recorded deaths are merely the tip of a much larger iceberg: conversely the number of deaths recorded might be a poor guide to the gravity of the situation. Should anyone be in doubt of this, then we have De Waal's account of famine in Darfur (Sudan), whose inhabitants made a clear distinction between famine which brought only hunger and destitution, and those 'famines that kill'.[8]

Secondly, and following Sen, we recognise at least the possibility of famine at moments when there is no overall shortage of foodstuffs, but some individuals are excluded from the market because they were unemployed or underemployed (which itself might be a dimension of high prices) and which left them without the income to enter the market and buy foodstuffs.[9] From at least the second half of the sixteenth century, there was an awareness in England that industrial artisan populations were vulnerable to downturns in employment brought on by high food prices which reduced the demand for non-essential goods – clothing or shoes, for instance. A correspondent of William Cecil's, James Ryther, referred to this in a letter sent in the dearth year of 1587 from Yorkshire:

---

of Husbandry and Trade (1692–1703)', in Alexandra Shepard and Phil Withington (eds), *Communities in Early Modern England* (Manchester, 2000), pp. 235–51.

[8]   Alexander de Waal, *Famine that Kills: Darfur, Sudan, 1984–1985* (Oxford, 1989), ch. 3.

[9]   John Walter and Roger Schofield, 'Famine, Disease and Crisis Mortality in Early Modern Society', in Walter and Schofield (eds), *Famine, Disease and the Social Order*, p. 44.

The causes of these extraordinary numbers of these [poor people] have greatly grown by the hardness of some rich men that have this year put away servants and workfolk, which in other years they usually kept; also the unableness of many that put servants away because they could not keep them, corn rising to so high a price and the trades of clothing falling to so low a rate as in the confines of this shire wool is sold for 2s. 4d. a stone.[10]

This introduces a degree of paradox into famine. Starvation, distress and death from starvation-related diseases *could* occur within a population when there was no shortage of foodstuffs overall, even in the presence of low prices, unless mitigated by charitable, local or state action. This is perhaps Sen's key insight into the nature of famines.[11] In reality though, it is a shortfall in production which causes prices to rise, demand for non-essential consumables to fall and for unemployment to rise, thus depriving people of the income they need to purchase foodstuffs.

A concentration on the market and its workings has tended to shift attention away from the agricultural basis of famine. In some respects this follows the preoccupation of contemporaries. Magistrates and local governors could not conjure additional foodstuffs up out of the air, but they could attempt to manage markets to achieve an equitable distribution of food and to avoid profiteering and hoarding. They often bought into the myth of hoarding, even in Bengal in 1944, and undertook searches to discover where foodstuffs were being held.[12] Despite considerable public rhetoric aimed at speculators (often the same corn factors who in normal years were indispensable for making the system work), speculators playing the market were rarely discovered, and one might suppose that the purpose of the searches was to show a hungry population that government was both concerned and active on their behalf. Moreover, the movement of food out of areas of high prices and empty stomachs into urban centres or even abroad could produce a tense situation and outbreaks of disorder as people attempted to impede the traffic or even seize it for distribution at fair prices. Disorder, and the fear of impending disorder, generates paper which historians have been only too ready to analyse.[13] What the records of government

---

[10]   W.J. Craig, 'James Ryther of Harewood and his Letters to William Cecil, Lord Burghley, part II', in *Yorkshire Archaeological J.* 57 (1985), pp. 134–5.

[11]   Starvation could also occur in rather different conditions, when states denuded areas of essential foodstuffs. Early modern states were never powerful enough to do this: but they could enforce emigration though by the destruction of crops or foodstuffs as a tactic against civilian populations in war.

[12]   Cormac O'Grada, 'The Ripple that Drowns: Twentieth-Century Famines in China and India as Economic History', in Hindle and Humphries (eds), *Feeding the Masses*, pp. 25–8.

[13]   For examples, J. Walter and K. Wrightson. 'Dearth and the Social Order in Early Modern England', *Past and Present* 71 (1976), pp. 22–42; Walter, 'The Social Economy of Dearth in Early Modern England', in Walter and Schofield (eds), *Famine, Disease and the Social Order*, pp. 55–128. S.

do not contain, though, are systematic records of productivity and yield. Data of this sort was rarely been gathered before the nineteenth century and, as O'Grada has shown, is even elusive for even the Bengal famine of 1943–44,[14] but more can be discovered from the extant accounts of farming estates and individual farmers than has generally been acknowledged.[15] It would be our contention that recent historians have mistaken famine for a *human* phenomenon when in truth it is first and foremost an agricultural *phenomenon*.

This bears on the idea, an application of Malthusian thought, that famines are an indication of overpopulation. As we all recall, Malthus saw the increase of population outrunning any potential increase of food supply. Of course, he no more calculated on gains in agricultural productivity than on the development of contraception: but the idea has taken root that famines effect the operation of the positive check, scything back a population which has outrun its resources. So, in mid nineteenth century Ireland, the population had grown to unsupportable numbers and was bound to be trimmed back.

This, though, betrays a failure to understand how farmers work. Producing food costs money. Few pre-modern societies have the capacity to carry a stock of foodstuffs from one year to the next: moreover, to do so costs money which means that it is hardly in the interests of farmers to do so. Grain shrinks in volume through insect and rodent infestation; old grain is less valuable. Other than the costs of keeping grain from one year to the next, the prudent farmer would have been much better off selling his grain in the year it was produced than seeing it command a diminished price in a later year. The only people who could keep stocks from year to year were in towns.[16] Hence farmers judge the quantity that they can produce and sell: they do not produce foodstuffs which they cannot sell, or sell only at a loss. What happens in famines is that the supply of food is cut back abruptly through either adverse weather or plant disease, by factors which cannot be predicted or allowed for. Hence one might go so far as to say that this aspect of the Malthusian 'positive check' is never seen operating in pre-industrial history when, on the contrary, there is plenty of evidence for the operation of the preventive check. What did for the west of Ireland in 1845–46 was not overpopulation: it was the unexpected and unprecedented collapse of a staple crop due to a previously unknown plant disease. I would concede that in retrospect at least, having a potato monoculture was incautious even if no one

---

Hipkin, 'The Structure, Development and Politics of the Kent Grain Trade, 1552–1647', in Hindle and Humphries (eds), *Feeding the Masses*, pp. 99–139 for tensions within the area provisioning London in years of shortfall.

[14]   O'Grada, 'The Ripple that Drowns', pp. 21–4.

[15]   For the use of estate archives, see 'Famine as Agricultural Catastrophe: The Crisis of 1622–3 in East Lancashire', *Economic History Rev.* 63 (2010), pp. 974–1002 and for farm accounts, below, pp. 85-98..

[16]   The idea that foodstuffs could be carried over from year to year is present in the literature but has rarely been identified in practice: Cormac O'Grada, *Famine: A Short History* (2009), pp. 140–42.

anticipated the arrival of a new and destructive plant disease: having a range of grains growing, and planted at different times of the year, which spread the risk should one or more fail, was far more prudent as we shall see.

Famines then arise as the result of sudden and abrupt shortfalls in food supply, normally brought about by adverse climatic conditions, although plant disease can be factored in as an independent element. This is to say that in normal circumstances, people do not create famines. They cope with famines as best they can, and through the forms of food allocation they adopt, they can either ameliorate famines or make them worse. But ultimately a famine arises from a shortfall in food supplies, and the usual reason for this is the weather. The idea that weather was a driving factor has never quite been lost, although little attention has been paid to it in recent years. We are familiar with short-term runs in climate and it is recognised that the half-century between 1680 and 1730 was an especially cold phrase within a longer period of chill. Overton has suggested that the turnip was originally adopted as a stand-in fodder crop which could be sown should the hay harvest fail. In this first stage, farmers valued it for its green foliage rather than its root.[17]

One might advance a further proposition though. Because famines are largely dictated by weather, they also have the possibility of being essentially localised. We might take the analogy of an earthquake here. At its epicentre, it might bring down buildings with enormous loss of life. Further away, it might bring down ceilings and do cosmetic damage. Even yet further away still, it might be no more than a vibration, a rumble, a swaying of lights, an experience of curiosity and interest, but not life-endangering. The implication of this for historians is that the nation state is the wrong level from which to look at famines. As essentially localised phenomena, what imperils life in one location may count as no more than belt-tightening in another. And, as natural phenomena, some famines are worse than others just as some earthquakes devastate all and others merely raise dust.

The severity of a famine, measured, for instance, in terms of the heightened death rates it caused, is the outcome of the interplay of two quite different factors: the scale of the agricultural shortfall, and the success of the human efforts to alleviate that failure.

Hence, whilst historians have often adopted a Whiggish linearity, holding that famines became less damaging because the capacity of both market and governments to cope with them improved. In this analysis what defeated famine was institutional sophistication, and the ability of society to find the resources to resist 'shocks'.[18] It is therefore easy to assume that the reason why

---

[17] Mark Overton, *Agricultural Revolution in England: The Transformation of the Agrarian Economy, 1500–1800* (Cambridge, 1996), p. 203.

[18] O'Grada. *Famine*, ch. 7 for a long perspective on these issues.

famine disappeared from England after the 1640s was that society became better able to cope with it whilst the less robust and more backward societies of northern France and Scotland continued to suffer from periodic moments of distress. Appleby, however, located the English escape from famine in terms of changes in agricultural practice and it is to this we turn after we have reviewed the price data.

II

Peter Laslett launched the discussion of famine in early modern England by asking 'Did the peasants really starve?': but it was Appleby who answered Laslett's question in the affirmative.[19] Appleby died prematurely, his work certainly incomplete, but in the space of less than a decade he carved out for himself a unique position in early modern economic history, and one which has remained unoccupied since. His paper, 'Grain Prices and Subsistence Crises in England and France, 1590–1740' was one of his last to be published (in 1979) and has become established – for lack of challenge – as the leading statement of how England escaped from famine.

Appleby offered a comparative discussion of price movements in the French famines of the later seventeenth and early eighteenth centuries and in the corresponding years in England. In France he showed showing upward movements of great amplitude in famine years. Moreover, the prices of all grains moved in parallel, so that they were symmetrical. This meant that in years of high prices, the poor had no means of surviving by trading down to poorer, cheaper grains: 'The poor were simply priced off the market.'[20] Appleby acknowledged diversification in northern France, but held that this had not proceeded far enough before the Revolution to make much of a contribution to 'the elimination of famine in the Old Regime'.[21] In England, by contrast, movements in grain prices in famine years were of much smaller amplitude than those found in France. Moreover, Appleby found that the movements in the cheaper grains, oats and barley, were nothing like as great as those in French markets. Indeed, there was only a limited correlation between the prices of individual grains. This was illustrated with graphs of annual grain prices at Norwich and Reading over the 1690s (Appleby's figures 2 and 3, reproduced here as Figures 3.1 and 3.2).

English price behaviour was therefore asymmetrical, and allowed the English to trade down, to live off grains which they would normally despise as human

---

[19] P. Laslett, *The World We Have Lost* (London, 1960, 2nd edn 1971): the quotation is the title of ch. 5; A.B. Appleby, *Famine in Tudor and Stuart England* (Liverpool, 1977).

[20] Appleby, 'Grain Prices and Subsistence Crises', p. 871.

[21] Ibid., p. 875.

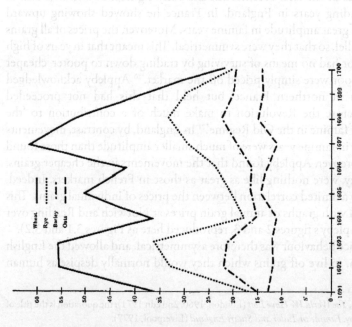

Figure 3.2   Grain prices in Reading, 1691–1700, after Appleby

Source: A.B. Appleby, 'Grain Prices and Subsistence Crises in England and France, 1590–1740', *Journal of Economic History* 39 (1979), p. 879.

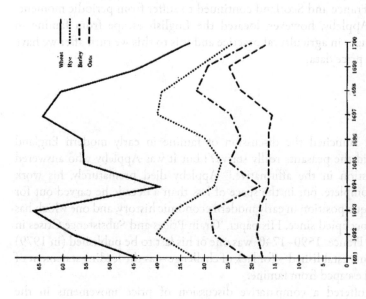

Figure 3.1   Grain prices in Norwich, 1691–1700, after Appleby

Source: A.B. Appleby, 'Grain Prices and Subsistence Crises in England and France, 1590–1740', *Journal of Economic History* 39 (1979), p. 878.

foodstuffs. Here Appleby cites William Harrison in his account of England in the 1560s, who says that in hard years the English poor were reduced to living off 'horse corn, beans, peas, oats, tares and lentils.[22] (Thirsk has since drawn attention to a Privy Council letter of October 1622 where the Council refers to barley, 'which grain being usually the cheapest, is in times of scarcity the breadcorn of the poor'.)[23] How England differed from France then was that in years of distress, the market for oats and barley continued to function at prices which allowed the poor the opportunity to purchase. And so he concluded:

> In short, the evidence suggests that a symmetrical price structure and subsistence crises went hand in hand. When all grains were costly at the same time, food shortage had an impact on both mortality and fertility: when one or another grain remained cheap, the demographic after effects were absent. In England, those who were priced off the wheat market could substitute barley, whereas those who customarily ate barley were protected by the considerable stability of barley prices, or else they could turn to oats. The complete lack of correlation between oat and wheat prices in Norwich in the 1690s suggests, indeed, that few people turned to oats.[24]

On the basis of some long-run data from Winchester, Appleby suggested that this asymmetrical pattern had appeared by 1660.[25]

At this moment, we have to note a difficulty with this argument. Even at a first glance, Appleby's data is probably less asymmetrical than he would like us to believe. And one is left with a puzzle. If lots of people were trading down from one grain to an inferior grain, why did the price of the inferior grain not rise in response? It is one thing to say that people were living off horse provender: but surely there was a continued demand for horsemeat from horses who could not simply be taken off their rations for a year to free up food for humans?

To continue with Appleby, though, this price structure was, in his mind, to be attributed to a switch from winter-sown grains, wheat and rye, to spring-sown grains, barley and oats, both of which were more tolerant of adverse weather conditions. A shift within the portfolio of grains grown 'was an increase in the supply of oats (and to a lesser degree, barley) which kept their prices stable and have the poor cheap grains to eat when the wheat and rye crops failed'. It was

---

[22]   Ibid., pp. 879–80. William Cecil in a recollection of the severe conditions of the 1550s, said that men had then been 'glad to make their bread of acorns'. D.M. Palliser, *The Age of Elizabeth: England under the Later Tudors, 1547–1603* (2nd edn, Harlow, 1992), p. 222.

[23]   Joan Thirsk, *Food in Early Modern England: Phases, Fads, Fashions* (London, 2007), p. 63, citing *Calendar of State Papers Domestic, 1619–23*, p. 455. A copy is printed in George Chandler, *Liverpool under James I* (Liverpool, 1960), pp. 271–2, the quotation from the latter.

[24]   Appleby, 'Grain Prices and Subsistence Crises', p. 882.

[25]   Ibid., p. 880.

Table 3.1   Norfolk: Acreage committed to differing grains, 1584–1640 and
                 1660–1739 (per cent)

	1584–1640	1660–1739
Wheat	28.7	19.8
Rye	16.4	11.4
Maslin	0.6	1.5
Barley	44.0	54.4
Oats	10.3	12.9
Total	100.0	100.0

Source: Taken from B.M.S. Campbell and M. Overton, 'A New Perspective on Medieval and Early Modern Agriculture: Six Centuries of Norfolk Farming, *c.*1250–*c.*1850', *Past and Present* 141 (1993), Table 2.

the failure of French agriculture to follow English agriculture in securing this balance between winter and spring crops which condemned it to intermittent famines through the eighteenth century.

Again, we might comment that this analysis seems to be pregnant with problems. That there was a switch from wheat and rye growing in Norfolk to barley and to a small degree oats comes through from Overton's work on probate inventories (Table 3.1). Glennie found a similar trend in Hertfordshire, although here the growing of rye had more or less disappeared by the end of the seventeenth century (when his study ends): the slack had been taken up by barley.[26] The area committed to barley growing in north Kent though seems to have dropped between the opening and closing decades of the century, but to have increased elsewhere in the county. In the Oxfordshire uplands, the trend was away from barley to wheat.[27] The shift that Appleby postulated seems to be proven in some areas even if one would be reluctant to claim it as a general trend. And it is possible to offer two examples of the trading down in grains which Appleby supposed took place, but which he was unable to show for the late seventeenth century. A Shropshire diarist noted in 1697 that 'there was a very bad crop in Wales ... so that after the harvest there was scarcely any bread made of corn [wheat] but only mixed with barley, oats or pease'. More surprisingly, similar expedients to stretch the harvest were employed in southern England. In his weekly *Collection for [the] Improvement of Husbandry and Trade* (of which more in a moment), John Houghton observed on 27 May 1698 that 'I am told

[26]   P. Glennie, 'Continuity and Change in Hertfordshire Agriculture, 1550–1700: I, Patterns of Agricultural Production', *AgHR* 36 (1988), p. 61, Fig. 2.

[27]   Data from a number of studies is gathered in Overton, *Agricultural Revolutions*, Table 3.12 (pp. 94–5).

that of late since corn has been very dear in several places about London, the poor have made their bread from three parts oatmeal and one part barley'.[28]

Barley does not make a satisfactory bread unless a mixed flour is employed as in the instance noted by Houghton.[29] In the late seventeenth century it seems to have been largely a malting crop, that is, that its primary outlet was into beer and spirit production. Hungry (and penurious) people perhaps drank less of both, so allowing the price of barley to fall although any shortfall in demand for barley for processing might have been taken up by a rise in demand for barley as a milling grain.[30] But Appleby does not notice either that or the fact that by the end of the century there was a significant export trade in both barley and wheat and that the crown was paying a bounty or export subsidy in some years in the later part of the century, which came into effect when the domestic price of grain had fallen below a threshold price. The amount paid in subsidy for the years 1689–98 has long been available in print and shows significant swings which surely match the domestic price (Table 3.2).

Of course, in 1694 and 1698, there may have been much less available for export, but part of the solution to the problem of barley prices may be that production, which in normal years was destined for foreign markets, was retained at home to make good a local shortfall. It is also possible to show that the export trade was actually reversed in 1694–95, for Houghton quotes a digest of customs for this year (and which is not otherwise known to be extant) which shows imports of wheat and barley and oats into London on a sizeable, if not substantial, scale. The 26,000 quarters of wheat imported need to be weighed against Chartres' estimate of a total London consumption in *c.*1700 of 575,000 qr of corn for bread alone, or the estimate of the coastal trade of corn into London in 1680 of 192,000 qr, or Houghton's report that 300,000 qr of corn were brought into London by barge along the River Lea from the grain growing districts to the north of city, some of which we will investigate later.[31] Nonetheless, the export of relatively small proportions of overall production or the import of equally small proportions of overall consumption could have a significant impact on prevailing prices.

---

[28] Jenkins, 'Demography', p. 88; *Collection*, no. 305, 27 May 1698.

[29] Thirsk, *Food*, p. 168.

[30] It may be possible, in time, to quantify the amount of beer produced for sale through the records of the excise. For the moment, Clark notes that the 1690s were a hard decade for the smaller innkeepers whose numbers fell sharply over the 1690s. He shows though that there was far more than simply a high price of malt running against them in this decade. P. Clark, *The English Alehouse: A Social History, 1200–1830* (Harlow, 1983), p. 208.

[31] John Chartres, 'Food Consumption and Internal Trade', in A.L. Beier and Roger Finlay, *London, 1500–1700: The Making of a Metropolis* (London, 1986), pp. 178–9; Houghton, *Collection*, no. 300.

Table 3.2   Corn bounty debentures, 1689–1698

	Outports	London	Total
1689	217	482	699
1690	7042	2273	9314
1691	16377	2472	18,849
1692	20136	925	21,062
1693	12452	2340	149791
1694	4318	74	4392
1695	13992	6402	20,284
1696	7314	7143	14,457
1697	11,094	2100	13,194
1698	4,480	520	5000
Average	9742.2	2473.1	25704.2

Source: Simplified from N.S.B. Gras, *The Evolution of the English Corn Market* (Cambridge, MA, 1926), p. 420, by rounding to the nearest pound.

This all suggests that there rather more to say about the 1690s than has been said so far. Appleby was at pains to say that 'my arguments here are intended to be suggestive rather than definitive' and he expressed caution about generalising too far from two comparative regional studies. Moreover, he was also careful to say that he had not discussed improvements in the transport of grain amongst other factors, 'and the general level of wealth in England and France'. And because this was one of his last papers, there is no way of telling how he might have developed his ideas into a more comprehensive examination of differential economic development in the two countries. The first difficulty is, though, that his identification of the 1690s as a period of asymmetrical prices is mistaken.

III

Appleby used price data which he acknowledged was far from ideal. His paper is really based on three series: annual prices in Norwich and Reading for 1691–1700 which he had from Thorold Rogers' venerable *History of Agriculture and Prices*, and a series for wheat, malt and oats for Winchester, 1630–1730 from Beveridge. Appleby wrote before the price series in the *Agrarian History of England and Wales, V, 1640–1750* were published (in 1984), and remarkably it

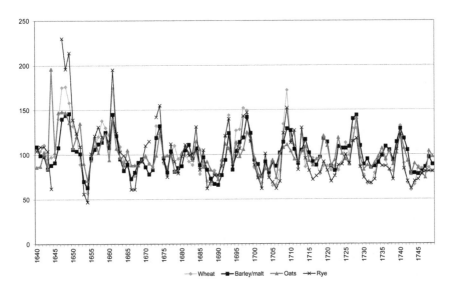

Figure 3.3   Grain indices, 1640–1749, after the *Agrarian History of England and Wales* (1640–1749 = 100)

Source: Peter J. Bowden, 'Statistics', Table A, in J. Thirsk (ed.), *The Agrarian History of England and Wales*, V (II), 1985.

seems no one has thought to graph this data to see whether it confirms his claims of asymmetrical movements. Figure 3.3 does so, apparently for the first time.[32]

What is clear is that even after 1700 the four grains track each other quite closely. Wheat, it is true, tends to have higher peaks and deeper troughs than the other grains. It also seems to move out of synch with barley at the end of the period (notice here the fall in wheat prices a year ahead of barley and the other grains in the 1740s). The last time that wheat and rye greatly exceeds barley in price is 1709: thereafter their prices move to broadly similar degrees in years of poor harvests (1728 and 1729, 1740), but in years of low prices wheat falls well below the price of barley and oats suggesting overproduction in good years.

In terms of correlations (Table 3.3), we find that the correlation between wheat and barley over 100 years is strong at 0.76122: but over the 50 years after 1650 it stands at 0.87165 whilst in the 50 years from 1700 it is 0.72799. There is then some evidence for the two series being less closely correlated over time. (A correlation with a year's lag is much weaker though.) The price of rye tracks that of wheat very closely indeed, but the relationship between wheat and

---

[32]   Peter J. Bowden, 'Statistics', Table A, in Joan Thirsk (ed.), *The Agrarian History of England and Wales*, V (II) (2 vols, Cambridge, 1985), II, p. 828–31.

Table 3.3   Correlations between grain prices, 1650–1749

Wheat v Barley	
1650–1749	0.76122
1650–99	0.87165
1700–49	0.72799
Rye	
1650–1749	0.90839
1650–99	0.89810
1700–49	0.92307
Oats	
1650–1749	0.66140
1650–99	0.68595
1700–49	0.61352

Source: Calculated from Peter J. Bowden, 'Statistics', Table A, in J. Thirsk (ed.), *The Agrarian History of England and Wales*, V (ii) (Cambridge, 1985).

oats is much weaker, and becomes progressively so. We can also view this data in a different way. The argument is that the price of wheat can be subject to substantial upward movements whilst the price of barley is much more stable. We can therefore look at these movements as a simple ratio, taking barley as 1.0. This is graphed in Figure 3.4.

The ratio of the two moves within a fairly narrow band. We do not see massive movements in the relative price of wheat over barley: indeed, after 1700, the price of wheat sags under that of barley. Again, this offers no support to the claim of asymmetrical price movements.

Of course, it is possible that this is simply a feature of the *Agrarian History*'s data. But if we look at a further price series – long available in print but not used by Appleby – the leet prices called at Lincoln each autumn, then again, we find no evidence of asymmetrical movements (Figure 3.5).

It therefore seems only appropriate to revisit Appleby's original graphs, which we have already seen as Figures 3.1 and 3.2 above. Appleby does not explain exactly what his data is. He says it is drawn from Houghton's *Collection* by way of Thorold Rogers. Houghton published weekly prices for some 48 locations – mainly southern English market towns – for not only grain, but a range of other commodities, including hay, tallow and wool. What Rogers did was to tabulate this data but in a rather odd way. He took for each year the prices given by Houghton but without any notice of how long the price prevailed. Hence, if barley in Borchester was at 16s. a quarter for 50 weeks, 17s. for a week and 18s. for the last week of the year, Rogers gave three prices. What Appleby may have done is averaged these prices, but it seems clear from his source note that he did not draw on the *Collections* themselves.

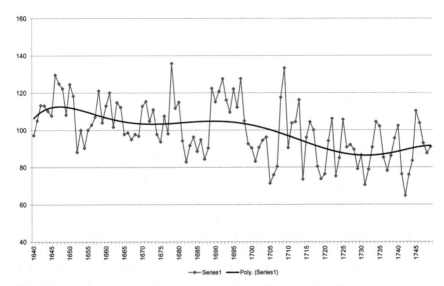

Figure 3.4   Annual ratio of wheat price to barley price, 1640–1749

Source: Calculated from data in Bowden, 'Statistics' Table A.

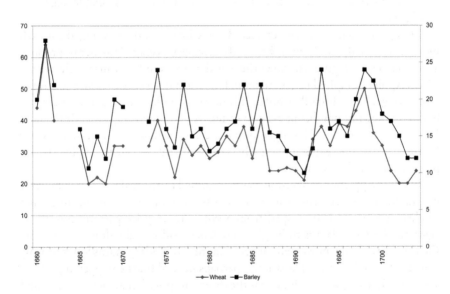

Figure 3.5   Lincoln leet grain prices, 1660–1704

Source: J.W.F. Hill, *Tudor and Stuart Lincoln* (Cambridge, 1956), p. 226.

A completely new series has therefore been created by keyboarding all the weekly prices for three towns: Norwich and Reading as used by Appleby, and two additional towns to the north of London but which were prominent entrepot for the London grain trade, Hitchin and (for reasons which will become clear later), Royston. In fact, the Houghton data has much more promise than it actually yields. The problem Houghton faced was that he was reliant on correspondents for local prices, and doubtless to his dissatisfaction, and certainly to ours, they were less forthcoming that he might have wished. Faced with no new news for months on end, Houghton continued to print the last price he had received. Of course, it may be that some of the long runs of unchanging prices really reflect markets which moved neither up nor down, but the truth is that the price data is less good than one would wish, especially for some of the more distant locations. Houghton himself recognised this by dropping some markets and substituting others where he doubtless believed that he had acquired a reliable correspondent. Royston is one of these markets: it was dropped early in 1697. Appleby in Westmorland, just the sort of location for which a good price series is really desirable, was reprinted unaltered for eight months before it was dropped in May 1697. For the markets under consideration, though, we may be fairly confident that the data is fairly reliable, simply because it does alter with a reasonable degree of regularity.

Houghton's data has been extracted week by week, then averaged for each month, and finally the 12 monthly totals have been averaged further to produce an annual figure. Figure 3.6 shows the new data in a similar format to the way in which Appleby graphed it. (Note though that it starts a year later and continues a year longer.) It is broadly similar. If however, we plot the data for wheat and barley on the same graph, but use two scales, we get something rather different as Figure 3.7 (a–c) shows. This suggests that there is a high level of symmetry except for the fact that the year of highest wheat prices is 1697, where the highest barley prices fall in the following year.

In effect Appleby's conclusion was determined by the scale on which he drew his graph: on further scrutiny it seems impossible to maintain the argument that English agriculture had escaped from a symmetrical price pattern, nor, if the *Agrarian History*'s data is to be given credence, had it really done so by 1750. On the contrary, the movement of prices in the two leading grains looks broadly similar, although some explanation is perhaps needed for the staggered peaks in 1697–98. If, then, we conclude that the divergent price behaviour of wheat and barley are not an explanation for the lack of famine in England in the 1690s, then what is? In order to investigate further, we now turn to the accounts of a single farmer from south Cambridgeshire, John Crakanthorp.

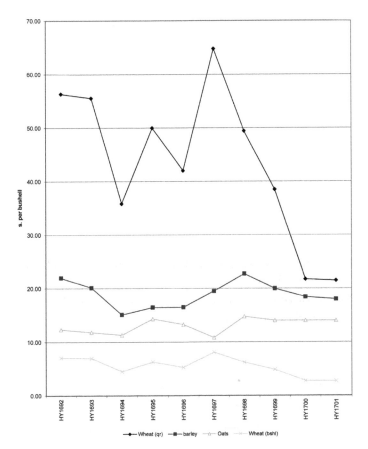

Figure 3.6   Grain prices, Norwich, 1692–1701, after Houghton

Source: Data extracted from Houghton, *Collection for Improvement of Husbandry and Trade.*

IV

Crakanthorp was a farming clergyman, the vicar of Fowlmere from 1667 to his death in 1719.[33] Crakanthorp perhaps thought of himself as one of the smaller farmers of the district but the best estimate is that he had about 60–75 acres in cultivation in any one year (Table 3.7). The majority of this was glebe but he also owned some land of his own in Fowlmere. He was therefore far from being a peasant, and is in fact best regarded as a specialist barley farmer in an area which by the beginning of the seventeenth century already had a high reputation for its

---

[33]   For Crakanthorp, see Paul Brassley, Anthony Lambert and Philip Saunders (eds), *Accounts of the Rev. John Crakanthorp of Fowlmere, 1692–1710* (Cambridgeshire Records Soc. 8, 1988).

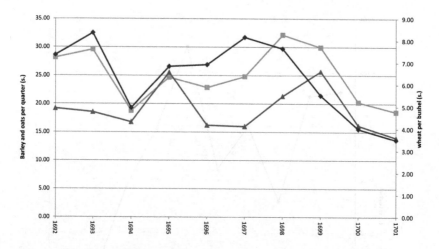

Figure 3.7a   Annual average prices, wheat, barley and oats, Reading,
               1692–1701

Source: Data extracted from Houghton, *Collection for Improvement of Husbandry and Trade*.
Note: data for 1692 for a part year only.

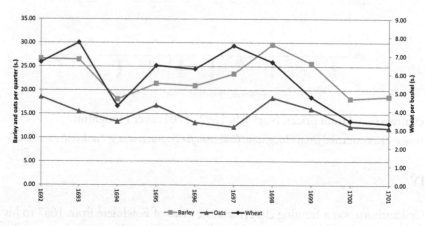

Figure 3.7b   Annual average prices, wheat, barley and oats, Norwich,
               1692–1701

Source: Data extracted from Houghton, *Collection for Improvement of Husbandry and Trade*.
Note: Data for 1692 for a part year only.

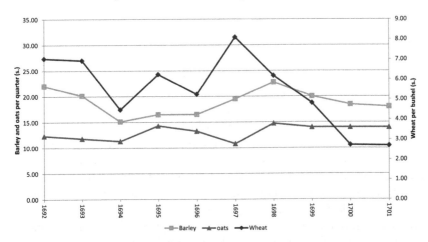

Figure 3.7c   Annual average prices, wheat, barley and oats, Hitchin,
1692–1701

Source: Data extracted from Houghton, *Collection for Improvement of Husbandry and Trade*.

Note: Data for 1692 for a part year only.

malt.[34] He was also growing a surprisingly large amount of rye and a small area of wheat. He was also a tithe collector and this introduces a degree of complexity into his account.

Crakanthorp has already attracted attention from historians. A first tranche of his records, part of what had once been a large archive, was published in 1988 by Brassley, Lambert and Saunders. These fall into two categories. The first is an orthodox household account book, the sole known survivor of at least seven, covering the years 1705–10 when his children were mature. Crakanthorp assigned his farming interests to his son Nathaniel when he married in 1708. Secondly, and more useful for our purposes, throughout his farming life Crakanthorp also maintained what Brassley et al. called 'harvest books', an annual account of all the corn Crakanthorp received and what he did with it. The books are arranged by the five crops (wheat, rye, barley, oats and peas) and then by each 'dressing' or threshing of the crop, its preparation for sale. For each tranche 'dressed', Crakanthorp tell us how it was used, and for crops sold off the farm, he invariably tells us the price they secured and usually who their purchaser was. Brassley et al. have published the 'harvest accounts' for 1682–89: the identification of two further books of 'harvest books' for 1680–82 and 1690–1702 allow us to offer detailed figures for the production of all four grains for 22 consecutive years including the decade of the

---

[34]   Ibid., pp. 17–18.

crisis.[35] It must be mentioned however, that the books are not as straightforward in their interpretation as this suggests. Crakanthorp was in receipt of tithe as well as the product of his own farm. Whilst he is careful to tell us how much he grain he sowed and over what area, he never distinguished between the produce of his own farm and the tithe he received, perhaps doing so in other account books which are either not extant, or remain unidentified. This means that a calculation of yield using the harvest books produces figures which are too high to be plausible.[36] In fact it is possible to estimate that Crakanthorp produced between about 5 and 12 per cent of the corn that passed through his barn so that he cannot have been farming much more than a few per cent of the cultivated area of the parish.[37]

Before turning to the production data, we might consider the price data. As has been remarked, Crakanthorp grew oats but almost entirely for use on the farm, and so it is not possible to construct an oat price index from this data. For the other crops, Crakanthorp sold small quantities locally, sometimes to his farm labourers, sometimes to named individuals from Fowlmere, sometimes simply 'at home'. The major part of his produce though was sold in bulk to grain dealers in Royston and a number of neighbouring villages, and we may guess that most of this went into malting and thence to London. There is no real difference in price between the two outlets.

Figure 3.8 is therefore based on a simple division of the amount of each grain sold off the farm divided by the income received in each harvest year. The most obvious feature are the high price years of 1692 and the three successive years, 1696–98, in all of which wheat was at over 6s. a bushel. This was unprecedented: in four years in the late 1680s the price had been at under 3s. a bushel and the average for the whole decade was only 3s. 4d. Even in the two years of relative remission, 1694 and 1695, wheat prices remained high compared to those to which people were accustomed. The same is true of rye and barley. The average

---

[35] The books for 1682–92 are published by Brassley et al. (eds), *Crakanthorp*, pp. 35–119. Those for 1680–82 and 1693–1702 which were discovered subsequently are University of Reading, MERL, D60/18–19. The threshing books have been databased and categorised according to the type of transactions as follows: consumed on the farm; given in charity to the poor etc.; consumed in the household; sent for malting; sold (in volume, to a dealer); sold locally (at the farm gate, in small parcels), sown; 'tail' (light grains) sold; grain given as wages; with a miscellaneous category and a category of balancing transactions.

[36] Brassley et al. (eds), *Crakanthorp*, pp. 29–31.

[37] The logic underlying this estimate needs explaining. We know the area sown by Crakanthorp and the amount of grain passing through his barns. If we assume that wheat produced 10 bushels per acre then Crakanthorp was producing about 3 per cent of the total: if we assume 15 bushels per acre, then about 4.5 per cent. For Barley, if we assume a lower bound figure of 12 bushels per acre, then about 4 per cent; if a higher one of 23 bushels per acre, then around 12 per cent. To take a different approach, if the yield of wheat was about five times that sown, the Crakanthorp's share of production was about 5 per cent; if we assume an eightfold return, then about 13 per cent. For barley, for a fivefold return about 4–5 per cent and for an eightfold return about 12 per cent.

price of rye in the 1680s had been about 2s. 4d., falling to between 1s. 6d. and 1s. 8d. in three years: but it was almost invariably above this price throughout the 1690s, peaking at over 5s. in 1693 and selling at over 3s. 0d. a bushel in five consecutive years in the later part of the decade. Barley retailed at an average of 2s. 4d. throughout the 1680s but fetched over 3s. 0d. in 1693, 1698 and 1699. The worst year was 1698 with an average of slightly over 3s. 6d. for the year, but in February 1699 barley was selling at around 30s. a quarter or 3s. 9d. a bushel. If we look at these prices and ask whether they are symmetrical or asymmetrical, then they are surely more the former than the latter: that is that a year of high prices in one grain is generally mirrored in high prices in the others. It might also be noted that the year of highest prices for rye and barley trails the year of the highest price by wheat by a year, so 1692 and 1693, 1697 and 1698.

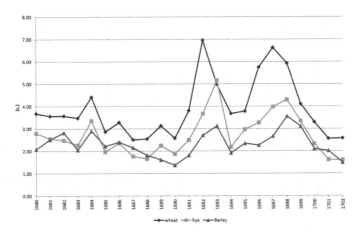

Figure 3.8   Crakanthorp prices, 1680–1702

Source: Crankanthop threshing books, *passim*.

Next, let us look at annual production. Table 3.4 gives the 'production' of the four grains on the Crakanthorp 'farm' (in reality the mixture of his own farming endeavours and the tithe passing through his barns). Volume per year is given, and this is also expressed as the percentage of average production over the 22 years for which we have data. The three grains normally used for human consumption are given a subtotal column.

The production of all four grains falls below 20 per cent of the average in three years, 1686, 1693 and 1698; 1680 was also a thin year with close to a 10 per cent shortfall in production. If we look at the years in which the supply of human foodstuffs falls more than 10 per cent of the average, then a slightly different pattern emerges. The year 1680 is a little more than 10 per cent deficient; 1686 is severely deficient at only 73 per cent of average output and followed on a year

Table 3.4   Crakanthorp: 'Production' of grains by year and the percentage of average production by year. Years more than 10 per cent below average in bold

	Wheat		Rye		Barley		Human grains		Oats		All grains	
	production	per cent of average	production	per cent of average	production	per cent of average	Production	Per cent of average		Per cent of average		Per cent of average
1680	121.75	**53.50**	386.00	**86.49**	1408.25	99.09	1916.00	91.45	236.00	**63.74**	2152.00	**0.88**
1681	323.25	142.04	457.19	102.44	1106.00	**77.82**	1886.44	90.04	348.00	93.99	2234.44	0.91
1682	236.25	103.81	288.88	**64.73**	1371.50	96.50	1896.63	90.53	358.75	96.89	2255.38	0.92
1683	270.75	118.97	423.25	94.84	1759.25	123.79	2453.25	117.10	561.00	151.52	3014.25	1.23
1684	129.13	**56.74**	302.25	**67.72**	1738.38	122.32	2169.75	103.56	478.00	129.10	2647.75	1.08
1685	222.25	97.66	583.50	130.74	1106.25	**77.84**	1912.00	**91.26**	483.50	130.59	2395.50	0.98
1686	126.75	**55.70**	367.25	**82.29**	1042.50	**73.35**	1536.50	73.34	344.50	93.04	1881.00	**0.77**
1687	247.25	108.65	658.25	147.49	1726.00	121.45	2631.50	125.60	348.50	94.12	2980.00	1.22
1688	205.00	90.08	418.00	93.66	1476.25	103.87	2099.25	100.20	287.88	**77.75**	2387.13	0.97
1689	282.00	123.92	336.63	**75.43**	1606.25	113.02	2224.88	106.20	332.00	89.67	2556.88	1.04
1690	365.75	160.72	474.13	106.23	1426.00	100.34	2265.88	108.15	485.50	131.13	2751.38	1.12
1691	220.75	97.00	450.25	100.88	1297.00	91.26	1968.00	93.93	358.50	96.82	2326.50	0.95
1692	280.38	123.20	623.75	139.76	1595.00	112.23	2499.13	119.29	253.75	68.53	2752.88	1.12
1693	156.75	**68.88**	281.00	**62.96**	1259.75	**88.64**	1697.50	**81.02**	218.75	**59.08**	1916.25	**0.78**
1694	292.50	128.53	642.50	143.96	1346.25	94.73	2281.25	108.89	293.00	**79.13**	2574.25	1.05
1695	160.38	**70.47**	621.25	139.20	1687.25	118.72	2468.88	117.84	314.75	**85.01**	2783.63	1.14
1696	198.50	**87.23**	346.75	**77.69**	1649.50	116.06	2194.75	104.76	609.25	164.55	2804.00	1.14
1697	113.75	**49.98**	181.00	**40.56**	1405.00	98.86	1699.75	**81.13**	693.00	187.17	2392.75	0.98
1698	231.00	101.51	496.00	111.14	1076.88	**75.77**	1803.88	**86.10**	150.50	**40.65**	1954.38	**0.80**
1699	281.00	123.48	526.38	117.94	1445.50	101.71	2252.88	107.53	370.50	100.07	2623.38	1.07
1700	273.50	120.18	297.25	**66.60**	1447.30	101.84	2018.05	96.32	266.50	71.98	2284.55	0.93
1701	277.50	121.94	647.50	145.08	1255.50	**88.34**	2180.50	104.08	353.50	95.47	2534.00	1.03
1702	218.00	95.79	456.00	102.17	1456.00	102.45	2130.00	101.67				
average	227.5707		446.3014		1421.198		2095.07		370.26		2463.74	
deficient years		7		9		6		4		6		4

which was itself slightly down; 1693 was nearly 20 per cent deficient but was followed by three better than average years before we have two poor years in succession: 1697, 21 per cent short and 1698, 14 per cent so. The reason why 1697 does not appear as a grossly deficient year when four grains is considered is the large production of oats in that year: the reason why 1698 was deficient was the poor oats crop. 'Watch the oats' will be a constant refrain in this chapter.

Let us turn to the performance of individual crops. Wheat comes out as being the most unreliable. In seven out of 22 years its production fell below 90 per cent of average, but in four years – 1680, 1684, 1686 and 1697 – less than 60 per cent of the average crop was produced. On the other hand, it produced more than 20 per cent of the average in eight of the years. Rye was even more volatile, with shortfalls of more than 10 per cent in nine of the 22 years in view. Barley had shortfalls of more than 10 per cent of the average in seven of the years, but only three times did it achieve a 20 per cent excess over the average. In the four poorest years it was round a quarter below average.

In 14 of the 22 years at least one crop was more than 10 per cent below average. In four years (1680, 1684, 1696 and 1697) wheat and rye were more than 10 per cent below average. In a single year (1698), barley and oats were both more than 10 per cent below average (and in fact substantially so) There are then two years – 1686 and 1693 and 1694 – in which both the wheat-rye combination and barley failed. In 1693 the performance of oats was also deficient. This was the sole year in which all four crops were more than 10 per cent below average, in which only barley supplied a creditable return.

Let us advance beyond this and see how shortfalls impacted on the market. Out of the total grain produced, some was bound to be reserved for the following year's seed, and one may assume that the producing household had preferential access to the balance. In normal circumstances there was also a tithe to be paid. This may have which may have been a fixed rent (a modus) or a fixed proportion of the unthreshed crop, but as Crakanthorp was a tithe gatherer, this is not an issue we can address here. We might think that the amount reserved for seed and used in the household would be much the same in volume terms from year to year, but the amount needed for seed varied from year to year as the extent of the area under crop varied and as sowing rates were adjusted (a point we turn to later). The amount used in the household might also vary. It is possible that they ate more wheat in years when it was cheap, and it may have been prudent for a clerical household to be seen tightening its belt when times were hard as an act of social solidarity. The amount of oats consumed rose and fell perhaps in relation to the price, but also in line with a factor which we cannot allow for here, the availability of herbage and fodder. So, in a bumper year, the proportion of the crop available for sale might be very high when the price was low: in a poor year the proportion might be very low when the market place price was high. Table 3.5 also gives the volume available and the proportion of the crop available for sale after seed had been set aside and provision made for household consumption (or farm usage in the case of oats). For wheat, about two-thirds of the crop was available for sale over 22 years, but this might fall below 50 per cent (1680, 1684, 1686 and 1697), but equally it might be above 80 per cent (1982, 1690, 1693). In volume terms, Crakanthorp was normally selling 160 qr of wheat, but in 1684 it was as little as 47.9 qr and in 1,697 63.8 qr. Occasionally it exceeded 200 qr. For rye, 84 per cent was normally available for sale. In only a single year did it fall below 75 per cent (the disastrous year of 1697) but it rarely exceeded 90 per cent. In volume the average was 380 qr, but this also fluctuated from under 200 (1697, 124 qr) to over 50 (1687, 576.3; 1692, 546.8; 1694, 541.3 and 1701, 579.8). Less than 10 per cent of barley was used at home in all years save one (1681), but again we can see large movements in the volume, from less than 1,000 qr in 1681, 1686 to over 1,500 in seven years of the 22: the average of 1,330 qr per year. Oats are almost the reverse of barley, with almost all production being consumed on the farm. Again though, one should watch for those years when quite considerable quantities – nearing a quarter or a third – were sold – as in 1683 and 1684, and again in 1691, 1696 and 1697.

The amount offered for sale of any particular grain could therefore vary dramatically from year to year, but the variability differed from grain to grain, with barley seemingly the most stable in its output. In normal years, as one grain fell, another tended to rise, and so the mix of winter and spring grains did indeed spread the risk. The danger arose when all three were deficient, which happened about every fifth year, but in 1697 and 1698 two deficient years followed each other.

Crakanthorp was also meticulous in describing how his grain was disposed of, and in the case of sales, to whom it was sold and for how much. We can therefore use his threshing books to calculate his income from sales and this is presented in Table 3.6. This shows the extreme variation in his income. Normally had made about £200 from his sale of grain, but in a single year less than £100 and in six years, all but one in the 1680s, less than £150. In two years, and one of them 1692, he made over £300 in grain sales. The question is then whether the years in which he made small profits were those of poor harvests or large harvests. Overall, there is a correlation between the total amount produced and income, but this is far from clear cut because there were four grains involved and even if, as we have seen, their prices tracked each other, the fact that the contents of the basket of grain that Crakanthorp had for sale differed in every year means that there is no simple correlation between output and income. In 1685 the supply of grains in total was three-quarters of average but income was only 65 per cent of average. In 1686 production was about average but the income was 70 per cent of average so a big increase in output brought only a small increase in income. In 1687 the production of grain was 20 per cent over average and income was close to average, but the following year the total produced was slightly over average but Crakanthorp's income was only 48 per cent of average. It remained low the following year even though the amount of grain produced was 12 per cent over the average. In 1693, 20 per cent deficient in all grains, income was 66 per cent above the average. In the following years of distress, income was well above the average although production was down. Obviously, any attempt to relate income to production needs to be conducted at the level of the individual grain, but it is the case is that Crakanthorp's income was much more stable in the 1690s than the 1680s; and was higher in the years after 1692.[38] Before 1692 he made an average of £169 a year: after that year £240 (a figure which would be higher had not his income tailed off at the end of the century). But whilst Crakanthorp earned much more from his farm and tithe collecting activities in the 1690s than 1680s, it is not immediately obvious that he was benefiting from dearth years. Indeed, it may be the case that the current price was determined less by the amount in the barns than by an assessment of the growing crop, so that years which were quite bountiful might have high prices because there were fears for the quality of the next harvest, whilst years which were quite thin could remain relatively cheap. In this way, years with quite similar levels of productivity could display quite different prices.

V

Measures of gross production conflate the yield per acre or seed with the extent sown. Regrettably, as we saw, we cannot distinguish the production of Crakanthorp's farm from his tithe and so it is impossible to calculate yield figures. In most years Crakanthorp tells us the area sown and in the others we can usually infer the area (Table 3.7). This too is partly dependent on the unequal distribution of his land between the fields of Fowlmere. From Table 3.7 we can see that Crakanthorp normally grew 6–8 acres of wheat (average 6.75 ac.), 15–20 acres of rye (average 16.53) and between 35 and 40 acres of barley (average 37.6). He normally sowed less than 10 acres of oats (average 9.4), but this varied widely from year to year. In fact the oats are the least well documented of his crops for his oat accounts lack detail. The appearance is that this, the most mundane of his crops, but also the one which brought least profit, never really commanded his attention. It is most likely that for Crakanthorp (and in Fowlmere generally), oats were normally horse provender and not a human foodstuff.

Confronted by a table such as Table 3.7, the historian's instinct is to try and relate it to prevailing prices from the previous harvest. And yet it is not the only approach. It is just as likely that the factor at the forefront of the farmer's mind was the weather, and whether he could successfully plough and sow a winter crop or whether waterlogging on the one hand, or early frosts on the other, prevented

---

[38]   Was a greater stability in the corn market the result of the introduction of the corn bounty?

Table 3.5 Crakanthorp: 'Production' of grains giving total passing through Crakanthorp's barn, total available for sale after deduction of household expenditure and seed used for sowing, and proportion available for sale

	Wheat			Rye			Barley			Oats		
	Total production	Total available for sale	Percent available for sale	Total production	Total available for sale	Percent available for sale	Total production	Total available for sale	Per cent available for sale	Total production	Total available for sale	Per cent available for sale
1680	121.8	53.3	43.7	386.0	320.5	83.0	1408.25	1289.5	91.6	236.00	36.5	15.47
1681	323.3	184.4	57.0	457.2	414.2	90.6	1106.00	972.3	87.9	348.00	3.0	0.86
1682	236.3	212.5	89.9	288.9	238.8	82.6	1371.50	1261.9	92.0	358.75	71.0	19.79
1683	270.8	188.3	69.5	423.3	351.0	82.9	1759.25	1708.3	97.1	561.00	150.5	26.83
1684	129.1	47.9	37.1	302.3	236.8	78.3	1738.38	1628.6	93.7	478.00	148.0	30.96
1685	222.3	142.1	63.9	583.5	441.0	75.6	1106.25	1022.0	92.4	483.50	16.5	3.41
1686	126.8	58.5	46.2	367.3	303.0	82.5	1042.50	928.8	89.1	344.50	21.0	6.10
1687	247.3	159.5	64.5	658.3	576.3	87.5	1726.00	1707.8	98.9	348.50	51.0	14.63
1688	205.0	150.0	73.2	418.0	371.3	88.8	1476.25	1334.3	90.4	287.88	29.5	10.25
1689	282.0	220.8	78.3	336.6	271.5	80.7	1606.25	1457.0	90.7	332.00	7.0	2.11
1690	365.8	310.5	84.9	474.1	425.1	89.7	1426.00	1353.0	94.9	485.50	29.8	6.13
1691	220.8	160.8	72.8	450.3	376.8	83.7	1297.00	1194.0	92.1	358.50	89.3	24.90
1692	280.4	173.4	61.8	623.8	546.8	87.7	1595.00	1535.0	96.2	253.75	0.0	0.00
1693	156.8	128.5	82.0	281.0	229.8	81.8	1259.75	1217.0	96.6	218.75	18.8	8.57
1694	292.5	210.5	72.0	642.5	586.8	91.3	1346.25	1253.3	93.1	293.00	2.0	0.68
1695	160.4	118.1	73.7	621.3	541.3	87.1	1687.25	1522.5	90.2	314.75	4.3	1.35
1696	198.5	145.5	73.3	346.8	280.5	80.9	1649.50	1519.5	92.1	609.25	179.8	29.50
1697	113.8	63.8	56.0	181.0	124.3	68.6	1405.00	1308.3	93.1	693.00	265.0	38.24
1698	231.0	168.5	72.9	496.0	402.3	81.1	1076.88	1058.4	98.3	150.50	9.0	5.98
1699	281.0	217.5	77.4	526.4	475.4	90.3	1445.50	1404.8	97.2	370.50	35.0	9.45
1700	273.5	189.8	69.4	297.2	242.9	81.7	1447.30	1429.1	98.7	266.50	28.0	10.51
1701	277.5	217.3	78.3	647.5	579.8	89.5	1255.50	1150.1	91.6	353.50	39.0	11.03
1702	218.0	172.3	79.0	456.0	408.8	89.6	1456.00	1345.8	92.4			
		160.6	68.6		380.2	84.16		1330.5	93.5		56.1	12.58

him from entering his fields. Frost could also be destructive of winter grains. If, by January, the winter grains looked weak, then there was an incentive to increase the acreage of spring grains provided that conditions were right for sowing. As we noted before, prices, of course, could also mirror this *actualitie* of the fields. We are, however, only talking about small variations in acreage – as Table 3.7 shows.

In the future, it might be possible to connect the micro-history of weather and ground conditions to the area sown, but not yet. Instead, we can make some broad suggestions. First, we can detect a degree of market responsiveness in Crackanthop's treatment of barley. Over the entire period (1680–1702), it appears that when the March price was 16s. per quarter or lower, then the mean acreage sown was 36.18 acres with a mean sowing rate of 3.15 bushels per acre; when the prevailing price was over 20s. per quarter, then the mean area sown was 38.8 acres and the mean sowing rate was 3.02 bushels per acre. Correlations between the rates are weak however, but there does seem to have been a tendency in high price years to sow more ground but skimp on seed. Second, we have the extreme variability in the area sown to oats and some suggestions can be made as to why. In 1683 and 1684 he sowed about 13 acres of the crop – twice what he had done in the previous two years. The 1683 harvest was not a bad one but the 1684 harvest was deficient in both wheat and rye. It is possible that the large area of oats sown was in recognition that the winter grains looked weak in the first weeks of January 1684. In both of these years, quite large amounts of oats were sold locally, at the farm gate, which is unusual for Crakanthorp.

It seems probable though that Crakanthorp deliberately increased the acreage of oats sown after 1693. In 1695 he sowed 13 acres at a high seeding rate. This, we must assume, indicates that during the winter of 1695–96 he was pessimistic about the future supply of grain. He then had a bumper 'crop' of 610 bushels of oats in the harvest of 1696 and cut back a little to 12 acres when he next sowed in January 1697. This brought an even larger 'harvest' of 693 bushels. When he sowed in the spring of 1698, he cut the area sown to an estimated seven acres. The impression is that in both the spring of 1696 and again in 1697 he sowed extensive areas of oats as a fall back out of anxiety that the winter grains would not perform well. There is a hint that he sowed and then increased the area sown in the harvest year 1697 (for the 1698 harvest.). Normally, the produce of one 'dressing' is marked in the accounts as sown, so we can assume that the sowing took place soon after that dressing had been made. In the harvest year 1694, this was 2 February 1695, in 1695, 22 January and 4 February, in 1696, 7 January 1697 and in 1698 29 December. But in 1697 1 qr 2b of oats from the dressing made on 11 December were sown, and further 1 qr 2b of oats from the dressing made on 31 March 1698. Crakanthorp must therefore have been pessimistic

Table 3.6   Crakanthorp: Computed income from sales (in £)

	Wheat	Rye	Barley	Oats	Total	Per cent of average
1680	8.77	42.57	110.85	2.86	165.04	81.35
1681	31.30	51.21	92.99	0.07	175.56	86.54
1682	36.09	27.32	163.95	6.50	233.86	115.27
1683	31.41	37.29	134.70	10.71	214.11	105.54
1684	9.82	37.13	204.63	14.25	265.82	131.03
1685	18.64	39.84	73.04	0.67	132.19	65.16
1686	9.06	34.31	98.51	0.23	142.11	70.05
1687	18.96	44.24	132.74		195.94	96.59
1688	17.68	29.04	50.09	1.30	98.11	48.36
1689	33.50	26.98	49.23		109.71	54.08
1690	39.22	39.20	57.01	0.66	136.10	67.09
1691	29.55	46.06	78.63	5.61	159.85	78.80
1692	59.32	97.42	180.08		336.82	166.03
1693	31.20	53.93	176.14		261.28	128.79
1694	37.03	61.09	107.90		206.02	101.55
1695	21.44	76.45	138.99		236.89	116.77
1696	40.94	43.11	131.35	14.10	229.51	113.13
1697	19.65	21.41	166.28	15.49	222.84	109.84
1698	47.36	81.02	168.82		297.20	146.50
1699	43.32	77.10	211.11		331.53	163.42
1700	29.65	27.15	142.30		199.11	98.15
1701	26.93	43.83	110.08		180.85	89.15
1702	21.47	29.52	84.49		135.48	66.78
	28.80	46.40	124.52		202.87	

about the 1698 harvest as late as the end of March, and this encouraged him to sow an additional area of oats.[39]

Moreover, the prodigious quantities of oats Crakanthorp handled in those two years must imply that that the sowing of larger than usual areas with oats must have been general within Fowlmere, for most of the oats in the accounts must have been tithe oats rather than the produce of his own land.

In the 1680s, when his oat 'crop' exceeded about 400 bushels, Crakanthorp moved to sell the excess. So, in 1683, he had 561 bushels and sold 150 bushels. In

---

[39]   There is no evidence that the second sowing of oats was made by ploughing up land already sown with winter wheat as is reported from 1740. In fact, the place names in the harvest books make it certain that this was not done. J.B. Post, *Food Shortage, Climatic Variability and Epidemic Disease in Preindustrial Europe: The Mortality Peak of the Early 1740s* (London, 1985), pp. 90–91.

1684 he had 478 bushels and sold 142, but 1685 583 and sold virtually none. In 1696 he had 609 bushels and sold 169. In 1697 he had 693 bushels and sold 246 bushels. The appearance is then that in these two years, he (and others) sowed an unusually large acreage of oats, used an unusually large amount within the household and farm and sold a large balance: 28 per cent in 1696 and 35 per cent in 1697. What is additionally significant is to whom the crop was sold. In previous years of excess, he had mainly sold in bulk into the trade or in large parcels to his neighbours. In the harvest years 1696 and 1697 he sold exclusively into the local market, as he says of the sales in late 1697, 'sold at home by the bushel and the peck', that is to people coming to the farm to buy for their own domestic consumption. These sales have their own logic: they fall during the summer and autumn of 1697. The amount he sold 'at home' fluctuates from year to year, but when seen over time, he sold relatively little wheat 'at home' in 1696 and 1697, relatively little rye, especially in 1697, but more barley in both years and an extraordinary amount of oats. One would not wish to press this too far, but the impression is that people in Fowlmere were switching from a diet of wheat and rye to barley and oats in just the way John Houghton reported in May 1698.

This suggests that Appleby was mistaken to read the price evidence as implying that 'few people turned to oats'. One wonders whether there was not a collective feeling amongst farmers that sowing a few additional acres of oats in these years would repay, both in that the demand was there, but also that it would serve to alleviate distress within their villages. As a result, the price of oats remained fairly flat, but the supply plentiful (perhaps helped by conditions which favoured it). Sowing additional oats may have been an act of social responsibility as much as charity. Crakanthorp was not giving his oats away and may have been selling them at a better than decent price. In May 1697 he was selling oats in Fowlmere at 1s. 8d. a bushel when they were (on Houghton's prices) 1s. 2d. in Hitchin and at the end of the year he was selling at 1s. 3d. or 1s. 4d. when the Hitchin price was 1s. 0d. This confirms the overall impression of the Crakanthorp accounts, that he gave nothing away that he could sell. There is a story to teased out of them about his sales of the light grain or 'tail'. In cheap years there was no demand for this and it went to his animals: in poor years it was sold to his labourers and others at a price which was plainly discounted from the going rate for 'the best', but was tied to it. Hence it would be wrong to suppose that Crakanthorp was doing this simply for humane reasons.[40]

---

[40] Crakanthorp also made gifts to the poor, but these only amounted to less than 200 bushels – mostly of rye – over the 22 years.

Table 3.7   Crakanthorp: Sown acreages

Year of sowing	Wheat	Rye	Barley	Oats	Total acreage sown
1680	4.5	14.125	38.75	7.8[a]	65.175
1681	2.6	9	40.25	6.5	58.35
1682	7.0	13.0	37.0	NI	
1683	4.0	15.0	40.5	13.25	72.75
1684	5.75	15.0	30.75	12.75	64.25
1685	NI	25.5[a]	30.5	NI	
1686	6.5	18.8	36.0[a]	7.04	68.34
1687	5.0[a]	14.5	NI	NI	
1688	8.3[a]	12.2	35.0	12.0	67.5
1689	4.5	17.6	43.0	11.7[a]	76.8
1690	6.5[a]	13.5	31.0	11.3[a]	62.3
1691	7.5	17	33.75	4.0	62.25
1692	7.5	19	42.5	6.0[a]	75
1693	6	14.5	41.0	9.5	71
1694	6.5	19.25	35.0	10.0	70.75
1695	6.5	19.4	43.5	13.0	82.4
1696	6.5	13.75	37.0	12.0	69.25
1697	11	20.0	31.0	7.0[a]	69
1698	8.5	23.0	42.0	7.0[a]	80.5
1699	7	13.5	47.0	6.0	73.5
1700	8	19.3	37.5	10.0	74.8
1701	10	21	38.5	11.5	81
1702	8.75	12.25	35.75	NI	
Average	6.75	16.53	37.60	9.4	68.8

Note: Years are the years in which the crop sown was harvested, so the figures for 1691 are for wheat and rye sown in 1690 and barley and oats for the sowings of spring 1691. Averages are based on years for which we have actual or inferred data. Figures for 1682–91 taken from Brassley et al. (eds), *Accounts*, Table 4, with missing figures interpolated (but note that this Table uses different dates). [a] Estimated from the quantity sown assuming a sowing rate of 3 bushels per acre.

VI

At the end, Appleby can be judged to be both right and wrong. His asymmetrical analysis seems not to hold water. The price of all grains tracked each other and it is simply not true to suppose that the price of barley and oats remained a constant. On the other hand, Appleby was right to focus on ready access to spring grains as the solution of the question why the English didn't display a famine mortality in the 1690s. Of course, a single farmer or village cannot speak for the experience of the whole nation, but Crakanthorp's account books do suggest that the answer lies in the recourse to oats. Even if hardly attractive as food, it sustained life. At a larger level though there was also barley. Whilst it is possible that the acreage of barley was also increased in response to fears about the wheat harvest, barley could also be diverted from the export trade and out of brewing. And here is perhaps a larger solution to the question. A prodigious quantity of barley was grown in the late seventeenth century for malting. This provided a margin, a cushion, which could be called upon when needed in hard years when, in any case, the demand for drink probably declined as the cost of food increased. This may be seen as a self-regulating mechanism – demand being transferred within the economy from one outlet to another – but we may suggest that it was the existence of this barley economy and the recourse to oats which allowed the English to pass largely unscathed through a succession of difficult years.

This is to suggest that there was never an absolute shortage of food in England in the 1690s although it may well have been the wrong type of food, and people were forced into eating less attractive grains. This compares with the situation with France where the range of prices suggests that there was a real shortage of food and the explanation here may well be that in some areas, the option for switching between grains was simply not there. The same may apply in Scotland. Whatever the shortfall in England, the crops were certainly not wiped out.

There is a secondary consideration here as well. As Sen has taught us, supply is irrelevant if it is not possible to convert demand into either acquisition through the market or by transfer payments. In England demand was almost certainly maintained by transfer payments through the poor law within the village and town. There is therefore a degree of circularity: what may well have been paying for the oats sold from Crakanthorp's farm gate may well have been his own poor rate. As has been acknowledged on a number of occasions, the 1690s saw an increase in poor law expenditure generally with per diem payments rising and driving up the overall cost of the poor. This inflation to take account of food price inflation was not followed by any reduction in rates once prices returned to more normal values. There was therefore a sort of ratchet effect which perhaps let the poor better off until attempts to retrench on costs began in earnest.[41] Again, in explaining why England escaped, the maintenance of demand by the poor law must play a part.

This takes us back to comments made earlier. In this chapter we have perhaps gone further than anyone else to describing agricultural conditions in England in the 1690s. Price information gets us so far. It identifies periods of interest

---

[41]   P. Slack, *Poverty and Policy in Tudor and Stuart England* (London, 1988), p. 179; S. Hindle, *On the Parish? The Micro-Politics of Poor Relief in Rural England, c.1550–1750* (Oxford, 2004), p. 255.

and tells us exactly what problems confronted the consumer in the marketplace when they went to buy foodstuffs. But prices tell us little about the cause of high (or low) prices, and to secure some understanding of this we need to change perspective and examine the behaviour of the individual farm. On a close-grained but narrow base provided from Crakanthorp, we can show the scale of short shortfalls in food supply in the 1690s. We can even speculate on the agricultural strategies used to ameliorate the shortfall in grains. This is all proper and appropriate. But there are then additional levels of complexity to be teased out: the impact of famine is not simply a question of agricultural supply alone, but how human society coped with shortfalls in supply. That the distress in both Scotland and France were so much greater may reflect the ability of those societies to cope with an agricultural catastrophe, but the scale of what had to be faced might well differ as well. England escaped lightly and it is possible to explain why to some extent. The French and the Scots may have been unequal to the task, but the magnitude of the problem they faced could also have been much greater too.

Chapter 4

The Farming and Domestic Economy of a Lancashire Smallholder: Richard Latham and the Agricultural Revolution, 1724–67

A.J. Gritt

There has been a long-standing recognition that small farmers were ubiquitous throughout Britain in the eighteenth and nineteenth centuries.[1] As late as 1870 more than one-quarter of English farms were under five acres with a further 28 per cent between 5 and 20 acres. Nevertheless, these data are subject to regional variation; in Cornwall and Middlesex, for instance, 60 per cent of farms were under 20 acres compared to only 35 per cent of farms in Cumberland and Westmorland.[2] The numbers of farmers occupying between 5 and 20 acres entered a period of uninterrupted decline in the 1880s but remained numerically dominant until 1970.[3] Whilst the preponderance of small farms has been acknowledged, their economic significance has gone largely unnoticed. They are often assumed to be insignificant, victims of the institutional and structural changes that characterised the eighteenth-century 'landlords' revolution'.[4]

A number of regional studies have pointed to the continued social significance of smallholding after the period of the classic agricultural revolution, but few have considered their wider economic role. Indeed, such studies tend to emphasise the fragility and peripheral nature of the smallholding economy.[5]

---

[1]   D. Grigg, 'Farm size in England and Wales from early Victorian times to the present', *AgHR* 35 (1987), pp. 179–90; Alun Howkins, 'Peasants, servants and labourers: The marginal workforce in British agriculture, *c.* 1870–1914', *AgHR* 41 (1994), pp. 49–62; Mick Reed, 'Nineteenth-century rural England: A case for "Peasant Studies"?', *J. Peasant Studies* 14 (1986), pp. 78–99. For a wider perspective see Fernando Collantes, 'Farewell to the peasant republic: Marginal rural communities and European industrialisation, 1815–1990', *AgHR* 54 (2006), pp. 257–73.

[2]   M. Overton, *Agricultural Revolution in England: The Transformation of the Agrarian Economy, 1500–1850* (Cambridge, 1996), p. 175.

[3]   Grigg, 'Farm size', p. 184.

[4]   For the distinction between the landlords' and the yeomans' revolution, see Robert Allen, *Enclosure and the Yeoman: The Agricultural Development of the South Midlands, 1450–1850* (Oxford, 1992).

[5]   Richard Moore-Colyer, 'Land and people in Northamptonshire: Great Oakley, c.1750–1850', *AgHR* 45 (1997), pp. 149–64; June A. Sheppard, 'Small farms in a Sussex Weald parish, 1800–60',

Reed, for instance, has argued that small farms were an anachronism, an economically marginal 'survival' from a previous era which provided a makeshift existence.[6] Market gardening has received some special attention partly because of its integration with commercial markets and urban food supply networks.[7] As labour-intensive, highly productive micro-holdings market gardens fit comfortably within taxonomies of the agricultural hierarchy. However, the general mass of smallholders is less well understood.

The longevity and regional dominance of smallholding is strongly suggestive of a significant economic role, and this has been confirmed by some focused studies. Donajgrodzki, for instance, has shown that in Swaledale 'peasant' farms were dominant even up to the Second World War. These 'self-employed family groups' often survived depression better than large capitalist farms, and formed a 'versatile and adaptive system' which operated fully within commercial markets. Indeed, 'they have to be regarded not as mere survivors or survivals, but as a mainstream component of the agricultural economy of the period ... their operations made sound economic sense ... and produced a solid economic contribution to British farming'.[8]

Searle's work on agrarian change in Cumbria emphasises the significance of the social and economic achievements of family farms. After a transitional phase in the early nineteenth century, family farmers were able to 'out-compete their capitalist neighbours' by the late nineteenth century, partly by concentrating more heavily on dairy farming. Family farmers also benefited from their ability to dispense with waged labour and rely instead on their own labour coupled with new technologies. Larger farmers, on the other hand, remained dependent upon waged labour to carry out the tasks which could not be carried out by machine.[9]

Work on smallholders in Lancashire has been particularly instructive. By the end of the nineteenth century – and possibly from earlier times – Lancashire had a greater concentration of farms of 20 to 50 acres than any other English county.

AgHR 40 (1992), pp. 127–41; Susanna Wade Martins, 'Smallholdings in Norfolk, 1890–1950: A social and farming experiment', *AgHR* 54 (2006), pp. 304–30; Ian Whyte, 'Parliamentary enclosure and changes in landownership in an upland environment: Westmorland, *c*.1770–1860', *AgHR* 54 (2006), pp. 240–56.

[6]   Mick Reed, 'The peasantry of nineteenth-century England: A neglected class?', *History Workshop J.* 8 (1984), pp. 53–77; id., 'Nineteenth-century rural England'.

[7]   F. Beavington, 'The development of market gardening in Bedfordshire, 1799–1939', *AgHR* 23 (1975), pp. 23–47; Malcolm Thick, *Neat House Gardens: Early Market Gardening around London* (Totnes, 1998); A.W. Ashby, 'The family farm', *Proc. of the International Conference of Agricultural Economists* (1934), p. 199.

[8]   A.P. Donajgrodzki, 'Twentieth-century rural England: A case for "Peasant Studies"?', *J. Peasant Studies* 16 (1989), p. 437.

[9]   C.E. Searle, '"The odd corner of England": An analysis of a rural social formation in transition, Cumbria, *c*.1700–1914', unpublished PhD thesis, University of Essex, 1983.

Winstanley has argued that Lancashire's small family farmers 'were far from being backward, subsistence peasants' and should be considered as a 'rural *petite bourgeoisie*'. Often located on the urban fringes or benefiting from a transport infrastructure that provided ready access to urban consumers, such farmers had an 'extensive dependence on the market economy'.[10] John K. Walton argued that Lancashire's farmers made a distinctive contribution and that the agrarian regime 'filled an appropriate ecological niche which would not have been responsive to Norfolk panaceas'. Small dairy farms and the intensive cultivation of vegetables on the outskirts of towns 'constituted effective and appropriate responses to the opportunities offered by urban demand under the prevailing circumstances'. In a very direct sense, agricultural production and urban markets were intertwined, and the agricultural regime 'suited the needs of farmers and their customers'.[11]

However, whilst the economic role of smallholders in nineteenth-century Lancashire has been established by Winstanley and Walton, they sidestepped the issue of the origins of this class of farmer. Were they simply fortunate peasants who, due to external economic and demographic developments, found themselves well placed to profit from industrialisation? Or were they a product of industrialisation and the intensification of land and labour markets? Little work has been done on long-term changes in average farm size and labour structure in Lancashire, though we do know that average farm size was around 30–35 acres in the period *c.*1700–1850. The relatively low levels of hired labour are not suggestive of the presence of large labour-employing farms. Indeed, whilst industrial capitalism emerged and matured in Lancashire, the structural changes of the classic eighteenth-century agricultural revolution largely bypassed the county: parliamentary enclosure was confined to upland waste, there was no upswing in average farm size and farm service did not enter a terminal decline.[12]

Smallholders generally fared well in the late Victorian agricultural depression ensuring their persistence into the twentieth century.[13] However, the dominant interpretation of contemporaries and historians is that Lancashire agriculture was anachronistic and farmers were slow to innovate or adopt the innovations

---

[10]   M. Winstanley, 'Agricultural and industrial revolutions: Reassessing the role of the small farm', in C. Bjorn (ed.), *The Agricultural Revolution Reconsidered* (1998), pp. 108–109; id. 'Industrialization and the small farm: Family and household economy in nineteenth-century Lancashire', *Past and Present* 152 (1996), pp. 193–4.

[11]   J.K. Walton, 'The agricultural revolution and the industrial revolution: The case of north-west England, 1780–1850', in Bjorn (ed.), *Agricultural Revolution Reconsidered*, pp. 74–5.

[12]   A.J. Gritt, 'Making good land from bad: The drainage of west Lancashire, *c.*1650–1850', *Rural Hist.* 19 (2008), pp. 1–27; id., 'The "survival" of service in the English agricultural labour force: Lessons from Lancashire, *c.*1650–1851', *AgHR* 50 (2002), pp. 25–50.

[13]   T.W. Fletcher, 'Lancashire livestock farming during the Great Agricultural depression', *AgHR* 9 (1961), pp. 17–42; id., 'The Great Depression in English agriculture, 1873–96', *EcHR* 13 (1960–1), pp. 417–32.

of others.[14] The extent to which Lancashire's urban populations were dependent upon foodstuffs produced outside the county does not help rescue this reputation.[15] Commentators from the late eighteenth century onwards noted the small size of the average Lancashire farm. In 1795, for instance, Holt observed that while most townships contained one large farm of 200 to 600 acres, 'the more general size of farms is from 50, 40, 30, down to 20 acres'.[16] Twenty years later, Dickson claimed that 'there are probably few districts in which the division of landed property into farms, is more minute than this'.[17] He was much more aware than Holt of sub-regional variation in farm size and, in general, farms nearer to towns were smaller than those at greater distance, with the largest farms being the upland sheep farms in the far north of the county. Small farms were equated with agricultural backwardness, undercapitalisation and low intelligence. Numerous contemporaries could be cited to demonstrate the prejudice against small farmers exhibited by regional and national writers, but one shall suffice. In the second of Lancashire's *General Views*, Dickson wrote:

> Men of this stamp are quite unfit for the management of land and besides they have neither the capital nor knowledge necessary for rendering land productive and beneficial. Whatever they perform about it is commonly done in the worst and most irregular manner and they seldom attend at all to any sort of improvements. If the lands are under grass they are usually overrun with weeds and if in tillage mostly left without manure or any proper cultivation. In short it appears to me from a pretty full examination of the subject that in this district nothing can be more prejudicial to the interests of the landed proprietors or more injurious to the community than the practice of annexing lands as small farms to cottages designed for weaving and other mechanical labourers. All they seem capable of rendering useful to themselves is a small portion of ground for raising garden vegetables and potatoes. Their rents are constantly paid from the loom or

---

[14]   J. Holt, *General View of the Agriculture of the County of Lancaster* (1795), pp. 26–7; J.C. Loudon, *An Encyclopaedia of Agriculture* (1825); L. Rawstorne, *Some Remarks on Lancashire Farming and on Various Subjects Connected with the Agriculture of the Country* (1843), pp. 5–7; W. Rothwell, *Report of the Agriculture of the County of Lancaster* (1850), pp. 106–107. This interpretation of backwardness in Lancashire's farming regime has been reiterated by historians. See A. Howkins, *Reshaping Rural England: A Social History, 1850–1925* (1992), pp. 141–2, citing A. Mutch, 'Rural society in Lancashire, 1840–1914', unpublished PhD thesis, University of Manchester, 1980; J.P. Dodd, 'South Lancashire in transition: A study of the crop returns for 1795–1801', *Trans. Historic Society of Lancashire and Cheshire*, 117 (1965), pp. 89–107.

[15]   R. Scola, *Feeding the Victorian City: The Food Supply of Manchester, 1770–1870* (Manchester, 1992), pp. 43–51; Dodd, 'South Lancashire', pp. 89–91, 97–8; C. Kinealy, 'Food exports from Ireland, 1846–47', *History Ireland* (1997), pp. 32–6; S.G. Checkland, 'Corn for south Lancashire and beyond, 1780–1800', *Business Hist.* 2 (1959), pp. 4–20.

[16]   Holt, *General View*, p. 19.

[17]   R.W. Dickson, *General View of the Agriculture of Lancashire* (1815), p. 113.

some other employment and they seldom care any thing about the land except for the little convenience it affords them by its natural produce of keeping a few half starved animals. Eight or ten customary acres often does little more than support a cow and horse in an indifferent manner.[18]

More succinctly, Loudon stated of Lancashire: 'Farms in general small; education and knowledge of most of the small farmers very circumscribed'.[19] A generation later Caird was still lamenting that 'Unfortunately the great proportion of the country [Lancashire] is held by small farmers, who, however industrious, do not possess the intelligence or capital requisite to meet the natural difficulties'.[20] As we shall see, the weaver-farmer of 10 customary acres closely describes Richard Latham and his household. It remains to be seen how backward and conservative he was.

I

Richard Latham's account book was transcribed and published under the editorship of Lorna Weatherill in 1990.[21] Her transcript met with a cool reception from the local scholarly community, one detailed review finding that the transcript contained 'serious deficiencies', a view that has more recently been echoed by Foster.[22] Critics have tended to focus on the quality and accuracy of the transcript and its publication has not stimulated a great deal of detailed analytical work. Weatherill, of course, has used the accounts in her work on consumerism, which is widely cited.[23] She provides an analysis of the household's expenditure as part of her study of consumer behaviour. Weatherill does not scrutinise the account to any great extent: the few pages she devotes to Latham provide an impression of a household economy sustained through mixed

[18]   Dickson, *General View*, p. 107.

[19]   Loudon, *Encyclopaedia*, p. 1119.

[20]   J. Caird, *English Agriculture in 1850–51* (1851, repr. London, 1968), p. 265.

[21]   L. Weatherill, *The Account Book of Richard Latham* (British Academy Records of Social and Economic History, new ser. 15, 1990). The manuscript is held at the Lancashire Archives (hereafter LA), DP 385.

[22]   C.B. Phillips, 'Review of *The Account Book of Richard Lathom* [*sic*], *1724–67*, *AgHR* 39 (1991), p. 83; Sylvia Harrop and Patricia Perrins, 'Review of *The Account Book of Richard Latham, 1724–67*, *Trans. Historic Society of Lancashire and Cheshire* 140 (1991), p. 235; Charles Foster, *Seven Households: Life in Cheshire and Lancashire, 1582–1774* (Arley, 2002).

[23]   Lorna Weatherill, *Consumer Behaviour and Material Culture in Britain, 1660–1760* (2nd edn, London, 1996); Sara Pennell, 'Consumption and consumerism in early modern England', *Historical J.* 42 (1999), pp. 549–64; Polly Hamilton, 'Haberdashery for use in dress', unpublished PhD thesis, University of Wolverhampton, 2007.

farming and spinning, enjoying a varied diet, having surplus cash for schooling, books and leisure, but never achieving great comfort or luxury.[24]

Charles Foster did not refer to Weatherill's analysis, but attempted a more rounded analysis of the Latham household economy. However, this study is deficient in a number of ways, notably his inadequate understanding of the economic context of agrarian change in south-west Lancashire. Nevertheless, Foster's study draws attention to the complexity of the accounts and provides valuable insights. He provides a sound analysis of Latham's management of his debts, the wider family structure, and uses individual transactions to reconstruct telling episodes in the evolution of the household. Despite Foster's great perspicacity, however, he relies on cherry picking entries for discussion rather than undertaking a thorough analysis of the accounts and his assumptions and lack of appropriate context renders his analysis deficient in places. Nevertheless, he concludes that Lancashire smallholders with three-life leases could enjoy a reasonably comfortable life, albeit one that was characterised by a variety of economic activities.

John Styles has undertaken the most recent and the most impressive analysis of Latham's accounts. Styles focuses on the production and consumption of textiles within the Latham household, but the detail he extracts from the accounts, whilst remaining conscious of external contexts, generates a study that is innovative and detailed without falling into the trap of being insular. Styles identifies three phases in the Latham household. The years 1724–41 was a time of household formation witnessing the birth of eight children and restricted household budgets. In this period expenditure on clothes was very limited. The period 1742–54 saw greater prosperity, undoubtedly the consequence of additional income earned at the spinning wheel by Latham's daughters. Expenditure on clothing increased greatly only to tail off after 1754 as children left home and increased amounts were spent on hired labour.[25]

Latham's accounts have thus been analysed from a variety of perspectives. However, the literature does not develop our understanding of Latham as a farmer, an innovator, or an individual responsive to market conditions as well as his own family's requirements for food, shelter and clothes. Indeed, agricultural historians have very largely ignored this account for two decades.

Richard Latham's account book is one of the most remarkable documents of the English agricultural revolution – and one that is easily misinterpreted. Foster contends that Latham 'shaped his household's lifestyle in traditional ways' and that his account 'may present a picture of how life was lived on these small farms

---

[24]   Weatherill, *Consumer Behaviour*, pp. 114–23.

[25]   John Styles, *The Dress of the People: Everyday Fashion in Eighteenth-Century England* (London, 2008), ch. 14. I am very grateful to Professor Styles for allowing me access to the typescript of his book.

in the seventeenth or even in the sixteenth century'.[26] Such an anachronistic reading of the account is difficult to understand. Latham's world view, such as we can divine, was very much of its time: his agricultural activities strongly suggest this, his early adoption of cotton supports this, his awareness of contemporary politics places this into context, and the purchase of fashionable items within his financial reach shows an awareness of contemporary consumerism. Latham lived through a time of social, economic and political change that saw Lancashire emerge from being economically backward and sparsely populated to become a dynamic, innovative region with a highly productive and adaptive agricultural base capable of supporting rapid urbanisation and industrial concentration. Latham's account, therefore, sheds significant light on how the innovations of this agricultural system contributed in distinctive and significant ways to underpin Lancashire's remarkable economic transformation of the later eighteenth century.

Nevertheless, Latham's accounts are not straightforward to use. The entries are jumbled, Latham's mathematics was sometimes poor, and there are undoubted problems with the transcript. The idiosyncratic method of accounting itself suggests that Latham saw his account book as part financial record, part journal. This fact is significant for, unlike more formal accounts, Latham's account book does not support detailed financial analysis. Indeed, an insight into Latham's mentality can be derived from the fact that the book records disbursements only, although aspects of the nature of his income can be reconstructed based on what he produced. However, keeping track of spending was clearly more important than monitoring income. Fluctuations in the latter have to be inferred through the imperfect mirror of the disbursements.

The book itself is structured chronologically with disbursements for each year from 1724 to 1767. Few individual entries are dated although those that are appear in chronological order, suggesting that the undated entries were also written chronologically. This is supported by the annual cycle reflected in the order of the entries within each year: purchase of seeds, 'bulling' of cows, haymaking, harvesting, an increase in the purchase of coal, candles, salt and meat, the settling of accounts, and payment of debts and wages. Such chronology suggests both a structure and a predictable pattern to the yearly cycle recorded in working accounts. Latham's account is much more than a record of disbursements: it is a form of life writing.[27] Indeed, a great deal can be reconstructed from relatively basic transactional details. The account provides not only a glimpse into Latham's life, but also those of his immediate family and the wider community. In part this is a product of additional comments he enters into the book that go beyond financial accounting, but it is also a consequence

---

26   Foster, *Seven Households*, p. 143.

27   Adam Smyth, *Autobiography in Early Modern England* (Cambridge, 2010).

of the fact that a large number of his transactions were with named individuals within the wider community. However, the bulk of the entries form a simple record of financial transactions, comprising a mixture of diverse items that are unlikely to have formed a single purchase. Typical entries are as follows:

	s.	d.
For flannel senglet 1s. 6d.: clog nails 1d: ½lb butter	1	9
For almaneck 6d.: butter 3lbs 11½d.: quarter of mutton	2	4½

The approach adopted here has been very labour-intensive, but provides a more thorough and more accurate analysis than has previously been attempted. Each individual purchase has been isolated and, where possible, ascribed a financial value. Thus, the entries above reproduced from Weatherill's transcript have been normalised for the purposes of analysis:

	s.	d.
For flannel singlet	1	6
Clog nails		1
½ lb butter		2
For almaneck		6
butter 3 lbs		11.5
quarter of mutton		11

This process resulted in Latham's 43-year long account being itemised into 11,245 individual entries. Each item has been categorised for the purposes of analysis, which was a challenge in itself due to Latham's idiosyncrasies. These fall into five main categories: phonetic and erratic spelling, obsolete language, regional dialect words, ambiguous language and obscure entries. These categories are not exclusive and there can be considerable overlap.

In the first category we can include entries such as Allos (aloes), bucels (buckles), chicin (chicken), chimly (chimney), fushtan (fustian), gacet (jacket), gug (jug), heters (heaters), hough (hock), inunipris (juniper), marckery (mercury), salet (salad). Obsolete words are frequently used, for example noger (a tool for boring) along with various tools, implements and accoutrements associated with dairying: pigin (a small pail), eshin/ashin/ashings (which is a pail or tub), chessfat (a cheese vat).[28]

---

[28]   Most of the definitions in this section are derived from the *Oxford English Dictionary*.

Regional dialect words include alicer, meaning vinegar, which was used widely in the north of England,[29] bag skin, a northern term for the salted stomach of a calf used as rennet[30] and birm, which is likely to be a variant of barm used by Latham in baking and/or brewing (as in barm cake). Regional names for plants can pose problems: sivete has proved to be untraceable; Elmery on the other hand is probably Ale Mary, a variant of Alecost or Costmary widely used in medicinal preparations.[31]

These problems are compounded by the ambiguities in Latham's language, which is not eased by the lack of context. In 1724, 1733, 1741, 1745, and 1764, for instance, Latham bought a nosel/nosle/nostl. There are several possible alternative definitions:

1. Nosle, as a variant of norsel, is defined as a 'band' or 'fillet' and as Latham regularly purchases bands and fillets this would certainly fit;
2. 'a loop on the traces of a harness';
3. 'numerous short pieces of cord by which a rope is attached to the sides of a fishing net'. Despite the fact that Latham lived near Martin Mere there is no other evidence of Latham being involved in fishing so this can probably be discounted;
4. An alternative definition is derived from nozzle, which is defined as 'a socket on a candlestick into which the lower end of a candle is inserted'.

It is very difficult to resolve this ambiguity, and the only clues are that Latham occasionally records that the nosels were made of leather, and that sometimes these purchases were in association with other expenditure related to the maintenance of his cart, suggesting that the second definition is the one that Latham intended.

A further example is that of gugons (gudgeons), which are pivots that can be part of a spindle or axle, or part of a hinge on a gate or door. While this may assist our understanding of this item as an object, it would be instructive to know if Latham was repairing spinning wheels, farm gates, barn doors, house doors or axletrees. He could, of course, have been repairing any of these at different points in time – although Latham does specifically refer to 'gugons' in the context of repairing the barn door on one occasion.

Latham's frequent purchase of fillets also poses some interpretative difficulties. 'Fillet' has a variety of meanings in use in the eighteenth century including a head

---

[29]   Joseph Wright (ed.), *The English Dialect Dictionary* (6 vols in 12, London, 1898–1905), I, p. 37.

[30]   T. Darlington, *Folk-speech of South Cheshire* (London, 1887), p. 114.

[31]   Elmery/alemary is not mentioned in the RHS horticultural database, but Alecost/Costmary has many regional names. It was used as a medicinal herb. See www.apps.rhs.org.uk/horticulturaldatabase/hortdatabase.asp?ID=17980 accessed 13 July 2011.

band worn as decoration, a fillet of meat or fish, 'a perforated curb to confine the curds in making cheese', a strip of material for binding (including for use with a horse), or a strip of any material. Any of these definitions could fit. Latham purchased fillets on 25 occasions, spending between 1d. and 7d. each time. On five occasions he purchased fillets in combination with thread, inkle, laces or tape. However, Latham also purchased fillets alongside halter reins (1733) and thongs (1735). Latham did not purchase fillets after 1750, despite the fact that he maintained a horse until his death. Some of his daughters had entered service by this time, and this was also at a time of peak expenditure on clothes, hats and shoes within the Latham household. The probability is that most of these fillets are narrow strips of material used by his daughters for decorative purposes.

A final example of the ambiguous entries is that of garth/garthing/gartering which he purchased on 15 occasions between 1724 and 1760, not including entries which unambiguously relate to garters as items of clothing. Garth is related to girth, and as such this can relate to a leather strap to hold a saddle in place, or a band to go round a barrel. Garth is used in these two contrasting ways by Latham: 'Garth for pilsh', purchased in 1733, clearly means 'saddle girth' (a pilsh is a light saddle), whereas 'Garthing washing tub and pigin' and 'Garthing and mending 2 ashings and piggin' refer to the definition of a wooden hoop for a barrel or tub. However, the vessels in question include dairy (ashings and piggin) and domestic (washing tub). 'Gartering piggin' is clearly different in kind from 'gartering 6 yds' which probably indicates the purchase of narrow cloth. Moreover, there are entries that lack context altogether where expenditure was simply for 'garth' or 'gartering'. Such entries remain ambiguous and determining their meaning with any precision is not possible.

The meanings of some entries remain elusive or uncertain: annel water, which is on one occasion recorded as annelseed water, may mean aniseed water which was a by-product of the process of distilling aniseed taken as a carminative. Aluberd, arfo, chorter, cimlin, filbeting, Mar puy, mata charpes, warles and wontey/woontey remain unknown.[32] Cetwecet proved elusive, but context and some internal cross referencing finally revealed its meaning – discussed below. Boolows/booloes/bulos might be taken to mean bellows, but as Latham on occasions buys these in quantities of 5 quarters and 8 quarts this seems unlikely. Coulering is used in the context 'coulering white and brown' which might, therefore imply paint for domestic maintenance. 'Dading gartering' (1737) probably refers to some sort of device designed to help a child to learn to walk. Filbow is possibly some sort of iron clamp. Salume may be salt pork, but this is

---

[32] Aluberd may mean halberd in the sense of a device to 'constrain a lame horse to tread or rest on his heel' as defined by Ephraim Chambers in his 1728 *Cyclopædia; or, An Universal Dictionary of Arts and Sciences.* See *Oxford English Dictionary.*

a derivation from Italian and, as the earliest reference to it in the *Oxford English Dictionary* dates from 1926, it seems unlikely.

Some of the linguistic problems are insurmountable, although work with dictionaries and a close reading of Latham's accounts have kept this to a minimum. The overall impact on the analysis is negligble and most of these entries have been placed in a residual 'miscellaneous' category which amounts to just 0.5 per cent of Latham's total expenditure.

Aside from the linguistic problems, there are also mathematical issues which need to be addressed. Latham occasionally omitted monetary values for his purchases, and although it is tempting to infer prices from the internal evidence, this has been resisted. The price of mumpins, for instance, varied between 4d. per pound and almost 5½d. per pound between 1727 and 1738. It would be unwise, therefore, to estimate the cost of the 6lb of mumpins purchased by Latham in 1733 for which no value was entered. Such omissions must remain blank. Of greater importance are inaccuracies in Latham's mathematics, demonstrated by the following examples.

		s.	d.
1733	sop 1d.: peper 1½d.: 1 measure of seed barly bought of June Barton	0	2½
1737	new cloath 1s.: sope 1d.: beesom 1d.: biskets 2d.: nut megs biskets 2d.: hopps 2d.: pins 11d.	1	9¼
1745	oyl 1d.: mace & nutmeg 3½d.: cups 3d.: spoons 9d.: candels	0	11½
1750	suger 4d.: trecel 6d.: salt 3d.: dying 9 yds of linen	1	1
1755	veal 1s. 3d.: mugs 5d.: suger etc 8½d: bag skin	1	9½
1764	suger 9d.: sack cloth 4½ yards 2s. 5d.: sop	2	8

These extracts are typical of the frequent errors or omissions in Latham's accounting. The 1733 entry omits a value for the seed barley, providing a total for the line in the account based on the cost of the soap and the pepper. The entry for 1737 includes a possible missing value of the nutmeg, but the total of 1s. 9¼d. should read 2s. 9d. Similarly, the entry for 1745 shows a missing value for the candles, but the line total has been miscalculated and should read 1s. 4½d. rather than 11½d. The entry for 1750 is added up correctly, but omits the likely significant expenditure for the dying of nine yards of linen cloth. The entries for 1755 and 1764 also omit values and underestimate the total expenditure. These are typical of a significant minority of entries in the account book. The result is that the annual totals of expenditure cited by Weatherill, calculated by adding up the line totals, are an underestimate of the purchases for which Latham accounted. These examples demonstrate that itemising the accounts not only facilitates closer analysis, but also corrects mistakes made at various stages of the account's production. If we assume that the prices of individual purchases are more likely to be correct than the summing up of several purchases which may have taken place on different days, then the itemisation can correct some of Latham's poor arithmetic.

The position of females in the Latham household is rather blurred by these accounts. There is evidence of their economic activities, access to money, and the purchasing of items by and for Nany and the daughters, but detail is often elusive, or at best suggestive and incomplete. As will be seen, Latham's wife and daughters were engaged in a range of domestic, industrial and agricultural pursuits, and Latham employed his daughters on the farm after they had left the parental home. The purchase of female work-clothes and shoes as well as silk dresses and handkerchiefs indicates clear areas of female consumption recorded by Latham in an otherwise male-dominated account. Medicines for Nany and the daughters as well as visits to relatives or to fairs and markets are also recorded, with Latham specifically recording the spending of money by the female members of the household on such visits. This might suggest that money earned at the spinning wheel contributed to a household economy which was controlled and accounted for by Richard. It is certainly the case that expenditure increased and lifestyle improved once the daughters were fully contributing.

Latham only recorded sexual activity on one occasion, in 1725. 'Nany my wife going to the Filde [Fylde] the 3rd of June. I did lye with her the same morning'. He does record the impact of childbirth on the household, largely due to the necessity of employing a female relative to undertake domestic and farm work during Nany's lying-in period. School fees were regularly paid for all of the children, indicating a belief in the value of education, Christian instruction and literacy for the girls as well as Dicy, his son.[33] Although it remains a possibility that the female Lathams retained some of their own earned income, and even engaged in their own entrepreneurial practices as did Peter Walkden's wife in Pennine Lancashire, there is no evidence for this and Richard's accounts provides a much stronger impression of a patriarchal family structure than Walkden does through his diary.[34] This may be a product of source material, as the richness of a discursive and reflective diary reveals complexities concealed by accounts. However, as the following analysis shows, a careful reading of accounts can provide important insights into a range of socioeconomic factors that are beyond simple financial transactions.

---

[33] Richard's son, also Richard, was consistently recorded as Dicy (i.e. Dickie).

[34] R.W. Hoyle, 'Farmer, nonconformist minister and diarist: The world of Peter Walkden of Thornley in Lancashire, 1733–34', *Northern Hist.* 48 (2011), pp. 271–94.

II

Richard Latham (*c.*1694–1767) lived in Barrison Green on the south-eastern edge of Scarisbrick in the parish of Ormskirk on the south-west Lancashire plain. Scarisbrick was a sparsely populated township extending to almost 8,000 acres with an 1801 population of 1,154.[35] Barrison Green was a small scattering of houses, not sufficiently cohesive to be called a hamlet. A 1675 survey of Scarisbrick listed only seven tenements in 'Narrow Moss' and 'Barazel Greene' between them.[36] Indeed, settlement across much of the township was extremely scattered. Scarisbrick was low-lying and fertile, but parts of the township were prone to flooding, in part because of the presence of Martin Mere, a large shallow lake that was both a major landscape feature and a source of food and income for the inhabitants on its shores.[37] In Weatherill's introduction to Latham's accounts she suggests that the Mere had been recently drained, but the situation was not as simple as this.[38] Thomas Fleetwood had secured the necessary lease, endorsed by Act of Parliament in 1695, and commenced work. There was some initial success and reclaimed land was being ploughed or grazed by the end of the seventeenth century. Court cases ensued as inhabitants claimed loss of livelihood, but the drainage fell into disrepair and Fleetwood died, heavily in debt, in 1717. There was some rudimentary management of the drainage system until 1753 when the lease finally expired, and the sluice gates were washed away in 1754. Drainage efforts were renewed in the 1780s under the direction of the landowner and improver Basil Thomas Eccleston who was awarded a gold medal for his achievements by the Society for the Encouragement of Arts, Manufacturers and Commerce in 1785.[39]

This tale of the drainage of Martin Mere is well known and frequently repeated, but in some respects it could be unintentionally misleading. The role of landowners as investors and improvers and of smallholders as litigious subsistence farmers, foragers and fowlers reflects the capital-intensive nature of large-scale drainage and the varied economy of the smallholder in the early

---

[35]   BPP 1801–2 VI.1, Abstract of the answers and returns ... Enumeration part 1, England and Wales, p. 172; also 1833 XXXVI.1, Abstract of the answers and returns ... Enumeration Abstract I, p. 300.

[36]   LA, DDSc 25/40.

[37]   Martin Mere was two miles north of Barrison Green and actually had very little impact on Latham's life. It is not mentioned in the accounts.

[38]   Weatherill, *Account book*, p. xviii.

[39]   A.P. Coney, 'Fish, fowl and fen: Landscape and economy on seventeenth-century Martin Mere', *Landscape Hist.* 14 (1992), pp. 51–64; W.G. Hale and A. Coney, *Martin Mere: Lancashire's Lost Lake* (Liverpool, 2005); J.M. Virgoe, 'Thomas Fleetwood and the draining of Martin Mere', *Trans. Historic Society of Lancashire and Cheshire*, 152 (2003), pp. 27–50. For a wider discussion of drainage in the area see Gritt, 'Making good land from bad'.

Table 4.1　　　Occupational structure, Scarisbrick, 1682 and 1767

Occupational group	1682		1767	
	No	per cent	No	per cent
Husbandman	22	39	20	40
Yeoman/farmer	8	14	9	18
Labourer/servant	13[a]	23	8	16
Service/tertiary	6[b]	11	3[c]	6
Industry/artisan trades	8[d]	14	10[e]	20
Totals	57	100	50	100

Source: Norman Gardner (ed.), *Lancashire Quarter Sessions Records: Register of Recusants, 1682* (Wigan, 1999); E.S. Worrall, *Returns of Papists, 1767. Diocese of Chester* (Catholic Record Society, Occ. Pub. 1, 1980).

Notes: [a] Includes 12 labourers and 1 plowright. [b] Includes 1 alehousekeeper and 5 'gents'. [c] Includes 1 miller, 1 priest and 1 steward. [d] Includes 2 blacksmiths, 1 carpenter, 1 house carpenter, 1 plasterer, 2 websters, 1 wright. [e] Includes 2 blacksmiths, 1 apprentice blacksmith, 1 plasterer, 1 apprentice plasterer, 2 turners, 3 weavers.

eighteenth century. It was not until the later eighteenth century that mechanisms were found to generate the finances necessary to undertake effective drainage by a levy on landowners and occupiers in parts of south-west Lancashire. Indeed, Eccleston's much vaunted efforts after 1781 were within a framework of widespread investment in drainage: only his capacity for self-publicity and ability to wallow in limelight set him apart from many of his contemporaries.

Recusancy lists of the 1670s and 1680s indicate that agriculture and supporting trades were the mainstays of Scarisbrick's economy, and the 1767 Return of Papists shows that this had not altered a century later (Table 4.1). Indeed, there is remarkable consistency in the occupational structure at this admittedly crude level, with 25 per cent of the recorded male occupations in non-agricultural trades in 1682 compared with 26 per cent in 1767. The 1831 census may be flawed in many respects, but the 211 agricultural families, compared with 60 employed in trade, manufactures and handicraft (that is, 22 per cent non-agricultural) indicates that Scarisbrick's almost total dependence on agriculture continued into the nineteenth century. Scarisbrick was adjacent to the market town and legal centre of Ormskirk, which, with its burgeoning service industries, retail sector and artisan crafts, provided many of the non-agricultural needs of the population. There was also a nascent rural textile industry centred on Ormskirk which spread into adjacent townships. From the early seventeenth century onwards Scarisbrick leases and Quarter Sessions petitions and recognisances mention weavers, websters and linen websters.[40] However, it is likely that the textiles 'industry' was larger than mere occupational labels suggest and by-employments were undoubtedly of some significance. The Latham household, for instance, was fully engaged in textile production including wool, linen and cotton from as early as 1736, although Richard was never recorded with anything other than an agricultural occupation. Theirs was a typically mixed economy.

This economy is an undoubted consequence of the social structure. Scarisbrick was dominated by a mass of smallholders and there is little evidence of a significant village elite. The 88 Scarisbrick tenants of Robert Scarisbrick whose details were recorded in a 1716 survey collectively leased 2,648 acres at an average of 30.1 acres each (Table 4.2). More than four-fifths of landholders held less than 50 acres, accounting for half of the leased area. This compares with an average of 36.3 acres in Altcar on the nearby Molyneux estate. In Altcar, 77 per cent of landholders held less than 50 acres, but they accounted for only one-third of the land area. Although both communities were numerically dominated by smallholders, large farmers were notably absent from Scarisbrick. In part this was a product of the fact that the Molyneux estate leased the Altcar demesne to a single tenant whereas Scarisbrick still had a resident landlord. It should also be noted that many tenants had rights over the unenclosed commons or leased additional grazing land on short-term leases, and the figures given in Table 4.2 do not take account of this. The evidence suggests that as the owner of a life leasehold tenement of around 19 statute acres, Latham was entirely typical of the farmers who dominated not only Scarisbrick, but much of south-west Lancashire. Scarisbrick farms, as elsewhere in the region, did not employ large numbers of labourers.[41] There was neither the surplus population nor the demand for labourers and servants, and this smallholding society created a certain degree of communality where the distinction between farmer and labourer was somewhat blurred.

Landlord improvement was not much in evidence during the period Latham was farming in Scarisbrick. This was a period of a distinct lack of landlord investment, sandwiched between the excesses of Fleetwood and Eccleston outlined above. It was further compounded by the financial and political problems faced by Robert Scarisbrick, the major landowner in Scarisbrick. Robert Scarisbrick was implicated in the 1715 Jacobite rebellion, and after surrendering in July 1717 spent time in Newgate before being moved to Lancaster. He was bailed until his trial in September 1718 when he was acquitted.[42] The period of Robert Scarisbrick's imprisonment, bail and trial saw the estate temporarily

---

[40]   See the series of Scarisbrick leases at LA, DDSc 27. Quarter Sessions records include the following: QSB/1/26/7; 1/110/66; 1/118/51; 1/158/40; 1/158/57; QSP 723/27–8.

[41]   Gritt, 'Survival of service'.

[42]   B.G. Blackwood, 'Lancashire Catholics, Protestants and Jacobites during the 1715 Rebellion', *Recusant Hist.* 22 (1994), pp. 41–59; Paul Monod, *Jacobitism and the English People* (Cambridge, 1989).

Table 4.2   Farm size in Altcar and Scarisbrick, 1697–1716

Statute Acres	Altcar, 1697				Scarisbrick, 1716			
	Number	per cent of landholders	Total Acreage	per cent of land	Number	per cent of landholders	Total Acreage	per cent of land
Less than 5	27	33.8	62.3	2.1	11	12.5	33.1	1.2
5 to 10	9	11.3	64.6	2.2	11	12.5	85.1	3.2
10 to 20	5	6.3	77.8	2.7	21	23.9	337.1	12.7
20 to 50	21	26.3	723.3	24.9	28	31.8	887.3	33.5
50 to 100	13	16.3	893.1	30.8	14	15.9	937.7	35.4
100 to 250	4	5.0	616.5	21.3	3	3.4	368.6	13.9
Over 250	1	1.3	462.4	15.9	0	0	0	0
Total	80	100	2,900	100	88	100	2,648.9	100

Source: Lancashire Archives, DDM 14/9, Altcar survey, 1697; TNA FEC 1/1432, fol. 10.

forfeited, creating a period of some complexity in terms of estate administration and a certain amount of documentary confusion. No new leases were issued by the estate between July 1715 and November 1718, nor was the manor court held in 1716 or 1717, though it was held in October 1718.[43] However, forfeiture also generated records which go some way towards filling gaps or inaccuracies in local record keeping. The government undertook a series of surveys in 1716 and 1717 with a view to selling the estate. Tenants continued to pay rent, 'servants' still harvested and threshed wheat, cattle and horses were still grazed on the meadow. In many respects life continued as normal.[44]

This period of documentary confusion apparently coincides with Latham's inheritance of his father's leasehold. In 1699, Thomas Latham took out a lease for Mawdsley's tenement on 'Barewarshill Greens in Scarisbrick' for the lives of Richard, Edward and Thomas Latham for the annual rent of 9s. 9d. with the additional boons of two hens or 12d., one day 'heaveing' dung or 6d., two days shearing or reaping corn or 20d., the making of half an acre of grass into hay or 3s. 4d. in money. According to the 1716 government survey, the boons added almost 22 per cent to the annual value of the rent roll of the Scarisbrick estate.[45] Unusually, Thomas Latham's right to the use of the tenement was to last for a minimum of seven years irrespective of the lives of his three sons.[46] It

---

43   LA, DDSc 27.

44   TNA, FEC 1/1432, fo. 13.

45   TNA, FEC 1/1432, fo. 10.

46   LA, DDSc 27/97.

has previously been assumed that Richard inherited in 1723, enabling him to get married in August of that year, with his account book commencing within four months of marriage.[47] Foster has questioned this theory, suggesting that he inherited the leasehold in 1716 following the death of his father, Thomas Latham.[48] This theory is supported by central records. A government survey undertaken on 20 October 1716, which was not used by Foster, lists Thomas Latham as tenant three days before his burial was recorded in the parish register. The sale value of the tenement was reckoned at £48.[49] A second survey made four months later lists Richard Latham as tenant, despite local estate rentals indicating that Thomas Latham paid his rent and satisfied his boon obligations in each year 1716–19. Estate records name Richard Latham as tenant from 1720, paying his half-yearly rent of 4s. 10½d., 16s. for his half acre in 'Birskar' meadow, and paying in cash for his boons.[50] Richard was clearly in possession of his tenement from 1717, and had sufficient ready money to avoid undertaking boon labour, for at least four years before he commenced his account book. However, it seems likely that Richard was not farming the tenement himself for several years after his father's death. Even after local records name him as tenant, it may well be that he was engaged in paid work elsewhere, perhaps saving wages earned as a servant, while the tenement on which he paid rent was sublet. What is certain is that the 29 year-old Richard Latham married Anne Barton at Ormskirk parish church on 25 August 1723.[51] Within four months of marriage he commenced his account book and the process of stocking his farm.

III

It is without question that for much of his life, Latham was undercapitalised. He had access to local credit, but this was limited by what he could afford and at times his household economy was extremely stretched. Latham's overall expenditure shows significant peaks in 1728 and 1760, when he paid entry fines of £40 to renew his lease plus other associated costs (Figure 4.1). Latham borrowed money to purchase these leases.[52] The entry fine he paid in 1728 accounted for 75 per cent of his expenditure in that year, and heralded the start of some lean years in

[47]   T. Steel (ed.), *The Registers of the Parish of Ormskirk, 1715–70* (Lancashire Parish Register Soc. 170, 2009).

[48]   Foster, *Seven Households*, p. 143.

[49]   TNA, FEC 1/1432, fo. 10.

[50]   LA, DDSc 25/51; 25/53; 25/55; 25/57.

[51]   Latham's age is given in his marriage allegation issued at Chester on 24 Aug. 1723. See Cheshire Marriage Allegations, images, *FamilySearch* (http://www.familysearch.org).

[52]   See A.J. Gritt, 'The operation of lifeleasehold in south-west Lancashire', *AgHR* 53 (2005), pp. 1–23.

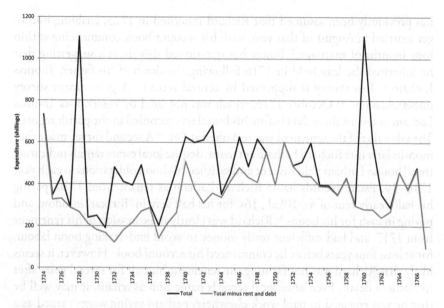

Figure 4.1   Latham's total expenditure and expenditure less payments for
rent and debts, 1724–47

the Latham household. Total annual expenditure fluctuated, but expenditure
after rents, fines and debts had been paid saw a marked downward trend from £16
in 1725 to a trough of just over £6 in 1732. With the eldest four children born
in 1726, 1727, 1729 and 1731, these cannot have been easy years. Not only did
expenditure on furniture and domestic implements fall significantly following
the renewal of the lease, expenditure on farm livestock was also reduced, and
expenditure on clothes and shoes and meat was curtailed. The household budget
recovered somewhat from the low point of 1732, but the period 1730–48 was
dominated by repaying debts. Indeed, over these 19 years, expenditure on debts
fell below 25 per cent of the annual expenditure on only eight occasions; in only
three of them did it fall below 10 per cent of outgoings (Figure 4.2).

The renewal of the lease in 1760 caused much less disruption to the Latham
household. The £42 13s. capital was raised with loans of £10 from James Prescot
and Thomas Tomson. Latham does not record repaying the former of these, but
as he only records paying interest on this loan once with a payment of 2s. 6d. in
1761 it could be assumed that it was repaid by 1762. The loan from Tomson was
repaid with interest in May 1761. Further loans from Elin Wright were repaid
in 1761 and 1762 with total payments of £10 16s. 6d. Crucially, Latham did
not have to borrow the full sum so he had obviously been building up capital
during the 1750s to pay towards this renewal. Saving may well be indicated by
the declining expenditure of the 1750s (Figure 4.1). Debts accounted for over

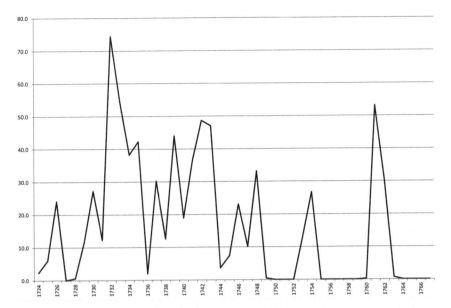

Figure 4.2   Latham's expenditure on debt as a percentage of total expenditure, 1724–67

half of Latham's expenditure in 1761 and over one-third in 1762. However, the impact on other expenditure was much less noticeable than in the 1730s, with expenditure, after rent and debts had been paid, reducing from over £21 in 1758 to a trough of £12 in 1762, recovering to over £20 per annum by 1764.

The fluctuations in Latham's domestic economy are reflected in the family's consumption of meat, which in turn is indicative of some of his farming activities. Latham purchased a considerable quantity of food, especially meat, fish and bread, but also more exotic items that he could not produce himself. Latham purchased meat and fish on 1240 occasions between 1724 and 1767, and with the exception of the lean years 1730–33, and his final two years of life, Latham never spent less than 10s. per annum on meat (Figure 4.3). However, consumption varied over time in a significant fashion: it fell from an average of 25s. 10d. per annum 1724–27 to 8s. 7d. per annum in the straitened years 1728–33. His meat consumption shows a clear upward trend in the two decades after 1745 during which time he rarely spent less than 30s. per annum on meat. In the more affluent years 1755–62 he spent, on average, 51s. a year. The types of meat consumed also varied over time. Apart from offal, beef was the cheapest meat available. Consequently Latham purchased beef much more frequently than any other meat (Table 4.3). Pork cost him an average of 2½d. per pound, veal was almost 2¾d. per pound, bacon 3¾d. per pound and mutton almost 4½d.

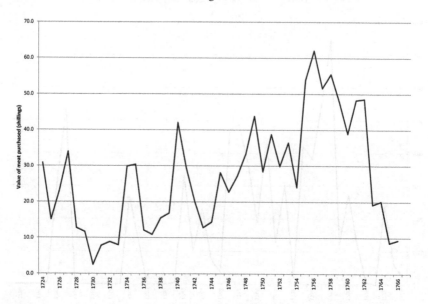

Figure 4.3   Latham's expenditure on meat, 1724–67

per pound.[53] In the first four years of his marriage, Latham's expenditure on the cheapest offal was minimal, spending more than £1 per annum on beef, pig meat and mutton. However, the years 1728–48, when the family was growing and debts needed servicing, were rather different: expenditure on beef, pork, bacon and mutton was reduced whilst purchases of offal became much more common. There was a further reversal in the more affluent years of the 1750s with large quantities of beef and mutton purchased. Offal almost disappeared from the Latham diet in the 1760s whilst consumption of other meats also reduced.

Over the course of the account book Latham spent £58 on meat which, allowing 3d. per pound, amounts to 4,668 lbs purchased over 43 years. However, Latham's meat consumption was not entirely dependent upon purchased food stuffs. Comparing his meat purchases and husbandry practices is instructive. The purchase of bees, chickens, cows, ducks, geese, pigs, sheep and a turkey indicate that Latham was clearly producing animal products, and this broad range of livestock might indicate production for domestic consumption. On his marriage Latham stocked the farm and in the first year of the account he purchased four cows. He maintained a small herd of cows over the 43 years of the account book and recorded paying a total of 55s. for the 'bulling' of his cows on 99 occasions. In addition to the calves he bred, he regularly added new stock, with approximately 50 calves and cows purchased for a sum of around £100. It

---

[53]   He occasionally bought fish and shellfish but never in sufficient quantity to facilitate analysis, and it is unlikely that they formed a significant part of the family's diet.

Table 4.3 Latham's expenditure on meat, 1724–66

	Head and pluck			Beef			Mutton			Pork/bacon		
	Average price per lb: not available			Average price per lb: 2 d.			Average price per lb: 4½d.			Average price per lb: pork: 2½d.; bacon 3¾d.		
	No of purchases	Total cost (s.)	Average expenditure per annum	No of purchases	Total cost (s.)	Average expenditure per annum	No of purchases	Total cost (s.)	Average expenditure per annum	No of purchases	Total cost (s.)	Average expenditure per annum
1724–27	2	0.5	0s. 2½d.	22	44.8	11s. ¼d.	14	17.6	4s. 4¾d.	3	27.8	6s. 11½d.
1728–48	97	88.8	4s. 2½d.	66	207.3	9s. 10½d.	32	28.6	1s. 4¼d.	19	40.0	1s. 10¾d.
1749–59	29	18.3	1s. 8d.	43	218.5	19s. 10¼d.	34	115.2	10s. 5¾d.	2	1.9	0s. 2d.
1760–66	5	2.5	0s. 4d.	22	110.7	15s. 9¾d.	21	36.3	5s. 2¼d.	1	0.7	0s. 1¼d.
Totals	133	110.1	2s. 6½d.	153	581.3	13s. 6¼d.	101	197.7	4s. 7¼d.	25	70.4	1s. 7½d.

is highly probable that he sold most of his livestock on the hoof. Latham only recorded paying for the slaughter of cattle on six occasions and he only recorded eating meat from his own cattle twice.

The cattle plague that affected most of England at some point between 1745 and 1758 hit Lancashire in 1749 and caused widespread loss.[54] There was a highly organised response from the Lancashire Justices and a watch was set up at various points of entry into Lancashire as early as 1747.[55] However, the losses were severe. Latham only records selling hides on two occasions: in January 1750 Latham paid for the slaughter of one of his cows and sold the hide, having paid 1s. for the 'cetwecet' (certificate), according to the regulations.[56] However, in February 1751 he lost three cows in 10 days, almost certainly the result of cattle plague, and on this occasion he records selling two of the hides, rendering some of the fat to make candles with no reference to the required certificate. It would seem that Latham had contravened the regulations, not wishing to lose income. While he was deficient in livestock he incurred additional expenditure for milk, butter and cheese. He purchased a cow from a neighbour in April 1751 but an important new direction for Latham was that he mainly restocked with Scottish cattle. He purchased a 'littel' Scotch cow in August 1750, one more a year later and two in August 1752. Scotland had escaped the cattle plague, so there was a good chance that these cattle would be disease free. This was clearly a successful experiment and Latham went on to purchase further Scottish stock in later years, long after cattle plague had disappeared, indicating his involvement in an increasingly sophisticated national market for Scottish cattle in the century after 1750.[57]

On the other hand, Latham's pig production was clearly for domestic consumption and is reflected in the low levels of pig meat he purchased. Latham recorded the purchase of pigs or swine on 47 occasions, and records their slaughter on 40 occasions. It might be expected that the straitened years of the 1730s would be the period of maximum domestic meat production, but in fact the opposite was the case. Latham made no purchases of pigs in 1729, 1731, 1733, 1735, 1737–38 and 1740. Slaughtering followed a similar pattern, with payments for the slaughter of 10 pigs in the 18 years 1724–41 and 30 pigs in the 26 years 1742–67. Perhaps Latham undertook his own slaughtering in these years, but at 6d. for the killing of a pig, the savings would not have been significant. It seems more likely that the initial outlay and the cost of food (or

[54]　John Broad, 'Cattle plague in eighteenth-century England', *AgHR* 32 (1983), pp. 104–15.

[55]　See for instance Lancashire archives: QSP 1597/6; 1597/7; 1598/5; 1598/20; 1598/21; 1598/22; 1601/5; 1601/6; 1602/4; 1602/5; 1602/7; 1602/8; 1602/17.

[56]　'Cetwecet' is likely to be a mistranscription of 'cetivecet'.

[57]　J. Blackman, 'The cattle trade and agrarian change on the eve of the railway age', *AgHR* 23 (1975), pp. 48–62.

the lack of surplus kitchen waste), precluded the keeping of pigs in years of restricted domestic economy.

Latham purchased 35 young 'pigs' and 12 slightly older 'swine' paying, on average, just over 6s. and 14s. 6d. respectively. On no occasion did Latham pay for the services of a boar and there is no evidence at all that Latham was breeding pigs. Latham was clearly purchasing young pigs and fattening them for the table. Latham does not record the weight or value of this deadstock but the average weight of 113 pigs slaughtered on Basil Thomas Eccleston's demesne farm at Eccleston 12 miles to the south of Scarisbrick between 1759 and 1787 was 308 lbs, worth an average of £4 5s.[58] If Latham's pigs were of equal weight to Eccleston's, then the 40 slaughtered pigs would have weighed 12,320 lbs, providing 355 lbs of pig meat per annum in the 26 years 1742–67 (or 7 lbs per week) compared with 171 lbs per annum (3¼ lbs per week) in the 18 years 1724–41. This clearly made a significant contribution to the dietary needs of the family and it undoubtedly explains why Latham made only three purchases of pork and bacon after 1749.

IV

Early modern Lancashire's agrarian regime was largely devoid of a permanent pool of hired labour. Indeed, few people of any age claimed their occupation as labourer or farm servant. With a low average farm size and undercapitalised farmers, there was not the demand for a large landless labour force, and with very low population density throughout most of the early modern period, population growth in south-west Lancashire was largely sustained by piecemeal reclamation and enclosure. The result was an economy dominated by small family farms who sustained themselves through a combination of farming, labouring and textile production. Eighteenth-century Lancashire was certainly not a place where gentlemen farmers engaged in refined pursuits while a large poor labour force toiled in the fields or threshing barn. Latham's occupation was recorded as '*agricola*' (farmer) in 1724 and in his own will he referred to himself as a yeoman.[59] He served as a collector of the land tax in 1738 and as surveyor of the highways in 1746 indicating that he had some status within the community.[60] This perceived status may help explain why he apparently had no difficulty in obtaining credit from within Scarisbrick, yet 20 acres of leasehold land did not provide a life of any great refinement. The smaller yeomen were family farmers,

---

[58]   A.J. Gritt and J.M. Virgoe (eds), *The Memoranda Books of Basil Thomas Eccleston, 1757–1789* (Record Society of Lancashire and Cheshire, 139, 2004), pp. 12–192.

[59]   LA, WCW, Ellen Latham, Scarisbrick, 1725; WCW, Richard Latham, Scarisbrick, 1767.

[60]   LA, PR 2816/1, Scarisbrick Township book.

and many of the husbandmen were poor, not quite landless labourers, working for other husbandmen and also for larger farmers. The labour requirements of households were sporadic and largely dependent upon the dynamics of the family life cycle.

In the early years of his marriage up to 1731 Latham spent between £1 and £2 a year on hired labour, with almost 62 per cent being spent on ploughing. In 1732 his labour costs were reduced to almost zero, reflecting the straitened circumstances of the household in that year. Latham spent an average of just 13s. per annum on labour between 1733 and 1739, or enough to pay for around 20 days' unskilled labour at 8d. per day. By the 1740s his children were getting old enough to work, but rather than reduce the amount spent on labour it actually increased during this time, no doubt reflecting the fact that seven of Latham's eight children were girls. Undoubtedly his daughters were engaged in textile production and in the dairy, but they were not recorded doing heavy manual work as was his son, Dicy. In the period 1740–47, Latham spent an average of almost £1 per year on hired labour, not counting the £10 spent on marling in that period. Dicy died in April 1748, and this caused an immediate increase in farm labour costs, to over £2 per year in 1748 and 1749. However, the major increase came after 1750. Richard had bouts of illness from this time, recording payments to doctors and for medicine for himself in 1748, 1752, 1756, 1760 and 1764. His average expenditure on medical goods and services was three times higher in the period 1748–67 compared with 1724–47. This is reflected also in his labour costs. His annual expenditure on labour was over £3 on average in the period 1753–67 and over half of his total expenditure on labour was in these years.

Latham employed individuals to undertake a wide variety of farming tasks: burning mossland, ploughing, sowing, mowing, haymaking, harvesting, threshing, ditching, digging for peat and tending livestock. It would seem that some jobs were only ever done by outside contractors. Latham recorded paying for ploughing in 40 of the 44 years covered by the accounts: he never referred to undertaking ploughing himself, nor did he spend money on plough repairs. Like other small farmers, Latham could not afford to maintain his own plough team.[61] Mowing, on the other hand, was paid for in 29 years and threshing in only 11 years, 10 of which were after 1749. Latham purchased a plough and a harrow in 1724 for 5s. 6d. and 2s. 6d. respectively when he was initially stocking his farm. The harrow lasted over 20 years as in March 1746 Latham purchased 'one new harrow frame of John Modsley' for 2s. 8d. closely followed by expenditure on 'sharpening 30 harrow teeth & 6 new ones' at a cost of 1s. 9d. The plough, on the other hand, was not mentioned again, which might suggest that it was longer lasting, or alternatively that he sold it. From a labour perspective, it

---

61   Hoyle, 'Walkden', p. 286.

would seem that while Latham was happy to undertake harrowing, harvesting and threshing, he preferred to hire in a plough team. In 1742, for instance, he recorded 'ploughing moss field 2 times over by John Worthington I sowd & harrowed it the 27th [and] 28th of April'.

Latham and his family were clearly engaged in diverse activities. This is indicated partly by the absence of payments for specific jobs, and partly by payments for the purchase and repair of tools and equipment. Latham purchased or paid for the repair of flails, forks, pikels (pitchforks), scythes, sheep shears, sickles and spades as well as regular repairs to his wheelbarrow and cart with associated equine tack. Other non-agricultural tools included an awl, a variety of axes, chisels, a hammer, nogers, a pick, a plane, riddles, sieves, saws, a weigh beam and weights. He purchased and repaired dairying equipment: cheesefats, jugs, mugs, barrels and churns. Predictably, dairying, like domestic work, was regarded as female work with women being paid to undertake washing and milking when Nany was ill or visiting relatives. Tools and equipment related to textiles production were also heavily focused on the female members of the household. Various spinning wheels were bought or repaired between the 1720s and 1760s, as were wool cards, cotton cards and knitting needles.

Nevertheless, the Latham household was not self-sufficient in yarn until the 1740s by which time the daughters were productive and able to work as outworkers, generating increased income which led to a rise in the standard of living.[62] The textile production included flax, wool and cotton, with some of the flax and wool being produced on the farm. In the case of flax in particular, this necessitated further expenditure on labour for the preparatory stages. In this context a swinglehand was purchased for 18-year-old daughter Betty in 1744. Other textiles tools were purchased for named female members of the family and as late as 1760 Nany's old spinning wheel was repaired for Latham's 27-year-old daughter Ann, who had probably left home by this time.

As well as the unpaid family labour that is implicit in the account, Richard also paid various family members to undertake certain tasks. Richard employed his brother and sister-in-law John and Catherine (Katy) Latham over a number of years. John was born in 1697 and married Catherine in 1719, and these two were the main source of labour from the extended family. Latham paid his brother 10d. per day, whereas the going rate for his female relatives was 6d. per day.[63] John was primarily employed to undertake mowing and delving, with much of this activity concentrated in the period 1748–53. Even at the age of 67 in 1764, however, John was employed to do some mowing. Katy, John's wife, also did paid work for Richard. Apart from a day's domestic work in 1726 when

---

[62]   Styles, *Dress of the People*, ch. 14.

[63]   These male rates are consistent with those paid by Basil Thomas Eccleston until the mid 1760s. See Gritt, '"Survival" of service', p. 39.

Nany was ill, and a day and a half shearing with her husband in 1729, all the work that Katy did was later in life, after 1754, and she always worked alongside Betty. There were at least four different Bettys: two of Richard's nieces, born 1718 and *c.*1720, his wife's sister, and his eldest daughter born in 1726. It is not clear which Betty was employed. Betty and Katy were something of a small labouring gang in the 1750s and over a period of 10 years acquired some expertise in managing mossland as they undertook moss burning, delving and 'tenting' the moss ground. Betty, Richard's daughter, had married in 1753 and with children born in 1754, 1755, 1757, 1760, 1761, 1763, and 1766, working in her father's fields might not have been an option for her.[64] Richard employed another Betty to fulfil part of his boon obligations in 1734 and 1736 by working four days at haymaking. At the time his daughter would have been 8 or 9, and this Betty is likely to have been his sister-in-law. Less ambiguous is the employment of his other daughters. Sarah (b. 1729) and Ann (b. 1733) were employed by Richard in 1764 and 1765 to 'shear' wheat and burn moss. Sarah was also employed for haymaking in 1764. It is likely that both daughters had left home by this time, and perhaps were continuing to do for money jobs that had previously been done as part of a family economy. Latham only records paying for burning of moss on nine occasions, eight of them after 1749, including five in the period 1760–66. On six occasions names are recorded and all are female. Either Latham was not burning his moss land before this time, or, more likely, it was a task performed by unpaid family members, and therefore unrecorded.

It is difficult to know exactly what the balance was between family labour and hired labour, but it is clear that the amount of hired labour fluctuated. Some individuals were only ever employed for specific tasks, such as James Smith who ploughed Latham's mossfields 1759–62, or Jon Draper who was frequently employed to do ploughing and mowing from the mid 1760s on. A John Draper, yeoman, had taken out a lease in 1753 and 65-year-old John Draper was listed in the 1767 Return of Papists as a husbandman, with his 31-year-old son, John, apparently also still resident in the parental home.[65] The individual undertaking the ploughing and mowing for Richard Latham is likely to be John Draper jun., and undertaking this work away from his father's farm was no doubt a valuable contribution to the household economy.

John Prescott undertook a variety of tasks for Latham in the 1720s and 1730s: carting coal, hay and turf, delving, haymaking, ploughing and harrowing. Most of these tasks required a horse, and it may have been the demand for horse power as much as manpower that dictated this need although the additional traction brought by Prescott may have supplemented Latham's own. Latham did

---

64 Steel (ed.), *Ormskirk Parish Registers, 1715–70.*

65 LA, DDSC 27/260; E.S. Worrall (ed.), *Returns of Papists, 1767* (Catholic Record Soc., Occ. Pub. 2, 1989), p. 29.

have his own horse, but whether that was in use for other purposes is not clear: Foster has speculated that Latham may have earned money trading and carting.[66] However, in 1729 it would seem that Prescott's employment was on more than a casual basis as expenses of £1 9s. 6d. were recorded for 'ploughing & harrowing by John Prescott for me Richard Latham for this year'. John Prescott does not appear to have been a contracted servant, but he undertook a significant amount of work for Latham; 70 per cent of Richard's expenditure on labour in this year went to this one individual. However, John Prescott was more than a labourer. It is possible that John Prescott lent Latham £10 for the renewal of his lease in 1760, but this may not have been the same John Prescott that took a lease in 1701. John Prescott was included in the 1716 survey with three customary acres or approximately six statute acres.[67] Latham also records John Prescott supplying other goods and services beyond labouring: two varieties of potato sets, wheat and a calf, all of which imply that there was little social distance between Latham and his hired labour.

Latham continued with this sort of arrangement later in life. In the 1740s this role was filled by John Worthington who, as well as undertaking ploughing and carting, also supplied barley, oats, and a sheep. If we exclude the heavy investment in marling in 1746, 38 per cent of Latham's expenditure on labour went to this one individual between 1742 and 1750. Between 1756 and 1767, much of Latham's hired labour was provided by one man: Richard Wilson. Wilson undertook a wide variety of tasks with 43 per cent of Latham's expenditure on labour going to him in the final 12 years of the account. This includes several occasions when Latham settles an annual account: 'Rich Wilson work for me 2 years 1 day, 7th January, £2 12s. 4d.' in 1764 or 'Richard Wilsons work for us this year, £1 9s. 3d.' in 1766. Richard Wilson has proved elusive, but on only one occasion does he supply goods to Latham, with all other transactions reflecting labour performed. However, as Latham also regularly pays Wilson for casual tasks, in addition to settling an annual account, it seems unlikely that he was hired as a farm servant. Indeed, these wages are well below the going rate for a contracted farm servant in this district.[68] In addition, Wilson appears to have had his own horse, which would not normally be expected of a servant. Nevertheless, settling an annual account for a casual labourer at a time when Latham's household was relatively prosperous is contrary to Wilson's likely need for more rapid payment. Latham did make frequent payments to Wilson scattered throughout the year and the recording of an annual total may simply have been for Latham's accounting benefit. It is clear that the annual sums paid, whilst representing a significant

66   Foster, *Seven Households*, p. 150.

67   LA, DDSC 27/106; TNA, FEC 1/1432, fo. 10.

68   Gritt, '"Survival" of service'; Gritt and Virgoe (eds), *Memoranda Books*.

proportion of Latham's annual expenditure, did not provide a living wage to Wilson and he must have carried out paid work for other farmers.

Despite the fact that Latham had periods of years when much of his labour requirements were met by one individual, this should not hide the fact that he employed a large number of people for individual jobs or for specialist tasks. Latham provided the names of people he employed on his farm on 229 occasions – and he lists a total of 81 identifiable distinct individuals. In a community where landless labour was not abundant, and where farm service was not common, this is indicative of a community of smallholders working with and for each other. The account book very clearly identifies that individuals who worked for Latham also provided Latham with livestock, seeds, tools and implements. Richard Waddington, for instance, undertook mowing, carting, ploughing, threshing, marling and filling dung between 1746 and 1760. However, he also supplied Latham with bees, two calves, oats, oatmeal, oat straw, and rye straw between 1752 and 1760. Henry Bell undertook carting and ploughing for Latham. He also supplied pigs, hens, coal, barley, hay, oats, oatmeal, straw and wheat and Latham rented grazing from him for six weeks in 1756. 'Bel's wench' also undertook some burning of Latham's mossland in 1749. Henry Bell, yeoman, took out a lease in 1734 and in terms of social and economic status there is nothing to distinguish him from Latham.[69] Latham and Bell were clearly more than employer/employee and Bell's marriage in December 1751 is recorded in Latham's account. Latham recorded glimpses of the lives of people who were very much like himself and it would seem to be entirely logical to suggest that Latham undertook tasks for his neighbours at various times. But this was a society where hard cash mattered; helping a neighbour was not seen as a favour which would be repaid. For instance, when in 1742 Richard's colts were 'lost' he paid an unspecified individual 2d. to help him find them. Although there was an active system of bartering, goods were exchanged for goods, or were taken in payment for goods, and it appears to be rare for work to be paid for in goods of any kind.[70]

V

As we saw before, John Holt, like most eighteenth-century agricultural commentators, was highly critical of Lancashire agriculture. However, he did recognise a spirit of improvement in places, evidenced most clearly by Lancashire's

---

[69]   LA, DDSc 27/214.

[70]   This world of local credit has been discussed for elsewhere in Lancashire at a slightly earlier date: Hoyle, 'Walkden'.

Table 4.4   Latham's investment in marling, 1740–55

Year	Cost of marling	Proportion of annual expenditure (per cent)
1740	£5 8s. 10d.	17.2
1746	£4 16s. 5d.	15.4
1753	£2 17s. 9d.	11.4
1754	2s. 0d.	0.3
1755	1s. 1d.	0.3

saving graces: 'marl, manure and markets'.[71] The extent to which smallholders engaged in the practice of marling is difficult to assess, as most of the direct evidence available refers to demesne farms and the experiments of improving landlords. Nevertheless, there is evidence that from at least the seventeenth century many landlords used very large quantities of marl, and encouraged their tenants to do the same.[72] Marl is a calcareous substance, a mixture of clay and calcium carbonate found in deposits beneath the top soil across much of west Lancashire.[73] It was described by Holt as the 'great article of fertilization, and foundation of the improvements in the agriculture of this county'.[74] As Holt also observed, however, marling was very expensive with labourers paid 2s. 6d. per day for this task in 1780:

> Getting and filling marle is very laborious work, and requires the utmost exertion to obtain these wages; and which, after all, can only be effected by men young and in their prime, cheared by the company of fellow labourers and frequent refreshments.[75]

The importance of marl was also recognised by Arthur Young who saw in this practice signs of an improving mentality amongst Lancashire farmers.

Richard Latham undertook major investment in marling on three occasions, 1740, 1746 and 1753 (Table 4.4). Of course, it may be that he marled his land on other occasions, doing the work himself. By 1740 he was around 50 years old, and perhaps no longer fit enough to undertake the arduous task of digging out marl for periods of four or five consecutive days. However, given his financial and domestic circumstances from 1728 it seems likely that 1740 was the first

---

[71]   Holt, *General View*, p. 206.

[72]   See A.J. Gritt 'Aspects of agrarian change in south-west Lancashire, c.1650–1850', PhD thesis, University of Central Lancashire, 2000, ch. 6.

[73]   For a discussion of the chemical composition and general value of marl see W.M. Matthew, 'Marling in British agriculture: A case of partial identity', *AgHR* 41 (1993), pp. 97–110.

[74]   Holt, *General View*, p. 37.

[75]   Ibid., p. 40.

time he had undertaken this work. Marling cost Latham 19s. per day in 1740 and 1746. It is not clear how many labourers shared this money, and it probably also included the cost of a horse and cart, but nevertheless this was a significant investment.

Latham's marling activities represent strategic and piecemeal improvement of his holding. It is not clear which part of his holding he marled in 1740 but in 1746 his attention was focused on one field, identified as Middle Moss Field, and in 1753 he marled 'Moss Field'. Latham does not record his agricultural activity in sufficient detail to reconstruct rotations or calculate yields, but we can detect some of the impact that marling had on his farming activities. It was a clear attempt to bring land into more intensive cultivation and he appears to have followed Holt's broad description when he suggested that 'Long experience has sufficiently proved the propriety of the general practice of the county; which is, to lay the marle upon grass lands'.[76]

In May 1724 Latham had ploughed Middle Moss Field and sown clover. He did not record any further activity in this field for the next 10 years. In 1735 the field was brought back into cultivation, being ploughed in May and sown with wheat. It was ploughed and harrowed again the following April but Latham did not record sowing or harvesting. The field was ploughed and sown with oats in April–May 1739, and ploughed again in 1744, but again no crop was recorded. After marling this field in 1746, it was cropped much more heavily. It was ploughed in 1747 with no crop recorded and ploughed and sown with rye in 1749. It was ploughed twice in June 1750 and sown with wheat in September of that year. After the wheat crop was harvested in 1751 it seems that the field was rested and laid down to grass as it was mown each year from 1753 to 1756, usually in August. It was ploughed and burned in 1757, and ploughed again in 1758 and 1759, being sown with clover in 1760 which was harvested in September of that year. It appears to have been rested again for the next two years being ploughed, burned and sown with oats in 1763. Oats appear to have been cultivated here in 1764 also; it was ploughed again in 1765, when it may also have been limed, and in 1766 a crop of clover was harvested.

In 1740, when Latham first invested in marling, his domestic finances were beginning to emerge from the difficult period of the 1730s – although he was still some way from being debt free. Money earned at the spinning wheel was possibly supporting not only purchases of better food and clothes, but also investment in the farm. In 1740–41, Richard paid legacies totalling £7 12s. 2d. to his two nieces, the daughters of his deceased brothers, under the terms of his sister's will of 1725, representing an initial sum of £6 plus interest. Whether Latham had used this capital to support his own domestic and farming economy in the meantime is uncertain, though probable. A further £16 17s 8d was paid

---

[76]   Holt, *General View*, pp. 38–9.

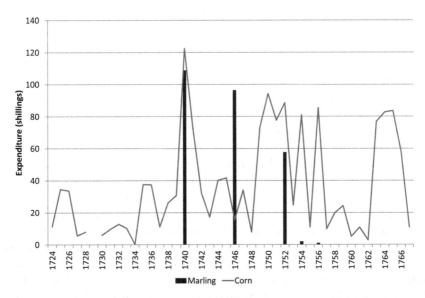

Figure 4.4   Latham's expenditure on marling and on corn, 1724–67

in interest and capital on debts owed by Latham in the same years. At the age of 50, Latham must have felt like he was finally getting his domestic finances under control, and it is no surprise that he took this opportunity to invest in his farm. That marling had an immediate impact on his farming activities is also evidenced by his expenditure on corn (Figure 4.4).

It is not always possible to distinguish between seed corn and corn purchased for consumption, so this analysis is somewhat crude, but 1740 marks a clear divide in terms of Latham's purchase of corn. Admittedly this was initially short-lived in 1740, but the period from 1749 to 1756 marks a period of more intensive arable cultivation, as does the period 1763 to 1766. It was also noted above that most of Latham's expenditure on threshing came after 1749.

The significance of this marling activity, along with liming, manuring and the rotation of crops, is that Latham clearly had an understanding of the preservation of soil fertility. Holt criticised the long-standing over-cropping of land in the Fylde, but elements of best practice advocated by Holt in the 1790s were being pursued by Latham in the 1740s. Dickson's easy dismissal of the smallholder economy on the grounds that 'Eight or ten customary acres often does little more than support a cow and horse in an indifferent manner' certainly does not apply in Latham's case. Not only was Latham preserving soil fertility, he also grew a phenomenally wide range of crops including at least four varieties of oats,[77] three different varieties of wheat,[78] rye, barley and clover. He grew six different sorts of potato[79] along with carrot, onion, cabbage, lettuce, leek, fennel and possibly turnips. His fruit production included apples, scarlet apples, cherry, currants, gooseberries and pear. His garden seeds included various herbs, garlic, caraway, chives and liquorice. In addition he also grew limited quantities of hemp and flax. Significantly, he bought large quantities of seed off-farm, mostly from neighbours. All of his grain and cereals were grown as field crops, as were his potatoes, although not on a grand scale. The rest of his produce was no doubt for domestic consumption, and with the addition of purchased food stuffs, the household had a varied and nutritious diet. However, from an agricultural perspective this wide variety of crops shows that Latham, and his neighbours, were experimenting with different crops and different varieties of familiar crops. Even vegetables and fruit grown in kitchen gardens served to increase the experience and skill level of Lancashire's smallholders. In the case of turnips, for instance, Holt claims that in Lancashire no turnips 'had been sown but in the gardens' until 1760.[80] Turnips and clover, along with potatoes, carrots and other vegetables for which the Scarisbrick district was to become known, had been known to Richard Latham from the 1720s.[81] By the time these crops were extended to large-scale field production tenants had decades, and generations, of experience honed in the kitchen gardens and small-scale field production.

VI

In many respects much of what Richard Latham did was small-scale, and it would be exceptionally easy to miss his role in the agricultural revolution. Nevertheless, we must bear in mind that Latham farmed just 20 acres in a community of undercapitalised smallholders and for the first two decades of married life his domestic finances were under considerable pressure. Within this context, and if Latham was typical, the evidence of four decades that included £12 spent on marling, growing unfamiliar types of potatoes, oats and wheat, experimenting with turnips, growing clover for fodder as part of a rudimentary crop rotation and purchasing Scotch cattle after the losses caused by an outbreak of cattle plague constitute a highly innovative agrarian regime. One man does not constitute a regime, nor could Latham have transformed the agricultural economy alone. However, he would have found it extremely difficult to operate

---

[77] 'oats', 'black oats', 'Scotch oats' and 'Polish oats'.

[78] 'wheat', 'French wheat', 'duck-bill wheat'.

[79] 'potatoes', 'little potatoes', 'kidney potatoes', 'rough whites', 'red potatoes', 'New sort Oughtendo'.

[80] Holt, *General View*, p. 34.

[81] Rothwell, *Report*, p. 37.

in a way that contravened the culture and practices of the wider farming economy. Indeed, the evidence of the accounts suggests that he was highly typical in his practises, ingenuity and pragmatism. This regime provided a platform for both the transformation in the agricultural landscape of south-west Lancashire, and a significant contribution to the wider economy in later decades. Far from being economically marginal, small farmers like Latham were central to the industrial revolution, both as industrial and agricultural innovators.

Latham's family economy benefited greatly from money earned from spinning, and the early adoption of cotton in 1736 alongside flax and wool is evidence of enterprise and alertness to opportunity. Latham was clearly part of a textile revolution, but this should not blind us to his farming activities and innovations. Money earned from textiles was reinvested in the farm. Latham's motivation was more likely to be the domestic comfort of himself and his family rather than any grandiose plan to effect agricultural change in south-west Lancashire, but the self-reliance and communality of the smallholder economy generated an environment in which the small steps taken by Latham were undoubtedly entirely typical of the majority of his neighbours. Latham was purchasing seed and livestock from his neighbours – and he may well have offloaded his surplus to them. He worked alongside them in his own fields, and no doubt in theirs too. However, this was not a closed system: *somebody* was introducing the Scottish cattle, foreign varieties of oats and wheat and new varieties of potatoes. This may have been landlords, it may have been the consequence of visits to markets and fairs in the Fylde, in Preston and Liverpool, it may have been other tenants, it may have been stockmen and seedsmen peddling their wares. It would be mere speculation to suggest which of these is the case: it is likely to be a combination. The crucial thing is that this was a smallholder society open to external influence and ideas. Richard Latham was a regular reader of newspapers and religious texts and took an interest in political affairs: it is not beyond the realms of possibility that he had read adverts or other texts advocating unfamiliar crops or breeds.

There remains a conflict between the dismissive comments of contemporaries and the evidence of Latham's accounts. This is difficult to explain, except from the perspective that agricultural commentators were often looking for large-scale, capitalist production of grains and cereals. A mixed rural economy dominated by a system of quasi-communal smallholdings largely devoid of agricultural specialisation and landless labour undoubtedly looked rather backward from the outside. This is not the place where contemporaries, or agricultural historians, have looked with any conviction for evidence of a dynamic agricultural regime, not least because small farms, family labour and a degree of communality fail to fit preconceived notions of the superiority of large, capitalist farms coupled with the influence of improving landlords. But Richard Latham emerged from the precarious financial position of the 1730s caused by his family situation and debt, to arrive at a position of much greater comfort, if not luxury, by the 1750s.

Latham's success was predicated on cautious innovation. He recognised, and took advantage of, his opportunities, and invested money in appropriate places. Having only one son who died aged 20, and two brothers who also died in their early twenties no doubt worked against him in terms of the long-term costs of agricultural labour, and a family with a different demographic would perhaps have behaved differently. But having six daughters survive to adulthood placed the family in a very favourable position to benefit from the growing demand for female labour in textiles in the middle decades of the eighteenth century. Latham's success was not down merely to good fortune, however. Some of his experiments failed, such as his attempt at home-dyeing, and his attempt to keep geese and turkeys was small-scale and short-lived.[82] However, Latham and his contemporaries laid down the foundations of an agricultural system that would provide a very large proportion of the green crops consumed by Lancashire's workers during the industrial revolution. Indeed, the rich farmlands of south-west Lancashire were to facilitate an unprecedented period of prosperity in the nineteenth century and in this environment smallholdings, communality and a distinct rural culture thrived into the twentieth century.

---

[82]   Foster, *Seven Households*, p. 162.

Chapter 5

The Seasonality of English Agricultural Employment: Evidence from Farm Accounts, 1740–1850

Joyce Burnette

Seasonal fluctuations in agricultural employment have important economic and social consequences. If work is seasonal, some workers must be unemployed in the slack season, or workers must be brought in for the busy season. If workers were unemployed part of the year, then their incomes were correspondingly lower. Even if the daily wage rate stayed the same, living standards could fall if the number of days a labourer was employed fell.[1] Feinstein adjusted his real wage series for seasonal unemployment in agriculture, assuming that 10 per cent of agricultural day-labourers in counties with primarily arable agriculture were unemployed for five months per year.[2]

The seasonality of work affected institutions; it has been argued that poor law allowances of the early nineteenth century were designed to deal with seasonal agricultural employment. Blaug supports this claim by noting that the Speenhamland system appeared in regions of arable agriculture, where employment was more seasonal.[3] Boyer also sees poor law allowances as a way of dealing with seasonality; he argues that workers had to be paid incomes sufficient to prevent them from emigrating to the city, and farmers preferred to use poor law payments to subsidise incomes because part of the relief bill was paid by other ratepayers.[4]

The seasonality of employment also affected the technology used. The use of the threshing machine was delayed by the Swing Riots of 1830, in which many machines were destroyed. Hobsbawm and Rude argue that the reaction

---

1 Peter Lindert and Jeffrey Williamson, 'English Workers' Living Standards during the Industrial Revolution: A New Look', in Joel Mokyr (ed.), *The Economics of the Industrial Revolution* (London, 1985), pp. 188–91.

2 Charles Feinstein, 'Pessimism Perpetuated: Real Wages and the Standard of Living in Britain during and after the Industrial Revolution', *J. Economic History* 58 (1998), p. 647.

3 Mark Blaug, 'The Myth of the Old Poor Law and the Making of the New', *J. Economic History* 23 (1963), pp. 151–84.

4 George Boyer, *Economic History of the English Poor Law, 1750–1850* (Cambridge, 1990).

to the threshing machine was so hostile because it took away one of the few forms of winter employment.[5] The exchange of labour between agriculture and industry meant that agricultural seasonality could also influence the path of industrialisation. Sokoloff and Dollar argue that, since English agriculture was more seasonal than US agriculture and cottage industry could be more easily combined with seasonal agricultural work, the English had more cottage industry, while the US had more factory production.[6]

In spite of the importance of seasonality in the historical literature, most historians have relied on indirect measures. Timmer constructs a seasonal labour pattern based on the tasks necessary on a farm running the Norfolk rotation. His conclusions are based on a hypothetical farm, and are not checked against the labour patterns of actual farms.[7] Other approaches measure some variable affected by fluctuations in employment. When unemployment is high, more people would need poor relief, so Goose used the number of paupers as a measure of the seasonality of unemployment.[8] An increase in the demand for labour should also increase wages, so Sokoloff and Dollar employed the ratio of harvest to winter wages as a measure of seasonality.[9] The wage is itself an important economic variable, but does not tell us how much employment changed. An increase in the demand for labour should increase both wages and employment, but the size of the wage increase does not tell us the size of the employment increase unless the elasticity of supply is known. Large increases in wages are compatible with either large or small changes in employment. Relatively few measures of seasonality are based on reports of the number of workers employed. Boyer calculated unemployment rates based on the number of unemployed labourers reported in the 1834 'Rural Queries'.[10] Burnette used wage accounts from a farm near Sheffield to measure seasonality and showed that employment was highly seasonal for females and less seasonal for males. However, this one farm, which was the home farm of an estate, may not be representative of English farming as a whole.[11]

Since seasonal unemployment has been indirectly measured, estimates of winter unemployment for the early nineteenth century vary widely. Blaug

5   E.J. Hobsbawm and George Rude, *Captain Swing* (London, 1968).

6   Kenneth Sokoloff and David Dollar, 'Agricultural Seasonality and the Organization of Manufacturing in Early Industrial Economies: The Contrast between England and the United States', *J. Economic History* 57 (1997), pp. 288–321.

7   C. Peter Timmer, 'The Turnip, the New Husbandry, and the English Agricultural Revolution', *Quarterly J. Economics* 83 (1969), pp. 375–95.

8   Nigel Goose, 'Farm Service, Seasonal Unemployment and Casual Labour in Mid- Nineteenth Century England', *AgHR* 54 (2006), pp. 274–303.

9   Sokoloff and Dollar, 'Agricultural Seasonality'.

10   Boyer, *Economic History*.

11   Joyce Burnette, 'Labourers at the Oakes: Changes in the Demand for Female Day-Labourers at a Farm near Sheffield during the Agricultural Revolution', *J. Economic History* 59 (1999), pp. 41–67.

suggested that there were high levels of unemployment during the early nineteenth century: 'during slack seasons, which comprise from one-third to one-half of the calendar year, as much as half the labour force may be idle'.[12] As noted above, Feinstein assumed a much more modest 10 per cent unemployment.[13] Boyer estimated, based on the 1834 'Rural Queries', that 17.0 per cent of labourers were unemployed in the winter, and 6.6 per cent in the summer.[14] Whether the unemployment rate was closer to 10 or 50 per cent would have a big impact on the standard of living of agricultural labourers, so this chapter measures seasonality directly from employment records. Farm accounts offer the potential for providing a direct measure of seasonality. One farm may not be typical, but a large sample of farms should provide a reliable measure of employment patterns. This chapter will measure the employment of farm labourers directly from employment records, thus providing improved measures of the seasonality of employment.

Paid farm workers in Industrial Revolution England were either 'indoor' farm servants, who lived with the farmers and received room and board in addition to their annual wages, or 'outdoor' farm labourers, who lived in their own homes and received daily or weekly wages. While farm servants were hired for the whole year and theoretically would not have seasonal unemployment, Snell has shown that in fact there was a seasonal pattern of unemployment for farm servants. Males were least likely to be unemployed in July and August. For females the seasonal pattern was the same in the eighteenth century, but by the nineteenth century the nadir of female unemployment had shifted to the spring in the south-east.[15] This chapter will focus on farm labourers rather than farm servants. Labourers were more vulnerable to unemployment than servants because they did not have annual contracts, and thus might be hired, or not, on a daily basis.

If farms employed more workers in some seasons than in others, additional workers had to be recruited for the busy season. Extra labour may have come from local farm workers who were unemployed in the winter, from migrant workers, or from local non-agricultural workers who switched temporarily to farming work. English farmers used all these sources. High poor law expenditures in the early nineteenth century suggest that many workers were unemployed in the winter. Boyer suggests that the poor law was used to prevent workers who were needed in the harvest from migrating out of the parish.[16] Collins suggests that during the pre-industrial period farmers relied on local industrial workers to provide

---

12   Blaug, 'Myth', p. 154.

13   Feinstein, 'Pessimism Perpetuated', p. 647.

14   Boyer, *Economic History*, p. 89.

15   K.D.M. Snell, *Annals of the Labouring Poor: Social Change and Agrarian England, 1660–1900* (Cambridge, 1985).

16   Boyer, *Economic History*.

extra harvest labour, and that migrant labour took over this role when cottage industry declined.[17] There is evidence of workers in other industries leaving their normal employment to work in the fields. Handloom weavers were not available for weaving work during harvest.[18] Collins finds that 'there was no difficulty with summer labour as long as hand weaving kept up'. Work arrangements were flexible enough that workers did not necessarily show up every day for their jobs. Kirby finds that miners on the payroll of the Wylam Colliery in Northumberland were absent about a fifth of the time.[19] This degree of flexibility in work schedules would leave non-agricultural workers with the opportunity to work for brief periods during the harvest. There were also many migrant harvesters. Scottish and Welsh workers travelled south and east.[20] Some Irish migrated to England in the eighteenth century, but in the nineteenth century, as transportation costs fell, they came in much greater numbers.[21] During the Napoleonic Wars labour was scarce and sometimes soldiers who were stationed locally helped with the harvest.[22] In August and September 1795 the Essex farmer Henry Joslin spent £5 9s. 6d. hiring soldiers to help with the harvest.[23]

Considering the important consequences attributed to the seasonality of employment, the subject deserves more careful measurement. This chapter will measure the seasonality of employment directly, by counting the number of days worked in each quarter. I find that seasonal fluctuations were greater for women than for men, though they were still substantial for men. I also find that harvest wage premiums are not good measures of seasonal changes in the number of workers employed because the elasticity of labour supply varied across regions.

I

Almost half a century ago Jones and Collins called attention to the value of farm accounts and sought to save as many of them as possible. Many farm accounts have now been collected at the Museum of English Rural Life at Reading, and others exist in county record offices.[24] While the accounts that survive are not

17   E.J.T. Collins, 'Migrant Labour in British Agriculture in the Nineteenth Century', *Economic History Rev.* 29 (1976), p. 40.

18   Alan Armstrong, *Farmworkers in England and Wales: A Social and Economic History, 1770–1980* (London, 1988), p. 26.

19   Collins, 'Migrant Labour', p. 40. Peter Kirby, 'Attendance and Work Effort in the Great Northern Coalfield, 1775–1864', *Economic History Rev.* 65 (2012), pp. 961–83.

20   Armstrong, *Farmworkers*, pp. 25–6, 51.

21   Collins, 'Migrant Labour', p. 49.

22   Armstrong, *Farmworkers*, p. 51.

23   Essex RO, D/DJn/E5.

24   E.L. Jones, and E.J.T. Collins, "The Collection and Analysis of Farm Record Books', *J. Society of Archivists* (1965), pp. 86–9.

representative of farms that existed, farm accounts can provide information that is not available elsewhere.

Many of the surviving accounts are the records of the home farms of large estates. While most of an estate's land was rented to tenant farms, an estate usually kept some farm land 'in hand'. A home farm was usually managed by a bailiff, who owed his employer an account of all the money he spent for the farm. Some account books were signed periodically by the owner, indicating that the bailiff's accounts were checked. Some accounts were made for absentee owners, as were the accounts kept by Richard Greenwood for Hall Hill Farm in Stateley, Durham, which he mailed fortnightly to Mr Henry Moore in Lincoln.[25] While some estate farms were owned by dukes, many were the estates of lesser gentry. William Bagshaw of Derbyshire owned 782 acres, of which 210 were 'in hand'.[26] Some estates were owned by institutions; Isbury Charity owned a farm in Swell, Gloucestershire, and paid its bailiff £40 annually.[27] Food grown on the farm might be used in the owner's household, or might be sold. The accounts of Sir John Thomas Stanley of Alberley, Cheshire, record the value of food going 'to the house' and grain used as feed for animals as well as farm products sold to others. Of the farm's products, about one-fifth went to the house, one-fifth went to feed the animals, and the remaining three-fifths were sold.[28] More often, though, detailed records of the output consumed on the farm or in the household were not kept.

Tenant farmers were spending their own money and not their employer's, so the need for accounts was less urgent. Still, some farmers kept useful records, a few even keeping records of every penny they spent. George Wilson of Shavington, Chester, listed not only wage payments to labourers and £75 for rent, but also 1s. 8d. for a pepper mill, and £1 11s. 0d. for 'Universal History [in] 8 vols'.[29] A few farmers tried to keep track of the value of their capital, and their profits or losses. The accounts of Chancellor's farm in Somerset seem designed to determine whether the farm was making a profit. Expenses incurred before the fiscal year began were charged to the current accounting year if they were preparation for the crops grown that year.[30] Benjamin Stimpson's farm in Norfolk lost money in 1830, 1831 and 1832.[31] The farm of Wagstaff and

---

25　Lincolnshire RO, SE 19/3.

26　Sheffield Archives, OD 1400.

27　MERL, GLO 1/2/1.

28　Cheshire RO, DSA 241/11. The animal feed included was for both farm and non-farm animals such as coach horses. Products going to the house were mainly meat, but also included milk, flour and potatoes.

29　MERL, CHE 2/1/1, 1826.

30　For example, the 1776/67 account is charged £13 for 'the plowing & sowing 4 acres of wheat, which must be deducted from last year'. Somerset RO, DD/TD box 17, extracts from which are published in Thelma Munckton, *Chancellor's Farm Accounts, 1766–1767* (Weston-super-Mare, 1994).

31　Norfolk RO, MC 561/49.

Ward needed accounts because the farm was undertaken as a partnership, with each partner taking half of the profits. Unfortunately, once the hired man was paid, there were losses in each of the five years covered by the account book. Some of the farmers were women. Captain William Lukin managed his farm in Norfolk in 1804 and 1805, but in 1806 he went to sea and his wife took over its management.[32] Benjamin Stimpson rented a farm in Alderford, Norfolk, and when he died in 1831 his wife Mary took over.[33]

By the beginning of the nineteenth century a farmer could buy a pre-printed account book with pages dedicated to the value of various kinds of stock, and to weekly accounts for expenses and receipts. Harding of London printed a book used by Earl Cowper's estate in 1808.[34] Apley Park in Staffordshire (owned by Thomas Whitmore, Esq.) used 'Harding's Farmer's Account Book' from 1833 to 1839, and 'Taylor's Improved Farmer's Account Book' in the 1840s.[35] William Umbers of Warwickshire used the fifth edition of the *Swinborne's Farmer's Complete Account Book* in 1825.[36]

Wage accounts were sometimes mixed in with all expenses, and sometimes kept in a separate book. At Buckland Abbey in Devon daily wages were kept in the labour book, and piece-rate payments for jobs such as draining were included in the general accounts. Usually payments to male and female labourers were kept in the same book, but occasionally they are recorded in separate books.[37]

II

This chapter is based on wage records from a sample of farm accounts from 65 different English farms. The wage accounts provide information on the name of the worker, the number of days worked during the week and the daily wage. The name of the worker is used to determine the worker's gender. Occasionally women or boys were listed as a group rather than by name. For example, the accounts of the Harewood estate list men by name, but give only the number of boy and women hired each day.[38] Wagstaff and Ward's accounts generally list

---

32   Norfolk RO, WKC 5/233.

33   Norfolk RO, MC 561/44.

34   Hertfordshire RO, D/EP EA 26/5.

35   Staffordshire RO, 5586/5/17.

36   Warwickshire RO, CR1097/73.

37   At Gibside in Durham accounts of women's labour was kept in a completely separate book (Durham RO, D/St/E5/21/68 and 69). At Stoneleigh in Warwickshire, accounts for male and female workers were kept in separate sections of the same account book (Shakespeare Birthplace Trust, D18/31).

38   West Yorkshire Archives, Leeds, WYL 250/3/222. See also Buckland Abbey, Devonshire RO, Drake 346M/E6–E17.

payments to a 'man' or 'boy' rather than naming the individual.[39] More often, though, individual workers were identified by name in the wage accounts. Age is more difficult to determine, but in other work I argue that boys can be identified by their lower wages, so males with wages one-half of the median male wage or less will be counted as boys.[40] Wage payments varied in frequency. Some farms paid wages weekly, fortnightly, or monthly. Some farms, often smaller farms with fewer workers, paid wages irregularly. For this chapter I do not use records from farms that paid their workers less frequently than every two weeks.

For each farm I calculated the total number of days worked by men, boys and females. I then divided the total days worked by each type of labourer into quarters of thirteen weeks each.[41] The division of the year into quarters closely matches important transition dates in the agricultural year. The two most important days in the farming year were Lady Day and Michaelmas. Rent was usually due at these days, and in the south and east servants were hired on Michaelmas.[42] The transitions into the first and third quarters are marked by Christmas and St John's Day. The first quarter is approximately, but not exactly, Christmas to Lady Day, and the second quarter is approximately Lady Day to St John's Day.

The employment numbers reported here describe only the outdoor labour force, and do not include any farm servants hired annually. The use of farm servants declined in the nineteenth century, but the institution had certainly not disappeared by 1851.[43] If, in addition to the labourers described here, the farms also employed servants throughout the year, then the absolute variation between the quarters would remain the same, but these absolute variations would be a smaller portion of the total labour force. Below I examine whether seasonal fluctuations among labourers were greater at farms with servants.

Figure 5.1 shows the location of farms in the sample. While the sample is not random, I did make an effort to get farms from all regions of England. Farms with a greater portion of total employment in the third quarter are shown

39   Nottinghamshire RO, DDSJ/36.

40   See Joyce Burnette, 'Child Day-Labourers in Agriculture: Evidence from Farm Accounts, 1740–1850', *Economic History Rev.* 65 (2012), pp. 1077–99. The determination of the wage levels for boys is based on wage profiles constructed in Joyce Burnette, 'How Skilled were English Agricultural Labourers in the Early Nineteenth Century', *Economic History Rev.* 59 (2006), pp. 688–716. I do not separate female labourers by age because girls were rarely employed.

41   I define the first week of the year as the week ending in the range 4 Jan. to 10 Jan. In years that contain 53 paydays, one is dropped. Where labourers were paid fortnightly, pay periods that fell in two quarters were split evenly.

42   Ann Kussmaul, *Servants in Husbandry in Early Modern England* (Cambridge, 1981), pp. 50–51.

43   Alun Howkins and Nicola Verdon, 'Adaptable and Sustainable? Male Farm Service and the Agricultural Labour Force in Midland and Southern England, c.1850–1925', *Economic History Rev.* 61 (2008), pp. 467–95.

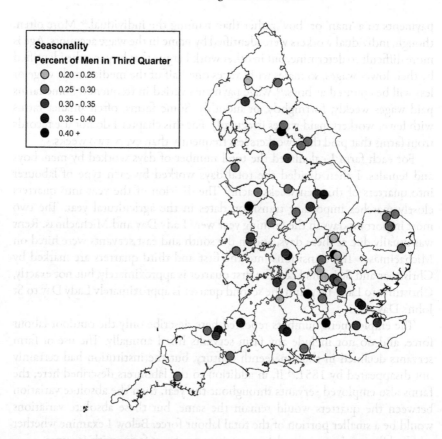

Seasonality
Percent of Men in Third Quarter
○ 0.20 - 0.25
◔ 0.25 - 0.30
◑ 0.30 - 0.35
◕ 0.35 - 0.40
● 0.40 +

Figure 5.1   Farm locations

in a darker colour. The east is generally thought to have much more seasonal employment than the west. Surprisingly, the map does not show a pronounced east/west divide. As we will see, reliance on wage measures of seasonality has led historians to overestimate the difference in seasonality between the east and the west.

III

To begin the analysis, I average values for multiple years at the same farm, creating a data set with 65 observations, one for each farm. Figure 5.2 shows the average over the 65 farms of the percentage of days worked in each quarter (numbers are given in the appendix). Overall 32 per cent of total days worked were worked in the third quarter, about 50 per cent more days than were worked in either the first or fourth quarters. Females were hardly employed at

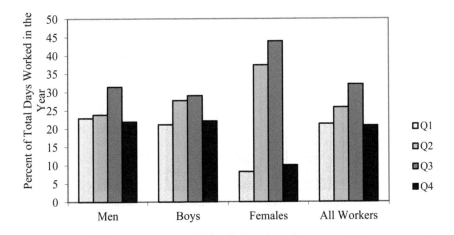

Figure 5.2   Percentage of days worked in each quarter

all in the fall and winter; these quarters account for only 18 per cent of female employment, compared to 45 per cent of employment for adult men, and 43 per cent of employment for boys. The flexibility of female employment allowed male employment to fluctuate less than total employment. However, even large seasonal patterns in female employment only modestly dampen fluctuations in male employment because females were such a small percentage of the labour force. Even at their peak, in the third quarter, female employment only provided 17 per cent of days working during that quarter.

Armstrong noted that high levels of seasonal unemployment were not universal. He notes that 'seasonal fluctuations were much less in evidence in pastoral areas where livestock provided year-round work, on small estates where a country house and its supporting farm or farms were run as an integrated enterprise, or where alternative occupations were readily available'.[44] My data confirm that work was less seasonal on estate farms, and on pastoral farms. Figure 5.3 shows the distribution of work across quarters for different types of farms.

Farms are divided into estate, yeoman, and tenant farms. Tenant farms are those for which the occupier paid rent. Estate farms were owned and occupied by someone who received rent from other land. Yeoman farms were occupied by a farmer who neither paid nor received rent. The fourth category includes farms where the ownership type is not known, and probably contains a mix of the three types. There is evidence of differences in seasonality across farm types. Estate farms had less seasonal fluctuation than tenant farms. This confirms Armstrong's view that estates were more likely to have winter jobs such as 'laying

---

44   Armstrong, *Farmworkers*, p. 64.

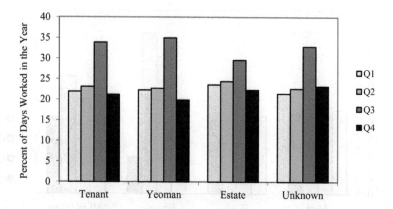

Figure 5.3   Seasonality of men's employment by farm ownership

drains, carting dung, coal, and timber, hedging, ditching and fencing'.[45] Estate farmers were also less likely to employ servants or family labour, so there was more year-round employment for labourers. While most of the surviving farm accounts are from estates, tenant farms were more typical of English agriculture, so my sample underestimates the seasonality of employment. Below I re-weight the results to account for the fact that I have under-sampled tenant farms.

Farms devoted to arable crops had greater seasonal fluctuations than farms focusing more on livestock. For about half of the farms I have information on farm revenues. I divide these farms into arable, mixed and pastoral farms. I define arable farms as those that received more than three-fourths of their revenues from the sale of grain, and pastoral farms as those receiving less than one-quarter of their revenues from grain. Figure 5.4 shows that arable farms had more seasonal employment than pastoral farms. Employment in the third quarter was 36 per cent of total employment at arable farms, 33 per cent at mixed farms, and 30 per cent at pastoral farms.

Since farm servants provided regular work throughout the year, farms that hired servants should, other things equal, have more dramatic changes in the number of day-labourers employed. For most of the farms I determined whether or not any servants were hired. Figure 5.5 compares the seasonality of male employment at farms with servants to that at farms without servants. As expected, the employment of labourers was more regular at farms employing no servants. At farms with servants, much of the regular work of the farm could be done by servants, leaving less employment for day-labourers in the slack seasons. Third quarter employment of male labourers was 40 per cent greater than in the

---

45   Ibid., p. 23.

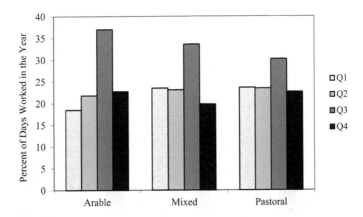

Figure 5.4   Seasonality of men's employment by type of output

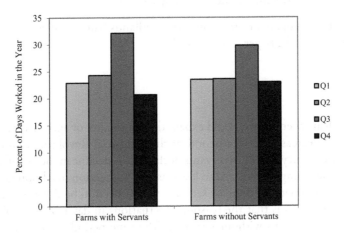

Figure 5.5   The effect of servants on men's day-labour employment

first quarter at farm with servants, and only 27 per cent greater at farms without servants.

While patterns of seasonality by farm ownership and output follow the expected patterns, regional patterns do not. While the arable south-east is expected to have the greatest seasonal variation in employment, it does not. Figure 5.6 examines the seasonality of employment in four different regions. About half of the farms in the sample are located in the south-east. The seasonal pattern of male employment in the south-west is very similar to that in the

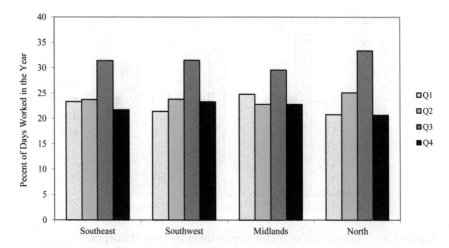

Figure 5.6   Seasonality of men's employment by region

south-east.[46] Compared to the south, the midlands had a smaller seasonal peak and the north had a larger seasonal peak.

IV

It is not clear whether we should expect the seasonality of agricultural work to increase or decrease over the period of the Industrial Revolution. During the nineteenth century the use of servants declined.[47] A decline in the use of servants should, other things equal, lead to less seasonal fluctuation in labourers because regular tasks previously done by servants would need to be done by labourers. (Figure 5.5 confirms that the seasonal fluctuations in day labour employment were smaller at farms without servants.) The time period examined here also includes extensive enclosure. Enclosure may have increased the seasonality of employment if it caused a shift from pastoral to arable farming.[48]

In order to examine whether there were changes over time, I use a sample that does not average across years within a farm. This sample contains 161 observations, one for each year of data collected. On average each farm has 2.5

---

46   The south-east includes Bedfordshire, Berkshire, Buckinghamshire, Cambridgeshire, Essex, Hampshire, Hertfordshire, Huntingdonshire, Kent, Middlesex, Norfolk, Northamptonshire, Oxfordshire, Suffolk, Surrey and Sussex. The south-west includes Devon, Dorset, Cornwall, Gloucestershire, Somersetshire and Wiltshire. The midlands include Derbyshire, Leicestershire, Nottinghamshire, Staffordshire, Shropshire, Warwickshire and Worcestershire. The north includes Cheshire, Cumberland, Durham, Lancashire, Lincoln, Northumberland, Westmoreland and Yorkshire.

47   Kussmaul, *Servants in Husbandry*.

48   Armstrong, *Farmworkers*, p. 36.

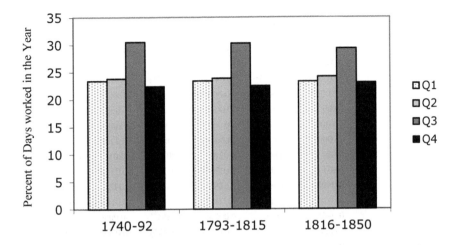

Figure 5.7   Changes over time in the seasonality of men's employment

years of data. The largest number of years contributed by any one farm is 21. Figure 5.7 compares the seasonality of men's labour during three different time periods, 1740–92, 1793–1815, and 1816–50. There is a slight decline in the percentage of work done in the third quarter (from 30.5 per cent to 29.3 per cent) but the difference across the three time periods is small and not statistically significant.[49] In contrast to men's employment, the employment of boys and females became less seasonal over time (see Figures 5.8 and 5.9). The percentage of days worked in the third quarter declines from 35 per cent to 26 per cent for boys, and from 57 per cent to 44 per cent for females.

To control for all of the farm's characteristics simultaneously I use regression analysis. Table 5.1 reports regressions predicting the percentage of total days worked in the third quarter for men, and for all workers. The low R-squareds indicate that there was a great deal of variation in seasonality which is not explained. There was no significant trend in the percentage of men's employment that occurred in the third quarter, but for the entire labour force there was a significant lessening of seasonality over the 1740–1850 period. This is consistent with the evidence of the declining seasonality of boys' and female employment in Figures 5.8 and 5.9. The seasonality of labourers' employment was significantly greater at farms with servants, but controlling for servants does not have much effect on the overall trend. Specialisation in grain has a positive effect on third quarter employment, but the effect is not statistically significant.

An important change during the 1740–1850 period was the wave of parliamentary enclosures that peaked in the first decade of the nineteenth

---

49   t=0.84.

Table 5.1   Determinants of third quarter employment

	Men	Men	Men	All Workers	All Workers	All Workers
Constant	0.3104*	0.3105*	0.3444*	0.3482*	0.3357*	0.3519*
	(0.0181)	(0.0174)	(0.0420)	(0.0171)	(0.0179)	(0.0318)
Trend	−0.0002	−0.0002	−0.0005	−0.0007*	−0.0006*	−0.0007*
	(0.0002)	(0.0002)	(0.0005)	(0.0002)	(0.0002)	(0.0003)
Size	−0.0007*	−0.0009*	−0.0005	−0.0011	−0.0011	−0.0001
	(0.0007)	(0.0008)	(0.0014)	(0.0007)	(0.0008)	(0.0010)
Tenant	0.0275	−0.0055	0.0201	0.0082	−0.0111	0.0138
	(0.0145)	(0.0147)	(0.0266)	(0.0136)	(0.0152)	(0.0201)
Yeoman	0.0498*	0.0491*	0.0495	0.0332	0.0325	0.0266
	(0.0202)	(0.0178)	(0.0378)	(0.0190)	(0.0184)	(0.0287)
Unknown	0.0405	0.0056	0.0953	0.0351	−0.0080	0.1503*
	(0.0268)	(0.0277)	(0.0628)	(0.0253)	(0.0286)	(0.0476)
South-west	0.0114	0.0116	−0.0102	0.0137	0.0166	−0.0029
	(0.0184)	(0.0161)	(0.0292)	(0.0174)	(0.0166)	(0.0221)
Midlands	−0.0101	−0.0134	0.0032	0.0270*	0.0232	0.0210
	(0.0136)	(0.0131)	(0.0319)	(0.0128)	(0.0136)	(0.0241)
North	0.0023	−0.0204	−0.0146	0.0384	0.0282	−0.0175
	(0.0167)	(0.0172)	(0.0349)	(0.0157)	(0.0178)	(0.0264)
Servants		0.0438*			0.0353*	
		(0.0135)			(0.0139)	
Per cent Grain			0.0392			0.0508
			(0.0451)			(0.0342)
R^2	0.10	0.20	0.15	0.12	0.16	0.29
N	161	135	69	161	135	69

Note: Dependent variable = Portion of days worked in the third quarter

century.[50] Unfortunately I have little information on the enclosure status of the farms in the sample. I do have data on one particular farm before and after enclosure. For The Oakes in Norton, Derbyshire, I have data for 1772–75 before the parish was enclosed, and for 1831–48 after enclosure. Figure 5.10 shows the seasonality of men's employment at The Oakes. There is a clear decline in third quarter employment after enclosure. After enclosure The Oakes raised more sheep, which require the most labour in the spring.[51]

Since the sample used for this chapter is not representative of farm size or ownership, I construct an estimate of seasonality by re-weighting the sample by

50   Mark Overton, *Agricultural Revolution in England: The Transformation of the Agrarian Economy*, 1500–1850 (Cambridge, 1996), pp. 148–50.

51   Burnette, 'Labourers at the Oakes'.

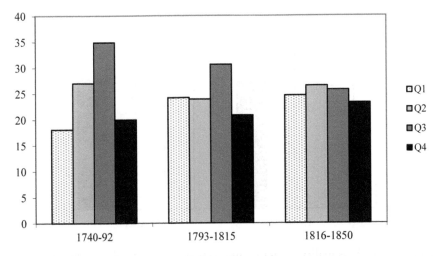

Figure 5.8   Changes over time in the seasonality of boy's employment

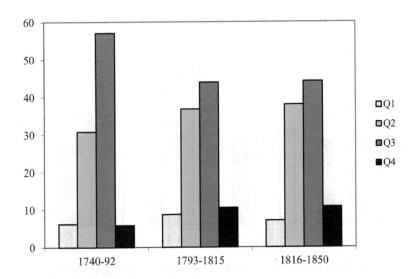

Figure 5.9   Changes over time in the seasonality of female employment

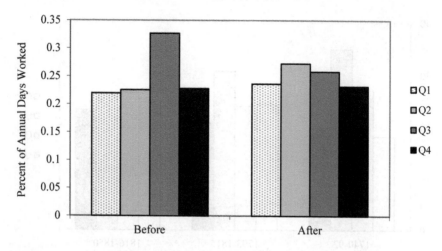

Figure 5.10   Seasonality of men's employment before and after enclosure at
the Oakes in Norton, Derbyshire

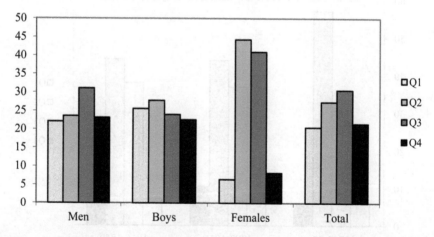

Figure 5.11   Percentage of days worked each quarter, reweighted averages

Table 5.2   Per cent distribution of employment, re-weighted by farm size and tenancy

Weighted by Employment

	Men	Boys	Females	Total
Q1	22.1	25.6	6.4	20.5
Q2	23.6	27.8	44.3	27.4
Q3	31.1	24.0	40.9	30.6
Q4	23.2	22.6	8.2	21.5
Q1/Q3	0.71	1.07	0.16	0.67
Q1/Q2	0.94	0.92	0.14	0.75

Weighted by Farms

	Men	Boys	Females	Total
Q1	21.7	25.8	5.5	20.0
Q2	23.8	27.4	42.1	27.5
Q3	31.5	24.2	44.7	31.2
Q4	23.1	22.5	7.4	21.3
Q1/Q3	0.69	1.07	0.12	0.64
Q1/Q2	0.91	0.94	0.13	0.73

farm size, tenancy and region.[52] I constructed two sets of weights, one weighting each category by the percentage of male employment in that category, and one weighting each category by the percentage of farms in that category. Table 5.2 and Figure 5.11 present the results of this calculation for each type of worker and each quarter. Figure 5.11 is similar to Figure 5.2, suggesting that the biased sample did not lead us too far astray.

---

52   Appendix Table 5.A3 shows the weights used for size and tenancy. I began with the number of farms and the average male employment in 14 size categories from the 1851 census. The employment weights will emphasise larger farms, and the farm weights will emphasise smaller farms. In each case I assumed that 80 per cent of farms were tenanted and 20 per cent were estate farms. (Thanks to Leigh Shaw-Taylor for this rough estimate.) To calculate a re-weighted value for the per cent of days worked by men in the third quarter, I first regress the percentage of each type of labour in each quarter on a time trend, farm size and dummies for farm ownership. Using these regressions I calculate a predicted percentage for each type of labour in each quarter in each size/ownership category. For example, for tenant farms of the smallest size I use 0.07 as the size and a value of one for the variable 'Tenant'. I also assume a value of 80 for the trend, so that employment patterns are predicted for 1820. For each region I calculate 28 such numbers and I then use the weights in Table 5.A3 to find a weighted average. I then weight each of the four regions according to the number of agricultural labourers in the 1851 census to find the overall averages in Table 5.2.

The numbers in Table 5.2 suggest that, for men, winter employment was only about 70 per cent as high as summer employment. If no harvest workers were drawn from other locations or industries, this would imply winter unemployment rates of 30 per cent. Of course, there is ample evidence that agriculture was able to draw on non-agricultural or migrant workers for the peak season. If workers were imported from other occupations or locations in the third quarter, then second quarter employment may be more accurate measure of the size of the local agricultural labour force. Relative to the second quarter, winter unemployment was only about 6 to 9 per cent. This level of unemployment is slightly lower than Feinstein's unemployment estimate of 10 per cent. Boyer estimated unemployment rates of 17 per cent in the winter and 6.6 per cent in the summer. This would imply that 89 per cent of those employed in the summer were also employed in the winter, which is similar to the results for men in Table 5.2. While I cannot determine what portion of harvest workers were imported, my estimates are broadly consistent with Boyer's findings.

V

Are wages a good measure of employment seasonality? One reason that the south-east is thought to have more seasonal employment than the south-west was that it had higher harvest premiums.[53] However, wage premiums do not tell us where harvest employment was the highest. Wages increased during harvest because the demand increased, but the relationship between the change in price and the change in quantity will depend on the elasticity of supply. In England the highest harvest premiums did not occur where harvest employment was highest because the supply of labour varied by region.

To examine the relationship between wage and employment fluctuations, I need a measure of the harvest wage premium. For each farm I identify three wages: winter, summer and harvest. The winter wages is the median wage for the period October through May. Harvest wages are median wages during the four to six weeks of the highest wages. Summer wage is the median over the period June through September, excluding the harvest period. I calculate two measures of the harvest premium: the harvest wage divided by the winter wage, and the harvest wage divided by the summer wage.

Table 5.3 shows both descriptive statistics and correlations with employment measures. Harvest premiums are positively correlated with third quarter employment and negatively correlated with both first and fourth quarter employment, which suggests that the wage changes were driven by demand

---

53   Sokoloff and Dollar, 'Agricultural Seasonality'.

Table 5.3   Wage premiums

		Harvest/Winter	Harvest/Summer
Average		1.52	1.45
Std. Dev.		0.61	0.60
Min		1.00	1.00
Max		4.00	3.81
N		146	145
Correlation with Per cent Men, in quarter	1	-0.09	-0.09
	2	0.02	-0.01
	3	0.11	0.14
	4	-0.06	-0.08

shocks. However, the correlations are small, suggesting that wage premiums are not very accurate predictors of quantity changes.

Because of the large harvest wage premium found there, the south-east of England is thought to have highly seasonal agricultural employment. Table 5.4 confirms that the south-east had the highest harvest wage premiums. I find that harvest wages were 88 per cent higher than winter wages. In the south-west, by contrast, harvest wages at the median farm were only 19 per cent higher than winter wages. The wage pattern, however, does not match the employment pattern. Employment fluctuations were greater in the south-west than in the south-east, and were greater in the north than in either of the southern regions. What explains why the seasonality differences in employment were so much different from the seasonal differences in wages?

Table 5.4   Harvest premiums and seasonal employment for men by region

Region	Harvest Wage/ Winter Wage	Third Quarter/ First Quarter Employment	Per cent of Families in Agriculture
South-east	1.88	1.35	44.8
South-west	1.19	1.47	34.2
Midlands	1.22	1.19	29.3
North	1.28	1.61	22.4

Note: Uses the data set with one observation per farm (multiple years are averaged).

If different regions had different supply curves, then an increase in the demand for labour at harvest would translate into different wage changes in different regions. Where the supply curve was inelastic, wage changes would be large and quantity changes small. Where the supply curve was elastic, wage changes would be small and quantity changes large. Figure 5.12 shows the effect of an increase in demand in two situations. Part A shows an inelastic supply curve, and Part B shows an elastic supply curve. Note that the wage increases the most in Part A, while the quantity of labour employed increases the most in Part B.

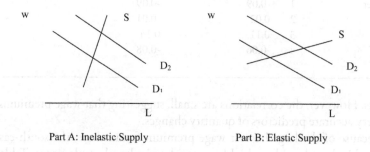

Part A: Inelastic Supply Part B: Elastic Supply

Figure 5.12 The effects of increased demand with inelastic and elastic supply

The patterns of wage and employment fluctuations suggest that the supply of labour was relatively inelastic in the south-east, and relatively elastic in the south-west. Table 5.4 shows that the harvest wage premium was largest in the south-east. At the same time, the quantity change in this region was smaller than in the south-west or the north. This suggests that the supply curve was relatively inelastic in the south-east. By contrast, the south-west had a more elastic supply curve; employment could expand substantially in the third quarter without much increase in the wage. The north also had relatively elastic labour supply, and seems to have had a larger demand for third quarter employment than the south-west, perhaps because of its greater use of servants.

The supply of labour to agriculture should be more elastic where there are people engaged in non-agricultural occupations who can easily be drawn into agriculture in the peak season. To test this hypothesis, I examine whether agricultural employment expanded more in counties with a smaller percentage of families listed as agricultural in the census. Table 5.4 also includes a measure of the percentage of families in the county that were listed as employed in agriculture in the 1831 census.[54] The south-east was most specialised in agriculture. Since there were fewer non-agricultural workers to draw on,

---

54 The percentage of families in agriculture was taken from the 1831 census. BPP 1833, XXXVI and XXXVII.

the supply of labour to agriculture would have been relatively inelastic. The percentage of the population in agriculture was the lowest in the north, and there the increase in employment from the first to the third quarter was the greatest. This expansion of agricultural employment could be accomplished with a relatively small increase in the wage because labour supply was elastic. The first three columns of Table 5.5 show the result of regressing men's third quarter employment on the harvest wage premiums. The relationship between the wage premium and third quarter employment is not significant. However, the percentage of families in the agriculture does have a significant effect on employment in the third quarter. Counties with greater specialisation in agriculture had a lower percentage of total male employment in the third quarter. This means that third quarter employment in agriculture expanded more in counties with more diversified employment. The labour supply curve was more elastic where workers in other industries could be drawn into agriculture.

Seasonal changes in wages have been used as an indicator of the seasonality of agricultural wages. However, the strength of the demand shock was not the only factor affecting the size of the wage change. The elasticity of supply was an important determinant of the wage change. Regions with the greatest seasonal wage change were regions with the most inelastic supply of labour. Labour supply was more elastic in areas where relatively more people were employed in non-agricultural occupations.

VI

The first successful threshing machine dates from 1786, but its adoption was slow.[55] One reason farmers were reluctant to use threshing machines was opposition of workers. During the Swing Riots of 1830 many threshing machines were broken, and many were saved only because farmers promised not to use them. In their classic analysis, Hobsbawm and Rude attribute this hostility to the fact that the threshing machine took away employment during the winter, when employment was particularly scarce. This section will compare employment at farms with threshing machines to employment at farms using hand threshing. Only farms with evidence of either machine or hand threshing are included in the sample for this section; other farms are dropped. My sample contains four farms that had threshing machines, and 29 farms with evidence of hand threshing. The earliest date that a threshing

---

55 Armstrong, *Farmworkers*, p. 50.

Table 5.5   Regressions of per cent employment in third quarter on wage premiums

	Q3	Q3	Q3	Q1
Constant	0.2780*	0.3153*	0.4035*	0.2344*
	(0.0141)	(0.0259)	(0.0341)	(0.0361)
Harvest	0.0106	0.0025	0.0128	
Premium	(0.0086)	(0.0108)	(0.0107)	
Trend		−0.0004	−0.0004*	
		(0.0002)	(0.0002)	
Size		−0.0005	−0.0009	0.0008
		(0.0007)	(0.0007)	(0.0024)
Tenant		0.0148	0.0167	−0.0246
		(0.0144)	(0.0138)	(0.0349)
Yeoman		0.0480*	0.0381*	0.0032
		(0.0197)	(0.0190)	(0.0414)
Unknown		0.0413	0.0432	−0.0354
		(0.0248)	(0.0237)	(0.0369)
South-west		0.0087	−0.0070	−0.0164
		(0.0190)	(0.0187)	(0.0553)
Midlands		0.0010	−0.0204	0.0474
		(0.0149)	(0.0153)	(0.0386)
North		−0.0110	−0.0571*	0.0112
		(0.0184)	(0.0215)	(0.0424)
Per cent in			−0.0023*	
Agriculture			(0.0006)	
Threshing				−0.0476
Machine				(0.0419)
R2	0.010	0.113	0.197	0.114
N	146	146	146	33

Note: Dependent Variable = Portion of Days Worked by Men in the Specified Quarter

machine appears is 1822.[56] The farms with threshing machines were located in Hampshire, Norfolk, Nottinghamshire and Shropshire.

The effect of the threshing machine seems to have been to move men's employment from the first quarter to the fourth quarter. Figure 5.13 shows the distribution employment for machine-threshing and hand-threshing farms. Machine-threshing farms use more men in the fourth quarter, and fewer in the first quarter. There is also evidence that they use more boys and females in the fourth quarter, perhaps because boys and females could be used for operating the threshing machine.

---

56   Accounts of Lascelles Iremonger. Hampshire RO, 41M63/5.

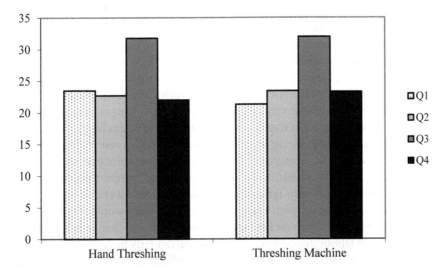

Figure 5.13   Differences in the seasonality of male employment by use of the threshing machine

As has been claimed, threshing machines did reduce winter employment. How much unemployment did a threshing machine cause? First quarter employment was lower at farms with threshing machines, but only by about 7 per cent. To see if the threshing machine has a significant effect, after controlling for other things, I regress first quarter employment on a dummy variable indicating the presence of a threshing machine. The fourth column of Table 5.5 shows the results. The presence of a threshing machine does have a negative effect on first quarter employment, though the effect is not statistically significant. The size of the effect is to reduce the portion of employment in the first quarter by 5 percentage points, which is 23 per cent of the mean of that variable. Though not significant, the point estimate suggests a substantial reduction in winter employment, and is consistent with the threshing machine causing winter unemployment.

VII

This chapter has used direct measures of employment from farm accounts to measure seasonal fluctuations in agricultural employment. For adult males first quarter employment was only 91 to 94 per cent of second quarter employment and only about 70 per cent of third quarter employment. Since migrants and industrial workers were used for harvest, winter unemployment was probably closer to 6 to 9 per cent than it was to 30 per cent. The employment of boys was less seasonal than men's employment, and the employment of females was much more seasonal.

Seasonal fluctuations in employment were greater at arable farms than at pastoral farms, but pastoral farms still employed more workers in the third quarter than in other quarters. Threshing machines reduced relative employment in the first quarter but increased relative employment in the fourth quarter.

Seasonal wage fluctuations are not good measures of fluctuations in employment because the elasticity of supply varied. In some places seasonal demand for harvest labour resulted in relatively large changes in employment with only small increases in wages, while in other places wage changes were large and employment changes were small. This suggests that harvest wage premiums should not be used as measures of seasonal employment fluctuations. Labour supply was relatively inelastic in the south-east, where a greater portion of the population was employed in agriculture. Since there were fewer non-agricultural workers in the south-east, even a large increase in the wage would not draw very many workers into the harvest labour force. As a result, the change in increase in the quantity of labour during harvest was not particularly high.

This study has demonstrated the value of collecting direct data from farm accounts. Harvest wage premiums did not tell us the whole story; seasonal changes in total employment had a different geographical pattern. Luckily, detailed farm accounts recording where and when workers were hired are available. Surviving records are not a random sample of farms, but we can re-weight the sample to provide better estimates of the seasonality of employment. The potential exists for using farm account data to answer other questions as well. Did an 'industrious revolution' lead to an increase in the number of days worked per year? Did the number of workers per acre decrease over time? The farm accounts needed to answer these and other questions are available in the archives, waiting for the historian to analyse them.

Appendix

Table 5.A1   Distribution of days worked by quarter, farm averages

	As Percentage of Days Worked Within Type				As Percentage of Days Worked by All Workers		
	Men	Boys*	Females+	Total	Men	Boys	Females
Q1	22.9	21.1	8.2	21.3	17.3	2.8	1.2
Q2	23.8	27.7	37.8	25.8	17.9	3.5	4.4
Q3	31.4	29.0	43.9	32.1	23.2	3.5	5.4
Q4	21.9	22.1	10.0	20.8	16.4	3.0	1.4
Min/Max	0.70	0.73	0.19	0.65			
Estate (n=38)							
Q1	23.6	21.0	7.9	21.8	17.6	3.0	1.2
Q2	24.4	29.4	39.4	26.5	18.2	3.8	4.5
Q3	29.6	29.7	41.7	30.9	21.8	3.6	5.4
Q4	22.3	19.9	11.0	20.8	16.5	2.9	1.5
Min/Max	0.75	0.67	0.19	0.67			
Yeoman (n=7)							
Q1	22.3	18.0	20.4	21.7	17.0	2.3	2.4
Q2	22.7	24.4	18.7	22.6	17.4	3.0	2.3
Q3	35.0	23.8	48.1	34.8	26.7	3.0	5.3
Q4	19.9	33.9	12.8	20.9	14.8	3.8	2.3
Min/Max	0.57	0.53	0.27	0.60			
Tenant (n=14)							
Q1	21.9	18.6	5.7	20.0	16.6	2.7	0.7
Q2	23.1	26.9	44.1	26.8	17.2	3.4	6.2
Q3	33.9	30.7	43.3	33.0	24.6	3.4	5.1
Q4	21.2	23.8	6.9	20.2	16.0	3.0	1.2
Min/Max	0.63	0.61	0.13	0.61			
Unknown Ownership(n=6)							
Q1	21.4	29.9	3.7	20.6	17.5	2.5	0.5
Q2	22.6	21.7	32.4	23.0	18.2	2.3	2.5
Q3	32.9	25.7	55.4	34.5	24.8	3.2	6.4
Q4	23.2	22.7	8.5	22.0	18.3	2.7	1.0
Min/Max	0.65	0.73	0.07	0.60			
Arable Farms (Grain more than 75 per cent of sales) (n=7)							
Q1	18.5	16.2	3.9	17.0	13.3	3.1	0.5
Q2	21.8	29.5	36.7	24.1	15.5	4.9	3.8
Q3	37.0	33.7	48.9	38.7	25.5	5.6	7.6
Q4	22.7	20.6	10.6	20.2	15.9	2.8	1.6
Min/Max	0.50	0.48	0.08	0.44			

Mixed Farms (Grain between 25 per cent and 75 per cent of sales) (n=16)

Q1	23.5	23.4	11.3	22.7	18.1	3.1	1.5
Q2	23.1	25.4	42.5	26.0	17.1	3.5	5.5
Q3	33.6	27.2	38.0	31.9	24.3	3.3	4.1
Q4	19.8	24.1	8.3	19.4	14.9	1.5	1.2
Min/Max	0.59	0.86	0.20	0.61			

Pastoral Farms (Grain less than 25 per cent of sales) (n=8)

Q1	23.6	24.0	8.3	21.1	17.2	2.0	1.9
Q2	23.4	28.0	35.3	25.7	17.1	2.5	6.2
Q3	30.2	32.1	45.8	32.8	22.3	2.4	8.1
Q4	22.6	15.9	10.7	20.4	16.4	1.6	2.4
Min/Max	0.75	0.50	0.18	0.62			

Farms with Servants (n=21)

Q1	22.9	22.1	8.7	21.6	18.0	2.6	0.9
Q2	24.3	27.9	44.5	26.1	18.9	3.5	3.7
Q3	32.1	25.1	38.8	32.2	25.0	3.1	4.1
Q4	20.7	24.8	8.1	20.1	15.9	3.0	1.2
Min/Max	0.64	0.79	0.18	0.62			

Farms without Servants (n=37)

Q1	23.5	21.0	8.1	21.8	17.4	3.0	1.3
Q2	23.6	29.0	34.6	25.5	17.6	3.8	4.1
Q3	29.8	29.4	46.1	31.1	22.0	3.7	5.4
Q4	23.0	20.6	11.2	21.6	16.9	3.1	1.5
Min/Max	0.77	0.71	0.18	0.69			

South-east (n=33)

Q1	23.3	21.6	5.3	22.0	18.1	3.5	0.5
Q2	23.7	28.3	42.5	25.7	18.5	4.1	3.1
Q3	31.4	26.5	45.6	31.4	23.9	4.0	3.4
Q4	21.7	23.5	6.7	20.9	16.8	3.6	0.5
Min/Max	0.69	0.76	0.12	0.67			

South-west (n=7)

Q1	21.4	20.8	13.7	20.1	14.6	2.7	2.7
Q2	23.8	37.9	30.5	26.8	16.5	4.6	5.7
Q3	31.5	25.5	38.1	31.6	21.9	3.3	6.4
Q4	23.3	15.7	17.7	21.6	15.8	2.4	3.4
Min/Max	0.68	0.41	0.36	0.64			

Midlands (n=13)

Q1	24.8	21.5	5.2	21.7	18.6	2.4	0.8
Q2	22.8	23.4	37.9	24.9	17.2	2.7	5.0
Q3	29.6	33.8	46.3	32.6	22.1	3.0	7.5
Q4	22.8	21.2	10.6	20.7	16.9	2.7	1.1
Min/Max	0.77	0.63	0.11	0.63			

North (n=12)							
Q1	20.8	18.9	16.8	19.3	15.4	1.3	2.6
Q2	25.1	23.8	28.4	26.7	17.8	2.0	6.9
Q3	33.4	34.1	40.1	33.9	23.2	2.5	8.1
Q4	20.7	23.2	14.6	20.1	14.9	2.0	3.1
Min/Max	0.62	0.55	0.36	0.57			
Farms with threshing machines (n=4)							
Q1	21.3	20.8	6.9	20.2	15.9	3.5	0.8
Q2	23.4	25.9	50.5	25.9	17.3	4.0	4.6
Q3	32.0	25.9	34.2	31.2	23.5	4.1	3.6
Q4	23.3	27.5	8.4	22.6	17.6	4.1	1.0
Min/Max	0.67	0.76	0.14	0.65			
Farms threshing by hand (n=29)							
Q1	23.5	23.0	8.7	22.2	18.1	2.9	1.2
Q2	22.7	24.7	39.2	24.6	17.7	3.3	3.6
Q3	31.8	30.7	44.8	32.6	24.3	3.5	4.8
Q4	22.0	21.6	7.3	20.6	16.8	2.9	1.0
Min/Max	0.69	0.70	0.16	0.63			

Notes: *Excludes three farms that did not employ any boys. +Excludes one farm that did not employ any females.

Table 5.A2   Distribution of days worked by quarter, annual sample

	Men	Boys*	Females+	Total	Men	Boys	Females
1740–92 (n=39)							
Q1	23.4	18.1	6.2	21.4	18.9	1.8	0.6
Q2	23.8	27.0	30.8	24.9	19.3	2.3	3.2
Q3	30.5	34.9	57.1	33.4	24.1	2.6	6.8
Q4	22.4	20.0	5.8	20.3	17.9	1.7	0.7
1793–1815 (n=31)							
Q1	23.4	24.2	8.7	21.2	16.3	3.0	1.9
Q2	23.9	24.5	36.8	25.8	16.7	3.6	5.5
Q3	30.3	30.6	43.9	31.8	21.6	4.0	6.1
Q4	22.5	20.8	10.5	21.2	15.6	3.2	2.3
1816–50 (n=91)							
Q1	23.3	24.6	7.1	21.7	17.7	3.0	1.0
Q2	24.2	26.5	38.0	26.7	18.3	3.7	4.7
Q3	29.3	25.7	44.2	29.7	21.8	3.3	4.6
Q4	23.1	23.2	10.8	21.9	17.4	3.2	1.3

Notes: *Excludes 10 farms that did not employ any boys. +Excludes one farm that did not employ any females.

Table 5.A3.   Distribution of Farm Size in 1851

Farm size	Average male Labourers	Average Total Labourers	Number of Farms	Weight by Employment		Weight by Farms	
				Estate	Tenant	Estate	Tenant
Under 5 acres	0.06	0.07	18,975	0.0003	0.0013	0.0133	0.0533
5–<10	0.13	0.15	25,299	0.0010	0.0038	0.0178	0.0710
10–<50	0.60	0.66	93,025	0.0161	0.0642	0.0653	0.2611
50–<75	1.44	1.59	33,515	0.0139	0.0556	0.0235	0.0941
75–<100	1.99	2.20	19,759	0.0113	0.0452	0.0139	0.0555
100–<150	3.03	3.35	34,044	0.0297	0.1187	0.0239	0.0956
150–<200	4.36	4.83	18,463	0.0232	0.0928	0.0130	0.0518
200–<250	4.83	5.34	15,492	0.0216	0.0862	0.0109	0.0435
250–<300	7.02	7.76	7,111	0.0144	0.0575	0.0050	0.0200
300–<400	8.96	9.91	9,031	0.0233	0.0932	0.0063	0.0254
400–<500	11.65	12.89	4,067	0.0137	0.0546	0.0029	0.0114
500–<600	14.37	15.89	2,248	0.0093	0.0372	0.0016	0.0063
600–<1000	18.54	20.51	2,816	0.0150	0.0602	0.0020	0.0079
1000+	22.32	24.68	1,132	0.0073	0.0291	0.0008	0.0032

Source: A. H. John, "Statistical Appendix", in Joan Thirsk, ed., *The Agrarian History of England and Wales*, vol. VI, *1750–1850*,(1989), pp. 1072-3. Calculations exclude farms of unknown acreage. Average male labourers is somewhat underestimated because I use the lower bound of each interval. (For farms with between 10 and 14 labourers, I estimate 10 labourers.) To obtain Total Labourers, I assume that female labourers were 10.6 per cent of the total labour force.

Data Sources

Bedfordshire, Eversholt, MERL, mic P245, Poddington, Bedfordshire RO, OR 1370; Buckinghamshire, Drake, Amersham, Buckinghamshire RO, D/DR/2/166 and 168; Chicheley, Chicheley, Buckinghamshire RO, D/X 958/1; Cheshire, Stanley, Alderley, Cheshire RO, DSA/1B, 2–14; George Wilson, Shavington, MERL, CHE 2/1/1; Derbyshire, The Oakes, Norton, Sheffield Archives OD 1518 and 1531; Devonshire, Buckland Abbey, Buckland Monachorum, Devon RO, Drake 346M/E6 to E17; Dorset/Devon, Bragg, Throrncombe, Dorset/Devon, Dorset RO, D83/22; Durham, Strathmore, Gibside, Durham RO, D/St/E5/21/68 and 69, Satley, Lincolnshire RO, SE 19/3; Essex, Petres, East Hordon, Essex RO, D/DP/A214; Joslin of Codham Hall, Great Warley, Essex RO, D/DJn/E5; Ulmes Farm, Latchingdon, Essex RO, D/DOp/E15; Crix Farm, Springfield, LSE Coll Misc 0031, vol. 5; Gloucestershire, Mangursbury and Swell, Glos., MERL, GLO 1/2/1; Hampshire, Iremonger, Clatford, Hampshire RO, 41M63/5, Edward, Fyfield, Hampshire RO, 2M37/343 and 341, Bury Lodge, Hambledon, Warwickshire RO, CR114A/357, Clanville Lodge, Andover, Warwickshire RO, CR114A/353; Hertfordshire, Cowper, Cole Green, Hertfordshire RO, D/EP EA 50/1, 50/3, and 26/5, Radcliffe, Wellbury, Hertfordshire RO, 48686, Radcliffe, Hitchin, Hertfordshire RO, D/ERE110, Rumbold, Watton on Stone, Hertfordshire RO, D/EB 1297 E2 and E3, Wymondly, Hertfordshire RO, 61589; Huntingdonshire, Tebbot, Bluntisham, Huntingdonshire RO, 157/1/1, Barnard, Brampton, Huntingdonshire RO, ddM 5/5, Barnard, Ellington, Huntingdonshire RO, ddM 44D/7; Kent, Tylden, Milstead, Kent RO, U593/A7 and A10; Blackall Farm, Sevenoaks, Kent RO, U269/A49/2 and 3; U269/A60 and A61; Lancashire, Hesketh, Rufford, Lancashire RO, DDHe 62/25–9; Lincolnshire, Scorer, Lincoln, Lincolnshire RO, Scorer Farm 1/ 2 and 1/7; Norfolk, Stimpson, Alderford, Norfolk RO, MC 561/44 and 49, Earsham Hall, Earsham, Norfolk RO, MEA 3/16 to 3/21, Lukin, Felbrigg, Norfolk RO, WKC 5/233, Felbrigg Hall, Felbrigg, Norfolk RO, WKC 5/229 and 5/250, Tompson, Great Witchingham, Norfolk RO, MC 561/42 and 47, Stody Hall, Stody, Norfolk RO, MC 3/89; Northamptonshire, Fitzwilliam, Longthorpe, Northamptonshire RO, F(M) Misc. vol. 106, 239; Northumberland, Featherstone Castle, Haltwhistle, Northumberland RO, ZCLA, ZHW 4/23 and 3/ 4; Nottinghamshire, Cullen, Rolleston, Nottinghamshire RO, DD 1571/11, Webb Edge, Strettey, Nottinghamshire RO, DDE 1/5, 1/12, 28/2, 3/24, Nevil, Thorney, Nottinghamshire RO, DDN 213/21, Wagstaff and Ward, Nottinghamshire, Nottinghamshire RO, DDSJ/36; Oxfordshire, Buscot, Buscot, Oxfordshire/Berkshire, Berkshire RO, D/ELV E71, E72, Fuller, Thame, MERL, OXF 11/1/1, Buscot, Wooton, Berkshire RO, D/ELV E68, Shropshire, Coton Hall Farm, Bridgnorth, MERL, SAL 5/1/1, Oakley Park, Bromfield, Shropshire RO, 552/10/849–50, Apley

Park, Stockton, Shropshire RO, 5586/5/17/22–36; Somerset, Crowcombe, RO, DD/TB/Box 14/7 and 11, Dunster Castle Farm, Dunster, Somerset RO, DD/L 1/5/16 and 16; D/DL/1/31/33, Marq. of Bucks., Lilistock, MERL, BUC 11/1/11, Chancellors Farm, West Harptree, Somerset RO, DD/SS 100–102; Wm. Thompson, Abbots Bromley, MERL, mic P262, Thentham, Chiaki Yamamoto, 'Two Labour Markets in Nineteenth-Century English Agriculture: The Trentham Home Farm, Staffordshire', *Rural Hist.* 15 (2004), pp. 89–116; Surrey, Pyrford Green Farm, Pyrford, MERL, SUR 2/1/1; Leigh, Stoneleigh, Shakespeare Birthplace Trust D18/31; Umbers, Wappenbury, Warwickshire RO, CR1097/73; Westmorland, Atkinson, Kirby Thore, MERL, mic P242; Yorkshire, Clifton, Durham RO, D/Sa/E181, Fryer, Tanfield Hall, Mickley, North Yorkshire RO, Z862/1, Mumforth, Bromakin Grange, Exelby, North Yorkshire RO, Z1026; Harewood, Plompton, West Yorkshire Archives Service (Leeds), WYL 250/3/253.

Chapter 6
Farmers and Improvement, 1780–1840

John Broad

Historians of rural society and agricultural change have found difficult to unravel how innovation was transmitted through rural communities which are often viewed as being cautious and conservative in their attitude to change. Farmers have left relatively few personal accounts of their enterprises, and when they have, have rarely projected themselves overtly as 'improvers'. The Culleys, for instance, farmed multiple enterprises on a grand scale and were famed for their advanced methods and techniques, but their extensive farming letters and diaries are virtually silent on how they introduced innovations.[1] We know that great landowners learnt about innovations through travels at home and abroad, and that improved estates received streams of visitors from home and abroad.[2] Their estate stewards and land agents fostered improvement on great estates through careful scrutiny of farmers' performance, and the judicious use of covenants in leases. Some of them were active experimenters.[3] Yet the great estate and resident steward directly influenced only a small proportion of English villages, much smaller than the percentage of land held by the great landowners.

The dissemination of improved farming practices from elite home farming can only be a partial explanation of how ideas circulated in agrarian society. Other means by which knowledge of improvement was spread can be identified. The modest output of farming literature turned into a stream from 1780 onwards, with the works of Arthur Young, William Marshall,

---

[1]   Anne Orde (ed.), *Matthew and George Culley: Farming Letters 1798–1804* (Surtees Soc. 210, 2006), and her *Matthew and George Culley: Travel Journals and Letters, 1765–98* (British Academy Records of Social and Economic Hist. 35, 2002).

[2]   See, for instance, the stream of English and overseas visitors to Basil Thomas Eccleston's Lancashire estates around 1800 recorded in his estate records (A.J. Gritt and J.M. Virgoe (eds), *The Memoranda Books of Basil Thomas Eccleston, 1757–1789*, Record Society of Lancashire and Cheshire 139, 2004, p. xvii) suggesting that the thirst to observe improved agriculture was not confined to lowland great estates and the 'Norfolk system'.

[3]   D.R. Hainsworth, *Stewards, Lords and People: The Estate Steward and His World in Later Stuart England* (Cambridge, 1992); G.E. Mingay, 'The eighteenth-century land steward', in E.L. Jones and G.E. Mingay (eds), *Land, Labour and Population in the Industrial Revolution: Essays Presented to J.D. Chambers* (London, 1967), pp. 3–27. For an example of the experimental land steward, see Bedfordshire and Luton Archives and Record Service R4/608/27 for a large file on Robert Salmon's experiments with implements, machinery etc. at Woburn, 1794–1816.

and the Board of Agriculture reports to the fore. This was widely and rapidly disseminated amongst landowners, but how far it was read outside the ranks of the landed classes is difficult to gauge. Arthur Young himself felt that the Board of Agriculture had become a 'Gentleman's Club' by 1805 and that too many men who knew nothing of farming had been employed to write the Board's County Reports.[4] Another way was through the growth of regional and county agricultural societies, and agricultural shows, beginning with the formation of the Bath and West Society in 1781, which offered prizes and ran competitions such as ploughing matches to spur agricultural improvement. The emergence of a farming press in the early nineteenth century provided both price information and a forum in which an agricultural interest group was created, but few farmers wrote about their use of it.[5]

Explanations for the development of a culture of improvement in the English countryside have fallen back on generalisations about the economic, social and cultural environment. The high level of national market integration for all agricultural products, and the quality of market information, certainly contributed to a heightened awareness of market conditions and a growing propensity for farmers to adjust cropping patterns in response the short- and medium-term price changes.[6] The shift from land ownership to leasehold tenancies amongst farmers in the course of the seventeenth and eighteenth centuries also made English rural society more mobile as well as more profit-orientated.[7] Farmers often moved to take new farms, but usually only within a 15-mile radius. Farmers in inland Lincolnshire or in Kentish parishes accessible to Romney Marsh rented pasture on coastal marshes that could be 20 or 30 miles away. Personal knowledge of London, the dominant urban centre, was available to one in six families in Myddle in Shropshire, more than 150 miles away, even in the late seventeenth century.[8] There were well-developed information flows even before the increasing local availability of printed newspapers from around 1700, and the explosion in the numbers of local publications after 1780.

---

[4]   M. Betham-Edwards (ed.) *The Autobiography of Arthur Young: With Selections from His Correspondence* (London, 1898), pp. 242, 244.

[5]   N. Goddard, 'Agricultural literature and societies', in G.E. Mingay (ed.), *The Agrarian History of England and Wales*, VI, *1750–1850* (Cambridge, 1989) pp. 361–83.

[6]   R.W. Hoyle, 'Why Was There No Crisis in England in the 1690s?', Chapter 3 in this volume; M. Overton, 'Agricultural productivity in eighteenth-century England: Some further speculations', *EcHR* 37 (1984), pp. 244–51.

[7]   David R. Stead 'The mobility of English tenant farmers, c.1700–1850', *AgHR* 51 (2003), pp. 173–89 demonstrates effectively that this mobility was a gentle one, with farmers staying a mean period of c.15 years, and some farming families remaining static for two generations.

[8]   D. Hey, *An English Rural Community: Myddle under the Tudors and Stuarts* (Leicester, 1974), p. 192.

The rush of public and publishing interest in farming came at a time when urbanisation and industrialisation were drawing people out of the countryside and away from agricultural employment. A separate farming interest and lobby emerged after the Napoleonic wars as a consequence. Yet if we want to judge how farmers engaged with improvement, and indeed what defined a modern farmer in the period, there are relatively few clear distillations of the idea in the literature. In 1811 Arthur Young printed a lecture on three eminent improving farmers of his day given to the Board of Agriculture as part of his endeavour to speed the diffusion of agricultural innovation. One was Robert Bakewell, about whom he stressed his meticulous care and economy in feeding his animals as well as his breeding skills. His other two examples have long been forgotten. Arbuthnot of Mitcham and Ducket of Petersham were extolled for their skills in soil preparation and management, by improving draining, plough design, and the management of manures and rotations. Young noted that observation and experimentation were key identifiers of the progressive farmer, and concluded that their practical skills needed to be matched to the science of men like Humphrey Davy 'under the enlightened patronage of the Board'.[9]

Attempts to abstract the characteristics of a 'modern' farmer at the period were rarer. Thomas Robertson did so in his summary of what the first *General Views* said about British farm sizes. He extracted five key characteristics: (1) that his time was equal to his business, (2) he does not perform manual labour 'not that this is below him but that he has higher matters on his mind', (3) 'he has no bailiff nor delegate whatever', (4) 'he has a lease, and is under no improper restrictions and services' and (5) he pays an adequate rent.[10] The implied model is very much that of what European writers described as the English model of large tenanted farms in which the farmer's capital was employed stocking the in farm and his enterprise use significant amounts of farm labour.

This chapter uses the words of three farmers of the period 1780–1840 to explore how they saw agricultural change, and reacted to it. Did real improving farmers who were not in the limelight follow the patterns and precepts described by Young and Robertson? The first example, John Carrington of Bramfield near Hertford, farmed 160 acres in partnership with his son. This was land rented first from a copyholder absentee landowner, and then from Earl Cowper of Panshanger who bought out the copyhold of the land that immediately adjoined his park. Carrington's activities are observed through the prism of his diary, which runs from 1798, the date of the death of his wife, through to 1810 when he died. W. Branch Johnson edited the diary for publication in the 1970s, and also

[9]   Arthur Young, *The Husbandry of Three Celebrated Farmers* (London, 1811).

[10]   Thomas Robertson, *Outline of the General Report upon the Size of Farms* (Edinburgh, 1796), pp. 53–7.

produced a separate account of Carrington's affairs.[11] The second diarist is Peter Davis, who farmed substantially larger farms on the Shropshire/Worcestershire borders from the 1830s. This is not a continuous narrative but two diaries, the first describing a tour he made in June 1835 proceeding north up the west side of the country into Scotland and across to Edinburgh and the Lothians, returning via Yorkshire, and the other covering the formative years 1836–37 when he was seeking out his first farm. The final farmer is the extraordinary John Mastin, son of a Nottinghamshire husbandman, whose career took him to London, Hertfordshire, Leicestershire and finally Northamptonshire where he trained for the ministry, becoming vicar of Naseby (and several other parishes) for many years. Unusually, his autobiography says much more about his agricultural business than any spiritual journey. His life from 1747 to 1828 is colourfully portrayed by a man who was proud of his achievements and the social recognition he obtained. All three men were literate and fluent writers, and this in itself may make them unusual in the farming community of their period. But their stories provide valuable testimony of how agricultural improvement was viewed and assimilated.

I

John Carrington was born in 1726 at Watton at Stone, just north of Hertford. His father was a gardener at Tewin Water, one of many country seats flanking the River Mimram as it ran west of Hertford. Hertfordshire was renowned for its agriculture and in the mid eighteenth century benefited from the flourishing malt and barley trade centred on Ware and Hertford, which provided the great London brewers with their raw materials.[12] In the 1750s Carrington was employed as a gardener by Richard Warren of Marden Hill in the parish of Tewin, with whom he developed a close and lasting professional relationship. From 1760 Carrington farmed Warren's copyhold in the adjoining parish of Bramfield as tenant. Bacons Farm consisted of 160 acres close to the edge of the parish, adjoining the perimeter of Earl Cowper's Panshanger House and

11   W. Branch Johnson (ed.), '*Memorandums for ...*': *The Diary between 1798 and 1810 of John Carrington, farmer, Chief Constable, Tax Assessor, Surveyor of Highways and Overseer of the Poor, of Bramfield in Hertfordshire* (Chichester, 1971), hereafter cited as *Memorandums*; idem, *The Carrington Diary, 1797–1810* (London, 1954). The latter is Branch Johnson's account, the former his edited and annotated transcript; a new fuller transcript is in preparation by Susan Flood for publication by the Hertfordshire Record Society, but a copy of Branch Johnson's fuller transcript of Carrington's diary is available on the open shelves at Hertfordshire Archives and Local Studies (and is cited here as 'original transcript').

12   P. Mathias, *The Brewing Industry in England, 1700–1830* (Cambridge, 1959), pp. 442–7, 463–4.

park. The farmhouse was a substantial two-storey building, with two gabled cross-wings, probably dating back to the fifteenth or sixteenth century. Here Carrington farmed successfully until his death in 1810, in the years of his diary in partnership with his younger son William. Carrington began his diary in 1798, after his wife's death, when he was 72. It was written on scraps of printed paper such as redundant taxation and constabulary documents and covers the last 12 years of his life.

Farming forms only a limited part of the subject matter of the diary, but there is regular and precise documentation of prices and farming events, and for the last eight years of the diary monthly reflections on farming conditions. Carrington wrote rather more about a lifestyle and outlook of semi-retirement. Though he was active on the farm, buying and selling crops and livestock on a regular basis, John enjoyed his seventies in the knowledge that his son William undertook much of the day-to-day work. He spent a great deal of time eating and drinking with friends, neighbours and business contacts. Until the last two years of his life he remained very active, walking long distances, riding further, and participating fully in harvest and sheep shearing.

This lifestyle reflected Carrington's character and reputation, but also the non-agricultural roles which he had taken on. He was the only overseer of the poor at Bramfield during the years of the diary. The overseers' accounts show the parish frequently owed him money, and that he was the only vestry member who signed the accounts – the other two or three members simply made their marks.[13] Since 1771 he had also been one of the head constables of the Liberty of St Albans, and Tax Assessor for the same area. This meant that he was known personally to most of the landowners of the district, to parish officials, and to a wide range of farmers, craftsmen and labourers. As head constable he dealt not only with day-to-day matters of law and order, but was closely involved in ensuring parishes fulfilled their militia quotas during the period of the Napoleonic invasion scares.

Carrington was as much a businessman as a farmer, yet he began life at a fairly low social status, and despite considerable success remained within the lower echelons of the middling sort. His business and leisure activities both indicate a wide circle of friends and acquaintances in Hertfordshire and in London, and that they extended beyond the farming community. Although he says almost nothing about his reading habits, he appears well informed about national and international events as well as local affairs. Above all he displays the characteristic that is at the heart of the economic and social changes of the later eighteenth and nineteenth centuries, a high degree of inquisitiveness across a wide range of subjects.

---

[13] Hertfordshire Archives and Local Studies (hereafter HALS), DP22/12/2, Bramfield Overseers' accounts and vestry minutes, 1803–18.

Carrington fits the John Bull stereotype very nicely. He vigorously supported Tory candidates at elections. He was the heart and soul of any party. Indeed, a recurrent feature of the diary is his recital of his visits to alehouses and taverns. He even records his remorse at episodes of over-indulgence. Branch Johnson counted over 80 pubs and taverns at which Carrington ate and drank in Hertfordshire and in London. There can have been few local banquets and celebratory feasts in the neighbourhood to which he was not invited: tenants' rent day feasts, vestry annual meals, Friendly Society banquets, Rogation Day feasts at the walking of the parish bounds, and a variety of other occasions. His elder son's presence running the pub in the adjoining parish of Tewin meant he was invited to all the events there as well as in Bramfield. There were additional one-off events outside the annual cycle: election dinners, feasts for George III's golden jubilee in 1810, and others.

His work kept him in touch with farmers, parish officials, and local landowners on a daily basis, and he was a frequent visitor to many elite houses in the area. However, his primary point of contact there was with the upper servants – bailiffs, stewards and housekeepers – with whom he often ate. His relationship with the elite was a distanced one. He was known to them because of his regular attendance at Quarter Sessions and Assizes, and because he assessed their taxes. Yet when he went to Bayfordbury House in 1805 on a tax-collecting mission and was 'made exceedingly welcome' personally by Squire Baker's wife, he felt the attention was both surprising and unusual.[14]

Carrington's official position was not the only channel of access to a wider view of the world than might be open to most tenants of modestly sized farm in Hertfordshire. His house at Bacons provided more space than he and his wife needed and they took in lodgers. In May 1800 he notes the death of one of these, a retired naval officer who had lived in the house for over 20 years, and often related to Carrington stories about his life and career across the world.[15] Another lodger was Joseph Strutt, the London antiquarian and engraver. In the 1790s Strutt and his son, together with an assistant, lodged in the attics at Bacons for some years after Strutt's wife's death. Strutt seemed to have engendered (or perhaps merely fostered) Carrington's continuing interest in antiquarian artefacts that surfaces intermittently in the diary.[16] The relationship between the Strutt family and the Carringtons continued when the Strutts returned to

---

[14] *Memorandums*, p. 111 (30 Jan. 1805).

[15] *Memorandums*, p. 47 (5 May 1800).

[16] On Strutt see his *ODNB* entry. He was a pioneer in the history of costume, and of sports and games, illustrating the books himself with colour lithographs. See Joseph Strutt, *A complete view of the dress and habits of the people of England, from the establishment of the Saxons in Britain to the present time* (2 vols, London, 1796–99) and his *Glig-Gamena Angel Deod, or the sports and pastimes of the people of England, from the earliest period to the present time, illustrated by engravings selected from ancient paintings* (1801, 2nd edn 1810).

London. Carrington spent time there with Strutt, sometimes staying with him, and attending Strutt's neighbourhood club at the Hole in the Wall in Hatton Garden. Strutt and his family came back to Hertfordshire, staying at Tewin with Carrington's son on two occasions before Strutt died in 1802.[17] Carrington retained his links with Strutt's London circle, noting visits to the Hole in the Wall club in January 1806 and May 1808.[18] Another man of some interest with whom Strutt rubbed shoulders on a regular basis was the Hertford printer Stephen Austin. Austin published the first (short-lived) Hertford paper, the *Hartford Mercury* in 1778, but for several years he was employed as parish clerk at Bramfield where Carrington would have regularly dealt with him. Austin's firm established a long-term presence in Hertford, reviving the local newspaper, providing bookselling services to the East India Company college at Haileybury (just the other side of Hertford from Bramfield), and developing a specialism in oriental typefaces and printing that lasted well over a century.[19]

Carrington also had financial as well as commercial expertise. The high degree of 'credit' provided by his successful farming and long public service involving large sums of money gave Carrington a special position in the local community. He knew his way around the financial and administrative worlds of London. His diaries and papers detail two occasions on which he led the appeal process against sentences of transportation and death.[20] He regularly spent time in London receiving dividends on investments and government stock, and buying and selling bonds. He did this on his own account, but also on behalf of family members, and also local Friendly Societies. In 1809 he was also dealing with the local bank in Hertford.[21]

As a farmer, Carrington was fully integrated into market processes at a sophisticated level, but was no hard-bitten capitalist, as his social concerns were widespread. They went far beyond his assistance to local Friendly Societies, for whom he acted as banker and investment manager, as well as winding one up while it was still solvent as its membership fell away. As poor overseer he inspected and helped improve Bramfield parish poor house, supervised the temporary housing of inmates when one inmate set fire to it, and oversaw the rebuilding process. He regularly gave a feast to the village poor at Christmas, on one occasion bringing the elderly poor of both Bramfield and Tewin to his house, and taking them home in his cart.[22] He records spending whole evenings

17   *Memorandums*, pp. 49 (June 1800), 58 (Mar. 1801), 64 (Sept. 1801) and 70 (Mar. 1802).

18   Ibid., pp. 126–7, 172.

19   Ibid., pp. 38, 44 (26 Mar. 1799).

20   Ibid., pp. 26 (1796); 194 (June 1807).

21   Ibid., pp. 75 (July 1802); 114 (Apr. 1805); 126–7 (Jan. 1806); 160 (June 1807); 173 (May 1809); 172 (May 1809).

22   Ibid., p. 151 (Dec. 1807).

talking with his less fortunate contemporaries in the poor house over a few beers. He also sold under-priced flour and wheat for the poor in the difficult harvest years 1799 and 1800. In 1800, much to his later embarrassment, he agreed to sell wheat to an 'association of poor men held at Campbell's the Green Dragon for 10s. a bushel' – well below the market price – and a fortnight later he found the men wanted to chair him through the market. He fled and hid, though the commotion caused some of the dealers in Hertford market to 'fly'.[23] Carrington's son was less generous, refusing to sell below the market price, but Carrington did sell loads of wheat at a small discount to help feed the poor of other parishes.[24]

Regular attendance at market was a major source of farming intelligence and a potential location for discussion of agricultural innovation. Carrington generally attended Hertford market every week, constantly recording market fluctuations in cereal supply and prices, particularly regularly in the crisis years around 1800. Livestock and other prices were intermittently mentioned in the diary when remarkable: for instance he noted low livestock prices in 1808 when fodder was scarce and there was effectively a forced sale. He noted his market coups, and also his small disasters. He attended other markets, and bought and sold elsewhere. His regular dealings with the Hoddesdon wool dealer Mr Scate apparently involved him selling his wool for an agreed minimum price and handing it over physically, but the dealer did not pay him until he had sold, settling matters at a later Hertford market.[25]

Carrington also invested and speculated in property, regularly attending nearby farm sales. In March 1806 he set off for a farm auction at Great Amwell, a village just the other side of Hertford to buy a bull 'for 9 guineas', but he instead bought 'three little tenements'. These are probably the houses he recorded paying for on 15 September, one of which he had already sold on.[26] In 1802 he had bought a house in Tewin, to which in 1804 he added a rebuilt barn adjoining his son's house there, which was converted into a shoemaker's shop at his tenant's request.[27] In July 1807 he attended a sale of Essendon and Little Berkhampstead properties, close to Hertford, where he bought four cottages, two of them newly built, for 200 guineas, and immediately sold them on for 325 guineas. He bought a further cottage at How Green for £58 and sold it for '£5 advance'.[28]

---

23   Ibid., p. 52 (27 Sept. 1800).

24   Ibid., pp. 47 (12 Apr. 1800); 51 (12 Sept. 1800).

25   Ibid., pp. 101 (7 July 1804); 117 (5 July, 20 July 1805). It is not clear why this procedure was followed, perhaps because the quantity of his wool was too small to sell on its own. The early July date is recorded as the Midsummer fair in one year.

26   Ibid., pp. 126 (12 Mar. 1806); 134 (15 Sept. 1806). He paid £176 15s. for the three, and the two he retained were transferred into the names of his daughter and niece at the Amwell manor court in Nov. 1808: p. 163 (19 Nov. 1808).

27   *Memorandums*, pp. 73 (May 1802); 85 (Jan. 1804).

28   Ibid., p. 146 (8 July 1807).

In November 1808 he reported travelling to nearby Essendon, where he had recently bought cottages from Samuel Whitbread, to see the tenants there, and there must have been further purchases for in August 1809 a number of elite proprietors all wanted to buy them from him and he found it 'Very odd to have a doctor, lawyer and parson all consulting me altogether'.[29] Carrington's social position never changed, but greed and profits resulted in professional people deferring to him. There were properties elsewhere. In Bengeo (now a suburb of Hertford) he attended the Manor Court in October 1807 to pay quit rent on property he left to his daughter.[30] While Carrington's eye of property brought him profits, his attempt to purchase the copyhold he had farmed as a tenant for more than 40 years ended in failure. The matter is fully documented in Branch Johnson's book, but looked at in a wider context, Carrington's attempts to purchase the property from the second reversionary interest was highly speculative and was doomed to failure as Earl Cowpers' interest in a property that flanked his park was understandably strong. When Carrington found the property had been sold over his head by the copyholder in possession, he made no complaint. At the same meeting Manor Court where Cowper's possession was confirmed, he was granted the right to build a cottage on land he held in Tewin. His continued belief in his right to the farm is firmly stated in the diary, the grant perhaps some compensation for his decision not to fight Cowper.[31]

Carrington's knowledge of the land market had other aspects. In August 1801 he notes that he bought a farm in Datchworth ('Cheretree Farme and Steels wood'), paid the deposit for it on 4 August, only to sell it on on 9 August.[32] In this case we may wonder whether he had been employed to act for another in the sale. He was certainly employed to investigate possible tenancies and purchases for others. In September 1801 he looked over a farm at South Mimms for a neighbour in Bramfield before journeying into Berkshire to appraise another at Bradfield. Both were deemed unsuitable.[33] When another neighbour's farm in Bramfield fell vacant, Carrington went to London to see if he could take over the lease, but although willing to bid £200 for the remaining four years of the lease, found it sold for more than twice as much. It led him to reflect on the rapid rise in rents. The same farm had paid £90 rent 70 years before, had then risen to £100 and only four years before to £120. It was now to be let for £220 a year.[34]

29 Ibid., p. 177 (12 Aug. 1809).

30 Ibid., p. 150 (26 Oct. 1807).

31 Ibid., pp. 173–4 (27 May 1809). For Branch Johnson's detailed account of the twists and turns of Carrington's claim on the copyhold of Bacons' see *Memorandums*, pp. 7–10.

32 Ibid., pp. 62, 64 (1, 4, 24 Aug. 1804).

33 Ibid., p. 64 (15 Sept. 1801) and HALS Transcript for the following days.

34 Ibid., pp. 120, 122 (1 Oct., 9 Nov. 1805).

Despite the range of Carrington's interests he was above all a practical farmer. His interest in new methods and technology was always a critical one, based on observations in his neighbourhood, not books, newspapers, or formal farmers' clubs. John and his son William ran the farm as an informal partnership. Joint decisions appear to have been made about cropping and soil preparation, but they sold stock and produce as individuals: at one point John distinguishes his wheat for sale from William's. Animals appear to have belonged to individuals. John treated the sheep flock as his own enterprise, supervising shearing and wool sales. In 1805 he rented agistments on Hertford Heath for his heifers.[35] Other evidence suggests some kind of share farming agreement, perhaps informal, of which no copy has survived.

Bacons Farm consisted of 19 separate fields totalling 162 acres, and the Carringtons at one point rented a small additional acreage in Hertford. In September 1804, John Carrington set out the fields and acreage at the end of harvest: 32 acres of wheat, 13 acres of barley, and 15 acres of oats and peas. This was just over a third of the total acreage, and we can only speculate on how the remainder was farmed. There were fields planted with turnips, which were sold as well as fed, others with potatoes. Carrington's frequent monitoring of hop prices, and occasional purchases of hops suggest some land was used as a hop ground. If these crops took up 20 more acres, we can suggest a mixed farm split almost evenly between arable and pasture. There is no mention of fallows, and the 28-acre field named as growing wheat in 1805 but which was not cropped in 1804 suggests most of the land was under rotation. Some land was set aside to raise a hay crop, while fields were sown with clover, for two cows were 'busted' with clover in May 1804 (one dying), while in June 1805 Carrington noted he had not gone to market because he was concluding the clover harvest, 'the finest hay ever known'.[36] On the livestock side, a dairy herd, pigs and sheep were regularly kept, together with guinea fowl, turkeys and geese.

The evidence for the adoption of innovations is largely incidental to the diary. The presence of turnips, hops, potatoes and clover, show that new crops had been adopted. The apparent absence of fallow indicates that the Carringtons farmed in a way typical of Hertfordshire, which was known for its advanced agriculture. A proportion of all crops grown were sold at market, and fodder crops were bought in when necessary. In addition to rotations, soil quality was improved by 'chalking': much of the southern end of the farm underwent this in 1801–02. Four new pits were dug, a local man, his wife, and four children (three daughters, one son) 'did their work alternatly', and John Carrington reckoned the

---

35   Ibid., p. 119 (Aug. 1805).

36   Ibid., pp. vi includes a map of the farm; 103 for field details, more fully delineated in the original transcript; 119 (25 Aug. 1805); 115 (26 May 1805); 145 (27 June 1807).

whole had cost him £100.[37] In 1804 Carrington notes the planting of potatoes in field crops in rows allowing them to be harvested by careful ploughing, to be picked up by local women and children. He reckoned to have taken 400 bushels from a single acre. That this warranted a note in the diary suggests it was a new practice.[38] John Carrington notes trips to buy seeds: in 1804 an agreed purchase of barley seed from a neighbouring farming in Tewin Hill was converted into an exchange for white oats seeds; in April 1806 a detour from market to Ware Park to inspect the potatoes grown there by Squire Byde resulted in a return trip several days later to buy 35 bushels of seed potatoes.[39] In February 1809 he notes selling three acres of 'sweed turnips', the first mention of the crop, suggesting a recent adoption.[40]

Carrington learnt about innovations from visits to farms, great houses, at market, and probably from time spent at market or on their farms with neighbouring farmers. He often records travelling with his neighbours whilst when an adjacent farm acquired a new tenant he was quick to visit and was soon regularly conversing.[41] New machinery was observed at market, for instance the multi-functional chaff cutting machine displayed at Hertford in 1804 that could grind beans and barley and cost 12 guineas. Carrington attended the county ploughing matches held in neighbouring parishes in 1807 and 1808 where the gentry and farmers also showed their prize livestock.[42] When Marden Hill (his old landlord's estate) was bought by the Flowers family in 1807, they invested in a threshing machine and three new patent ploughs, and Carrington went across to see them in action. The following year, despite increasing illness, he returned to observe further improvements. In the same month he travelled with a neighbour to Tewin Bury to observe a major stream diversion for a water mill to power the tenant's threshing machine.[43]

Carrington's diary shows an experienced farmer who, even in his late '70s when in declining health, was curious about 'improvements' and who was adopting new crops and systems on his farm piecemeal rather than in a grand experimental manner. But beyond that there is a constant concern for numerical precision and profitability. He notes prices and profits carefully, but also the weights of his three fat pigs, and a large bull. He also counts precisely the numbers of mice and rats killed when the open wheat stack – the 'hovell' – was

---

[37] Original transcript, p. 140 (Annual summary, end 1802) gives full details. The process of marling was relatively simple in this part of Hertfordshire where Chiltern chalk was overlaid with glacial clay deposits. Digging through the clay brought easy access to chalk.

[38] Ibid., p. 104 (24 Sept. 1804).

[39] Ibid., pp. 97 (15 Mar. 1804); 129 (29 Apr., 3 May 1806).

[40] Ibid., p. 168 (7 Feb. 1809).

[41] Ibid., pp. 129 (26 Apr. 1806); 124 (25 Dec. 1805).

[42] Ibid., pp. 100 (9 June 1804); 149 (25 Sept. 1807); 162 (11 Sept. 1808).

[43] Ibid., pp. 162 (2, 15 Sept. 1808); 182 (26, 21 Nov. 1809).

cleared in 1806 and 1809.[44] The importance of order, neatness, and profitability runs through Carrington's diary whether it is concerned with farming, taxation, or financial affairs. That, and a constant interest in novelty and innovation, tempered by scepticism about the cost benefits of their application, were at the heart of Carrington's view of the world.

II

The diaries of Peter Davis show us the life of a young man setting out on a farming career. Peter was born in 1811 and brought up on the family farm at Dean Park in Burford, close to Tenbury Wells in Shropshire but adjacent to both Worcestershire and Herefordshire. There are two fragments of diary. One describes a farming tour made in June 1835 when he was 24. The other covers the 22 months from January 1836 to November 1837 detailing the end of his farming 'apprenticeship'. This was marked by the valuation and transfer of many of his father's assets to him in April 1837, and his father's death the following August. While the travel diary is self-contained, the other fills a single notebook which starts and ends in the middle of a month, suggesting that further diaries existed but have not survived.[45]

The Davis family had lived at Burford since before the turn of the century. Samuel senior and his wife had three sons (William, Samuel and Peter) and a daughter (Eliza), soon after whose birth in 1813 Peter's mother died. In 1836, William, the eldest, was a leasehold tenant to a 480-acre farm, Dean Park, in Buraston township nearby, while his father Samuel, who had been the previous tenant at Dean Park, had moved to the Rectory at Burford, but retained two leases from other landlords and continued farming.[46] Samuel jun. had been sent to Cambridge University, and become a married clergyman in Devon, but moved back to Burford to seek better employment, while their sister Eliza's marriage on 9 August 1836 is described in the diary.[47] Peter, the third son, was 24 at the time, seven years younger than William, and lived initially with his father at the Rectory. Some indication of the scale of their farming can be gauged from the farms Peter Davis looked at as potential tenancies in 1836–37.

---

44   Ibid., pp. 113 (Mar. 1805); 128 (4 Apr. 1806); 171 (25 Apr. 1809) 'it is a great loss to the farmer to stack wheat abroad whear the virmen can take it & in barns if not soon thrashed, my loss £10 in this'.

45   The diaries were discovered by Peter's descendants, Bruce Coates and Martin Davis, and published as M. Davis (ed.), *The Diary of a Shropshire Farmer* (Stroud, 2011). Much background and personal information about the Davis family and individuals mentioned in the diaries is drawn from their work.

46   Ibid., pp. 10–11, 16.

47   Peter Davis's diary 1836–37 (hereafter *PD*), 9 Aug. 1836.

A farm of 133 acres was deemed too small, and others were considered ranging from 250 to 440 acres.[48] The family also owned an unknown acreage of land in the neighbourhood which they let out. It was not inconsiderable. One copyhold alone was of 84 acres.[49] When Samuel Davis senior died, his probated moveable wealth was just under £2,000, and this was after he had made over most of his farm stock and tackle, and household items to Peter. Just before he died Samuel changed his will to divide his residual wealth between his two farming sons, but leaving Samuel junior two pieces of land.[50] Local people considered the family wealthy: when in October 1836 father and son attended a land sale as observers, one farm was sold for £8,025, well above the expected price, because a bidder thought the Davises were in the market.

The Davises moved in circles just below the level of the gentry – farmers, clergy, lawyers and doctors – and the young Peter was keen to join local clubs and attend balls and social gatherings. William was elected overseer at Burford in 1835, and when the Poor Law Union was formed at Tenbury, he became a Guardian as well.[51] The Davises' landlord, Mr Rushout, was elected MP for Evesham in the 1837 general election, and the family were much involved in the feasts and celebrations locally that marked his return.[52] Many visits to friends and relatives were recorded in the diary, as were the comings and goings of farmers, salesmen and tenants. Landlord/tenant relationships are portrayed as amicable, and usually conducted in conjunction with a meal.

Peter did not go to Cambridge, but diary entries indicate that he read across a range of subjects. He had some knowledge of farming literature,[53] dipped into history, was reading Southey's essays, and borrowed the latest copy of the *Athenaeum*.[54] In 1837 he tried to set up a Reading Room in the Swan Inn in Tenbury, enquiring about hiring a room, and negotiating an annual contract for the supply of national and regional newspapers.[55] When there was a brilliant display of Aurora Borealis he made diary comments on various explanations, giving an indication of general scientific reading.[56] This was a reasonably educated man, but the diary is terse and has no literary pretensions.

---

[48] Ibid., 6 Sept. 1837.

[49] Ibid., 10 Apr. 1836.

[50] Ibid., 6 Sept. 1837; 20 Apr. 1837. M. Davis (ed.), *Diary*, p. 22.

[51] *PD*, 25 Mar., 26 July, 29 Aug. 1836.

[52] Ibid., 16 Feb. 1837.

[53] Travel Diary (hereafter *TD*), June 1835, 13 June 1835.

[54] *PD*, 18 Mar., 3 Mar., 9 Mar. 1836.

[55] Ibid., 10, 28, 31 Mar. 1837. His business plan was based on at least 20 people buying an annual subscription of one guinea. His interest in the project may have been sparked by seeing the public reading rooms in Liverpool and Edinburgh during his 1835 tour. Both merited specific mention and discussion. *TD*, 9, 15 June 1835.

[56] *PD*, 18 Feb. 1837.

The family farm in Burford was a mixed enterprise, with wheat and barley regularly grown, together with turnips, swedes and clover. There were sheep and cattle, but no evidence of much dairying, since cheese was bought in occasionally. There were hop fields, and various expeditions made by the two sons suggest that this was a developing aspect of the business, since they visited other farms with hops, and inspected drying kilns and equipment. Beyond these, there was a cider orchard which seems to have been put to commercial use, since cider was sold and not just used as a beer substitute for farm labourers. We do not know how many labourers were employed on the farm, and without any indication of acreage we cannot make an informed guess. However, when Samuel senior died, six labourers were the under-pallbearers.

At the opening of the main diary Peter was working on the farm which his father and brother William ran as an informal partnership. William lived at 'Park' while his father and Peter were living in Burford Rectory. When brother Samuel moved up from Devon, Peter was sent to live with his brother.[57] Crops and stock sold were defined as belonging to William or his father, but Peter moved between the two, working as required. All three men regularly attended markets and fairs, whether or not they had planned business. Some days, father would be at one market, William at another, so on 12 December 1836 William set off for Bewdley fair while Samuel senior was at Ludlow market.[58] Although ownership of crops and stock was clearly separate, William and Samuel senior automatically did business on each other's behalf, and Peter acted for both. For example on one occasion Peter took his father's wheat samples and William's barley samples to market, and sold a load of barley, but no wheat.[59] Some of Peter's trips involved receiving cash for produce sold, others to undertake business at their bank in Worcester. The farm was then jointly managed and output was clearly assigned to either father or son.

Between January 1836 and April 1837 Peter never seems to be acting on his own account, but on 20 April 1837 a valuer came to Burford charged with dividing effects 'between Father and myself' and this marked a fundamental shift in the enterprise. From this point, Peter took over his father's role on the farm. Peter records 'Everything valued to me excepting two lots of wheat, the one at Nash, the other at Burford Granery', while he also received most of the furniture in the Rectory apart from a bed, bedsteads and a number of other pieces.[60] Four days later Peter attended Bewdley fair and bought a lot of barren cows and bullocks on his own account. On 1 May he hired a lad and housekeeper, suggesting that he now formed a separate household, and on 4 May he notes that

---

57   Ibid., 3 Mar. 1836.
58   Ibid., 12 Dec. 1836.
59   Ibid., 31 Mar. 1836.
60   Ibid., 20 Apr. 1837.

his father dined with him.[61] The decision to make this division was timely. On 23 June 1837 Samuel senior was unwell. On the following day he fell violently ill, never fully recovered and died on 30 August.

For much of the diary Peter was learning the ropes of the business. Much time was spent on tasks such as delivering money for contracted sales, organising sheep-shearers and hop-pickers, taking hops to Stourport to be weighed, and a variety of routine tasks.[62] He and his brother joined the sheep-shearers and hop-pickers, and attended the dinner and dancing at the end of the hop harvest.[63] He undertook horse hoeing, selling William's hop poles, collecting purchases of turnip seed, and drilling swedes.[64] In the same period his father was taking him to inspect land owned by the family, measuring timber, mending ponds and hedges, and negotiating repairs and improvements with the tenant.[65]

If it was not premonition of coming ill-health that led Samuel senior to give Peter full rein on the farm in Burford in April 1836, it may have been the increasing exasperation expressed by Peter about not being able to take on a tenancy of his own elsewhere. Throughout the diary he constantly visited farms which had been advertised to let, or which were rumoured to be becoming available. He spread his net wide, travelling not just to farms within a 15-mile radius of Tenbury, but making trips to stay with relatives just east of Bridgnorth, some 20 miles away, to look at a number of farms west and north of Wolverhampton.[66] Sometimes he went on his own or with his brother, on others with his father. Some of the early visits resulted in his being told the farm was not available, or was already promised elsewhere. Perhaps this was a polite way of telling him that he was not considered suitable. On later occasions he went with his father, particularly when terms were being discussed.[67]

Peter was champing at the bit to run his own farm. After viewing and liking one farm between Bromyard and Hereford, his father and he made a bid £20 below the asking price which was declined. In one of the more charged entries in an otherwise even-tempered, even anodyne diary, he declared he felt 'very angry with my father for not closing on it'. He perhaps persuaded his father to change his mind, but returning to increase the offer the next day he was told the farm was now let.[68]

[61] Ibid., 24 Apr., 1 and 4 May 1837.
[62] Ibid., 3 Aug., 5 Oct. 1836.
[63] Ibid., 10 June, 26 Sept. 1836.
[64] Ibid., 30 Apr. and 5 May; 10 May, 21 June, 5 June 1836.
[65] Ibid., 21 May; 11 June; 22 July 1836.
[66] Ibid., 15 June, 14 Nov. 1836, 11 Jan., 2 Feb. 1837.
[67] Ibid., e.g. 28 Oct. 1836, 2 Feb. 1837.
[68] Ibid., 28, 29 Oct. 1836.

In Peter Davis's diary we see the coming of age of a young farmer. How did he learn about current good practice and what was his attitude and approach to farm improvements? As with John Carrington 30 years earlier, little is explicit, yet much can be gleaned. Take the farm visits in search of a tenancy. In the 10 months from April 1836 to February 1837 he explored the possibilities of 15 farms spread across about 50 miles of the west Midlands, west of Birmingham. His terse diary entries suggest a growing confidence in appraising the quality not just of the land, but of the potential of the enterprise, the importance of state of repair, and the tithe liability.[69]

Learning to judge land and farms was only one part of the apprenticeship. He combined it with various episodes that engaged him with innovative practice. The most formal was his two-week tour in June 1835 when he was 24, described in a separate diary. There is no preamble discussing the purpose of the journey, but as he concluded it with the statement 'Thus ends the first tour of any distance from home I ever made', and had undertaken it alone, it was effectively a rite of passage. He travelled up the west side of England to Carlisle, crossing into Scotland at Gretna and then proceeding to Edinburgh where he spent two full days before returning down the east coast to Nottingham, Leicester and Northampton, from there cutting across country to Banbury, Evesham and home. The farming tour was a well-established phenomenon dating back to the eighteenth century when men such as Arthur Young (and on one occasion William Marshall) published their views on agriculture and improvement in the form of tours. Foreign observers of Britain, such as Per Kalm and Rochefoucault frequently published their observations in the form of travelogues.[70] The tours of less celebrated writers and practitioners have occasionally been analysed.[71] Some idea of the scale of agricultural tourism can be seen from the estate's side in the case of Eccleston estate in south Lancashire in the late eighteenth century where a continual stream of British and overseas visitors inspected the improvements.[72]

The tour gave Peter a taste of city life. In Liverpool he examined the docks, visited two American ships, public buildings, and the Exchange, and he noted the news rooms. He took the train on the Liverpool to Manchester railway, opened in 1830 and still a novel experience. Manchester he 'soon tired of' and spent only a morning before leaving. In Edinburgh he visited many of the tourist spots – the Castle, Holyrood, New Town, Arthurs Seat (at 5.30 in the morning), attended the Kirk, listened to a natural history lecture at the university – and

---

[69]   In June 1837 he borrowed a copy of the Tithe Commutation Act and another book on church revenues. *PD*, 19 June 1837.

[70]   Pehr Kalm (trans. Joseph Lucas), *Kalm's Account of His Visit to England on His Way to America in 1748* (2 vols, London, 1892).

[71]   G.E. Mingay, 'Professor Symond's Tour 1790', in C.J. Wrigley and J. Shepherd (eds), *On the Move: Essays in Labour and Transport History Presented to Philip Bagwell* (London, 1991), pp. 9–21.

[72]   Gritt and Virgoe (eds), *Eccleston*.

saw the Law Courts and Leith docks. However, a great deal more space in the diary was devoted to observations on the quality of farming and on agricultural innovations. As he passed through the countryside, often in stage coaches but also walking, he recorded the landscape, soils, crops and quality of farming that he observed.

We do not know whether by 1835 Peter Davis was performing an unusual journey for a farmer of his age, experience and background, but the route he followed, up one side of England to Scotland, where the Lothians were renowned for their advanced agriculture, returning down the other side of the country, was certainly following in other's footsteps. Peter noted farming practice that he considered good, such as drilling swedes, planting potatoes in four-foot wide beds with squared ditches around them (whether in gardens or fields) which he found in Cheshire, Denbighshire and Flintshire. He was generally impressed by the quality of northern English agriculture, whether on the Cheshire plain, north of Lancaster to Burton and Slyne, northwards from Penrith, Carlisle and the border (where he found drilled turnips and potatoes 'in a scientific manner') and 'turnip, barley, wheat and seed grown to the greatest perfection'. He found the 'people more intelligent and industrious than in the southern and midland counties', but after chatting to a farm servant for some time found him 'deficient in the details of his own business'.[73] Passing Netherby Park near Longtown, much improved by the Graham family, Peter noted that 'it was more interesting to me having read the report of the farm published in the Farmer Series'.[74] Approaching within 10 miles of Edinburgh he found the land 'cultivated more like a garden than fields and far excels anything I have met with before'.[75] Apart from sightseeing in the city, he made a point of visiting two large nurseries, Henderson's and Dickinson's, the latter extending to 50 acres and employing 40.[76] Making his way south from Edinburgh he made a point of visiting a farm where a steam-driven threshing machine was installed, and finding new and well-designed farm buildings and high quality cultivation there. Passing through the heart of improved Lothian agriculture, near Haddington, he noted the largest arable fields he had ever seen and the planting of beans two and a half feet apart to allow horse hoeing.[77]

---

[73] *TD*, 12 June 1835.

[74] Which series is referred to is unclear. *The Farmer's Magazine* (Edinburgh, 1800–25) has one brief mention of Graham and his tenants' association to improve farming. Its successor, *The British Farmer's Magazine* (London, 1826–) includes articles on famous farmers in editions from 1826–28, but Graham was not among them, and they ceased thereafter. There are no mentions of Graham's farming in the journal through to 1838.

[75] *TD*, 13 June 1835.

[76] Ibid., 15, 16 June 1835.

[77] Ibid., 16 June 1835.

Travelling south through Northumberland and Durham he noted that Scottish techniques and systems were used on poorer soils, reserving his praise for the agriculture he found south of Northallerton, and more particularly between Tadcaster and Doncaster. There he noted rape cake from Leeds used as manure, flax, teasels and woad grown, and lucerne double-cropped, pronouncing the area 'the richest and – except East Lothian – the best cultivated district of the Kingdom'.[78] Moving south to Nottingham, Leicester and Northampton he noted the changing agricultural landscape, the crops and breeds observed, and features such as lime works. Around Towcester, he noted the absence of drilled crops and good farming, but as he turned west on his homeward leg, found interesting good practice around Banbury and Evesham.[79]

Peter Davis's tour diary shows he was stimulated by the farming practice he observed. Can we see any transfer into his own farming practice the following year? If we hypothesise that apart from recording key moments in the farming cycle – sheep shearing, hay making, and grain harvests – and natural disasters such as floods, this rather terse diarist mentioned farming events because they were novel and hence noteworthy, then it is interesting that both drilling swedes and horse hoeing, both observed on his tour, are noted in the diary.[80] It is also possible that his observations on the large orchards attached to farms in east Yorkshire may have some link to the investment in new cider-making equipment at home in August 1836 and the commercial production of cider on the farm.[81]

While there is no explicit discussion of 'improvement' in the 1836–37 diary, there is nevertheless explicit evidence of systematic exploration of novel and good practice, and a searching out of good farming. One example is hop growing. The Davises grew hops on their Burford farm, but in the summer of 1836 William and Peter seem to have made a point of looking at what other farmers in the neighbourhood were doing. On 31 August they travelled into Herefordshire looking at three different farms growing hops and on one examined a newly installed hop kiln built to a Kentish design. It seems likely that they were either intending to expand production, or to update their practice.[82] In the following May, when Peter visited Albrighton fair to the north of Burford, he stayed on to visit the Teddesley Park estate at Penkridge to the west of Cannock Chase. There he spent three full days being shown round by the agent, John Bright, meeting tenants, seeing advanced farm buildings such as milking stalls, as well as the water-powered threshing machine that used water taken mainly from the farm drains, which, after it turned the wheel, was used to float water meadows. His

78   Ibid., 19 June 1835.
79   Ibid., 21 June 1835.
80   *PD*, 30 Apr. 1836, 5 June 1837.
81   *TD*, 19 June 1835; 1, 31 Aug. 1836; 4, 10 Nov. 1836.
82   *PD*, 31 Aug., 4 Sept. 1836.

final comment on his trip was that it 'has afforded me a great deal of pleasure and instruction'.[83] Another innovation taken up by Peter soon after he took control of the farm, was to purchase a pair of working oxen, which as Ted Collins has recently shown, had been revived as an economical source of farm power at this period.[84]

How then can we sum up Peter Davis's attitudes to improvement revealed in the diaries? Firstly, he was interested in improved farming and made significant efforts to learn more through tours and visits. This was part of a wider interest in science, innovation and modern commercial practice revealed in his interest in railways. He rode the Liverpool to Manchester train, and made a point of talking to the engineer constructing the new Liverpool to Birmingham line. When on tour, and also on trips to Bridgnorth and Birmingham, he noted commercial and industrial enterprises that caught his attention.[85] The part played by agricultural books and periodicals in his professional development is shadowy, but he clearly read and sought access to wider national and regional newspapers, again indicating that while his immediate horizons were regional in the west Midlands (he did not leave the area over nearly two years), he had a wider perspective.[86] When he and his father went to Hereford in September 1836 it was 'partly on purpose to see the agricultural show' but largely to take forward negotiations on a possible tenancy nearby.[87]

Peter Davis's diary shows an inquisitive young man, spending much time seeing markets and farms and the landscape of a widening region across four counties (Shropshire, Worcestershire, Herefordshire and Staffordshire). It seems likely that he pursued some of the innovations he saw on tour or elsewhere, and introduced some on the farm at Burford. But he was also close to his father, whom he described in the diary at his death as 'my best friend on earth', and probably adopted from him that most English of attitudes to improvement, summed up in his assessment of John Bright, the agent to the Teddesley Park estate as understanding 'the business of farming both scientifically and practically'.[88]

---

[83] Ibid., 24–27 May 1837.

[84] Ibid., 12 May 1837; E.J.T. Collins, 'The latter-day history of the draught ox in England, 1770–1964', *AgHR* 58 (2010), pp. 191–216.

[85] *PD*, 14 June, 8 and 9 Dec. 1836.

[86] Davies notes his brother's visit to London in May 1836 as his first excursion there. *PD*, 25 May 1836.

[87] *PD*, 19 Sept. 1836.

[88] Ibid., 30 Aug., 24 May 1837.

III

John Mastin (1747–1829) wrote his *Memoirs* (effectively an autobiography) towards the end of his life. It was begun before 1822, and its last chapters were written in two other hands after Mastin became blind in 1825. Much of the material was written in retrospect, though his editors suggest that the precision of many dates in the 71-page text meant that Mastin probably referred to diaries that have not survived.[89] This means that his text is not strictly comparable with Carrington and Davis, for he was consciously framing his life. His views on agriculture and improvement are more overt because central to his perception of his own life and career.

In recalling his upbringing and education, Mastin highlighted his delicate childhood, the notice taken of him by a local gentleman, and his schooling. He was first in a brutal dame school, then at the age of seven in a school in the next village where the master was a 'most excellent master, accountant, land surveyor &c &c' who taught him a range of advanced arithmetic including square and cube roots, fractions and the measurement of areas and three-dimensional objects. At 11 or 12 he was sent to Nottingham to perfect himself in writing, boarding with an aunt, but making visits home on the local butcher's cart. By the age of 13 he was reckoned a 'good scholar'. Despite this emphasis on education, he was kept back from school to help on the farm, and husbandry was the 'occupation he was at that time designed for'.[90]

His father rented land, and later tithes, from a local clergyman, and when at 13 Mastin began work, it was as servant to another Nottinghamshire clergyman, a post secured through family connections, and the transition eased by the presence in the household of a coachman from his own village. After two years there he changed employer to another clergyman, the post on this occasion secured through the local butcher. He reflected that life with his first employer gave him a taste for polite society, and a distaste for 'the rough uncouth manners of the country plebeian', his father's labourers.[91] At his second post, where he stayed four years, he grew up, became highly competitive, and learned skills such as bell ringing and wrestling while writing songs and poetry.[92] There he lived in a farm environment, for his employer farmed his own tithe and his farmyard was stocked with poultry.[93]

---

[89]   Christine Vialls and Kay Collins (eds), *A Georgian Country Parson: The Reverend John Mastin of Naseby* (Northamptonshire Record Soc. Victor Hatley Memorial volume, 1, 2004) (hereafter Mastin, *Memoir*), pp. x-xi.

[90]   Mastin, *Memoir*, p. 4.

[91]   Ibid., p. 6.

[92]   Ibid., p. 7.

[93]   Ibid., p. 8.

Mastin's employer took him on journeys to various places including London and Oxford, and these wider horizons made Mastin form 'a resolution of quitting a place he now found was of little consequence'.[94] He returned to his parents' house to find his father about to leave his farm because the landlord wanted to give it to his own brother-in-law. A search for a new farm, using clerical connections in Leicestershire, failed, but a farm at Countesthorpe in Leicestershire was found through the local newspaper. Taking it on a 21-year lease from the blind rector of the parish, Mastin senior found the parish in the throes of enclosure, and John Mastin was fully engaged in the extensive work with hedges, gates, pits and pens, and with the construction of barns and stables paid for by the landlord by deduction from rent. Mastin expressed relish at the change: 'This was a new scene, a new country, new connexions were to be formed, new schemes were to be executed for improvement; and it was here he first became a proficient in agricultural pursuits'.[95]

Mastin's next employment was triggered by fickle aristocratic promises. His father had given Earl Howe assistance in an enclosure dispute in Epperstone, and in recompense Howe offered to 'do something for' Mastin that used his writing and accounting skills if he would present himself in London, but when Mastin made the journey, there was nothing available.[96] Mastin stayed on with relatives in London, sought work through newspaper advertisements and eventually secured a post as 'house and land steward, to pay all country bills, and superintend a large farm' in Loudwater near Rickmansworth, Hertfordshire. His reaction to the very different farming environment mirrors that when his father moved to Leicestershire:

> This was quite a new country to Mr Mastin, the mode of agriculture, and implements of husbandry were equally strange. The two-wheeled plows of the county were almost prodigies, and the knee-fan he had never before seen. The method of cleansing corn by throwing, he was quite unaccustomed to; and many of their terms he did not understand.[97]

Mastin presents himself in the *Memoir* as a resounding success in the post. He won over the local farmers and tradesmen by promptly paying bills (unlike his predecessor) and this was easy because his master 'was extremely [*sic*] rich'. He found himself invited into local houses, and to join the club at the Swan, Rickmansworth. At the same time he endeared himself to his master who went fowling with him and left him in control when he went travelling. Indeed Mastin

---

[94]   Ibid., p. 9.
[95]   Ibid., p. 11.
[96]   Ibid., p. 13.
[97]   Ibid., pp. 14–15.

claimed 'he was more a companion to him to him, when in the country, than a servant'.[98] He was offered better jobs in London, or in India, but turned them down on the grounds of preferring country life.

Mastin's time in Hertfordshire spanned only two years (1770–72) and ended with a romantic courtship and marriage. His beloved was the 17-year-old orphaned daughter of a local farmer and wheelwright who had both freehold and copyhold property. The couple eloped to Gretna Green, but Mastin's practical streak ensured that he first checked her father's will at Doctors Commons, and took legal advice in London. He further ensured his own family's support by calling on them with his bride to be on the way north. She was quickly accepted, and Mastin's father accompanied the couple on their journey north. While the couple were also quickly reconciled to her family in Hertfordshire, Mastin draws a discreet veil over his relations with his employer, but clearly left his employment.[99]

From the romantic world of a Gretna wedding the couple faced the reality of married life in Leicestershire, close to Mastin's father. John failed to secure the schoolmastership of Gilmorton, and earning a living became an increasingly urgent problem as three children were born to the couple in the first three years of the marriage and seven in eight years. After the second birth, Mastin's wife's guardian allowed her just under £40 in advance of her coming of age. With this Mastin bought some land in Blaby (Leicestershire), 'pulled down the house, took credit for some materials, and with the assistance of his father's team as to carriage &c., he built a small but neat cottage of two rooms on a floor with a vestibule'. At this point he seized a career opportunity when his father's cousin offered him presentation to a Nottinghamshire rectory if Mastin would qualify for holy orders. He did this by doing a deal with a local clergyman to give him the first year's salary of the living in returning for bringing him to the necessary educational standard. Mastin worked on the farm during the day, took lessons at night, and within two years was fluent in Greek and Latin, and could translate between them.[100]

Times were difficult in the last 18 months before his wife's majority. Mastin survived by borrowing £30 and 'a few Bills with Tradesmen were run'. The promised rectory on ordination was lost. A fourth child was born in January 1777. However, when his wife's inheritance came in he sold the copyhold, and with the money and a cash inheritance cleared the debts and also bought part of the farm his father rented, providing an income of £15 a year.[101] When his tutor pronounced him ready for examination he sought a curacy, and eventually

98   Ibid., pp. 15–16.
99   Ibid., pp. 19–25.
100   Ibid., p. 26.
101   Ibid., p. 27.

found one paying £51 a year at Husbands Bosworth through contacts his father had made whilst supervising enclosures nearby. After a successful examination at the Bishop of Lincoln's residence at Buckden he was ordained deacon in 1777 and was priested in 1779. As he took up residence on the curacy, he also rented 41 acres of farmland of newly enclosed land in Walton and Kimcote which soon produced good crops.[102] Later in the year he added the curacy of Naseby (Northants.), adding £27 a year to his income, but requiring Mastin to own a horse to travel between parishes. He renovated the parsonage at Husbands Bosworth and was taken into the circle of the resident squire, who introduced him to the world of the Meynell hunt. However, within a short time he acquired the vicarage at Naseby which became his enduring home.

By 1779, at the age of 32, Mastin had consolidated his career as a churchman, combining this with considerable agricultural, land management and valuation skills. These were the basis of his life for the next 50 years. Within 10 years he had enhanced the living at Naseby from £27 to over £70 a year, with help from the impropriator and Queen Anne's Bounty funds, investing the Bounty money in land during a downturn in the land market. He took one additional curacies from time to time, and much later patronage brought him two further vicarages worth over £500 a year, one of which he gave to his brother, who had also become a clergyman. Yet throughout his life, Mastin continued to engage in 'country business' as he called it.

This meant renting land and improving it. He rarely held more than 50 acres, and the place and type of land were continually changing. When the 200 acres of glebe lands at Husbands Bosworth were untenanted for two years after the American War of Independence, Mastin took on 50 acres.[103] He also farmed 20 acres of glebe at Naseby.[104] In November 1788 he took a 15-year lease in Clipston, adjoining Naseby. This:

> very poor land run over with goss hassock rushes and other trumpery, in the present state worth but little, however Mr Mastin ventured to give for it £8 per annum. He began to cleanse this land by stocking the goss, paring and burning the turf, and by proper management, it soon brought good crops of corn and bread clover. He built a small barn of two bays at his own expense upon the premises.[105]

---

[102]   Ibid., p. 30.
[103]   Ibid., p. 35.
[104]   Ibid., p. 30.
[105]   Ibid., p. 36.

In 1795 he took on a 35-acre farm in Husbands Bosworth: 'rough uncultivated land, under the idea of improving the same and making it better worth the rent, which it afterwards turned out to be'.[106]

In 1808 Mastin bought a close he was renting in Clipston for £300 'because he might other wise have lost the use of it'.[107] After 1810 he was increasingly incapacitated by severe gout, and reined in his agricultural enterprises. His description of the appalling weather and harvest of 1816 implies its impact was on his neighbours, not himself.[108] However, when the parliamentary enclosure of Naseby took place in 1821–22 following the Act of 1820, Mastin suddenly recovered from his sickness. He:

> found himself very inactive, soon tired with walking, and in fact growing the old man apace. However, to draw him out, and give him exercise, he took to rent, 20 acres, in two allotments, very near the Village, tho' at the opposite ends. This renewal of his favourite pursuit, tho' on a small scale, became to him pleasing and satisfactory. It was a convenience he looked up to, not so much for profit, the land being high rented: and the produce of it very low in price. He entered on the land at old Lady Day 1822.[109]

This enterprise went on for two years (by which time he was 77 years old) until the end of 1823 when 'Mr Mastin relinquished all his grazing business finding, by experience, that it did him no good. He grew old, and tired of all country business'.[110] In all these farming activities Mastin combined farming profitably with efforts to improve poor land. He does not express this explicitly as setting an example to his neighbours, but that was a recurrent theme.

Mastin's experience and expertise also found him much in demand for land appraisal and assistance, even farm management. In 1794 he became the man of business for 'Mr Payne the Banker', first in buying a house and then farms of over 500 acres to form an estate. One of the sellers, a Mr Sturges, decided to shift his business from grazing to becoming a 'Hertfordshire farmer' and tasked Mastin to find a farm there, and then with running it. Meanwhile, in 1795 Mastin switched in the opposite direction, selling his wife's freehold property in Hertfordshire to set up and learn the grazing business on the Northamptonshire/Leicestershire borders, at first enduring losses.[111] These activities brought Mastin a considerable and profitable clientele amongst the local clergy and gentry, mainly for assistance

---

[106] Ibid., p. 40.
[107] Ibid., p. 48.
[108] Ibid., p. 56.
[109] Ibid., p. 63.
[110] Ibid., p. 67.
[111] Ibid., pp. 38–40.

in land valuation, but after a time 'upon mature reflection, he began to think it rather inconsistent with his clerical character, and gave it up entirely except sometimes giving his advice privately'.[112] However he continued to engage in rural business, on commissions to consolidate local livings in 1800, was offered appointment as a J.P. in 1801 (which he turned down), as sequestrator of Welford cum Silbertoft, commissioner for Grand Union canal works in 1814, in rate disputes at Marston Trusswell (1802), taking on manorial work for various gentleman there and at Silbertoft, and in 1819 becoming a manager (overseer) of the short-lived saving bank at Welford.[113]

Mastin lived and worked in the world of the country gentry, professionals and tradespeople, but his origins, upbringing and farm training gave him credence as someone understanding farming in a variety of modes and a practical manner who could deal with local people. He claimed to have been a popular vicar in all the parishes he served, and was active in the building and endowing of a large school for 80 in Naseby in 1814.[114] However, when in 1825 the Methodists set up a chapel in the village his reaction was one of sorrow, but at 78 he did not have the fight to challenge them.[115] His social status remained very ambivalent. He hunted and dined with the gentry and aristocracy, kept a hunter, and bred a prize pack of hounds. His history of Naseby achieved a subscription list of 700 including aristocrats, gentry and clergy and university dons across most of England, without him ever advertising it.[116] He clearly had a certain celebrity outside his immediate locality. However, it was a personal status, and did not elevate his family. Indeed, there appears to be a measure of diffidence in his attitude to crossing the divide into gentility. When he published his history of Naseby, he was asked to join the Society of Antiquaries, but refused, citing the cost of the annual membership fee. He claimed he declined the invitation to become a JP 'because he could not reconcile Mrs Mastin to his acting as a Magistrate'.[117] Despite his increasingly comfortable financial situation, his daughters' marriages to a carpenter and joiner, to a cutler (though nephew to a gentleman), and to a farmer, suggest little social aspiration.[118]

Mastin's projects himself as busy, inquisitive and highly personable, with good relationships with rich and poor alike. He adapted easily to new farming territories and throve on challenge. His agricultural and land management

[112] Ibid., p. 49. cf. J. Broad, 'Clergé anglais, agriculture, et société rurale', in F. Quellier and G. Provost (eds), *Du Ciel à la terre: Clergé et agriculture, XVIᵉ-XIXᵉ siècle* (2008), pp. 209–10.

[113] Mastin, *Memoir*, pp. 41, 50, 54, 43, 42, 61.

[114] Ibid., p. 54.

[115] Ibid., p. 69.

[116] Ibid., p. 38.

[117] Ibid., p. 44.

[118] Ibid., pp. 40, 41.

skills were considerable, based on good numerical skills learnt at a local school, farming techniques absorbed working with his father both on the land and in enclosure work, and through his own initiatives. In a sense, his clerical career seems incidental, though there is a thread of connection with church matters that runs right through his life even before he sought to enter the church for what appear to be entirely material considerations. There is not a single note of spirituality in the *Memoir*. In his farming enterprises, which were all on a modest scale, he portrays himself as an experimenter and pioneer, and by implication, though never explicitly, as setting an example in improvement to his neighbours. His contribution to improvement went beyond practical trials. His comments on the themes of the Board of Agriculture Premium topics in 1801 merited the award of silver medal, and were published in the *Communications to the Board of Agriculture* in 1805. They dealt with the subject of paring and burning to prepare land for cultivation, and the 'Exhalation of dung'. In the latter he reported an experiment in which he had dissolved nitrate fertiliser and allowed it to re-crystallise, demonstrating by its constant weight that the fertiliser would work whether worked into the soil while wet or allowed to dry.[119]

IV

These three farming lives contrast different areas of the country, and focus on different parts of the life cycle, but there are common threads that elaborate our understanding of how farmers engaged with agricultural change. Firstly, by definition, all three were literate, and in the case of Mastin and Carrington this was demonstrably combined with good numeracy, with particular skills in valuation, and a facility with money and accounts. None made much of farming books and the farming press: Mastin and Davis were familiar with some of the literature, and Mastin contributed to it in a minor way. Its use appears to have been internalised. Nowhere in all three works is there any mention of any kind of farming club or society playing a role in innovation and thinking, or of agricultural shows influencing practice significantly.

Our farmers learnt primarily from their neighbours and a natural inquisitiveness and openness to change. All three were frequently in contact with stewards or land agents on great estates on a regular basis. They garnered techniques from fellow farmers and from journeys across a wide geographical range. Mastin farmed in at least four different counties (Nottinghamshire, Leicestershire, Northamptonshire and Hertfordshire), while the young

---

[119]   Ibid., p. 43. The pieces are printed in the Appendix. The silver medal was awarded at the Board of Agriculture meeting on 16 Nov. 1801, and the pieces were originally published in *Communications to the Board of Agriculture on Subjects relating to the Husbandry and Internal Improvement of the Country* (7 vols, London, 1797–1811), IV, pp. 115, 135.

Peter Davis not only made a farming tour to Scotland, but searched for a tenancy across another four (Shropshire, Worcestershire, Herefordshire and Staffordshire). Carrington operated over much of central Hertfordshire, was regularly in London, and assessed farms in Middlesex and Berkshire as well as his own county. Davis and Carrington both made visits to specific farms in the course of their everyday activities to see 'improvements' involving considerable capital expenditure. These were often on large estates, or where new owners had just bought farms with the intention of 'improving'. Davis's comments are of wonder, the older Carrington is constantly questioning the profitability of the investment. The tenant farmers in our case studies were much more likely to trial and adopt new crops and techniques, but are rarely explicit about it, and the novelty can often only be inferred.

All three farmers in the case studies displayed a business-like approach and kept a close eye on the bottom line. Carrington and Davis worked on 'family' farms, in the sense that other family members were active participants and partners in the enterprise, but these businesses were not corporate. Fathers and sons must have agreed cropping patterns, rotations, and strategies on the basis of pooled enterprise but outcomes and profits were personally earmarked. Each had a clear notion of which crops and livestock were theirs, and bought and sold independently of one another, though mutual trust permitted them to do business for one another: they were not competitors. Farming was a business, and one that most country people could turn their hand to. Carrington notes two of his neighbours who moved in and out of farming. One was a gardener who in 1800 threw up a safe job to take on a farm, but went bankrupt in 1809. A neighbouring farmer, John Randall, had previously been a servant to a local gentleman, but took up farming in 1794, only to sell up his farm in 1801 to become a coal merchant in Brighton.[120] Mastin records how a Leicestershire neighbour suddenly decided to shift his enterprise from livestock to become a 'Hertfordshire farmer'.[121] This ability and confidence to shift business was part and parcel of the growth of non-agricultural employment in the countryside that is such a feature of rural social structure in England in the post-medieval period.

Three case studies of farmers in the period 1780–1840 cannot provide definitive answers to the question posed at the beginning of the chapter, and their fluent literacy in itself may make them un-typical. Yet they showed many of the traits mentioned by Young and Robertson discussed earlier. Their characteristic numeracy and attention to profit, wide general interests outside farming, inquisitiveness combined with scepticism, and constant mobility, made them part of the wider movement of experimentation and innovation that

---

[120] *Memorandums*, 17 Nov. 1801.

[121] Mastin, *Memoir*, p. 39.

characterised British society in that seminal period. Farming shows, clubs and the trade press played only a minor part in their perception of what influenced them. An important element, particularly in the cases of both Carrington and Mastin, was participation in the valuation, appraisal, and taxing of land in their neighbourhood. Their contacts with landowners, and their stewards and land agents were important to all three, but not in the formal sense of providing models and imposing restrictive lease clauses on their farming. It was another part of the constant interchange of everyday life, no different from the regular contact with other farmers, dealers and urban craftsmen that was the stock in trade of farming life throughout the period.

Chapter 7

Farmers of the Holkham Estate

Susanna Wade Martins

'A good understanding between landlord and tenant' was the toast drunk at the Holkham audit in the days of Thomas William Coke, and the landlord-tenant system of farming as practised over much of Britain by the nineteenth century was seen as the ideal method of promoting 'improved' farming. Although the encouragement of new farming techniques through the example of the home farm, the granting of long husbandry leases and the personal interest of the landlord and his agent were regarded as of importance, it was the division of financial responsibility between the landlord and tenant which was seen as of greatest significance.[1] This freed up the tenant's capital for the working and stocking of the land and made the landlord responsible for fixed capital investment such as buildings and fencing, resulting in an efficient and highly capitalised industry. Thus, the role of the landlord was seen as crucial in providing the infrastructure for 'improved farming'. This view has been broadly supported by historians from Lord Ernle through Chambers and Mingay to Beckett, although more recently Elizabeth Griffiths and Mark Overton have reminded us of the importance of share farming in the English agricultural system.[2]

The debate over the respective roles of the tenant and the landlord in agricultural improvement in the early nineteenth century goes back almost to the contemporary literature. Arthur Young appreciated the importance of the farmers themselves, and listed 56 Norfolk men and one woman, of whom seven were Holkham tenants, who he saw as leaders in their class, describing them as 'famous for their improvements, the excellency of their management and the hospitable manner in which they live and entertain their friends'.[3] However, his praise was almost always confined to large farmers (those working over 300 acres). 'Small farms are detrimental to the occupier and the public in the smallness of

---

[1]   H.J. Habakkuk, 'The economic functions of English landowners in the seventeenth and eighteenth centuries', *Explorations in Entreprenurial History* 6 (1953), pp. 92–102.

[2]   R.E. Prothero (Lord Ernle), *English Farming, Past and Present* (1st edn, 1912, 6th edn, London, 1961), p. 161; J.D. Chambers and G.E. Mingay, *The Agricultural Revolution, 1750–1880* (London, 1966), p. 21; J.V. Beckett, *The Agricultural Revolution* (Oxford, 1990); E. Griffiths and M. Overton, *Farming to Halves: The Hidden History of Share Farming in England from Medieval to Modern Times* (Basingstoke, 2009).

[3]   A. Young, *A General View of the Agriculture of Norfolk* (London, 1804), pp. 31–6.

their produce ...'.[4] Marshall also described Norfolk farmers as 'strongly marked by a liberality of thinking, and by an openness of manner and conversation'.[5] There is no doubt that those who took on large farms had to be men of capital if they were to stock and work them and so were likely to be educated and willing to try new methods.

Equally, it is clear that while not all small farmers were laggards, some larger-scale operators did not come up to the highest standards.[6] However, information on tenant farmers is difficult to come by. E.L. Jones wrote in 1968 'Of the three agricultural classes, landowners, farmers and labourers, it is surprising that we know least about the economic condition of the middle group'.[7] This statement is still almost as true now as when it was written and so any study that can help in the understanding of this little-discussed group must be a valuable one.

It is for this reason that the remarkable survival of the diaries of two Holkham tenants, Thomas Moore of Hall Farm at Warham and John Leeds of Beck Hall, Billingford, covering the years of the Napoleonic Wars and the 1820s respectively, is very important, allowing us to study the activities of two farmers and the estate through the farmers' own eyes, but with the benefit of the detailed records of the estate. They can help us answer important questions such as how intensive and progressive were the farming methods, how much influence did the estate have over the day-to-day running of the farm, did tenants actually keep to the terms of their leases and finally, what sort of person was a Holkham tenant?

I

The Holkham estate is one of the best documented in Britain, famous for its role in the promotion of the 'improved farming' of the agricultural revolution. This role, much publicised by Mrs Stirling in 1908 and R.E. Prothero (Lord Ernle) in 1912, has been reassessed more recently.[8]

The estate, much the largest in Norfolk, covered about 40,000 acres in two blocks. That near the centre of the county around the original family seat at Godwick, near Tittleshall, was of mainly mixed soil: the other on the north

---

[4]   A. Young, *The Farmers' Letters to the People of England* (London, 1767), p. 94.

[5]   W. Marshall, *The Rural Economy of Norfolk* (2 vols, London, 1787), I, p. 37.

[6]   S. Wade Martins and T. Williamson, *Roots of Change: Farming and the Landscape in East Anglia, c.1700–1870* (Agricultural History Review Supplement 2, 1999), pp. 194–6.

[7]   E.L. Jones, *The Development of English Agriculture, 1815–73* (London, 1968), p. 25.

[8]   Prothero, *English Farming*, pp. 217–20; A.M.W. Stirling, *Coke of Norfolk and his Friends* (2 vols, London, 1908); R.A.C. Parker, *Coke of Norfolk: A Financial and Agricultural Study, 1707–1842* (Oxford, 1975); S. Wade Martins, *A Great Estate at Work: The Holkham Estate and Its Inhabitants in the Nineteenth Century* (Cambridge, 1980) and eadem, *Coke of Norfolk, 1754–1842* (Woodbridge, 2009).

coast around Holkham consisted largely of lighter soils. Here, a sheep-corn husbandry based on a foldcourse system whereby the sheep of the lord of the manor were grazed across the strip fields of his tenants, had developed in the middle ages. By the early eighteenth century this system was breaking down and many foldcourse rights were being let. As the growing of winter crops such as turnips and improved grasses increased, the value of enclosed land outstripped that of half-year land and foldcourses. Landlords, anxious to maximise their incomes, enclosed fields and gradually the landscapes of the north-west Norfolk estates took on their familiar appearance of large rectangular fields with hawthorn hedges bounded by straight, wide enclosure roads. This change had begun in the seventeenth century and increased in pace during the eighteenth, to be completed on the Holkham estate during the long ownership of Thomas William Coke from 1776 to 1842.

Alongside the enclosure of farms on the part of the landlord went the development of new farming practices by the tenants. Fodder crops such as grasses and turnips could be grown in the fallow year, allowing more animals to be kept and more manure produced to enable heavier crops to be harvested on land which had previously been some of the least productive in the county. Now that the open fields had gone, the soil structure could also be improved by heavy applications of marl, often over 30 loads an acre. As a result, in many areas both the landscape and farming practice changed totally within two generations.

The name of Thomas William Coke of Holkham (1754–1842, created first Earl of Leicester of Holkham in 1837) is inextricably linked with these developments. Coke was made famous in his own lifetime by writers such as Arthur Young, both in his *Annals of Agriculture* and his county survey as well as by reports in the Norfolk newspapers and a eulogistic pamphlet published by Edward Rigby of Norwich in 1817.[9] Much of his reputation resulted from his highly publicised annual 'sheep shearings' which were run on an informal basis from the time Coke took over the estate in 1776, but became important enough to be reported upon at length in the newspapers from 1798 until 1821. These notices ensured that news of the improvements made on his estates circulated not only within Norfolk, but amongst Coke's parliamentary colleagues, the aristocracy, gentry and progressive farmers generally. Beyond the charismatic personality of Thomas William Coke himself, the fame of Holkham was based on some apparently solid achievements. These included the fulfilling by the estate of its role as provider of the appropriate infrastructure for the intensive farming of the early nineteenth century. Nearly all the 70 farms on the estate went through at least one phase of rebuilding during Coke's lifetime. New brick and tiled, carefully laid-out premises alongside good residences, designed to

---

[9]   A. Young, *Annals of Agriculture* (44 vols, London, 1784–1806), II, p. 353; idem, *General View ... Norfolk*; E. Rigby, *Holkham, its Agriculture etc* (3rd edn, 1818).

attract intelligent farmers with capital, were built. This was accompanied by the final phase of enclosure which left all the farms with regular fields, nearly always with good access to a lane or driftway, and well-placed farm buildings, often with a field barn for the more distant fields.

While extravagant claims have been made for the effects of Coke's management of his property and the income it generated,[10] the documents at Holkham have allowed these to be checked in recent years. The first audit book dates from 1707 and there is a continuous run from 1720. Letter books begin in 1816. There are also several eighteenth- and nineteenth-century farm surveys. This means that it has been possible to study the estate's management and policies in detail over a period of immense importance in agricultural history. We know the level of interest taken and amount invested in estate improvements. The audit books show a figure in the region of £150,000 was spent on farm improvements during Coke's lifetime, sometimes amounting to over 30 per cent of income from rent, while rents rose from about £15,500 to £35,000 over the same period.[11] It is true, therefore, that in general Coke invested heavily in the improvements to farm buildings and their layout and this enabled his tenants to implement the more intensive methods being advocated, and so pay higher rents.

It was not only through providing the framework for improved agriculture that the landlord could influence the farming on his estate, although this was probably the most important; he could also hope to persuade the tenant of the advantage of new techniques through the example of the home farm and the encouragement given by his agent. There is very little information at Holkham about the home farm before 1840, but account books for the years 1817 to 1827 show that it was being intensively cultivated, with 160 cattle and 2,004 sheep kept in 1817 to provide the manure for the 1,800 acre holding. Crops of wheat, barley, turnips, swedes and mangel wurzel were grown as well as various grasses such as clover, sainfoin and linseed.[12] The farm was visited by those who came to the sheep shearings, the crops admired and the finer points of the animals discussed.

The influence of the agent could also be significant, and Francis Blaikie, estate steward from 1816 to 1832, was the most important here. On his arrival at Holkham, he visited all the farms of the estate and wrote a description, not only of the farms, but also of the farmers themselves, looking especially at the younger generation for potentially progressive tenants.[13] While Blaikie was full of praise for Thomas Moore's brother, Tuttell Moore, he was dismissive of his neighbour, Mr Ward, who was in high spirits when Blaikie met him. 'He talks

10   Prothero, *English Farming*, pp. 217–20; Parker, *Coke of Norfolk*, pp. 71–82.

11   Wade Martins, *Great Estate*, p. 86.

12   Ibid., pp. 77–78.

13   Holkham MS, E/G9; Report on the Holkham Estate by Francis Blaikie, 1816.

of improving, but at present everything is wrong'. Of John Leeds, the father of the diarist at Beck Hall, he wrote, 'This is altogether a very fine farm and a very intelligent and well-informed farmer'. The impression is that Blaikie had a good working relationship with most of the tenants and understood their personalities and weaknesses. He also appears, from his copious letter books, to have been in regular contact with them,[14] although, as we shall see, his influence was sometimes minimal.

A final tool at the landlord's disposal was the lease. Long leases (up to 21 years) had been usual, but by no means universal, on the Holkham estate from the middle of the eighteenth century. They had usually contained some sort of stipulation as to how the land should be cropped. In common with other estates, these restrictions were becoming more detailed as the century progressed, and especially during the period of high prices sparked off by the French wars when the temptation to grow more grain crops than the soil could really stand was a very real one.[15] It was Blaikie who was responsible for formalising a series of rotations suited to the various soils of the estate which he felt should be included in leases. A book containing Blaikie's model leases survives in the estate archive.[16] Although we know what these leases stipulated, it is much more difficult to be sure how far they were kept, and how important they really were in influencing farming practice. We shall see that here the evidence of John Leeds's diary is particularly significant.

II

Over recent years a re-evaluation of the balance between the role of landlord and tenant in improvement has shifted emphasis in favour of the tenant.[17] The actions of the great landowners such as Coke of Holkham were important in providing the infrastructure for improved farming, but it was the work of the tenants themselves which made places like Holkham famous. In his book written in 1851, James Caird describes the work of Coke of Holkham in glowing terms and then goes on to praise the tenants, saying that their investment in feeds and fertilisers was equal to that of Coke in permanent improvements: 'No farmers in England have more right to rest content with the point they have

---

[14] Blaikie's correspondence with General Fitzroy, tenant of Kempstone Lodge Farm, has been analysed by Mary-Anne Garry in *An Uncommon Tenant, Fitzroy and Holkham, 1808–1837* (Dereham, 1996).

[15] Parker, *Coke of Norfolk*, pp. 100–5.

[16] Holkham MS, E/G19.

[17] Arthur Young in his *Farmer's Tour through the East of England* (4 vols, London, 1771), written shortly before Thomas William Coke inherited described the improved farming of many of the Holkham tenants, without mentioning the estate at all. See also Wade Martins, *Great Estate*, pp. 108–10.

reached than the best of Lord Leicester's tenants'.[18] Richard Bacon, in his essay on Norfolk agriculture of 1844, lists the 'first generation' of Norfolk improvers, amongst whom were several Holkham farmers such as Mr Tuttell Moore and Mr Bloomfield of Warham, while the 'second' (that is, 1840s) 'generation' was entirely made up of Holkham tenants.[19]

However, it is clear from Blaikie's description of the tenants in 1816 that not all farms had such progressive occupiers, although most tenants were described as 'zealous', 'industrious', 'good' and 'deserving'.[20] From the Holkham estate records we know the names of the tenants, and about 80 different family names cover the period of Thomas William Coke's ownership. About 25 of these held more than one farm and remained on the estate for nearly all of the period. It may well be that they were related by marriage to other tenants. In 1850, 18 of the Holkham farms were held by only five families. By this date the Holkham tenantry was headed by a small group of progressive farmers with sufficient capital to improve their large farms and bring them to a high standard of intensive cultivation, whilst a few farms were still occupied by 'old-fashioned' and 'backward' farmers.

We know the level of rent tenants paid and arrears they accumulated in years of depression. As elsewhere, they were prepared to accept high levels of rent increases during the Napoleonic Wars and the middle years of the nineteenth century, whilst feeling the effect of low grain prices and collapse of confidence in 1821–22 and 1825–26. The letter books contain correspondence with them, usually about rents or requests to depart from the terms of a lease. One of the most important differences between Holkham tenants and many of their contemporaries was the size of the farms they occupied. Of the 70 estate farms of 1850, 6 were over 1,000 acres and 28 more than 500. If we accept Mingay's minimum figure of £2 per acre as the working capital needed by a farmer at the beginning of the nineteenth century,[21] it is clear that there would be a limited number of potential tenants. Some tenants were small landowners in their own right; General William Fitzroy, who was tenant of Kempstone Lodge Farm from 1808 to 1837 was the younger son of an aristocrat, and an enthusiastic 'improver', but a tenant of such high social status was unusual.[22]

There are drawn surveys of all estate farms in 1789. The two major written estate surveys of 1816 and 1851 describe the farms and give the agent's assessment of the tenants' abilities as farmers. Whilst all this is enormously valuable, it only

---

[18]   J. Caird, *English Agriculture in 1850–51* (1851, repr. London, 1968), pp. 164–5.

[19]   R.N. Bacon, *The Report on the Agriculture of Norfolk* (London, 1844), pp. 110–11.

[20]   Holkham, MS E/G9.

[21]   G.E. Mingay, *Enclosure and the Small Farmer in the Eighteenth Century* (London, 1968), p. 22.

[22]   Mary-Anne Garry, *An uncommon tenant. Fitzroy and Holkham, 1808–1837* (Dereham, 1996).

tells us about the farmer insofar as the estate impinged on his activities, and so the information to be found in the diaries is of immense interest.

III

Thomas Moore's diaries are now deposited in the Holkham archive. They were kept in red leather-bound annual volumes of 'The Norfolk and Norwich Gentleman's Memorandum Book' covering most years between 1799 and 1811.[23] John Leeds's Journal is now in the Norfolk Record Office. It was kept in a single note book entitled the 'Agricultural Journal, Memoranda, etc. as continued from my former book, J.P. Leeds' and runs from September 1823 to January 1828, with gaps in August and September 1825.[24] Daily entries vary in length. They include both the business of the farms and Leeds's social engagements, providing not only insights into the running of large tenant farms but also the daily life and activities of the prosperous farmers of the time.

Both families were well thought of and long-standing Holkham tenants, but they were farming very different farms and their diaries cover contrasting periods of agricultural prosperity. That of Thomas Moore describes conditions during the high prices of the Napoleonic Wars on a light-land farm near the centre of the Holkham estate, while that of John Leeds was written during the agricultural depression of the early 1820s on a farm of mixed soils on the fringes of estate influence.

The Moore Family at Warham

William and Sarah moved to Warham from Shottesham (to the south of Norwich) some time between the birth of their sons William (born in Shottesham in 1767) and Thomas (born in Warham in 1771). Thomas William Coke bought the Warham estate from Charles Turner in 1785 by which time William Moore senior was a tenant paying a rent of £321. In 1794 he was granted a lease for Grove Farm. He retired in 1796 and his son, Thomas (the writer of the journal), took over the farm. In 1806, when the lease was renewed, the rent was reduced to £286 but by 1820 it had risen to £366 which included payment for an increased acreage and a percentage towards the cost of new buildings.[25] Thomas had moved from Warham by the time of his death and his son had taken over the tenancy. Members of the Moore family continued to be tenants at Warham into the twentieth century.

---

23   Holkham MS, T/M/1–7, Moore papers.
24   Norfolk RO, MC 681/1 802x7, hereafter cited as L[eeds] D[iary].
25   Holkham MS, A/Au, Audit books.

The Tuttell family were long established in Warham and it is possible that the Moore family's move to the parish was linked to the marriage of one of William Moore's sisters to a member of the Tuttell family, as by 1791 a scion of the family was known as Tuttell Moore and was renting a Warham Farm. It was Tuttell Moore who was regularly praised by Bacon as one of the first generation of Norfolk 'improvers'.[26] He was named by Francis Blaikie in 1816 as a 'zealous, indefatigable and practical farmer – and no theorist'.[27] He retired in 1827 and died in Wells in 1844. The grandeur of the Moore and Tuttell family table tombs in Warham St Mary's churchyard indicate that both were families of considerable social standing.

Thomas Moore was in his thirties at the time he was keeping his diary and so presumably at the height of his farming career, during the period of agricultural prosperity that accompanied the Napoleonic Wars. It was also the time when his landlord, Thomas William Coke, was at the peak of his agricultural and political influence.

Soon after Thomas Coke bought the Warham estate he commissioned the land agent Nathaniel Kent to undertake a survey of his new purchase. Kent described the buildings at Moore's farm. The farmhouse was 'good', there were two large barns, two stables, three cart houses, a cow house and 'sundry sheds'. The farm covered 474 acres with 149 acres of sheep walk.[28] Moore's diary describes the building of new barns and extensions to the house. In May 1811 the red bricks for the house were being fired on the site, but the white bricks were brought from Holkham. On 13 August 1811 'the new part of my house was covered with blue tiles' and at the end of September he 'removed all my spirits etc. into my new cellar'. A new field barn, built at a cost to the estate of £330 18s.[29] was nearly burnt down in June 1811 'when a tar bucket boiled over ... and set fire to the reed on the roof'. In 1816, when Blaikie visited the farm he described it as in 'complete repair' although 'too extensive and expensive for the extent and rent of the farm'.[30] This was typical of Blaikie's attitude to new buildings on the estate. He was critical of the extravagant building schemes that had been undertaken by Coke and favoured retrenchment in the less favourable post-war climate, writing, 'It would be greatly to the advantage of the tenants as well as to the landlord, and much to the credit of the former if they would condescend to be guided by my sound advice that I give them in regard to the buildings on their farms'.[31] A plan of 1828 shows the layout of the farm. The

26   Bacon, *Norfolk Agriculture*, p. 110.
27   Holkham MS, E/G9.
28   Holkham MS, E/G7, Nathanial Kent's report, *Plans and Particulars of Norfolk Estates,* 1789.
29   Holkham MS, A/Au, Audit books.
30   Holkham MS, E/G9.
31   Holkham MS, E/C1, Letter books, 1827, p. 86.

fields were all regular and dissected by good farm tracks; the field barn was built at their intersection, which helped compensate for the fact that the main farm buildings were on the edge of the village on the eastern side of the land.[32] The soil itself was varied with light sandy soils to 'good useful land' producing a 'good quality of grain'. Some of the pastures were rather boggy.[33] In 1819 Chalk Hill Farm was built by T.W. Coke for Thomas's son, Thomas Sewell Moore, where his family remained for several generations.

John Leeds's Farm at Beck Hall

Beck Hall, Billingford, was purchased by Sir Edward Coke in 1606. The agricultural history of this block of land in the centre of the county was rather different from that of the Holkham area. Here the soils were generally heavier than the light chalklands of north-west Norfolk. Piecemeal enclosure had taken place in many parishes by the mid eighteenth century and only small areas of open fields with foldcourse rights and common were left to be enclosed by parliamentary act.

A Robert Leeds took a 21-year lease of Beck Hall in 1725 and one William Leeds in 1776. When that lease came to an end, William Leeds moved away and it was 1810 before a member of the Leeds family returned to Beck Hall. By this time the landscape of Billingford had been changed by the enclosure of the commons and open fields in the north of the parish. It was probably at this time that the acreage of the farm was increased to 653 acres. We know that John Parmeter Leeds, the writer of the journal, was born in 1802 on the Leeds family farm (now called Oak Farm) at Kerdistone, a few miles from Billingford, to Thomas Leeds and his wife, Sarah. Oak Farm covered 270 acres and the house was a modest, but genteel, Georgian residence to which John retired when he gave up the lease of Beck Hall in 1858. His mother's family, the Parmeters, were a well-established family in the nearby market town of Aylsham where, according to White's directory of 1845, Robert was a solicitor, agent to the Blickling estate and Clerk of the Peace while Samuel was a corn miller and maltster. John Leeds' cousin John Parmeter was vicar of the tiny parish of Alderford, just south of Reepham. When the family moved back to Beck Hall in 1810, Thomas Leeds was 42 and John eight years old. He was probably the eldest son. The diary suggests that he had three sisters, Mary, Ann and Sarah. There is a gravestone in Billingford churchyard to Thomas Womack Leeds who died aged 11 in 1820. The inscription commemorates two further children, Christian and William who died as infants. John's grandfather, John, died in 1823, aged 88, and was buried in the family vault at Reepham, next to his wife, Sarah, who had

---

32   Holkham MS, E/G11, Kent's survey of Warham, 1785–89, p. 22.
33   Holkham MS, E/G12, H.W. Keary, 'Report on the Holkham estate', 1851, pp. 40–42.

died earlier the same year. The existence of a family vault suggests an affluent and well-established background. The death at the age of 49 of John Parmeter Leeds's mother is recorded in the diary in 1824 and she was buried in the nave of Billingford church.

The arrival of Thomas at Beck Hall heralded the beginning of a period of improvement. In 1815 a thatched field barn was built in the recently enclosed fields to the north.[34] Leeds mentions the feeding of cattle and the threshing of wheat at the fieldbarn in May and June 1827. When Blaikie visited the farm in 1816 there was 'a very great extent of young hedges'. The poor soils were being improved by marling and as a result, produced 'abundant crops of corn'. The bog land (the area of Pinchings Common) was about to be seeded for pasture and a new 21-year lease was promised as soon as the improvements were complete and was granted in 1816 at a rent of £465. The farm was suitably run under a five-course shift. It was 'generally clean and in good heart', the stock good and the corn fine.[35] The lease was renewed for a further 21 years in 1839 by Thomas's son (the author of the journal) at a rent increased to £560, a reflection of the general trend in increases on the estate during the profitable mid nineteenth century years.

Improvements continued into the 1820s and work on the new house and premises was being paid for in the period of the diary (1822–29),[36] although they are not mentioned in it. Possibly work was finished by 1823 but was financed over a longer period, a typical method of accounting at the time. There are few references to land improvement although gravel carting is mentioned twice.[37]

As one of the larger farms on the estate, Beck Hall, needs to be seen as one of a small group of about a dozen particularly desirable farms on the Holkham estate and as such was likely to attract a tenant from amongst the elite set of gentry-tenant families which led farming society in Norfolk. The fact that the Leeds family were also landowners on some scale meant that they mixed socially with the minor gentry. Indeed, *White's Directory* (1845) included Beck Hall in its list of 'seats of the nobility, gentry and clergy' together with only two other Holkham farms. One further fact that distinguished Beck Hall Farm from many other tenanted farms was that its tenant leased the shooting rights, presumably because it was so far from Holkham that the landlord could not easily enjoy them himself. This allowed the Leeds family to indulge in a pastime usually limited to landowners. The diary makes it clear that it enabled them to cross the social divide into the minor gentry class.

---

34   Holkham MS, A/Au.
35   Holkham MS, E/G9.
36   Holkham MS, A/Au.
37   LD, 25 June 1824, 23 May 1826.

At 653 acres, Beck Hall was above average size, even for the Holkham estate. The soils varied from light gravels suited to sheep in the south, to stronger loams in the north. To the north of the field barn was 'good mixed loam upon excellent clay'. The fields in the centre of the farm were useful pasture lands 'some of it low lying and well-adapted for mowing'. The Holkham agent, William Keary, wrote:

> There is not perhaps on the Holkham estate a more desirable occupation, for although there are unquestionably farms which possess naturally a better soil, there are few which combine so many advantages and are capable of being turned to so good an account.

The mixture of soils meant that in all weathers and all seasons there was work that could be done and the occupier was able to withstand 'any sudden transition in the price of grain'. Wool, mutton and beef all formed an important part of the income of this truly mixed farm.[38]

IV

As Thomas Moore's diaries cover an earlier period than that of John Leeds, they will be considered first. They begin in January 1799, when the national average for grain prices reached an all-time high of 130s. a quarter. Moore noted in his diary that the price at the nearby market town of Fakenham was 42s. a comb (or 84s. a quarter) – still a very profitable price. Not surprisingly then, he was able to go to Holkham on 15 January and 'pay Mr Coke in full rent'. The reason for these high prices was the strengthening grip of the war with France and with it, increasing fears of invasion. Coke, who had argued in Parliament against the need for war, was persuaded of the need for a local militia to defend the country in the event of French troops landing and so set up his own Holkham cavalry.[39] To this the tenantry were expected to enrol and on 29 March, Thomas Moore attended its first meeting. On 6 May he 'dined with the troop to celebrate Mr Coke's birthday' and on 12 June he attended a muster in the park. There were further musters in July and August, but by the following year, with the signing of a truce with France, the danger seemed over and on 6 May, he attended 'Holkham with the cavalry to deliver up all our arms'. Other than this short episode, and the welcome high prices for wheat that it brought, the war seems to have impinged very little on Moore's life. High prices may have been very profitable for farmers, but there was a downside for the poor. In his diary Moore noted in January

---

38   Holkham MS, E/G12, Keary, 'Report'.
39   Wade Martins, *Coke of Norfolk*, pp. 73–4.

1802, 'Wheat meal being 2s. 6d. a stone, ordered that all children of my parish should have 3d. a head weekly and widows 6d'.

Mr Coke and other activities of the estate are frequently mentioned in the diary. Because Holkham was no more than five miles away from Moore at Hall Farm, there was likely to be frequent contact. The sheep shearing was an annual highlight. On 29 May 1799 Moore went to Holkham for the shearings and 'dined with 90 gentlemen, one of whom was the Duke of Bedford'. The following year he went over for each of the three days, dined with 200 gentlemen and bought some Southdown sheep in the auction on the final day. In 1801 he joined 300 guests for dinner and 'rode with a large party to Burnham to see a fly trap'. (This, he explains, was invented by Mr Paul of Starston to catch turnip fly. It won a prize in the implement category at the 1807 sheep shearings and is likely to have been a board, covered underneath with a sticky substance which could be drawn across the turnips and to which the fly would stick. Similar implements are described in farming manuals of the time.)

Arranging meetings with Coke himself could be difficult. On several occasions, Moore rode over to Holkham in the hope of discussing business such as the renewal of his lease, only to find he was not at home. Sometimes, however, there were informal contacts. In June 1809 Moore breakfasted with his landlord and then 'rode afarming with him'.

The Holkham estate steward at the time was Francis Crick and many of the dealings that he had with his landlord were through Crick. We know very little of Crick's responsibilities except that he kept the accounts. His salary of up to £300 a year was far less than Blaikie's maximum of £650, which suggests that his duties were rather fewer.[40] Sometimes Crick would go to Warham. On 4 January 1802 he went to pay for 30 lbs of butter for Mr Coke and on the 28 October 1805 he was there giving permission for the demolition of 'some old walls in front of the house'. In November 1807 Mr Crick came to Warham to 'settle the rental of this parish'. Again, at the end of 1809 'Mr Crick took in the Warham tenants' bills and all of them dined here'. Although it was Coke himself who presented Moore with his proposal for the new lease, it was Crick who carried out the detailed negotiations. In March 1805 'Mr Coke called and offered me my farm again'. In October Moore went to Holkham to see Mr Coke 'who delivered his proposals for the new lease' and a week later Moore delivered his response in writing. There were several breakfasts with Mr Crick at Holkham in 1805 when the terms of the new lease were discussed and finally he met Coke to agree the terms. It was not until 1809 that the lease, running from 1806 to 1827, was signed. Part of this agreement involved the building of an extension to the house and later in the year Mr and Mrs Crick came to Warham so that Mr Crick could measure the brick work. Some visits were more social. In May 1807

---

[40]   Ibid., p. 55.

Moore rode to Holkham 'and took some wine with Mr Crick' and again a few days later 'took tea and supper with Mr Crick'. Occasionally Mr Coke also came to Warham. In December 1807 he came 'on a farming ride', while in October the same year 'Mr Coke and a party of ladies and gentlemen came to shoot'. Moore was also on friendly terms with the Holkham farm manager, Edward Wright who died in 1809. Moore was a pall bearer at his funeral.

As well as visits to Holkham for business, Thomas Moore also went for pleasure. On 2 July 1799 he took Mrs Moore to see the hall and on the 28 June 1805 'went with a party to see the grounds at Holkham'. Other visits to the Hall and grounds are also recorded. In 1807 he attended shoots at Holkham when 1,457 head were shot in three days.

One of the duties of a tenant was to support his landlord politically and Moore regularly rode to Norwich at election time. July 1802 saw the first contested election for many years and Moore rode from Trowse on the outskirts of Norwich with the cavalcade of Coke's supporters to the polling booths where he spent most of the day. Voting took place over several days and it was 10 days before Moore returned home. In the election of 1807 Coke was returned with his fellow Whig, Sir Jacob Astley, unopposed, but there was still a cavalcade of supporters into the city.

It is clear therefore that his landlord and the estate played a part in Moore's life socially, politically and agriculturally. He went to the hall frequently to pay his rent, less often to discuss the terms of his lease and improvements to his house and buildings. Sometimes this involved meetings with Coke, but more usually with his steward. He also visited Holkham with family and friends to view the house and enjoy the grounds. On one occasion he went shooting there. The sheep shearings and the dinners which accompanied them were also highlights of the year.

Thomas Moore's diary contains some details of his farming methods. As we would expect, the farm was run as a mixed farm, with livestock forming an important part of the enterprise, providing the majority of manure used on the farm.

Both sheep and cattle were kept. In 1805 Moore describes clipping 145 breeding ewes with six shearers, but what breed these sheep were is not clear. Moore was farming at a period when Coke (along with other farmers) was trying new breeds of sheep to cross with the native Norfolk horn.[41] Initially, Coke favoured Leicesters and it was these that he was promoting at the sheep shearings, but later he turned his attentions to Southdowns and Moore records interest in both breeds. In August 1799 he went to a sale of Leicesters near Kings Lynn, but does not say whether he bought any. He describes putting 12 horned wethers

---

[41] S. Wade Martins, 'From black-face to white-face: An aspect of the Agricultural Revolution in Norfolk', *AgHR* 41 (1993), pp. 20–30.

on a 12-acre field and these are most likely to have been the native Norfolks. In 1802 he was selling both half-bred and Southdown wool and in June he hired and bought rams from Holkham. Again in 1805 he bought 10 [South] down shearlings from Coke at the sheep shearings. By 1809 he had developed a Southdown flock to the extent that he could produce a Southdown wether of a sufficiently high quality to win a cup at the shearings. It is clear therefore that he was amongst the leading farmers who were intent on improving the quality of their flocks by introducing the new breeds of sheep. No doubt he was influenced by the enthusiasm of his landlord.

Cattle were probably mostly bought in as stores and fattened for the London market. These are variously described as 'Scots' and 'Highlanders' and would have been driven down to London for sale. In 1802 Moore went to Smithfield himself to see them sold. Whilst turnips would have been their most important winter feed, Moore describes how in 1805, he was trying them on linseed cake. Whether he had been feeding cake before this is not clear, but he was certainly buying and grinding it in 1799. The use of oil cake, made from the byproduct of crushing oil-rich seeds such as rape and linseed, as a feed was beginning to become established at the end of the eighteenth century, but did not become widespread until the middle of the nineteenth century.

The diary reveals a little about the crops that were grown and methods of cultivation. Turnips are mentioned. In June 1799, Moore 'sowed some turnips myself with the engine' (presumably a seed drill). The diaries also record the drilling of peas (March 1805), wheat (October 1799 and November 1805) and barley (April 1805). Drilling was gradually replacing broadcast sowing and the more labour-intensive dibbling at the time. In March 1799 he bought one of Mr Cooke's cultivators and at the end of the year he paid Mr Archer for 'carriage of a cultivator from London, an engine from Thetford and a corn drill'. There is only one reference (in October 1802) to dibbling seed; this was occasionally favoured by farmers because it was less wasteful. Some of the oil cake was being used to feed cattle while some was also being used as a fertiliser, a practice found on the Holkham estate well back into the eighteenth century.[42] In April 1809 Moore was 'sowing oil cake for turnips' and then ploughing it in. When it came to harvest he adopted the newer method of mowing part of the crop with a scythe to enable a closer cut and thus producing more straw for yard bedding for in-wintering. In some fields he kept to the older method of reaping with a sickle leaving a high stubble which could be fed off to animals in the field.

Other than the seed drill, the main mechanical advance was the threshing machine, available by the 1790s, but only slowly taken up in the low-wage areas of southern Britain over the next three decades. In 1809 Moore bought his own

---

[42]   For instance, Holkham MS, Holkham Deed 1067; Labour accounts for 1732 list the purchase and breaking of 4,700 rapecakes amongst the expenses for marling and mucking the fields.

threshing machine at a time when there were very few in Norfolk. High grain prices and a lack of labour during the Napoleonic Wars may have encouraged this investment. However, there were problems. It arrived at the end of March, and on 4 April Moore records that 'Tuttell got the threshing machine to work about nine'. On the 12 April the machine worked all day, but the next day the horse wheel broke and the next week he took his wheat to Mr Coke's machine. By the end of the year it was working again and in November 'began to thresh barley with machine, being the finish of this year's crop'.

More important to the progressive farmer than the crops grown was the rotation under which they were cultivated. A field book for all the farms on the estate was kept up at Holkham from 1789 to 1805. This listed what crop was grown in every field on all the farms:

> The benefit which results from a check of this kind upon the tenants of a large estate is very great as it fully guards against any improper course of cropping and by showing what has been the past system of husbandry upon any particular farm, a landlord, or agent is the better enabled to judge what regulation to lay it under in future.[43]

Thirty-one arable fields are listed on Moore's farm, and in the few cases when it is possible to check the record against the diaries it appears that the field book is accurate. Wheat followed by turnips, barley and then one or two years ley was the norm (in other words the conventional four-course), although two consecutive crops of cereals were sometimes grown, but only after two years of ley.

There are many references in the diaries to the negotiations over Moore's new lease which ran for 21 years from 1806, but was not finally agreed until 1809.[44] As well as the general statement that the arable should be managed in a 'careful and husband-like manner' the acreages of each crop were also stipulated. While 140 acres of the farm would be growing cash crops in the form of wheat and barley, 260 acres would be under fodder crops such as turnips, tares and vetches, and grass of either one- or two-year ley. To keep the lighter soils of north Norfolk in 'good heart' and provide enough animal feed to keep the stock needed to provide manure before the days of artificial fertilisers, it was necessary that nearly two-thirds was under fodder crops.

Thomas Moore's farming was thus typical of that practised by other large light-land farmers of his time, with their own flocks of breeding ewes and bought-in young cattle for fattening. Crops would have included cereals and turnips as well as pasture and hay. New feeds and fertilisers in the form of oil cake were being tried as well as limited mechanisation in the form of seed drills

---

43 Holkham MS, E/G8, 'Field book'.
44 Holkham MS, T/M/11, Moore papers.

and threshing machines. He was trying new methods, such as mowing, in place of the more labour-intensive reaping of cereals. However, labour was cheap, and there were plenty of women available to Moore to weed his crops.

V

John Leeds was only 19 when he started keeping his diary although he noted that it was continued from 'my former book'. It is not certain what sort of education he had received. In January 1827, he went with his school friend, John Willis, to see his old teacher in Hingham, whom he had not seen for seven years, suggesting that he left school at 16. He may well have been a pupil at Hingham Grammar School, founded in 1727 and which by the 1840s was taking some 40 boarders. If he was, he would have acquired a conventional classical education. The first 60 pages of the book in which the journal is written is taken up by extracts made from a text book on English history and Johnson and Boswell's *Tour of the Hebrides*, as well as snippets of poetry and theology. The diary is written in a clear hand and in good English and contains quotations from Sir John Sinclair's statistical writings as well as various veterinary and agricultural text books. Leeds read widely and kept abreast with the news, noting significant details. He went to the theatre, to concerts and to Mr Jackson's lectures in Dereham on 'galvarism, electricity and so on explaining various subjects of which I had before but a very imperfect idea'.[45] All of this suggests a good education by the standards of the day as well as an enquiring, if perhaps not very lively, mind.

If John left school at about 16, we do not know what he was doing in the intervening years. It is possible that he spent a period as a farm pupil elsewhere. The diary suggests that at only 19, John Leeds was involved in the running of the farm although it was always rented in his father's name. It is possible that his father was running the farm at Kerdistone, especially after the death of John Leeds senior in 1823, leaving some of the day-to-day affairs of the Billingford farm to his son. We do not know why John kept his journal and it is may be that it was seen by his father as part of his 'apprenticeship' as a farmer. He was expected to go about the farm every day and keep a record of the progress of work as well as prices given and received for grain and stock. Occasionally he comments that the diary has not been kept fully, 'because of the lack of a book'.[46] Possibly he kept notes which he then copied up.

It is difficult to know how much influence the Holkham estate had on John Leeds's social and farming life, but it was certainly far less than on Moore. He attended the sheep shearings and either he or his father, the audit. On the 11

---

[45] LD, 9 Apr. 1827.
[46] LD, Feb. 1825 and Oct. 1827.

January 1825, 'being the first Tuesday of the month went to the audit; found Mr Coke and family in perfect health'. He went to the sheep shearings at the end of July. The entry for 24 July 1824 reads, 'Went to Holkham with a party. Messrs Tuck, Gilbert and Bullock – met a large farming party and had of course an agreeable visit'. More detail is given in 1827: 'Went to Holkham to the usual farming party with shepherds Whaites, Bullock and Gilbert. Met a large party of yeoman from most parts of the country. Mr C. in fine spirits, the party altogether a very pleasant one, the Park Farm looking very well in most respects'.[47]

Mr Blaikie is occasionally mentioned when he passed through on his way to the elections in Norwich (18 June 1826) or was holding a manorial court in the area (22 October 1824). Blaikie's name, so well known in Roxburghshire agricultural circles, gave Leeds and his companions an entree into farming society there when they travelled to Scotland in 1825, but there is no indication that Blaikie called to inspect the farm or discuss farming matters. This in sharp contrast to the situation at Warham. It is likely that Beck Hall was too far from Holkham Hall itself to be within the area readily supervised by the estate. Not until the opening of the railway line through Elmham from Wells to East Dereham in 1857 did agents make regular visits.

We know from the estate descriptions of Beck Hall that its great advantage was the variety of land which it contained, allowing its tenant to withstand crises in different sectors of the market. The light land was good sheep land with the heavier soils more suited to cattle. 'Wool, mutton and beef' on this farm were 'perhaps more important sources of profit than cereal crops',[48] and certainly the buying, fattening and selling of stock was an important activity recorded in the diary. It is difficult to be sure how many animals were on the farm at any one time. The number of sheep clipped is an indication of the number kept for more than one season. On the 10 February 1825 the 'last of the fat sheep', 200 in number, were sold, presumably as the winter feed was eaten up. In 1826 340 were shorn, whilst the following year, the number was 216, 'rather less than we usually have at this time of year'.[49] Frequently however, over 400 were being fattened on the farm. In May 1825 403 hoggetts were bought at 'an extravagant price' (34s. to 36s. a head) at Swaffham fair.

Sometimes the breed of the sheep is mentioned. Like Thomas Moore and many of his contemporaries, John Leeds kept Southdowns. Only in the first year of the diary is lambing mentioned, and then a Leicester tup was used. Possibly in later years the breeding flock was replaced by a fattening one.

The keeping of sheep was a risky business with great losses in many years. In 1824 scab was a problem, whilst the following year 50 were lost 'through extreme

---

[47] LD, 30–31 July 1827.

[48] Holkham MS, E/G12.

[49] LD, 11 June 1827.

bad luck; indeed never worse'.[50] The following January the flock were bled 'to prevent, if possible, further loss'. At the end of the month they were bled again, 'having such intolerable bad luck and what is worse, unable to account for the loss'. On the 15 February Leeds sold his flock, diminished from 340 to 300, but a few weeks later he was restocking with 60 sheep for which he paid 35s. each, 'Great chance if they pay anything for keeping'.[51] A final hazard was rustling. Sheep stealing occurred twice, on both occasions in November. Four were stolen the first time 'and what is worse, undetected', but only one two years later.[52]

Because of the problems of disease, it is difficult to be sure how much profit the sheep made. Lambs varied in price from 20s. to 25s. and hoggets (one-year-olds) from 33s. to 36s. When fat they could be sold for anything from 40 to 52s., which could represent a doubling in value over two to three years. However, without precise figures for the cost of feeding, this is a meaningless figure. Certainly Leeds was often rather depressed by their return.

Cattle appear to have been a safer venture. There is no mention in the journal of calves being reared on the farm. Instead, a mixture of homebreds and scots, usually weighing between 50 and 54 stones and probably four-year-olds, were bought from various sources including Norfolk's celebrated St Faith's fair. Prices varied from £9 to £11 10s. Fourteen 'pretty good heifers at £13' were considered 30s. too dear.[53] Usually just over a hundred cattle were kept through the winter, divided between three yards with some often housed at the Kerdistone farm. They were fed roots and, from early January, oilcake, bought at a cost of about £5 a ton. From 1823 Leeds was experimenting with beet (mangel wurzel) as a fodder crop which he found more productive and nutritious than turnips. It was being grown on the home farm at Holkham by 1817. Leeds, first growing it in 1823, described it as a 'tolerable crop' (4 November 1823). In 1825 he was pleased with the yield ('excellent produce – 20 bargains an acre').[54] In April the following year he quotes Messrs Lindsey and Newby on the advantages of mangel wurzel. According to them, 'Mr R.C. Harvey' claimed to have grown two-thirds more in weight of mangel wurzel than of swedish turnips. Leeds noted 'The enormous quantity of 54 tons has been grown per *acre*'. However there seems to have been some confusion with sugar beet because he continued:

Bonaparte caused this invaluable crop to be cultivated purposely to extract sugar (producing) 9 cwt of well-grained powder sugar and 130 gallons of rectified

[50] LD, 29 Mar. 1825.
[51] LD, 25 Feb. 1826.
[52] LD, 28 Nov. 1825, 6 Nov. 1827.
[53] LD, 2 Mar. 1825.
[54] LD, 12 Nov. 1825.

spirit besides the green leaves for the cattle and the dross of the distillation for pigs, etc.[55]

In May he wrote, 'going strong into beetroot'. It produced 20 tons an acre, which, Leeds regarded as 'prolific' although this was a very dry year.[56] On the 26 December 1826, he wrote, 'Ascertained that a smaller quantity of beet will suffice for the same yard of cattle. Ten and a half loads enough for 23 heifers or 12 stone a day for each beast'. The main problem seems to have been the labour needed to stack it. At the end of the previous October, he had recorded, 'Finished at last stacking beet – an expensive substitute for turnips, 1006 loads at Billingford and Kerdistone'. Nevertheless, he was pleased with its qualities as a feed and he grew it again the following year.

The collecting and preparing of 1½ cwt of turnips a day must have provided full-time employment for several men during the winter months. In the spring the beasts went out to grass and were sold, as they came ready, mostly to the local dealer. Leeds was usually pleased with the price, which varied from £16 to £24. For instance on 30 May 1826 he sold Mr Mayes 13 Scots beasts at £24 each, 'paying pretty well for a year's keep'. One bullock was bitten by a viper in September 1825 and a heifer had fallen into a clay pit the previous year. Generally, however, there do not seem to have been the same problems with the cattle as there were with the sheep, and Leeds admitted that they often fetched 'a very good price without any risk'.[57]

Like Moore, some 25 years before, Leeds relied on manure to fertilise his fields. The journal describes the removal of the manure from the yards and the spreading of it on the fields. The only other source of off-farm fertiliser was oil cake which was not only fed to cattle, but is recorded in 1824 and 1827 as being spread at about one ton per acre on land during the autumn before cereal crops and in June before turnips.[58]

A variety of crops were grown. Wheat, peas, barley, turnips, swedes and mangel wurzel as well as hay crops including trefoil, suckling and ryegrass are all mentioned. The usual seasonal pattern of land preparation, sowing, weeding and harvest can be followed in the journal. As at Warham, barley was spring sown and wheat an autumn-sown crop. Roots were sown in the late spring and early summer and consumed during the winter.

The Holkham field book shows what was grown on the Beck Hall fields before John Leeds's time.[59] Only a few fields were under a conventional four-

---

55   LD, 28 Apr. 1826.

56   LD, 28 Oct. 1826.

57   LD, 24 May 1825.

58   LD, 26 Sept. 1823, 14 June 1824, 6 Oct. 1825, 26 Mar., 6 June 1827.

59   Holkham MS, E/G8.

course, sometimes extended to five with grass being left for a second year. The six-course recommended by Kent[60] was followed in several fields (wheat, barley, turnips, barley followed by two years' grass). This allowed half of the shift to be in cereals, and sometimes one of the grass years would be replaced by peas. Of the 27 fields, the number under cereal in any one year varied from nine to 14 (a third to over a half). The result was a great variety of rotations across the farm. It was presumably to instil some sort of order that the husbandry covenant became more formalised under Blaikie after 1816. However, from the diary, we shall see that such tidy systems were easier to put on paper than enforce in practice. The practice of taking two crops of corn in succession continued into the 1820s.

The first surviving record of a four-course rotation (wheat→roots→barley→grass) being stipulated in a Holkham lease is in 1815, and with the appointment of Francis Blaikie as agent in 1816, it became a standard requirement.[61] Blaikie saw his role as one 'to convince a farmer that it is not to his advantage to take *quite* as many corn crops from the land he occupies as it will bear'.[62] Of course, this was not such a difficult task in the years of falling grain prices after the end of the Napoleonic Wars as it might have been earlier. As we have seen, when Blaikie visited Beck Hall in 1816, it was occupied 'under the promise of a lease for 21 years' (to commence at Michaelmas 1816), and farmed under a five-course shift. The evidence of the field book quoted earlier for the variety of rotations practised suggests this might be an over-simplification.

In 1817 Blaikie wrote his *General Form of leases to be Granted by T.W.C. Esq. on his Estate in the County of Norfolk with Forms of Covenants for Cultivating the Arable Lands and Approved of by Francis Blaikie Gentleman*, laying down a series of four, five and six-course shifts. In fact the six-course shifts were never used and nearly all farms were let under a four-course scheme (Blaikie's type A). Occasionally his type C, which imposed alternate four and five courses, with grass left for two years every other rotation, was used on poorer soils and this was the one discussed between Blaikie and Thomas Leeds when Blaikie visited Beck Hall to negotiate its lease. It stipulated that not more than four-ninths of the arable should be in cereals in any one year (somewhat less than that allowed to Moore). This is the lease under which John Leeds would have been expected to run the farm.

The survival in the letter books of numerous applications by tenants to depart from the terms of their leases suggests that they were taken seriously and that the tenants felt permission was required for even the smallest deviation. However, an analysis of the admittedly spasmodic entries in the journal, referring to crops grown in the various fields at Beck Hall, suggests that the regular rotations made

---

[60]   N. Kent, *General View of the Agriculture of Norfolk* (1813 edn), pp. 223–5.

[61]   Parker, *Coke of Norfolk*, pp. 100–105.

[62]   Holkham MS, E/C1/1, 1816 Letter Book, p. 129.

famous through the leases of the Holkham estate were not necessarily always practised here. The journal only covers five years, so it is not possible to follow through the full nine years which the four, followed by five-year shift of Blaikie's type C rotation would cover. In several fields a four-course appears to have been practised, whilst in others it was a five-course with two years of grass, suggesting that here the nine-year pattern was being implemented. Barley was sometimes replaced in the rotation by seeds or oats, and this would have been acceptable. There are five occasions when peas are mentioned. Under the five-course shift which was part of the rotation laid down in Leeds's lease he could choose to grow peas *instead* of grain after grass and before turnips. Under the six-course, which Blaikie had rejected, peas could be grown *between* wheat and barley. The five examples of peas being grown which are recorded in the diary show them *between*, not *instead* of grain crops, suggesting that Leeds had decided to take the law into his own hands and crop under the system as he thought best.

More serious, from the estate's point of view, there were two fields where the golden rule of no corn crops two years in succession was broken. On the Home Close wheat was even grown for four out of five years. No explanation for this is given in the diary, or in the Holkham letter books. The only conclusion to draw is that when it is possible to check what was actually happening on the ground, we find that the rotations laid down in the leases were not rigidly followed. There is no suggestion in the diary that Blaikie ever visited Beck Hall to check what was being grown and, perhaps because it was so far from Holkham, Leeds felt safe to do more or less what he liked. Fallow had by now been completely superseded, but in general, he appears to have carried on cropping much as his predecessors had 20 years previously.

Besides information on crop rotations, the diary gives further insights into arable farming. As at Warham earlier, roots were almost always drilled to ensure they grew in rows, allowing for hoeing to clean the ground between the rows. However, there is one entry which suggests that turnip seed was sometimes hand-sown, 'the ridge system being but a slow process, though I think, sure'.[63] This method was described to Arthur Young by Leeds' neighbour, Mr Blomfield of Billingford in 1802. The ridges were set out with a two-furrow plough and the manure laid in the furrows. The seeds were then sown broadcast and the ridges split into the furrows. 'The turnips came up regularly on flat land in rows at two feet'.[64] There are no references to this practice elsewhere; it must have been an idiosyncratic local method.

The cereal crops could either be drilled or sown. As with roots, drilling allowed for hoeing. In March 1824, a field of wheat was hoed 'being full of beggarly imposters'. In September 1825, Leeds wrote, 'As proof of sown wheat

---

[63]   LD, 18 May 1824.

[64]   Young, *Norfolk*, p. 225.

being sometimes advantageous, Mr Sam Bircham relates an instance of a field near Reepham producing nine combs 16 [pecks?] per acre'. In the autumn of 1826 he tried the labour-intensive system of dibbling wheat, costing 8*s.* an acre, 'a new plan here',[65] although common in other parts of Norfolk. There is no record of whether it was judged successful.

Harvest was always a worrying time with days lost through wet weather. Corn that had been cut and stooked but not carted might have to be turned to stop it rotting and there were years when Leeds bemoaned the fact that there was likely to be much black (or rotted) barley gathered. 1826 was a dry year which meant the crop was light, but its harvesting quick and easy. The previous year's harvest had been difficult and late, resulting in two harvests in 12 months on the farm.[66] No yields are given for cereals, so there is no way of judging comparatively the success or otherwise of Leeds' cereal farming methods.

Knowing when to sell grain could be as much of a skill as buying and selling stock and hardly a week went by when either John or his father did not go to Norwich to visit the corn dealers, who then met in St Andrew's Hall. Prices not only depended on the quality and availability of grain, but also on outside pressures; uncertainties over changes in the corn laws especially resulting in low prices. Leeds reported in May 1825, 'corn market rather dull today from the expected alteration with regard to the free trade in that article. A delightful prospect for the farmer'. The complex working of the Laws meant the level of import duty varied with the market price of the home-grown crop. In November 1824, Leeds wrote 'Price of corn lower today owing to the rascally tricks of a few speculators in endeavouring to force averages in order to open the ports to foreign barley, but happily seen through by inspectors' and, later that month, 'Lower [grain] prices anticipated owing to the ports being open for that article'.[67] Even the weather could affect prices with fewer people attending market on a wet day.

The general depression in 1826, following the banking and commercial crisis of 1825, had a severe effect on grain prices. In January 1826 wheat was sold to Mr Foster for 50s. a quarter, 'being a very good price considering the depressed state of things which appear to grow worse rather than better'.[68]

This was not a period, in East Anglia at least, when the development of mechanisation in agriculture was important. The availability of a large cheap labour force who would have had to be supported from the poor rate if unemployed, meant that it was hardly worth it. Leeds is typical of most farmers at this time in his slow adoption of new machinery. Seeds were still frequently

---

[65] LD, 24 Sept. 1826.
[66] LD, 4–10 Sept. 1825, 21 Aug. 1826.
[67] LD, 13 Nov. 1824.
[68] LD, 28 Jan. 1826.

sown broadcast, although seed drills were used for much of the barley and root crop.

The change from reaping with sickles to leave a high stubble, to mowing with scythes to produce more straw, was also a slow one and as at Warham, both methods were used in most years. In the harvest of 1824 the wheat was reaped and the barley mown. In 1825 some wheat was mown 'owing to the land being very fowl, a slovenly way in my opinion, although in this instance very essential in order to get the land clean'.[69] In 1826, Leeds had to admit that mowing was faster; 'able to get over the ground twice as fast, doing nearly one and a half acres a day with one scythe', but he still regarded it as 'slovenly'.[70] The reason for this prejudice is obscure. His neighbour, Mr Hart, in 1843, commented that he had mown his cereals for 20 years, 'the extra straw produced is well worth it'.[71]

Flails for threshing were certainly still used at Beck Hall throughout the period of the diary. However other methods were also employed. A treadmill for working a threshing machine is first mentioned in March 1824, and in November, Leeds wrote, 'Thrashing out old red wheat with the treadmill at 15d. per c[o]mb, much cheaper than by horse power, if otherwise harder' – an indication of the cheapness and abundance of labour in contrast to the wartime situation experienced by Moore. Two years later, however a two-horse power engine was being used and the threshing could be done for 1s. per comb (3d. cheaper than with the treadmill). Leeds admitted that it 'was doing the work very well'.[72] We can see therefore, that a gradual change was taking place as mowing was replacing reaping and seed drills and threshing machines were taking over from the more labour-intensive methods. By the 1840s, when R.N. Bacon wrote his survey of Norfolk agriculture, these changes were almost entirely complete, at least on the large farms his enquiries encompassed. All the Holkham tenants who answered his questionnaire generally drilled rather than dibbled their crops and threshing by machine in place of the flail was common practice.[73]

Leeds was farming through far more difficult times than those described by Moore. The early 1820s were not good years for the agricultural interest. The post-war dislocation and return to the gold standard, completed by May 1823, caused economic deflation, and a series of good harvests between 1821 and 1824 resulted in a fall in grain prices. Even the protection of the corn laws could not prevent prices falling. Wheat values fell from between 40 and 50s. a quarter in 1815 to as low as 16s. at the trough of the depression in 1822; 1821–22 were the worst recorded years for the Holkham estate, with arrears for 1821 standing

[69] LD, 3 Aug. 1825.

[70] LD, 4 Sept. 1826.

[71] Norfolk RO, MFRO 11, Bacon's questionnaires 1842.

[72] LD, 13 Mar. 1826.

[73] Norfolk RO, MFRO 11.

at £10,500 out of a total rental of just over £30,000. Farms were given up and rebates of up to 30 per cent had to be agreed.[74] When the journal begins, at the end of 1823, conditions were only just beginning to improve. Leeds records in September that 'The market for corn especially dull; quite as much so as it was last season'.[75] The price certainly seems to have been very volatile varying from 28s. ('hardly a remunerative price') to 70s. ('a fair remunerative price').[76] After harvest in 1824 'The corn mart very dull owing to the new being so good and plentiful; we being unfortunate enough to hold our last'. By the autumn the price had steadied to 66s. a quarter for wheat and 44s. for barley, 'a very remunerative price'.[77]

However, far more serious was the financial crisis of 1825–26. As soon as trade had recovered from the immediate post-war problems, there was a wave of speculation, particularly in the newly recognised states of South America. Much of this speculation was questionable and by March 1825, the government was issuing warnings to that effect. The crisis broke in November 1825, reaching a peak on 13–14 December when six London banks (on which many country banks relied) failed. Country banks were calling in mortgages and accumulating gold while the city and many provincial towns were swept by panic. Altogether, between harvest 1825 and harvest 1826 over 60 country banks collapsed across England.[78]

Leeds's journal give us an insight as to how the shockwaves of the banking crisis could percolate down to a farming community innocent of financial speculation. In December, Leeds noted:

> The price of grain just now very dull, as well as the general state of things, from the extreme depression of the money markets, the funds having fallen by 10 per cent and the mercantile and manufacturing interests equally unhinged and without any apparent cause at present assigned.

In Norwich Messrs Day were the main casualty, mentioned by Leeds as 'bringing great distress upon some of our nearest neighbours'.[79] His own family lost £57 10s. through the collapse of Squire and Edmonds, a bank of which no other record has been found.[80] Rumours were rife and on Christmas Eve he heard that

---

74   Parker, *Coke of Norfolk*, p. 148.
75   LD, 20 Sept. 1823.
76   LD, 20 Oct., 6 Dec. 1823, 28 Jan. 1824.
77   LD, 28 Aug., 20 Nov. 1824.
78   L.S. Pressnell, *Country Banking in the Industrial Revolution* (Oxford, 1956), pp. 489–90.
79   LD, 19 Dec. 1825.
80   LD, 27 Dec. 1825.

'the well known and respectable Mr Harvey of Alburgh' (a partner in the Crown Bank in Norwich) had 'fallen a victim to his hazardous speculations'.[81] In spite of these problems, Leeds' father managed to pay his rent throughout this crisis, with no arrears recorded against him in the audit books. The grain markets remained unsettled into January 1826, 'not knowing who to deal with in the midst of these broken times'.[82] By the end of February prices began to recover although they were still uncertain. Concern shifted back to the corn laws and in May, Leeds was complaining of the 'hazardous times during the premeditated alteration in the system of business'.[83] At the end of the year a meeting was held at the Kings Arms in Reepham to put together a petition against changes in their structure. Leeds was critical of the apathy of the local farmers, 'The farmers as usual sleeping over their interests, but few attended in proportion to their numbers'.[84] By 1827 prices seem to have steadied as confidence returned to the markets.

VI

Although the two diaries are 20 or so years apart the social activities described in them are very similar. Both men went regularly to market, Leeds to Norwich and Moore to Fakenham. Both attended the annual dinners to celebrate Coke's birthday and the sheep shearings at Holkham. A pastime frequently mentioned by Moore was to go 'afarming' with a friend. This seems to have involved riding around looking at the farms of neighbours. In May 1805 for instance, he went 'afarming with Mr Sewell this morning – dined at Barton – back by nine'.

Moore describes visits to family and friends, dinners with Mr Crick, trips to the theatre in Wells and the coursing club there. On the 20 May 1799 he attended the Association in Walsingham and went from there to Wells to see Mr Bloom[field's?] new ship – the 'Patriot' – launched. 'I spent a late evening at The Fleece'. There were occasional journeys to London where he would visit Smithfield and go to the theatre and in April 1799 he 'sat for my likeness'. Visits to Yarmouth included going aboard and touring a naval vessel and trips to Norwich included shopping and the theatre.

John Leeds enjoyed such country interests as shooting, fox hunting, dogs and horses, alongside occasional visits to the theatre, concerts and dances at the local assembly rooms. Friends came to stay and he went away for a few days at

---

[81]   LD, 24 Dec. 1825; for Harvey, W.H. Bidwell, *Annals of an East Anglian Bank* (Norwich, 1900), p. 258.

[82]   LD, 6 Jan. 1826.

[83]   LD, 17 May 1826.

[84]   LD, 14 Dec. 1826.

a time with them for short visits to Cambridge and London. There were family parties including entertainments and dancing. The diary describes in detail his six-weeks tour of Scotland and the north of England. He seems to have returned from Scotland with an illness which lingered on for nearly a year, and like Moore, health features prominently in the diary. In Moore's case, bleeding seems to have been the usual remedy. This concern over health was typical at a period when premature death was so much part of everyday experience. John Leeds himself had lost three siblings in their infancy or childhood: he carefully noted the deaths of friends in his journal. In November 1799 a still-born child was born to the Moores and Thomas records the purchase of a small coffin for 6s. In December 1802 he took the precaution of having two of his children inoculated.

The diaries suggest that these men were part of tight-knit communities with a small circle of friends, many of whom were relations. Thomas Moore regularly dined at the Tuttells, often in a 'large family party', as well as visiting the Sewells. Leeds's friends were drawn from the ranks of the minor landowners, who not only held small estates, but might also be merchants. Bircham and Parmeter were a firm of well-established brewers and maltsters in Reepham while Stephen Leeds of Whitwell was a tanner. The Parmeter family also included a land agent and cleric. Others were farmers. Beck Hall was frequently full of visitors, often staying for a week at a time, and there is no doubt that visiting, particularly between young ladies (John Leeds had three sisters living at home) was an important way of passing the time.

VII

The period of agricultural change associated with the Napoleonic Wars and their aftermath is one with which Thomas William Coke and his larger tenants were inextricably linked. It is noted for developments in husbandry techniques and the farming infrastructure such as enclosure and the laying out of fields, the improvement of soils through marling and draining, and the provision of farm buildings. At both Hall Farm and Beck Hall all these improvements were taking place. This was typical of many of the 70 Holkham farms at this time and so the estate can be seen as fulfilling its obligation in providing the framework for improved farming. This much is clear from the estate records. The questions to which tenants' records, as distinct from the estate records, should be able to provide an answer, are how far was the tenant an exponent of the improved farming, and how successful was he?

As far as cereal production is concerned, we know little of the yields produced on either farm, so we cannot judge whether productivity increased. This production had to be supported by having nearly half the land under fodder crops to provide the keep for the animals producing the manure. Moore was able to take advantage of the inflated wartime prices, and when the market was not distorted by outside factors, Leeds seems to have been reasonably pleased with grain prices and the returns from this side of the enterprise. We know that both were mixed farms, where the income from livestock was important. Leeds seems to have been extremely unlucky with sheep and much of the time this aspect of his business probably ran at a loss. The cattle, however, did better, and again he was usually pleased with the prices obtained. The farming system adopted was profitable enough to allow both men to pay their rents in full and on time.

In terms of husbandry techniques, it is clear that although a four- and five-course shift was the rotation adopted over most of the two farms, there were some fields where an extra crop of grain was taken and where two corn crops were grown in succession, almost certainly breaking the terms of Leeds's lease. There is no correspondence in the letter books suggesting that Leeds had permission to do so, but neither does the farm seem to have been inspected by the agent and so there was no check on what was being planted. This runs counter to the belief that Holkham tenants stuck rigidly to the rotations laid down in their leases and always asked permission if they wished to change.

Both men were prepared to try new methods. Thomas Moore and John Leeds's father were both highly regarded by Blaikie. John read widely, collected advice and medical recipes from friends and from books, which he then copied into his journal, and took an interest in farming techniques he saw on other farms, both locally and further afield. He experimented with growing beet, very much an innovative crop. That he did not slavishly follow strict rotations under all circumstances acts as a note of caution to those who emphasise the importance of this aspect of agricultural change at the expense of other more significant developments, such as livestock farming and the improvement of the soil by draining, marling and manuring.

In the long run, however, John Leeds was not as successful as his father. When the new agent at Holkham, William Keary, viewed the farm in 1851, he found it much out of condition', the crops were light, the stubbles fowl and the fences not well kept. Not enough stock were kept and 'it is feared that a want of capital is the root of the evil'.[85] However, the fault for this lack of capital may not have been entirely Leeds's own: he may have been damaged by some one else's failure. In a letter to the agent in 1844, John Leeds wrote to deny rumours of his intention to give up the farm and of the help his friends were giving him through temporary troubles. By 1849 he was behind with his rent and he told the steward that his affairs were being managed by his brothers-in-law. Exactly what had gone wrong is never made clear.[86] Leeds finally retired to the small

---

85   Holkham MS, EG/12.
86   Holkham MS, MM96729, Letter Books.

family estate at Kersdiston near Reepham in 1859 when the family finally gave up the farm. He died in 1872 and is buried in Reepham churchyard.

Both farming families were examples of the type favoured by the estate and continued to farm on the estate for several generations to come. But what the two diaries demonstrate is that although there is a quarter of a century between them, and both men were writing in very different economic circumstances, farming methods had hardly changed. Rotations, crops grown and the amount and types of machinery used were much the same. Both men used limited amounts of bought-in oil cake, both for cattle feed and fertiliser but still stuck to reaping part of their crop and Leeds still broadcast (sowed) part of his seed. It is clear that it was not the post-war depression that stimulated interest in change, but the improvement in farming prospects. The 'high farming' techniques promoted by the next generation, of whom the Holkham tenant, John Hudson of Castle Acre was a leading example, did not come to the fore until the middle years of the nineteenth century.[87]

---

[87]   Wade Martins, *Great Estate*, pp. 114–17; H.M. Jenkins, 'Lodge Farm, Castle Acre', *J. Royal Agricultural Society of England*, 2nd ser. 5 (1869), pp. 460–74.

Chapter 8

The Landowner as Scientific Farmer: James Mason and the Eynsham Hall Estate, 1866–1903

Peter Dewey

James Mason of Eynsham Hall, Oxfordshire (1824–1903) was a remarkable man, whose origins are shrouded in mystery. He was brought up by the widow of an architect named Mason, but, according to a memoir written by his grandson, was in fact the natural son of a man who came from 'a very well-known family'. The natural father provided a good education for James, who went on to attend the University of Paris.[1]

Mason's studies at Paris (which were probably at the School of Mines) included chemistry and metallurgy. Shortly after the 1848 French Revolution he moved to Spain, where he became manager of copper and lead mines for three English mining companies in the Bilbao region. At some point he met his future life-long business partner and friend, Francis Tress Barry, who in 1847 was appointed acting British Consul for the Biscay region. By 1856 they were partners in the firm of F.T. Barry & Co., importing British industrial goods and machinery into Spain.[2]

Mason was a man of considerable energy and wide interests. Not content with his management of the English-owned mines, he provided technical supervision for other mines in Spain, submitted articles to the *Mining Journal*, and kept in touch with the latest publications on mining, banking and bookkeeping. He was also an active investor on the London stock market. It is tempting to speculate that he was already a rich man when the next phase of his career opened. The companies for which he worked became unprofitable, and were wound up in 1857–58. Mason then moved to southern Portugal, into the Iberian Pyrites Belt, which had been mined (chiefly for copper) since Roman times. Of the concessions available in the Mertola region, he settled on the San Domingos

---

[1]   Museum of English Rural Life (MERL), University of Reading. Eynsham Hall archive, OXF 22/15/31, Memoir of James Mason by Michael H. Mason, Nov. 1966, p. 1. All following references are to the Eynsham Hall archive held by MERL.

[2]   'Barry, Sir Francis Tress', *Who Was Who* (online edition, accessed 2009).

mine. This was derelict, although littered with the spoil heaps of ancient mining activity. The concession had been granted by the Portuguese government to a Spanish company, La Sabina, in May 1858. In October 1858 La Sabina signed a contract with Mason and Barry. The contract was for the exploitation of the San Domingos mines by Mason and Barry on a royalty basis for 50 years.

The San Domingos contract was the route to the rapid acquisition of great wealth for both men. Mason was in charge at the mine site, employing the latest mining techniques and steam-driven machinery. Barry remained in England, responsible for sales and marketing. The site rapidly developed, at first opening up Roman deep shafts, and later using open-cast methods. By 1864 the mine employed 3,000 men, and the firm had built an 18-kilometre narrow-gauge railway to link the mine to the nearest river port and thus to the coast. Although primarily a source of copper, the mine's most successful product between 1859 and *c.*1866 was sulphur, derived from copper pyrites. During that period, the firm effectively monopolised the supply of sulphur to the British alkali industry. In addition, a method of extracting the copper from the pyrites was developed. Although by the later 1860s San Domingos was overshadowed by the resurgent rivalry of the Rio Tinto and Tharsis mines, Mason continued to innovate in order to find more economical means to extract copper, sulphur and iron from the mine and its spoil heaps.[3]

The scale of operations at the San Domingos mine was immense. Between 1859 and 1891 it yielded 7.3 million tons of mineral ore, and the cumulative profit to be divided by the partners in that period came to £2,818,000. Although it is not possible to estimate the amount of Mason's personal wealth before his death in 1903, there is no doubt that he was very rich indeed by Victorian standards.[4]

Mason did not live in Portugal for very long. Although at the start of the San Domingos operation he resided for several years at the mine (1859–62), he then returned to live in England, operating the affairs of San Domingos by letter, being in almost daily correspondence with his managers, and only visiting once a year.[5] By now a rich man, he turned to the matter of becoming a landowner. His grandson's memoir asserts that, from his earliest mining days, James Mason's overriding aim was to acquire an English estate and to experiment with scientific farming, mining being but a means to this end. There may be some truth in this, although he did not begin his scientific experiments for many years after buying his

---

[3]   The preceding paragraphs on the San Domingos mine rely heavily on the chapter by Maria Joao Ramos P. Silva, 'San Domingos Mine's English and Cornish Connections', in P. Claughton and C. Mills (eds), *Mining Perspectives: The Proceedings of the Eighth International Mining History Congress 2009* (Truro, 2011), pp. 187–93. I am indebted to Dr Silva for generously sending me a copy of her original conference paper.

[4]   OXF 22/2/335, James Mason's profits etc. 1859–91 (a note of 19 May 1891 on Eynsham Hall headed paper, in James Mason's hand).

[5]   Silva, 'San Domingos Mine's Connections', p. 191.

estate. It may also be the case that his urge to acquire land and the status that came with it was spurred by awareness of his paternity. In any case, he soon acquired his estate. This was the Oxfordshire estate lying about seven miles north-west of Oxford and known as the Eynsham Hall estate, although it is located next to the village of North Leigh, and is several miles distant from Eynsham.

The Eynsham Hall estate, when Mason purchased it in 1866, consisted of a large eighteenth-century house ('a capital mansion', according to the estate agents) and home farm in a ring-fenced park, and four adjacent farms, of small or middling size (Barnard Gate, 50 acres; Blindwell, 69 acres; Little Green, *c.*110 acres; Salutation, 125 acres). The total area of the estate was 1,074 acres. All the farms, including the home farm (*c.*420 acres), were let to tenants; the let area was 857 acres. The remainder of the estate (217 acres) was in hand and not farmed; it consisted of the mansion with its gardens, lakes and ponds and woodland. The bulk of the woodland was being grubbed up at the time of the sale, to leave only 59 acres of woods. A view of the layout of the estate at the previous sale, in 1862, is given in Figure 8.1.[6]

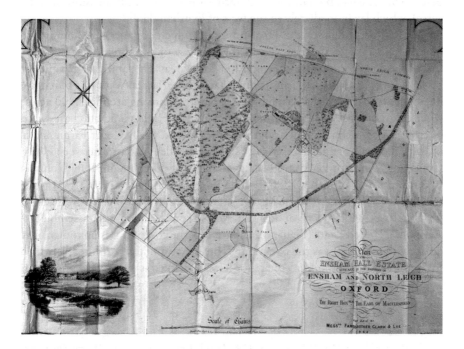

Figure 8.1   Map of Eynsham Hall estate, 1862

------

[6]   OXF 22/13/1, Report and Valuation on Eynsham Hall Estate, February 1866, by Debenham, Tewson and Farmer, London. (Note that Blindwell Farm was within the estate's ring-fenced home park.)

The asking price for the estate was £54,000. It is not known what price Mason paid for it, but the purchase did not by any means exhaust his capital. In the early 1870s he remodelled the Hall substantially, to the plans of the eminent designer Owen Jones, adding east and west wings and a fourth storey. He commissioned some notable pieces of furniture (some of which are now in the Victorian and Albert Museum) from Jones, and in 1878 the house was described as 'magnificently furnished'.[7]

Mason went on to increase his landholdings substantially. His biggest purchase was in 1875, when he bought the larger estate of South Leigh, adjoining Eynsham Hall to the south. This, which included the village of South Leigh, covered 1,430 acres. Although some of the farms are difficult to identify by name on the Ordnance Survey 25-inch maps, the largest ones were Tar Farm (348 acres), Church Farm (328 acres) and Station Farm (521 acres). The price paid for the estate is not known. At some point before this he had bought two small farms between Eynsham Hall and South Leigh – Brick Kiln (71 acres) and its neighbour, Ambury Close (area unknown). At an unknown date, but before 1877, he had bought the small farm called Osney Hill (possibly only 42 acres), which lay immediately to the west of Eynsham Hall.[8]

In 1885 he purchased the Freeland estate, which adjoined the home park of Eynsham Hall to the east. It was the smallest of the three estates now in his possession, comprising the mansion known as Freeland Lodge and its surrounding park (50 acres), and a single farm of 267 acres. With this purchase, he now had an almost unbroken block of land comprising around 2,800 acres, running south for several miles from Eynsham Hall. His last land purchases were of two farms which lay away from this central block, Holly Court Farm, north of Eynsham Hall, of 242 acres, and the smaller Puddle End Farm, between Holly Court and Eynsham Hall, of 59 acres. The date of purchase of Holly Court is uncertain; it was probably 1886. Puddle End was purchased in 1888. At their maximum extent in *c.* 1900, the Mason estates covered an estimated 3,193 acres.[9]

Thus over a period of at least 20 years, James Mason had assembled a substantial landed estate (Figure 8.2). Although the cost of this is unknown, it is unlikely that money was the paramount consideration. It is far more likely that his ambition was to build a coherent estate, as a look at the map of the estate

---

[7] *The Builder*, 9 May 1874, p. 385; C.A. Hrvol. Flores, *Owen Jones: Design, Ornament, Architecture and Theory in an Age of Transition* (New York, 2006), pp. 196–201; *Victoria County History, Oxfordshire*, XII, p. 122.

[8] OXF 22/15/10, Schedule of lands the property of James Mason Esquire of Eynsham Hall to be redeemed of land tax [1898]; *VCH, Oxfordshire*, XII, p. 243.

[9] Ibid., pp. 123, 220–23.

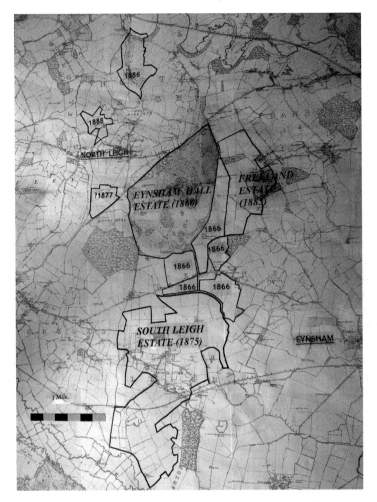

Figure 8.2   James Mason's Estates, 1866–88 (The estates and farms are
shown with their dates of purchase. Their boundaries are
shown here on 6" OS maps, second edition, 1883–4)

compiled here indicates. The somewhat outlying Holly Court and Puddle End
might just have been attractive propositions at the time.[10]

_____

[10]   Figure 8.2 has been compiled using the Ordnance Survey Field Numbers recorded on the 25
inches to the mile OS maps of 1876 onwards. The OS Field Numbers on the Eynsham Hall estate are
listed in OXF 22/15/10, Schedule of lands the property of James Mason Esquire of Eynsham Hall to
be redeemed of Land Tax [1898]. The estate and farm boundaries thus derived have been marked up on
6-inch OS maps (2nd edition, 1883–34), and photographed to obtain this map of the estate.

I

The soil quality on the Mason estates was not of the best. The agents in 1866 had described the Eynsham Hall estate as having a 'stiff loam and clay surface, with a clay subsoil'.[11] Daniel Hall described it thus:

> Practically the whole of this land lies on the Oxford Clay, which here forms a poor soil, unkindly and difficult to cultivate, and yielding a very unsatisfactory pasture for many years after it is laid down to grass.

Parts of the estate needed improved drainage, and some fields were liable to riverine flooding. As Mason's experience was to confirm, it was difficult to make good permanent grassland on these clay soils.

However, if the quality of the land was not of the best, it did not prevent Mason from investing heavily in the estate. His improvements to the Eynsham Hall mansion have been noted. He also put a lot of money into the estate's fixed capital.[12] Shortly after 1866 he enlarged and adapted the Hall lake so as to provide a water supply for the Eynsham (and later the Freeland) estate and the neighbouring villages. On the home farm, whose buildings had scarcely been mentioned by the agents in 1866, there was by 1897 a complete set of (timber) farm buildings, including cattle sheds and pig pens, a riding school, a timber yard, workshops for carpenters and wheelwrights, a smithy and a complete gasworks, with safety provision provided by fire hydrants. The estate had also a pair of steam ploughing engines valued at £1,008 in 1888, and it purchased a new 'traction engine' for £351 in the same year.[13]

II

The records of the Mason estates, which are deposited at the Museum of English Rural Life at the University of Reading, are substantial. They are particularly rich in financial accounts and farming statements relating to the home farm and to the Eynsham Hall estate. These records, kept in great detail in large ledgers in immaculate handwriting, with tables of contents, are of the highest quality. Mason's background in business, his scientific frame of mind, and his concern for the highest standards of accurate accounting, all mark these out from the

---

[11] OXF 22/13/1, p. 5.

[12] See n. 37 below.

[13] OXF 22/16/4/6, Plan of the Home Farm, timber yard etc. of the Eynsham Hall Estate; *VCH Oxfordshire*, XII, p. 122; OXF 22/13/2, The rating of lands in hand and for rating purposes, the property of J.F. Mason Esq, by F.W. Jones, Oxford (1904); OXF 22/2/278a, Farming Accounts for the year ending Michaelmas 1888.

common run of farm and estate records. They provide a fascinating view of how a very astute man of business and science tried to meet the challenges of contemporary farming.

The main bases of the Mason approach to farm accounts were twofold. Firstly, every field and every enterprise would be charged for the cost of work done for it, and the balance of profit or loss recorded; in essence, every productive unit was to be a cost centre. Secondly, allowances would be made for the imputed cost of rent not received on land in hand, and for interest foregone on the capital employed in the estate. So if land was not rented out, but worked by the estate, a notional allowance would be made for rent thus foregone; in practice, this seems to have consisted in charging the same per acre as paid by the tenants in rent. The addition of a notional charge for interest (5 per cent) on capital employed was a constant reminder that farming was a business, and needed to pay attention to its rate of return on capital, as compared with the return on other occupations in which it might have been employed.

The fine-tuning of the system related to enterprises (for example, crops in each field, or a class of livestock) which showed a deficit on the year, and in the handling of overhead costs. On loss-making operations, the deficit was carried over to the next year, and interest charged on it until the deficit was wiped off. Estate overheads, such as the poor rates, management time, and all miscellaneous expenditure otherwise unallocated, were lumped together as 'establishment charges', and divided up according to the acreage of each field.[14]

The practical working of this system may be illustrated from the farming statements of Eynsham Hall in 1890. Table 8.1 is the complete entry recorded *verbatim* for the growing and disposal of the oat and oat hay crop in Field No. 306 (the Ordnance Survey number) in 1890. This comprehensive account bears out the principle enunciated above, that is, of treating every enterprise (here meaning a field) as a cost centre, and is assiduous in entering every cost, including coal for threshing, and wear and tear on the threshing drum (how many farm accounts ever did this?). For products which were not sold off the farm, and thus did not have a market value (the green vetches sent to the stables, and the chaff rakings for the game birds), there are imputed credits. Both these items thus became inputs to other enterprises on the estate.

The concern with detail may have been somewhat overdone. Thus in drawing up the profit and loss account for the Eynsham Hall home farm in 1890, credit was allowed for the rabbits caught on the estate. There were 9,000 of these, and they were entered in the accounts as if all were sold, at the current price of 1s. each, realising a total of £450. This extra £450 made all the difference between

---

14   This analysis of Mason's accounting methods has been derived from the study of the accounts presented here. See also A.D. Hall, 'The agricultural experiments of the late Mr James Mason', *JRASE* 65 (1904), pp. 107–108.

Table 8.1   Cultivation costs and revenue for Field 306, Eynsham Hall estate,
              year ending Michaelmas 1890

To:		By:	
		Produce	
Cultivations to Michaelmas 1889 brought forward	15s. 6d.	Green vetches 22 tons 10 cwt	£20 5s. 0d.
[Cultivation] during year ending Michaelmas 1890:		Green vetches 6 loads to stables	£5 8s. 0d.
Horse labour	£10 0s. 3d.	Oat hay 10 tons @ 60s.	£30 0s. 0d.
Manual labour	£23 18s. 0d.	Green oats 1 ton 15 cwt @ 18s.	£1 11s. 6d.
Seeds	£5 16s. 5¼d.	Oats 55 [qtrs] 40 lbs per bush. @ 22s.	£60 10s. 0d.
Compound mixture	£23 15s. 0d.	Straw, chaff and cavings, 16 tons @ 30s	£27 0s. 0d.*
Coal for threshing	6s. 0d.	Rakings to game	£2 0s. 0d.
Wear and tear of Engine drum	£1 10s. 0d.		
Establishment charges	£5 10s. 9d.		
Balance, being profit for rent	£75 2s. 6¾d.		
[Total]	£146 14s. 6d.	[Total]	£146 14s. 6d.

Note: the vetches were presumably sown as an undercrop with the oats. * Error in the original: should be £24 0s. 0d.

Abbreviations: cwt/hundredweight; qr/ quarter; lb/pound (weight).

Source: OXF 22/2/280, Eynsham Hall, farming statements for the year ended [Michaelmas] 1890.

profit and loss, since the profit for the home farm came out finally at £350. The account assumed that all were sold, but this may not have been the case. Although there is no analysis of game disposals for that year, there is one for 1889, which shows that, of the 7,966 rabbits caught, only 4,197 were sold, the rest going as presents, or to the Hall kitchens, or to foxes and the kennels. Making an allowance for the benefits of imputed rabbit sales is of course as defensible in accounting terms as including the costs of imputed rent on land in hand, but it may have been going a bit too far to enter also a credit of £90 for the estimated value of dung dropped by the rabbits in the coverts.[15]

Aside from the actual accounting ledgers, the Mason archive contains much detail on the cropping of the land in hand, which grew substantially in the 1880s and 1890s. The farms of the original Eynsham Hall estate bought in 1866 had been entirely let, the largest lease being for the combined Home (*c.*420 acres) and Little Green (*c.*120 acres) farms. These two were still being worked by one tenant when the South Leigh estate was purchased in 1875. The combined Eynsham Hall and South Leigh estates were still largely tenanted in 1876, when the rent roll shows rent being paid on a total of 2,410 acres, the rest of the land being the 216 acres of home park woodland already in hand in 1866.[16]

Until this point, Mason had been content to be a rent receiver rather than an active farmer, but the economic depression in arable farming which commenced after the early 1870s led to farmers running into difficulties, and abandoning their tenancies. In South Leigh by 1878, all but two of the farms were vacant. John Bryan, who is shown as Mason's tenant in South Leigh for 521 acres in 1876 and 324 acres in 1885, is reported to have lost £5,000 of capital in the first five years of his tenancy through successive crop failures. He never recovered financially, and died insolvent in 1914. In the early 1880s, rent arrears on the estate grew; from £751 at Michaelmas 1881 to £1,224 a year later, and £1,632 at Lady Day 1883. Most of the latter debt was paid off by November of that year, but £851 was still outstanding. Bryan appears among the larger debtors during these years, and still owed £170 at November 1883.[17]

The result of the farming depression was that Mason took ever more land in hand. The next rent roll extant, of 1885–86, shows rent being received on only 1,309 acres of the Eynsham and South Leigh estates; to this could be added 268 acres of the newly acquired Freeland estate, which was still entirely rented. Another effect of the depression was that rents per acre had fallen. In 1876, 2,559 let acres had yielded £4,000 exactly, or £1.56 per acre. In 1885–86 the 1,577 let acres produced an income of £2,009, or £1.28 per acre.[18]

The amount of land in hand probably fluctuated with the fortunes of the tenants, but it grew in the longer run. In 1866 it had been 216 acres, consisting largely of home park woodland. In 1890 it may be estimated at 614 acres; 309 of this is listed as 'Home Farm', but this seems to have included the whole of the Freeland estate, which in all probability was now being worked as one unit with

[15] OXF 22/2/196, Game Disposal 1889; OXF 22/2/280, Home Farm. Common Form Profit and Loss Account 1890. ('Account created so as to include the Park and give proper Credit in respect of Rabbits (*sic*) production and manures from Rabbits wasted in coverts etc.').

[16] OXF 22/2/204, Rent Roll, 1876–1903.

[17] *VCH, Oxfordshire*, XII, p. 248; OXF 22/15/7, Statements of rents due, 1880–83.

[18] OXF 22/2/204, Eynsham Hall Estate, rent roll 1876–85; OXF 22/2/205, Rent book, 1885–1903.

the original Home Farm.[19] Not all of this was arable land; in 1892 James Mason himself, writing in the *Journal of the Royal Agricultural Society of England* about his scientific experiments, noted that he now farmed 450 acres of arable. A list of fields in hand for the whole of the Mason estates in 1900 gives a total of 1,263 acres in hand, of which 529 were arable, the rest (734 acres) being 'parks and pastures'.[20]

The arable must have been distributed widely over the whole estate, since a note of the land in hand in 1904 at Eynsham Hall and Freeland gives a total arable acreage of only 147 (and a pasture acreage of 517). It should perhaps be noted that the Victoria County History, following Daniel Hall, gives an upper estimate of land in hand as 1,800 acres, of which 800 acres was arable.[21]

III

Mason had withdrawn from active involvement with the Portuguese mining business in 1879, passing responsibility for it to his son (James Francis). This, combined with the growth of land in hand, seems to have spurred Mason to develop his scientific interests, in the form of experiments on the growth of plants, and in the practical application of the results to his land.[22]

His experiments were directed to one broad end; to utilise the biological resources of the soil more efficiently. These resources were nitrogen, phosphoric acid and potash (potassium). His aim, like that of many contemporary scientists, was to find out how a higher proportion of these nutritious agents in the soil could be used by plants. In practice, his experiments centred on three themes; the exploitation of the subsoil; the use of novel artificial fertilisers such as basic slag; and ascertaining which crops were best suited to fix nitrogen in the soil.

His experiments were described in two articles published in the *JRASE*; one by Mason himself in 1892, and one in 1904 by Sir Daniel Hall.[23] The first two themes (better use of the subsoil and of basic slag) were adequately described by Mason in his 1892 article. Beginning in 1887, four plots, which had been treated so as to reduce their natural nitrogen content, were dug deep, and planted with white and leguminous crops, being also treated with basic slag. The idea of the deep digging was to bring the nitrogen, phosphate and potassium in the subsoil into contact with the root system of the plants and thus make them available to

---

[19]   OXF 22/4/1, Home Farm Crop Book, 1890–93.

[20]   OXF 22/2/296, Profit and Loss Account, year ending 1900, pp. 120–2 (acreage actually planted).

[21]   OXF 22/13/2, 'The rating of lands in hand ...'; *VCH, Oxfordshire*, XII, p. 137; James Mason, 'Field experiments on the fixation of free Nitrogen', *JRASE*, 3rd ser., 3 (1892), p. 657; Hall, 'Agricultural Experiments', p. 107.

[22]   OXF 22/15/31, Mason, Biography of James Mason, p. 3.

[23]   Mason, 'Field Experiments', pp. 651–67; Hall, 'Agricultural Experiments', pp. 106–24.

the growing plants. At the same time, the utility of dressings of basic slag could be assessed.

The results of these experiments were rather surprising. The deep digging and basic slag seemed to have worked in supplying phosphates and potassium, but the surprising result was that, from plots which must have contained very little available nitrogen in the soil or subsoil, crops were got which contained a notable quantity of nitrogen.[24]

These results pushed Mason further into the question of how plants fixed nitrogen, and whether from the soil or from the air. This was at the time by no means definitely resolved. It was shortly before this that Hellriegel and Wilfarth had published their great work on symbiotic nitrogen fixation – in a brief report in 1886, and more fully in 1888. They showed clearly that the nodules on the roots of certain leguminous plants had the property of fixing nitrogen from the atmosphere. Their work was hailed immediately as epochal, but there was much more work to be done in refining their experiments and applying them to practical agriculture; the investigations set in train thereby continue to this day.[25]

The realisation that the nitrogen question was still not finally solved, coupled with his correspondence with leading agricultural scientists such as Lawes and Gilbert (of Rothamsted), set Mason off exploring further the processes governing the exploitation of nitrogen by growing plants. His experiments on this and other questions carried on until 1898.[26]

The practical lessons which Mason took from his researches were several. The idea of deep digging was in order to bring up the subsoil and allow its weathering, the better to allow potash and phosphoric acid (and possibly nitrogen) to be assimilated by the plants. The efficacy of Mason's deep digging was tested in the laboratory of the Royal Agricultural Society, where samples of his subsoils before and after weathering were tested. The results showed that the weathering was very effective in making the potassium compounds more available to the plants, although not the phosphoric or nitrogenous compounds. Due credit was paid to Mason, who had for the first time scientifically tested the already well-known practical advantages of weathering of the subsoil.[27]

His other practical lessons concerned artificial fertilisers, animal feeds and nitrogen fixation. By trial and error he tested several different formulae for top-dressings for his crops, and he worked at devising new and more efficient feed mixtures for his livestock. As regards the better fixation of atmospheric

---

[24]   Mason, 'Field Experiments', pp. 654–7.

[25]   P.S. Nutman, 'Centenary Lecture', *Philosophical Transactions of the Royal Society of London*, Series B, 317 (1987), pp. 69–106.

[26]   Hall, 'Agricultural experiments', p. 112.

[27]   OXF 22/15/8, Tabulated analysis of soils at Eynsham Hall. Analysis by Dr Bernard Dyer; Weathering of subsoils. Analyses by Dr Voelcker; Hall, 'Agricultural experiments', pp. 113–15.

nitrogen by legumes, he evolved a general scheme of growing two years of nitrogenous-fixing crops (for example, clover), followed by two nitrogen-consuming crops (cereals such as oats or wheat, or roots such as potatoes or mangolds). He at first used red clover, sown amongst beans, making the combined crop into silage for animal feed. However, this was unsatisfactory, the silage losing a lot of dry matter in the manufacturing process. It was also doubtful whether the soil was suitable for red clover in two out of every four years. Mason then changed to lucerne, laying down several hundred acres to it by the late 1890s.[28]

Mason's experiments were carried on at the same time that he was applying his ideas on all these subjects to his farming, and they were mutually interactive. This evolution can be followed from the cropping books kept in his own handwriting, for the years 1890–93. They cover all the fields in hand at the time (305 acres arable are recorded in total), with the cultivation procedures for each field detailed meticulously. Their flavour and content can best be appreciated by looking at part of one of these entries *verbatim*:

No. 122. 8a[cres] 1r[ood]   No red clover since 1866–7.

In 1887 this field was in the hands of Merry of Freeland. The crops were various. Farming poor and exhausting, and land badly drained. It was then drained and cleaned. During the winter it was dug and the subsoil forked – total depth about 16 inches. 8½ loads of dung were applied to 6¼a. On 2 acres no dung was applied. 16 c[wt] Basic [*slag*] per Acre was applied all over. 4 c. Basic per Acre was used in the Drill.

1888.

Mangolds:- On Apl. 28 10 lbs of seed were sown per Acre. From June 6 to July 25, 10 Dressings of Black Nitrate mixture were applied per a[cre]. In all 10 c[wt]. Horse hoeings 2; flat hoeing 1; hand hoeings 2.

Produce:- Oct. 8. Mangolds with Dung tested 17 T[ons] per A[cre]; without Dung, 13 T[ons] per A[cre]

Swedes:- The top-dressings were 10C per Acre in 10 dressings. Put on between June 6 and July 25. 2 horse-hoeings – 1 flat d[itt]]o. - 2 hand hoeings.

---

28 Hall, 'Agricultural experiments', pp. 117–18.

Produce:- Nov. 1 Swedes on the Dunged Part gave 26 T[ons] per Acre; On the not dunged part 19 T[ons] per Acre.[29]

Thus far, the record illustrates his emphasis on initial deep digging (which also brought the benefit of an increased and earlier dryness of the land after rain), the use of basic slag, his 'black nitrate' mixture (discussed below), and an experiment with and without farm dung. The next crop (1889) was barley, for which the land was ploughed once in January and February, and cultivated by steam in March. A top dressing of black nitrate was again used (3 cwt. per acre). The crop yielded 41½ bushels of best corn and 8 bushels of tail corn per acre; the straw chaff and cavings were 1 ton 10 cwt. per acre.

Having taken two 'white' crops, which consumed nitrogen rather than replacing it in the soil, he turned to what became his main cropping policy; to follow two white crops with two leguminous ones. In 1889–90 he planted winter oats and vetches, top-dressed with another of his 'mixtures', this one named 'leguminous mixture'. The land was ploughed once only, given one heavy harrowing before drilling the seed in, and one rolling and one harrowing after drilling. Testing the crop yield in July indicated a yield of 14 tons 9 cwt per acre. The crop was all made into silage. In 1890–91 he put in his second year of leguminous crops, namely winter beans with vetches, and red clover in the spring. The beans failed, owing to frost. The beans/vetches and clover were cut for silage in 1891.

Mason's final note for 1890–91 reads:

> This field like all the others when again steam-ploughed and subsoiled after the 1st or the 2nd crop of clover has been cut must be levelled up [*sic*] in Basic to 2 tons per acre – say put on 1 ton in following the plough and sow in such manner that part falls in the furrow and part on the ridges. It is very possible that I shall plough under the Second crop of Clover in this field ... especially if this is done in hot dry weather.[30]

1890–91 was the high point of his use of red clover. But his experiments in brick-built experimental 'tanks' with both red clover and lucerne from 1890 on were to show that lucerne was superior in accumulating nitrogen in the soil for the use of subsequent crops, and he then turned (more so after 1896) to lucerne on a large scale. By now his method had developed so far as to be succinctly summed up by Daniel Hall:

---

[29] OXF 22/4/1, Home Farm Crop Book, 6 Aug. 1890–25 Apr. 1893; entry for Field No. 122. The layout of the original has been simplified.

[30] Ibid.

Mr Mason's scheme was to open up the subsoil by deep steam cultivation, manure liberally with basic slag to furnish phosphoric acid and lime, trusting to the weathering of the subsoil to supply potash and to the lucerne crop to assimilate nitrogen.[31]

Unfortunately, the results of sowing lucerne were disappointing. It was sown without a cover crop, and 'as the seasons were dry this resulted in a bad plant, a defect from which the fields never recovered financially'.[32] Analysis of the financial results of laying down Field 38AB (35 acres) to lucerne in 1897 showed the cost of laying down as £171 16s. 0d.; the profit over all the seven seasons 1897–1903 only amounted to £137 19s. 0d. On the other hand, by this time the field was in a good state for grazing, and the slight profit had been struck after allowing for (imputed) rent of 20s. an acre, and interest on capital of 5 per cent. But the difficulties he met may account for the fact that, although he laid down several hundred acres to lucerne, Mason did not always follow his original intention, and follow with corn or roots, preferring to follow with grass seeds as the lucerne grew older, and thus create permanent pasture.[33]

Mention has been made of Mason's innovation of his own recipes for top-dressing crops. There were eventually three of these. The one most often referred to was called 'Black Nitrate Mixture'. Its main constituents were nitrate of soda, 'potash salts', basic slag, plus salt, soot and sawdust. This was noted as containing 56 lbs. weight of nitrogen per 10 cwt. The recipe antedates 1891, at which date some minor adjustments were made to it.

There was also a 'Plain Nitrate Mixture'. The only active fertilising agent in this was 3 cwt of nitrate of soda per 10 cwt of the mixture; the remainder was made up of 'dry dirt in dust from road scrapings', soot, and sawdust. The date of its origin is unclear, but Mason suggested two variations on its formula in 1895, and proposed a slightly revised version for use 'after the season of 1896'.

For his leguminous crops, he evolved a special mixture, referred to as the New Mixture. The main constituents of this were kainit (a potassium salt) and basic slag, plus soot and sawdust. This was presumably in use in the early and mid 1890s.

His final innovation was for a 'new Nitrate Mixture', the recipe for which is dated 29 September 1902. This was mainly basic slag, with nitrate of soda, lime, gypsum, soot and sawdust. The entry accompanying this proposal notes that: 'By making use of this new mixture it may not again be nec[*essary*] to apply Basic or Lime to the land and this will be done at small cost as it is necessary to top-dress the nitrate ...'. The purpose behind this appears to be to

---

31   Hall, 'Agricultural experiments', p. 118.
32   Ibid., p. 118.
33   Ibid., pp. 118–19.

save money by minimising the number of fertiliser applications on the land. Mason was, at the age of 78, still very active in agricultural innovation.[34]

Mason had more success with his experimental work on arable crops than in animal husbandry research. This work was concerned with extensive feeding trials for young beasts, especially bullocks. Detailed records were kept of the foods consumed, and the rate of increase of live weight under different regimes. At the end of each trial, balance sheets were drawn up showing the number of food units consumed for maintenance and for weight increase, with allowance made for the manure returned to the land by the animals.

While the results of the bullock feeding trials showed that rapid feeding to young stock was more effective than a slower method with older beasts and less concentrates, it also showed that the lucerne and silage raised on the estate were effective stock foods. But the financial calculations did not show a profit, unless an excessive credit was taken for the manure returned by the animals to the land. A.D. Hall's review of this part of Mason's farming concluded that 'The trials, in fact, from a financial standpoint, were vitiated by the want of the skilled grazier's eye in the buying and the selling'.[35]

By trial and error, Mason evolved an animal policy which suited the land, aided by his improved grass pastures. At Michaelmas 1900, the accounts showed a complement of 37 milking cows, 174 feeding cattle, 648 ewes and 148 lambs, and 1,339 sows or young pigs. There was also a poultry operation, of 631 fowls. These livestock operations all made a profit, but in most cases not a large one. The pigs were the most profitable, yielding a profit of £1,144 in 1900. They were mainly Tamworth-Berkshire crosses, kept in the fields and given some extra feeding, but never brought to a state of great fatness, as there was a ready market for them as bacon pigs.[36]

IV

The final question about Mason's farming policies is whether they were profitable or not. The Eynsham Hall archive does not supply a satisfactory set of estate accounts covering this entire period, but some suggestions may be made.

It is unlikely that Mason had profitability much in mind when purchasing the estate in 1866. He was already a rich man, with (one assumes) a fair book

[34]   OXF 22/4/1, Crop Book of Home Farm, 6 Aug. 1890 – 25 Apr. 1893. The recipes for these mixtures are given on the front endpaper of this volume.

[35]   Hall, 'Agricultural experiments', p. 122.

[36]   OXF 22/2/296, Home Farm profit and loss account, year ending Michaelmas 1900, pp. 102–103; Value of live and dead farming stock, cultivations etc. at Michaelmas 1900, pp. 117–18: Hall, 'Agricultural experiments', p. 124.

Table 8.2   Eynsham Hall: Financial results of farming land in hand, 1888
(profit (+) and loss (−))

Arable and pasture lands	+ £95 16s. 9d.
Livestock	− £7 0s. 11½d.
(A) Profit on arable, pasture and livestock	**+ £88 15s. 10½d.**
Parks	
Costs: poor rates, horse labour, manual labour, manures	− £1,124 12s. 10½d.
Benefits:	
Grazing at 4d. a day, except beasts which are charged ⅙ less	+ £340 15s. 3d.
Hay crop (50 tons @ 50s.)	+ £145 0s. 0d.
(B) Loss on parks	**− £638 17s. 7½d.**
Overall farming loss [(A) − (B)]	**− £550 1s. 9d.**

Note: at the end: 'Rabbits not included, though if they had been they w[oul]d have been rated at 1s. each, or 3½d. per lb. (and would have estimated no. of rabbits killed outside the parks).'

Source: OXF 22/2/278a. Farming statement for year ending Michaelmas 1888, p. 10.

knowledge of agriculture, and had been informed of the poor quality of the land. Few accounts survive from the early years of his ownership, but he was prepared to invest in land improvement from the start. Thus between August 1866 and October 1867, when he had only just taken possession of Eynsham Hall, he spent the large sum of £3,363 on drainage. At that time, two of the livestock operations (sheep and pigs) were making losses.[37]

For the next 20 years Mason acted largely as a receiver of rent. It was in the mid 1880s that he began to take large amounts of land in hand, and the financial results of his farming begin to be recorded in more detail. In 1888 he had 210 acres in hand (125 arable and 85 pasture), in addition to the parks of Eynsham Hall and Freeland. The result was a moderate-sized loss (Table 8.2).

The picture in 1888 is one in which the farming of the combined arable and pasture was more or less breaking even, but the farming account as a whole, when the costs of working the parks was taken into consideration, showed a moderately large loss. The nature of the work done in the parks is not stated, but it seems from the above to be grassland improvement, with a large investment in labour and 'manures' (the usual contemporary term for artificial fertilisers, as opposed to farmyard dung). The parks also had little in the way of saleable produce to offset their costs.

---

37   OXF 22/2/61, Estate Account Book, 1866–67.

Table 8.3   Eynsham Hall: Receipts and expenditure on farming land in hand, 1895–99 (£)

	1895	1896	1897	1898	1899
Rent[a]	1,219	1,279	1,521	1,772	1,768
Interest[a]	343	301	417	570	677
Artificial manures	333	367	781	408	111
Foods	1,994	3,340	6,392	8,488	10,304
Manual labour	1,714	1,466	1,926	2,331	2,601
Livestock purchases	1,338	1,135	3,007	6,142	3,741
(A) TOTAL EXPENDITURE RECEIPTS	8,378	9,456	16,373	22,380	21,905
Produce sold	1,346	458	1,395	468	200
Livestock sold	2,747	2,904	6,710	10,051	13,439
(B) TOTAL RECEIPTS	4,093	3,362	8,105	10,519	13,639
(C) SUPPLIED TO MANSION	2,470	2,263	3,564	3,991	3,145
LOSSES [(B) + (C) – (A)]	–1,815	–3,831	–4,704	–7,870	–5,121
OVERALL FARMING LOSS	–960	–2,403	–709	–1,195	–2,279

Note: [a] Imputed rent and interest.

Source: OXF 22/2/295, Financial and statistical summaries of farming operations, 1897–1900, p. 29.

The overall loss was apparently struck before making deductions for the imputed value of rent and interest, so in the accounts for the whole estate the loss would have been larger. In the period 1895–99, when there was much more land in hand, and the accounts did make deductions for imputed rent and interest, there are continuous losses (Table 8.3).

While the farming operations, if judged by simply subtracting expenditure from receipts, showed very high losses, as shown in the penultimate line above, the final line of the accounts in the ledger, shown here as 'overall farming loss', recorded much lower deficits. How the accountant managed to reduce the losses to the level shown in the last line is not clear, but losses there certainly were, for each of these years. As regards farming policy, it seems that Mason had reduced his use of artificial manures on the grassland, and was relying on high feeding with purchased foods to bring on the beasts for market, and to increase the manurial value of their dung on the grassland. It is also noticeable that there is little sale of produce, which suggests that much of the arable produce was going for animal feed on the estate.

One other change in Mason's policy had by this time affected the financial balance; the experiments with lucerne, which began *c.* 1896. This, which involved breaking up pasture, was expensive, and resulted in large losses; by Michaelmas 1901, the cumulative loss on lucerne was £2,611 16s. 1d. The consolation was that the quality of the pastures was thereby improved.[38]

Although the record is far from complete, the accounts presented here suggest strongly that Mason's direct farming was in the long run a loss-making business. Were the tenanted farms run at a profit, offsetting the losses on direct farming operations? Only one snapshot of the tenant account is available, in 1904, when the balance sheet of the estate's affairs was drawn up for the information of Mason's son, James Francis, on his succession to ownership. This shows that the let farms produced a small surplus of £896. The smaller operations (letting of cottages and sundry other small properties, allotments, and woods and forests) produced a small profit, of £21. The only other item at estate level was the commencement of the building of a new mansion, the incoming son having decided to demolish the old house; to date, this had cost £331. All told, the profits on the non-direct farming side of the estate came to £586. So, presuming that the losses on direct farming operations identified as recently as 1899 were still continuing, they would not have been offset by the tenant and other accounts.[39]

Finally, if the estate was making losses for a long period, how was it enabled to continue in business? The simple answer is that it was not in business. While it was by no means merely the plaything of a rich man, and was certainly in later years a laboratory in which important contributions to agricultural science were being made, its rationale was not that of profit maximisation. Fortunately for the family, Mason's resources were such as to put the losses attendant on direct farming in the shade. This may be seen in the money expended on domestic, pleasure and personal activities on the estate (that is, excluding all Mason's direct farming operations, and the balance of costs and revenues from renting farms to tenants). In 1887 these non-agricultural expenditures amounted to £30,072. In descending order, the largest items were: private and personal (£11,901); housekeeping (Eynsham Hall) and other expenditure (£10,086); game and sporting (£3,898); stables and kennels (£2,999). Towards the end of his life, the overall expenditure was smaller, and there was less spent on outdoor activities, but the total spending was still much larger than the losses from his farming. On average in the two years 1900 and 1901 the non-agricultural spending amounted to £18,680 a year, the largest item being private and personal spending (£9,226), followed by house expenditure (£6,595), stables and carriages (£1,603) and

---

[38]   OXF 22/2/300, Accounts and farming operations, 1902–3, p. 6.

[39]   OXF 22/2/134, Eynsham Hall. Estate and farm accounts. Presentation, 1904; capital account with J.F. Mason Esq.

gardens (£816). By then only £87 went on game, and the list concludes with £353 spent on buying horses. It can safely be concluded that these activities were being subsidised from Mason's private income, which also sufficed to defray the losses on his farming.[40]

V

The story of James Mason and his Eynsham Hall estate is that of a very successful businessman who fulfilled an ambition to become an English landowner. His acquisition of landed property was on a large scale, and the quality of the estate, or its financial attractiveness, was of secondary importance to him. He later took much land in hand, and improved it, at the same time making a practical contribution to agricultural science. Why he settled at Eynsham Hall is not known. Although his obituary in the *Oxford Times* hinted at snobbery (the estate lies close to the Blenheim Estate of the Duke of Marlborough, and the Prince of Wales was also reputed to be interested in buying Eynsham Hall), this seems an unlikely motive for James Mason, who had roughed it in Iberian mines for several years. For most of this period, the mere fact of landownership and its attendant honours (in 1869 he was appointed Justice of the Peace and served as High Sheriff of Oxfordshire in the same year) was probably prestige enough. His entry into direct farming was an unplanned accident. From then on, his scientific curiosity and the urge to improve the quality of the estate drove him forward. The results were beneficial to agricultural science, but not to his pocket. This does not seem to have worried him.[41]

In conclusion, this study may be offered as a contribution to the ongoing debate as to how far successful Victorian businessmen were seduced away from money-making by the attractions of adopting the lifestyle of the landed gentry. The extreme proponent of this seductionist view is Martin Wiener, who has written that, from the mid nineteenth century:

> Businessmen increasingly shunned the role of industrial entrepreneur for the more socially rewarding role of gentleman (landed, if possible). The upshot was a dampening of industrial energies, the most striking single consequence of the gentrification of the English middle class.[42]

---

[40] OXF 22/2/20, Estate expenditure, 1901–03.

[41] *The Oxford Times*, 4 Apr. 1903, p. 12.

[42] M. Wiener, *English Culture and the Decline of the Industrial Spirit, 1850–1980* (Cambridge, 1981), p. 97.

While Mason certainly did join the ranks of the country gentry, spent a lot on conspicuously remodelling his mansion, performed the honorific tasks associated with his new status, improved his estate, and enjoyed country pursuits, he did not give up money-making. His continuing involvement in the management of his mines until 1879 has been mentioned above. He was an active investor on the stock exchange both before and after he withdrew from direct involvement in the mining business, acquired a London mansion, and died with a fortune not too far short of a million pounds, in spite of losing money on the direct farming operations of his later years. This was not a case of landed gentrification sapping the entrepreneurial spirit; it was rather a case of the entrepreneurial spirit invigorating the landed estate.[43]

---

[43]   James Mason died on 2 April 1903. His estate was valued for probate at £869,316 (gross value); the value of his personal estate was £751,855 (photocopy of probate grant of September 1903, supplied by Her Majesty's Courts Service, 3 Feb. 2011). Some of his stock market investment activity is traceable in OXF22/2/235, James Mason's profits etc., 1859–91.

Chapter 9

The 'Lady Farmer': Gender, Widowhood and Farming in Victorian England

Nicola Verdon

In many respects Victorian farming was a man's world. As an industry that was progressively directed by scientific research and technological innovation, agriculture came to be dominated by a language and imagery that was predominately masculine. Contemporary observers increasingly subjected women who were involved in farming to adverse comment and criticism. Those who worked on the land as poorly paid labourers were advised that agriculture was not a suitable occupation for women as it removed them from their natural arena of the home. In the late 1860s the Reverend James Fraser famously warned that agricultural labour was liable to 'unsex a woman in dress, gait, manners, character, making her rough, coarse, clumsy, masculine'. To him it was work that generated a 'very pregnant social mischief, by unfitting or indisposing her for a woman's proper duties at home'.[1] His views on labouring women were by no means exceptional.[2] Status-conscious farmer's wives and daughters, on the other hand, were vilified for removing themselves from economically productive roles on the farm and cultivating a lifestyle of leisure and gentility. In 1880 Richard Jefferies demanded to know where the tenant farmers' wife who made butter and cheese and salted bacon, assisted by her daughters, had gone. In his words the wife had become 'a fine lady', travelling in dandy-cart, clad in silks, satins, kid gloves, ostrich feathers, with 'a suspicion of perfume about her'. Her daughters, 'pale and interesting', were now proficient in piano-playing and painting. Their once offices of work – the dairy, farmyard and kitchen – were directed by paid employees.[3] Portrayals like these helped to promulgate the view that women were marginal to the farming world in Victorian England and those that remained were an affront to their sex.

---

[1] British Parliamentary Papers (BPP), 1867–8, XVII, 'First Report from the Commissioners on the Employment of Children, Young Persons and Women in Agriculture', Report by the Reverend James Fraser, p. 16.

[2] For a wider discussion of the depiction of Victorian women workers on the land see Karen Sayer, *Women of the Fields: Representations of Rural Women in the Nineteenth Century* (Manchester, 1995).

[3] Richard Jefferies, *Hodge and His Masters* (1880; 1992 edn), p. 77.

Historians have now done much to dismantle these stereotypes. The participation of women as paid workers in agriculture, as both day labourers and hired servants, has generated a considerable body of academic literature that has drawn attention to intricate regional patterns of employment levels and wage rates in the nineteenth century.[4] Diaries and other records kept by farmers' wives have revealed the multifarious roles they performed in the late eighteenth century, and recent research has suggested that their vital economic contributions continued into the nineteenth century and beyond.[5] Within this current upsurge of academic interest in the working lives of Victorian rural women, one figure has been largely overlooked however: the female farmer.

Existing studies construct an account of the marginalisation of women farmers in a society that was increasingly dominated by a rigid demarcation of male and female spheres. Leonore Davidoff argues that the institutions of farming – the clubs and societies, market halls and Corn Exchanges, sporting pursuits and leisure venues – effectively barred the involvement of women over the late eighteenth and early nineteenth centuries, making it increasingly difficult for a woman to manage a farm. This practical exclusion ran alongside a conscious withdrawal of middle-class farming women from productive to domestic and familial roles. Davidoff claims that by the 'mid century "golden age" of high agriculture', the withdrawal of women 'with ambitions for gentility from active participation in the running of the farm was complete'.[6] Pamela Horn suggests that after the mid nineteenth century it continued to be 'comparatively rare

---

[4]   Joyce Burnette, 'Laborers at the Oakes: Changes in the demand for female day-laborers at a farm near Sheffield during the Agricultural Revolution', *J. Economic History*, 39 (1999), pp. 41–67; eadem, 'The wages and employment of female day-laborers in Agriculture, 1740–1850', *EcHR*, 57 (2004), pp. 664–90; eadem, 'Married with children: The family status of female agricultural labourers at two south-western farms in the 1830s and 1840s', *AgHR*, 55 (2007), pp. 75–94; Judy Gielgud, 'Nineteenth-century Farm Women in Northumberland and Cumbria: The Neglected Workforce', (unpublished DPhil thesis, University of Sussex, 1992); Celia Miller, 'The hidden workforce: Female fieldworkers in Gloucestershire, 1870–1901', *Southern Hist.*, 6 (1984), pp. 139–61; Pamela Sharpe, 'The female labour market in English Agriculture during the Industrial Revolution: Expansion or Contraction?', *AgHR*, 47 (1999), pp. 161–81; Helen V. Speechley, 'Female and Child Agricultural Day Labourers in Somerset, *c.*1685–1870', (unpublished PhD thesis, University of Exeter, 1999); Donna J. Ulyatt, 'Female agricultural labour on the Dixon Estate, Lincolnshire, 1801–17', *AgHR*, 54, (2006), pp. 79–92; Nicola Verdon, *Rural Women Workers in Nineteenth-Century England: Gender, Work and Wages* (Woodbridge, 2002), ch. 4.

[5]   Ruth Facer (ed.), *Mary Bacon's World: A Farmers' Wife in Eighteenth-Century Hampshire* (Newbury, 2010); Basil Cozens-Hardy, *Mary Hardy's Diary* (Norfolk Record Soc., 37, 1968); Nicola Verdon, '"... Subjects deserving of the highest praise": Farmers' wives and the farm economy in England, *c.*1700–1850', *AgHR*, 51 (2003), pp. 23–39; eadem, '"The modern countrywoman": Farm women, domesticity, and social change in interwar Britain', *History Workshop J.*, 70 (2010), pp. 86–107.

[6]   Leonore Davidoff, 'The Role of Gender in the "First Industrial Nation": Farming and the Countryside in England, 1780–1850', in Leonore Davidoff, *Worlds Between: Historical Perspectives on Gender and Class* (London, 1995), pp. 180–205 (at p. 200), first published in Rosemary Crompton and Michael Mann (eds), *Gender and Stratification* (Cambridge, 1986).

for women to be engaged as farmers or farm managers in their own right'.[7] The reason for this was the existence of significant gendered barriers to success: it was not appropriate for women to supervise farms with largely male workforces or to engage in corn and livestock marketing, their education did not prepare them for the application of scientific farming, and landlords were reluctant to give farm tenancies to women. Despite these impediments Horn goes on to provide a brief but tantalising outline of several women – both widows and single women – who did manage their own farms in Victorian England. She minimises their significance, however, by suggesting the 'scarcity' of women farmers was linked to the Victorian perception that 'women in business' were 'regarded as freaks'.[8]

The Victorian female farmer then remains an elusive figure, difficult to classify and hard to locate in the historical record. As Davidoff points out, the limited number of sources 'from the women themselves', wearied by the daily grind and 'social isolation' that a farming life often brought, has hampered the historians' task in the past.[9] But some sources do survive. This chapter will offer insight into the world of the Victorian woman farmer through the analysis of one the few extant memoirs written and published by a woman farmer in the nineteenth century. She was Louise Cresswell, the self-titled 'Lady Farmer'. Her book, *Eighteen Years on the Sandringham Estate* was published in 1887 and recounts the trials and tribulations of a widow tenant farmer on the Norfolk estate of the Prince of Wales.[10] Louise Hogge was born into a prosperous entrepreneurial Bedfordshire family in 1830. Their kinship networks often brought them to north Norfolk, where she met and married Gerard Cresswell, the fifth son of a similarly affluent family, in 1862. Gerard had been tenant on a 140-acre farm at Sedgeford since 1859 and with their mutual 'love of horses, dogs, sport and country life', Louise was attracted by the idea of 'husband and wife being able to work together' in farming.[11] The lease to a much larger enterprise on the Sandringham estate, Appleton Farm, was signed before their marriage and they moved there in October 1862. The farm covered some 900 acres, with more than 1,200 head of livestock and a large labour force. The Cresswell's dream of prosperous partnership did not last; Gerard died just three years later, leaving Louise a widow with a young child at the age of 35. She continued to manage the farm for the next 15 years, until 1880.

October 1862 was also the date that the whole estate officially passed into the hands of its new royal owner, having been sold for £220,000 by Charles Spencer

---

[7]   Pamela Horn, *Victorian Countrywomen* (London, 1990), p. 124.

[8]   Ibid., pp. 124, 218.

[9]   Davidoff, 'Role of Gender', pp. 199, 200.

[10]   Mrs Gerard Cresswell, *Eighteen Years on the Sandringham Estate* (London, 1887). She was christened Louisa but referred to herself as Louise.

[11]   Cresswell, *Eighteen Years*, pp. 3–4.

Cowper in February that year. The Prince of Wales viewed Sandringham as a private get-away, an escape from the prying eyes of his family, and a pleasure ground. It was acquired primarily as a sporting estate where he could indulge his passion for shooting, with gamekeepers employed to rear pheasants, partridges and hares, and the 'battue' style of shooting, with beaters driving prey into the line of fire, adopted enthusiastically. A clause in their contract reserved all sporting rights to the landlord. This would cause Mrs Cresswell great difficulty in the years to come.

The autobiography was not her first foray into print. Cresswell had previously published two well-regarded pamphlets on farming, *Norfolk and the Squires* and *Farming with Profit*, published in 1875 and 1880, the first whilst she was still a tenant on the estate, the second as she was preparing to leave.[12] Her memoir, however, was written some years after she left the farm. It is partly an act of retribution against her royal landlord who she believed had deceived and victimised her. It is by no means an undiscovered source. Cresswell's confrontation with her landlord over the damage done by his game, beaters and shooting parties has previously been cited by Richard W. Hoyle in his exploration of the relationship between royalty and field sports in the nineteenth century.[13] Cresswell has also been the subject of a recent popular biographical account by Mary Mackie. This traces Cresswell's familial background and examines in great detail the fractious relationship between farmer and landlord by consulting the extensive correspondence between Cresswell and Edmund Beck, Steward of the Sandringham estate, which is held in the Royal Archives.[14] Mackie points out that Cresswell is by no means a reliable commentator. Her deployment of dates and names throughout the autobiography is sketchy at best, and with years of resentment and fury stored up, the book was conceived and penned after she had been ousted from the farm as an 'act of vengeance' in which 'she frequently allowed bitterness to cloud both her judgement and her memory'.[15] There are clear discrepancies between Cresswell's version of events and those revealed through the private correspondence. However, her autobiography includes detailed and revealing passages about her position as a widow running a large East Anglian farm, cultivating a wide range of produce, with a varied workforce across the crucial Victorian decades, when farming lurched from prosperity to

---

[12]　Mrs Gerard Cresswell, *Norfolk and the Squires, Clergy, Farmers, and Labourers etc. by 'A Lady Farmer'* (London, 1875); Mrs Gerard Cresswell, *How the Farming in Great Britain Can Be Made to Pay* (2nd edn, London, 1881). This was first published as *Farming with Profit, or How the Farms in Great Britain Can Be Made to Pay* (London, 1880).

[13]　R.W. Hoyle, 'Royalty and the Diversity of Field Sports, c. 1840–1981', in R.W. Hoyle (ed.), *Our Hunting Fathers: Field Sports in England after 1850* (Preston, 2007), pp. 53–5.

[14]　Mary Mackie, *The Prince's Thorn: Edward VII and the Lady Farmer of Sandringham* (Cambridge, 2008).

[15]　Ibid., *Prince's Thorn*, p. 264.

Table 9.1   Farmers/graziers in England and Wales, 1851–1901 (all ages)

Year	Male	Female	per cent female
1851	226,515	22,916	9.2
1861	226,957	22,778	9.1
1871	225,569	24,338	9.7
1881	203,329	20,614	9.2
1891	201,918	21,692	9.7
1901	202,751	21,548	9.6

Source: Census of England and Wales, 1851–1901.

depression. In this respect it is a unique and untapped resource. It will be used here to explore the difficulties and opportunities that farming presented to widows in the nineteenth century. Cresswell writes about how she understood her own position as a woman farming, how she viewed the agricultural world around her and how she ran the farm on a day-to-day, season-by-season basis. Before we meet Cresswell, however, some context will be provided through an analysis of the nineteenth-century census data. How many women farmed in the nineteenth century? Where did women farm? How many of them were widows? Whilst this source presents women farmers through the official categories established by census administrators – and certainly doesn't allow the women to 'speak for themselves' – it offers an important overview of their place in Victorian farming.

I

How many women farmed in Victorian England? In an era where women were effectively barred from other professions on account of their gender, and feminist campaigners had to mount hard-fought and protracted battles to dismantle barriers to employment in areas such as the law and medicine, the number of women who were classified as farmers was relatively high. As Table 9.1 shows, between 1851 and 1901, although a period characterised by great flux in farming fortunes, and one that saw a steep decline in the employment of paid female labour on the land, the number of women farmers remained remarkably stable at around 22,000. This meant that throughout the second half of the nineteenth century just under one in ten farms in England and Wales was headed by a woman.

Women farmers were a feature of all the English counties. This is demonstrated in Table 9.2 for 1851. Although regional patterns were not paramount, the counties which account for the lowest percentage of women farmers largely lay in the south-west and south-east and those that include the highest were northern and border counties (with Cambridgeshire as a striking exception). Women farmers were not a homogeneous group though. A minority were women farming in their own right, often the daughters of farmers carrying on in the business in which they had been raised and schooled. The vast majority of female farmers were, however, widows. Although the nineteenth-century census summary tables did not provide a breakdown of the marital status of female farmers, the age profiles reveal the dominance of older women and the general census reports surmised that around three out of every four women farming were widows, living in households with their children and 'carrying on the farms formerly held by their husbands' until a son or other male relative could take the reins.[16] From the late nineteenth century farming also increasingly began to be viewed as an intellectually and physically stimulating profession for middle-class educated townswomen, stymied by an urban environment and attracted to the possibilities offered by an outdoor life but this is not an aspect of women farming that concerns us here.[17]

Where farms were tenanted, allowing a widow to step into the void left by the death of her husband was seen as a convenient and usually temporary measure by estate owners and stewards to ensure continuity of family occupancy, but it was a step which was sanctioned by them with great reluctance. Debate in the mid-Victorian feminist periodicals linked the unwillingness of landlords to offer tenancies to widows to women's exclusion from the ballot box and their inability to defend agricultural interests through the exercise of a vote. In 1866 Barbara Leigh Smith, a leading early campaigner for women's suffrage, traced several 'instances of hardship ... directly to exclusion from the franchise and to no other cause', citing the example of one estate in Suffolk 'on which seven widows have been ejected, who, if they had had votes, would have been continued as tenants'.[18] In reality, however, resistance centred on women's physical and psychological capabilities: were they able to negotiate the shift from being a partner in a farm within marriage to being the sole manager of a farm, particularly on a large enterprise? As an article by the Lincolnshire landowners' daughter Jessie Boucherett in the feminist periodical *The Englishwoman's Review* pointed out, women were 'objectionable as tenants ... because landlords are afraid that a

16   BPP, 1904, CVIII, *Census of England and Wales, 1901: General Report with Appendices*, p. 103.

17   For further analysis of these women see Nicola Verdon, 'Business and pleasure: Middle-class women's work and the professionalization of farming in England, 1890–1939', *J. British Studies*, 51 (2012), pp. 393–415.

18   Barbara Leigh Smith, 'Reasons of the Enfranchisement of Women', in C.A. Lacey (ed.), *Barbara Leigh Smith Bodichon and the Langham Place Group* (London and New York, 1987), p. 105. I would like to thank Karen Sayer for allowing me access to her unpublished paper 'A Fine Lady Farmer: Victorian Farm Women, Perceptions and Perspectives', which analyses in greater depth the arguments mounted by the Langham Place feminists over the place of women in farming in the 1860s and 1870s.

Table 9.2   Percentage of farmers who were female in the English counties, 1851

County	per cent	County	per cent
Bedfordshire	7.6	Lincolnshire	7.1
Berkshire	7.4	Middlesex	5.9
Buckinghamshire	7.7	Norfolk	6.9
Cambridgeshire	36.7	North Riding	10.1
Cheshire	11.9	Northamptonshire	10.1
Cornwall	6.4	Northumberland	10
Cumberland	10.9	Nottinghamshire	10.4
Derbyshire	12.1	Oxfordshire	8.6
Devonshire	4.1	Rutland	12.3
Dorset	5.4	Shropshire	11
Durham	8.6	Somerset	7.4
East Riding	6.2	Staffordshire	9.8
Essex	8.6	Suffolk	7.9
Gloucestershire	8.1	Surrey	6.1
Hampshire	6.5	Sussex	5.7
Herefordshire	10.2	Warwickshire	9.5
Hertfordshire	9.6	West Riding	9.5
Huntingdonshire	5.6	Westmorland	8.5
Kent	7.0	Wiltshire	8
Lancashire	10.1	Worcestershire	11.2
Leicestershire	9.4		

Source: Census of Population for England and Wales, 1851.

woman would not understand the business of farming and would consequently be unable to pay her rent'.[19]

II

This was exactly the type of opposition that confronted Louise Cresswell. On her husband's death she had wanted to remain on the farm to bring to fruition all the plans that they had laid down together. The hard work, she hoped, would act as 'an opiate and distraction'.[20] But there was considerable disquiet about such a move. Whilst Cresswell did not live alone, corroborating other studies

---

[19]   Jessie Boucherett, 'Agriculture as an employment for women', *The Englishwoman's Rev.*, 79 (Nov. 1879), p. 481.

[20]   Cresswell, *Eighteen Years*, p. 25.

that show few widows of any age group or occupation lived unaccompanied in the nineteenth century, her circumstances were relatively unusual.[21] Firstly she was a young widow, without the assistance of a male relative to manage the day-to-day running of the farm. Having an adult son in the household was seen as particularly desirable for female-headed farms as sons provided not only physical labour, but could also assist in directing the outdoor labourers (who were likely to have been men) and oversee the commercial activities of the farm in the marketplace. Cresswell's only son was a toddler when she was widowed in 1865 and it was clear that her tenancy was not meant as a temporary 'holding operation' until he came of age. Secondly, Cresswell was farming in a region that was seen as the pioneer of agricultural progression and viewed as the exemplar of English arable 'High Farming'. This was farming on a large scale that often bestowed social, economic, and in some cases, political status on its proprietors. It was farming that was also deemed inappropriate for a woman to undertake. Expert advisers in the second half of the nineteenth century constructed a gendered divide between 'proper' farming, which was large-scale, arable and male, and 'subsidiary' farming, which was small-scale and concentrated on the 'feminine' areas of production such as dairy and poultry. Writing in *The Englishwoman's Review* in 1880, J. Mackenzie expressed regret 'when widows came to manage an arable or grazing farm', because, he argued, 'they were never able to prevent plundering, or manage details well'. Instead he advised the active and intelligent woman 'to turn her mind to dairy, poultry and bee-farming', all 'as sure to pay well if well looked after'.[22] This was advice that lingered for several decades. In 1899 the agricultural writer Professor James Long argued that women should not be counselled to 'occupy broad acres, to manage flocks and herds and studs, and to undertake the multifarious and anxious duties of the agriculturist' but to 'undertake those forms of culture, whether they relate to animals or the soil, which come within their sphere'.[23] His fellow commentator Sir James Blythe explained that by 'reason of their habits of neatness' women were more suited to the cultivation of 'smaller articles of produce' of the dairy, farmyard, greenhouse and garden because 'muscular strength' was 'unnecessary' and women's 'physical inferiority' was 'counterbalanced' by a 'deftness' of touch 'in the lighter occupations'.[24] Cresswell would have scoffed at such suggestions.

---

[21]   See for example Richard Wall, 'Elderly widows and widowers and their co-residents in late nineteenth and early twentieth-century England and Wales', *History of the Family*, 7 (2002), pp. 139–55; Sonya O. Rose, 'Widowhood and Poverty in Nineteenth-Century Nottinghamshire', in J. Henderson and R. Wall (eds), *Poor Women and Children in the European Past* (London, 1994), pp. 269–91.

[22]   *The Englishwoman's Review*, 82 (Feb. 1880), p. 85.

[23]   Professor James Long, 'The farm for the new woman', *The Woman's Agricultural Times*, 1, no. 2 (Aug. 1899), p. 4.

[24]   Sir James Blythe, 'Women and agriculture', *The Woman's Agricultural Times*, 1, no. 1 (July 1899), p. 3.

Cresswell well understood the misgivings that were expressed by neighbours and acquaintances at her plans to take over the running of a large Norfolk farm. As she explained:

> The opposition encountered when I first expressed myself willing and capable of undertaking the management of nearly nine hundred acres of land, twelve or thirteen hundred head of live stock, a large staff of labourers and other addenda, could hardly be considered unreasonable. It seemed a desperate attempt for a woman, and every possible argument was brought to bear against it.[25]

These doubts were overcome by the good name of her husband in the local community and the use that Cresswell could make of the networks that he had built up. She recognised her indebtedness to the neighbouring farmers in her early years and felt that she owed 'a deep debt of gratitude' to them because of their 'kindness ... unselfish assistance when I most needed it, their time and valuable experience always at my service ...'.[26] It was only because of her connections 'that every objection was finally removed' and she was able to install herself, as she put it, 'in the new position of lady-farmer'.[27] Widow farmers therefore had to prove to landlords that they were capable of business acumen but they were often only taken seriously if they had the backing of 'some man of substance who was willing to stand security for her', as Boucherett put it.[28] In another case from the mid 1860s, the widowed Mrs Orphen was considered incapable of managing the two farms that came under the tenancy of her late husband in Essex. The land agent, John Oxley-Parker, believed that 'Unless the management is really under the control of a man of experience and knowledge of business there really is very little hope of her doing any good in the farm'.[29] Her younger son was also considered 'quite unequal' to the task and after finding herself in considerable rent arrears she was counselled to give up the farm, advice she reluctantly but finally took. Cresswell however was lucky in having the services of the substantial local farmer, John Groom ('Mr Broome' in her account), who had taken Gerard Cresswell under his wing at the beginning of his farming career in the late 1850s. 'Broome' guaranteed Cresswell 'his own personal superintendence' and insisted that she applied 'to him in any business difficulty'.[30] He subsequently kept a close watch over her decision-making and development throughout her time on the farm.

---

25   Cresswell, *Eighteen Years*, pp. 25–6.

26   Cresswell, *Norfolk and the Squires*, p. 25.

27   Cresswell, *Eighteen Years*, p. 28.

28   Boucherett, 'Agriculture', p. 481.

29   J. Oxley Parker, *The Oxley Parker Papers* (Colchester, 1964), p. 101.

30   Cresswell, *Eighteen Years*, p. 28.

Cresswell's young age at widowhood and the size of her holding marked her circumstances out as unusual, although as the census of 1861 reported, women could 'often display remarkable talent in the management of large establishments'.[31] In order to be accepted, however, she had to relinquish many of the social and personal accoutrements usually associated with Victorian middle-class womanhood. She understood that she could not simply continue 'to lead a woman's everyday sort of life' but instead had to become 'wholly engrossed' in the work of the farm, 'and do and think of little else from morning till night'.[32] This meant foregoing local 'society' activities (although 'occasional visitors and old friends were always welcome') and spending long solitary evenings 'studying the intricacies of my profession and keeping accounts'.[33] She understood that without the protection of a husband, widowhood placed her in a vulnerable position in terms of personal security, living in 'that lonely place ... with quite enough valuables in the house to make it worthwhile to rob and murder me'.[34] In her own estimation, Cresswell imagined that she worked as hard, if not harder, than any other member of staff on the farm, with the calls on her time being continuous. She explained that unlike the labourers she employed during harvest, she did not get regular morning or afternoon breaks ('elevens and fours') 'for when they were taking their siesta, I had to look round the stock, and the marsh farm' and that she took her meals in a 'promiscuous' fashion 'when there was a few minutes to spare, and was out again directly'.[35] She generally 'contrived' to be at home for five o'clock tea 'which fell conveniently between coming in from the land and milking time, and the last round of the yards' but often on 'thinking I had finished for the day, would have to be out again for hours', checking the livestock in the sheds and stables.[36] She took Sundays off to spend with her son, arguing that only when you 'lead a working life' could you really understand what a 'real' day of rest was.[37] Her appearance, clad in 'serge gown and thick boots', came to reflect that of a working farmer rather than a Victorian lady: but despite her protestations that she was 'comfortable in nothing else', she did dress 'like other people, and felt quite respectable' on Sunday visits to church or other 'great occasions'.[38] The physical and continuous nature of the work and the utilitarian clothing worn by women is common in other contemporary descriptions of female farmers. The autobiography of Fred Kitchen, a hired lad

---

31   BPP, 1863, LIII (i), *Census of England and Wales, 1861, III, General Report with appendix of tables*, p. 36.

32   Cresswell, *Eighteen Years*, pp. 26–7.

33   Ibid., pp. 98, 45.

34   Ibid., p. 36.

35   Ibid., p. 38.

36   Ibid., p. 112.

37   Ibid., pp. 98, 125.

38   Ibid., pp. 151, 108.

on a turn of the twentieth century Yorkshire farm run by a widow, includes this description of his 'missus':

> A tall, raw-boned woman she was, with skirts permanently tucked up aft, and wearing a black hat of no particular shape. She was as hefty as a young navvy, and as strong as a young horse. She tackled any kind of work that turned up, such as slicing turnips for the beasts, teaming loads of hay, or even assisting at calving a cow. She was never lost for a job, but was always on the go ... .[39]

For Cresswell, the hard work and the attire were badges of honour, symbols of her involvement in 'the endless variety of farm life'.[40]

Whilst Cresswell conceded that the running of the farm was 'a severe mental and physical strain', it provided a range of opportunities and rewards not usually available to Victorian widows.[41] Pat Jalland argues that widowhood often became a period of effective 'social exile'. As Victorian society dictated that middle-class women should be totally dependent on their husband, financially, socially and emotionally, women could experience a 'total disintegration of their lives' in their absence.[42] For many their financial security collapsed but it was virtually impossible to find meaningful and remunerate employment. Opportunities for middle-class women to enter the labour market were very limited in the nineteenth century, and widows, especially those with children, were excluded from the narrow range of jobs that were deemed acceptable for unmarried middle-class women.[43] Cresswell was therefore atypical in having a job, farming, that presented 'widespread interests and fascination'.[44] Historians have effectively traced the efforts made by Victorian feminists to open up the urban professions to women in the second half of the nineteenth century whilst ignoring the many women who were already accruing specialist skills and knowledge managing farms in the countryside. For some women farming would have been a way of life, inherited through family ties over generations, but for others from non-farming backgrounds like Cresswell, it became, as she described it, an 'occupation and profession'.[45] Although Cresswell does not meet all the criteria recognised by historians as constituting a 'professional' worker, not being formally educated or trained in agriculture for example, farming

---

[39]   Fred Kitchen, *Brother to the Ox: The Autobiography of a Farm Labourer* (London, 1942), p. 37.

[40]   Cresswell, *Eighteen Years*, p. 100.

[41]   Ibid., p. 224.

[42]   Pat Jalland, *Death in the Victorian Family* (Oxford, 1996), pp. 231, 235.

[43]   Cynthia Curran, 'Private women, public needs: Middle-class widows in Victorian England', *Albion*, 25 (1993), p. 229.

[44]   Cresswell, *Eighteen Years*, p. 225.

[45]   Ibid.

bestowed on her a range of personal rewards that women who engaged in more typical 'feminized' Victorian occupations did not experience.[46]

It is clear from the detailed descriptions she includes in her autobiography of work patterns across the days and seasons that Cresswell was knowledgeable about farming techniques and conversant with changing practices. Spring for her was the key season of the year with 'heaps of work crowding in together, seed sowing and lambing time in one', the former 'not so risky and distracting' as the latter.[47] Attention then turned to summer 'haysel', turnip hoeing and scouring, before the excitements of the harvest. From May to October her stocks were shifted back and forth for grazing on the marshes. Bullocks were then fattened in boxes, 'a pathway between ... and a roofed overhead, a sort of Burlington Arcade, only much more interesting, and a splendid place for walking up and down in winter'.[48] Her stock 'had been gradually improved' including her Norfolk pigs, who were 'little beauties', and 'the dark-faced ewes' who were 'a leading feature of the place'.[49] She also saw beauty in more mundane tasks, inspecting the growing mangolds and turnips with 'excitement and interest, and watching the effects of different manures and soils'.[50] She was proud that the farm became noted for 'its high state of cultivation, even in this far-famed agricultural county', with visits from royal dignitaries and 'distinguished' agriculturalists from up and down the land.[51] Cresswell expresses an authentic if somewhat florid appreciation of her working environment and local surroundings. Nature, she explains:

> is full of compensations, and if you want scenery in the Eastern Counties, you
> must look up instead of down, where with a little imagination you will discover
> Alpine peaks and mountains and Turneresque colouring to your heart's content

in the autumn skies and sunsets.[52] Although Cresswell was careful to dispel the romantic image that some of her friends may have acquired on their brief visits to the farm, the distinction she draws between her farming life and the narrow confines of life of a more typical middle-class Victorian woman is revealing. Her life was not 'all cakes and cream', she argued:

---

[46]   Harold Perkin, *The Rise of Professional Society: England since 1880* (London, 2002). For further exploration of the rise of farming as a profession for women after 1880, see Verdon, 'Business and pleasure'.

[47]   Cresswell, *Eighteen Years*, pp. 100, 104.

[48]   Ibid., p. 109.

[49]   Ibid., pp. 97, 180, 102.

[50]   Ibid., p. 103.

[51]   Ibid., p. 97.

[52]   Ibid., p. 104.

but I would not have led any other for the world, or exchanged it for the highest position that could have been offered me; while the *bona-fide* farm 'worrits' were bearable in the average course of things and had nothing of the petty galling nature about them that embitters so many women's lives. Cattle diseases, strikes, free trade, and other 'burning questions' you share with the rest of the agricultural world, and have a wide horizon for your cares, instead of a narrow, carking one. And supposing I were a little overworked and overdone sometimes out of doors, all was rest and peace within.[53]

Cresswell was certainly a hands-on farm manager with an eye for good stock and a direct manner. She performed the whole range of duties – hiring and firing of staff, giving orders, attending market and entering cattle shows – that many considered were off-limits for women. She chided farmers' wives and daughters for looking 'down upon manual labour' and regulating 'your position in society accordingly', arguing that they 'lead useless lives, doing fancy work in the best parlour ... considering themselves superior to their more useful and industrious sisters'.[54] Cresswell appears to have revelled in her outsider status, a woman blazing a trail. She was not afraid to 'lift up *my* voice' in her dispute with her landlord.[55] As we will see below she did not heed legal advice that it was 'unpleasant for a lady to appear in person' to defend herself in court.[56] On the farm she preferred to keep the 'management of the stock entirely in my own hands'.[57] She kept a close watch over mounting animal cake and meal bills, regulating 'the quantity for each lot'.[58] Her brother's solicitor commented in 1879 that she was 'out farming all day, and blows up her men, etc. in fact she won't let her Foreman do much'.[59] She professed to 'enjoying a business excuse for an outing and gossip' that the weekly Tuesday market at Kings Lynn offered.[60] She viewed the annual cattle shows as her 'field days', delighted by 'the opportunity of professional discussions' with fellow farmers from around the globe, the awards cementing 'a good name in the agricultural world'.[61] At the end of her tenancy Cresswell suggested that she could put all her knowledge and experience to good use as a

53 Ibid., p. 99.
54 Cresswell, *How the Farming... Can Be Made to Pay*, p. 28.
55 Cresswell, *Eighteen Years*, p. 66.
56 Ibid., p. 42.
57 Ibid., p. 110.
58 Ibid., p. 109.
59 Quoted in Mackie, *Prince's Thorn*, p. 215.
60 Cresswell, *Eighteen Years*, p. 119.
61 Ibid., pp. 177–8.

neighbourhood advice centre 'setting up as a sort of itinerant and professional "help" to landlords in difficulties'.[62]

Cresswell therefore operated in a public sphere, remonstrating, conversing and socialising with men at every level. All of these contravened dominant Victorian ideals of feminine respectability but Cresswell discloses no impediments based upon her gender. She does acknowledge, however, that 'from the unusual circumstances of being managed by a lady', her farm was considered by some to be 'more conspicuous, than the generality'.[63] Cresswell exudes a confidence based upon her social class. She was 'no cockney', rather 'a Tory of the old school', and all her 'grubbing' about on the farm 'on friendly gossiping terms with almost every dealer, drover and pig-jobber in the country side', had not led to a diminution in her social status. She had not lost 'in the smallest degree the position of a gentlewoman'.[64] It was her standing in the agricultural community as a good farmer that was most important to her. Her reputation as a lady was not in doubt. She was therefore concerned that her altercation with the Prince of Wales should not sully her professional repute, first and foremost. As she wrote in 1880:

> My character as a Lady can take care of itself, but anything that affects my agricultural reputation or the care of my animals touches a very tender point. This may seem very absurd but would an Officer like to be reported for neglect of his duty to the Commander-in-Chief? The farm is *my* 'Regiment'.[65]

But although Cresswell often depicts herself as a woman alone, contending unflinchingly with the vagaries of the farming world, she did not run the farm single-handed. Far from it. The 'rest and peace' within the farmhouse was made possible by the industry of a number of indoor servants. The housekeeping was appropriated by the faithful nurse, who stayed on as other servants came and went, and 'would do anything for us'. The governess 'wrote the letters and did the flowers and refinements'.[66] They were assisted by 'an antediluvian from the village, and a boy from the farm'.[67] The household servants, particularly those used on a part-time or irregular basis are largely invisible in her account but, as Jessica Gerard established some years ago, such workers were an essential cog in country life, giving households 'the flexibility to meet its varying needs

---

62   Cresswell, *How the Farming ... Can Be Made to Pay*, p. 12.
63   Cresswell, *Eighteen Years*, p. 67.
64   Ibid., p. 63; Cresswell, *How the Farming ... Can Be Made to Pay*, pp. 13–15.
65   Quoted in Mackie, *Prince's Thorn*, p. 223.
66   Cresswell, *Eighteen Years*, p. 99.
67   Ibid., p. 19.

while minimizing disruption to its formal organizational structure'.[68] Outdoors, Cresswell employed the customary range of permanent and casual workers that were essential to a large farm business, including gang labour to perform seasonal tasks such as pulling turnips.[69] Her view of the workforce sometimes represents a strain of Victorian paternalist benevolence, but it also often betrays a strong sense of condescension and even contempt. At the top of the occupational hierarchy she understood that the appointment of a reliable steward was essential 'upon all farms of extensive acreage'.[70] However, her first steward at Appleton Farm, 'Dinger' (her pseudonym for James Mingay), proved to be a disaster. Her dealings with him reveal some of the difficulties widows faced in the hiring and firing of staff. He came with glowing references from reliable sources and although looking back Cresswell was puzzled 'that anyone should have been willing to part with such a treasure', she goes on to confess 'being a little apt to be taken in by plausible roguery well done'.[71] After three months of 'irreproachable' work he began to transgress and was ordered to quit by Cresswell. This decision, however, was only taken 'subject to Mr Broome's approval, who came riding over in all haste, as he always did if anything was wrong'.[72] Far from going quietly, 'Dinger' 'organised a rebellion amongst the harvest men as a legacy' and later brought an action against Cresswell for loss of wages amounting to just over £14.[73] Both generated considerable local attention but Cresswell depicts them as personal challenges to overcome. She decided to let the harvest rebels go and was forced to hire a ramshackle crew of men from town. She again consulted Broome but asked him to allow her 'to see if I could pull through alone' in order to 'establish my authority' over the men.[74] She took 'the steward's place myself', installing the head ploughman, a Methodist with authority amongst the labourers, as foreman. Although Cresswell's concedes that not everything ran smoothly, her recollection of the harvest is imbued with sense of communal nostalgia and gentlemanly camaraderie:

> The *coup d'état* proved a great success, and whatever the antecedents of my scratch pack may have been, they behaved in the most exemplary manner, and were obliging, orderly, and respectful ... Tom, Dick, and Harry would have their joke

---

[68]   J.A. Gerard, 'Invisible servants: The country house and the local community', *Historical Res.*, 57, (1984), pp. 178–88.

[69]   Cresswell, *Eighteen Years*, p. 59. See also Nicola Verdon, 'The employment of women and children in agriculture: A reassessment of agricultural gangs in nineteenth-century Norfolk', *AgHR*, 49 (2001), pp. 41–55.

[70]   Cresswell, *Eighteen Years*, p. 49.

[71]   Ibid., p. 30.

[72]   Ibid., p. 31.

[73]   Ibid., p. 32.

[74]   Ibid., p. 33.

and chaff; but not one coarse word or remark did I hear, or anything that was not fit for a lady's ear ... when the last stack was topped-up and it was time for the party to disperse, I was both sorry and relieved; we parted the best of friends in a chorus of harvest cheers ... I suppose all is well that ends well![75]

Nor did a personal appearance in court create any anxiety 'in the great case of Dinger *versus* the Lady Farmer' as Cresswell believed she had little to lose and 'must take things as they come'.[76] Treated by the prosecution as an irresolute woman who 'knew nothing and understood less', it gave her the opportunity to publicly display her wide farming knowledge and allow the faithful Broome and trusted farm servants to vouch for her character.[77] She won the case. Her next steward, in contrast, Robert Faircloth, was 'a worthy man' whose tenure was long, loyal and uneventful.[78]

Cresswell recognised dependability in the other more permanent members of her workforce. These, as she explained in *Norfolk and the Squires*, were the 'superior' men, 'the trustworthy Norfolk labourer; hard-working and faithful, patient and enduring', who stood by their employer and who sometimes rose up the farming ladder to become bailiffs and stewards, and even exceptionally, small farmers themselves.[79] At Appleton Farm she viewed her stock-keepers as being men who were fond of their animals 'and less erratic and more reliable than the other men'.[80] Her yardman, 'Trusty' Trundle, is described as a loyal and diffident servant, 'the best man in the country, who stayed with me till the last, for not being able to read or write, his thoughts were concentrated on his work'.[81] Her farm labourers in contrast, are largely depicted as childlike, dim-witted and corruptible. In this she reflects the dominant mid nineteenth century elite characterisation of the farm labourer as 'Hodge', backward, debased and bestial.[82] John Dent, writing on the 'Present Condition of the English Agricultural Labourer' in 1871 argued, in counties of southern and western England, where agriculture was the dominant employment and modern transport networks had yet to permeate, the labourer was 'unimaginative, ill-clothed, ill-educated, ill-paid, ignorant of all that is taking place beyond his own village, dissatisfied with

---

75 Ibid., pp. 36–9.

76 Ibid., p. 42.

77 Ibid., p. 45.

78 Ibid., p. 49.

79 Cresswell, *Norfolk and the Squires*, p. 28.

80 Cresswell, *Eighteen Years*, p. 33.

81 Ibid., p. 110.

82 Mark Freeman, 'The agricultural labourer and the "Hodge" stereotype, *c.*1850–1914', *AgHR*, 49 (2001), p. 174.

his position and yet without energy or effort to improve it'.[83] Cresswell would have baulked at the suggestion that labourers were ill-paid but would otherwise have approved of Dent's description. She believed that during the harvest revolt of the late 1860s, 'Dinger' was able to stir revolt because 'farm hands are as easily led away as a pack of children, only to repent of their folly afterwards'.[84] She suspected some of them of more dishonest activities, 'pilfering and loitering', if she was absent from the farm for too long.[85]

It is not surprising then that the ferocity of the trade union movement of the early 1870s took farmers like Cresswell by surprise. We don't know whether any of her labourers were directly involved in union activities. However, her farm was situated in a region that was a focus of local unionism in the early 1870s and she would have been aware of events that were unfolding in the county.[86] The labourers, she argued, 'would never have thought of it for themselves', and had been 'goaded and excited into action' by paid agitators 'setting class against class, inciting them to lawless deeds'.[87] Cresswell assigns the breakdown of old paternalistic relations between employer and employee to the union movement, drawing a distinction between the halcyon days before the 1870s and the turbulent times that ensued. Before their appearance she claims that she had been 'on very pleasant terms with my men; I liked them and I think they liked me'. She cites the labourers' 'homely thrifty ways, true dignity and contentment' as evidence of them not 'being ashamed of looking and dressing like what they were'.[88] The union ruptured this harmonious scene. Now 'good feeling was at an end; old kindnesses and liberalities forgotten or ignored'.[89] The union turned them from compliant and content workers into surly and aggrieved men who cast 'sullen looks and dark insinuations', poured forth 'bitter invectives against their imaginary foes' and shirked work as if it was 'a deadly enemy' whilst still expecting 'the same pay on Friday night'.[90] She doubted that the labourers were 'happier nor better for what are called their improved prospects ... always craving for more'.[91] Cresswell is again representative of the wealthy farming class, who were convinced that the union had changed the labourer for the worse. As Alun Howkins shows, this was an attitude that was expressed again and

---

[83]   John Dent, 'The present condition of the English agricultural labourer', *Journal of the Royal Agricultural Society of England*, 2nd ser., 7 (1871), pp. 343–4.

[84]   Cresswell, *Eighteen Years*, pp. 32–3.

[85]   Ibid., p. 119.

[86]   See Alun Howkins, *Poor Labouring Men: Rural Radicalism in Norfolk, 1870–1923* (London, 1985).

[87]   Cresswell, *Eighteen Years*, p. 188.

[88]   Ibid., pp. 189, 200.

[89]   Ibid., p. 189.

[90]   Ibid., pp. 190, 192.

[91]   Ibid., p. 200.

again by farmers who gave evidence to the 1881 Richmond Commission and also underpinned the conclusion of the 1890s Royal Commission on Labour, that relations between master and man were irrevocably damaged.[92] One of the Assistant Commissioners, Aubrey Spencer, felt that in all the rural districts he had visited in the course of his enquiries in the early 1890s, the labourers:

> were said to be more 'independent' than they used to be, by which is meant, I think, that they regard their relation to the farmer more in a strictly commercial light than they used to, and that the quasi family tie which used to exist between farmers and labourer has now ceased to exist.[93]

Other changes were afoot that caused Cresswell alarm. The 1870 Education Act first established the principle of universal state elementary education for young children and permitted the building of schools funded by local ratepayers. Compulsion to attend was enacted in 1880. Many rural elites, including farmers who were afraid of losing access to a cheap source of local labour, were suspicious of this move. Like many of her contemporaries Cresswell thought that education would 'spoil' boys for agricultural work, into which, she argued, they should be initiated by the age of 9 or 10. She saw education as a 'town' affectation not suited to country life and whilst, to her eyes, it may have been necessary for 'mechanics and artisans' to be educated, the 'real and proper object of education consisted in training children for the position they will probably occupy in life'.[94] Labourers needed to know their station in life and any aspirations beyond this would have serious consequences for the fabric of agricultural work and rural life in general:

> With this new education craze I suppose another race of juveniles will be turned out, destitute of manners, religion, and no respecters of persons, and pretty useless they will be for agricultural purposes, shut up in those hot school-rooms for years, and idling about the village between times, their brains crammed with all sorts of rubbish, rendering them mentally and physically unfit for their work.[95]

Education, like the unions, was seen by Cresswell and her contemporaries as a disruptive force, unsettling social relations and widening labourers' horizons. Cresswell believed that Norfolk labourers were 'no longer clod-hoppers' by the

---

[92]   Alun Howkins, 'From Hodge to Lob: Reconstructing the English Farm Labourer, 1870–1914', in Malcolm Chase and Ian Dyke (eds), *Living and Learning: Essays in Honour of J.F.C. Harrison* (1996), pp. 219–21.

[93]   BPP, 1893–4, XXXV, Royal Commission on Labour: The Agricultural Labourer, I, England. Part V. Reports by Mr Aubrey J. Spencer, p. 19.

[94]   Cresswell, *Eighteen Years*, p. 128.

[95]   Ibid., p. 127.

early 1880s, yet when it came to granting agricultural labourers the vote in 1884, old assumptions about the essential backward nature of the rural working class still prevailed.[96] Cresswell was unsure that the Norfolk labourer would know how to cast his newly gained 'wote', surmising that any 'strangers' standing for Parliament would not be acceptable, 'for a labourer, being asked if he should be for Gladstone, answered indignantly that he "never heerd on him".[97] Here her attitude reflects the influential portrayal by Richard Jefferies of Roger, 'One of the New Voters', in 1885, drawn after a day's reaping to the public house to drink, smoke and talk, not about 'the last book, the last play; not saloon conversation; but theirs – talk in which neither you nor any one of your condition could really join. To us there would seem nothing at all in that conversation, vapid and subjectless; to them it means much'.[98]

Those at the forefront of the union were at pains to debunk the notion that all members of agricultural hierarchy, from landlords to labourers, were a united interest group. Joseph Arch told the 1881 Richmond Commission that it was a 'mockery to the agricultural labourer' to talk about the 'good feeling' between master and man, 'because the farmer had got all he could out of the labourer'.[99] But Cresswell pedalled the view popular amongst the farming elite during the agricultural depression that it was the farmers and landowners who were suffering the most. She complained that whilst the cost of most farm produce had 'risen enormously', expenses had 'risen in greater proportion', the balance sheet being 'very much the worse' for it.[100] She went as far as to claim that by the mid 1870s, the Norfolk farm labourer 'with privileges', was 'one of the best paid among the working classes'.[101] The double scourge of the trade unions and education had, according to Cresswell, therefore 'contributed their full share towards the great "depression"'.[102]

The late 1870s were indeed troubling times for Appleton Farm. After several years of relative calm and prosperity by the end of the decade, and having suffered a run of poor harvests, Cresswell was in rent arrears. Her sense of persecution at the hands of the Prince of Wales increased. The Prince's lawyer and land agent became 'the secret enemy'.[103] She was, she argues, 'hunted down', brought to 'submission' and could 'hardly see how I could have contended against the

[96] Cresswell, *How the Farming ... Can Be Made to Pay*, p. 22.

[97] Cresswell, *Eighteen Years*, p. 203.

[98] Richard Jefferies, 'One of the New Voters', in *The Open Air* (1885), p. 38.

[99] BPP, 1882, XIV, Royal Commission on Depressed State of the Agricultural Interest; Minutes of Evidence, p. 92.

[100] Cresswell, *Eighteen Years*, p. 187.

[101] Cresswell, *Norfolk and the Squires*, p. 32.

[102] Cresswell, *Eighteen Years*, p. 200.

[103] Ibid., pp. 218.

adverse circumstances that came crowding upon me all at once'.[104] She accused Edmund Beck, the land agent, of being a 'mischief' maker. Without mentioning any names her 1880 pamphlet identified a group of land agents who had such powers invested on them that they 'become the greatest possible drawbacks to peace and prosperity', harbouring resentment against farm tenants based upon their class and gender. Agents, she claimed, looked:

> with mortal jealousy upon any one above him in the social scale, or whose outspoken, straightforward ways are a standing reproach and contrast, and will probably contrive sooner or later to ruin and oust him from his holding, persuading the Squire by some cleverly devised misinterpretation (and it is marvellous the power these men so often acquire over their masters) that gentlemen and lady tenants are a grand mistake upon the property and the sooner they are got rid of the better ... .[105]

She believed that too few of the new model cottages of the estate had been allotted to her, worsening her ability to attract the best labour. But her main difficulties, she claimed, arose from the fact that she farmed on a shooting estate. She complained once more of her crops 'riddled again with game as in the former years'.[106] 'Broome' argued in a letter to the Crown Solicitor, Mr White, that Mrs Cresswell's losses were down to three factors, 'the large quantity of ground game', first and foremost, followed by 'the very bad times during the last four or five years' and 'the large increases of labour'. Although it is not clear whether other tenants faced such large arrears at this time, Beck scoffed that 'If Mrs Cresswell is so much injured' by the presence of game, 'I cannot imagine how it is that the two Flintham tenants do not suffer equally'.[107]

Her volatile personality and poison pen did not help her cause but ultimately Cresswell's status as a widow farmer, overseeing a large farm that was teetering on the edge of financial disaster during economically turbulent times, made her particularly vulnerable. In her words she 'fought a good fight ... and with a fair chance and fair play I might have held my own even through these disastrous times'.[108] She took solace in the community solidarity that emerged in response to her plight, claiming that even the labourers 'worked with a will to the last, trade unionism and any little grudges being quite forgotten':

---

104   Ibid., pp. 219, 225.
105   Cresswell, *Farming for Profit*, pp. 17–18.
106   Cresswell, *Eighteen Years*, p. 218.
107   Mackie, *Prince's Thorn*, pp. 227, 228.
108   Cresswell, *How the Farming ... Can Be Made to Pay*, p. 29.

Their sense of justice was fully restored, and they were earnest in their condemnation of the measure being meted out to me. I am told they still speak of me with kindness and regret, and that if they dare venture to make the request, they would plead that the woman who has 'sorely suffered' might go back to dwell among her own people.[109]

While she is coy about the state of her financial affairs in her memoir, by the time she left the farm, in 1880, Cresswell owed two years' rent. Although she claims that she was essentially hounded out of the farm and offered no concessions, personal correspondence reveals a protracted and complex set of interactions between Cresswell and various members of the royal and estate staff that eventually led to a formal notice to quit. There were no male relatives waiting in the wings who could have taken on the tenancy (should the estate have desired that) as her only son Gerard was only 16 years old at the time and still studying at Harrow. Cresswell does not come out of these dealings unblemished.[110] After she conceded defeat, she submitted a claim to the estate for over £1,500 to cover her expenses in improving the farm from the 'wilderness' it had been, but even the faithful 'Broome' could only secure a few hundred pounds compensation for her as 'a present' for her losses.[111] The sale of farm stock took place on the first day of October 1880 and included amongst its inventory 24 horses, 88 cattle, 520 sheep, 120 pigs, a steam plough, an eight-horse-power traction engine and a four-horse-power portable engine.[112] Her household possessions were auctioned a week later. She was forced into 'life-long exile and separation from nearly all that makes life worth having to me', dividing her time between Norfolk, London and Texas, where her son Gerard had emigrated to farm in 1883.[113] Her sense of bitterness went with her, although she reassured herself that 'though they had the triumph ... somehow I do not think they will ever feel quite safe and comfortable so long as I am above ground'.[114] She died in Texas in 1916 but her body was returned to Norfolk to be laid to rest in the churchyard at North Runcton.[115]

---

[109] Cresswell, *Eighteen Years*, pp. 226–7.

[110] This is analysed in detail by Mackie, *Prince's Thorn*, ch. 8.

[111] Cresswell, *Eighteen Years*, p. 234; Mackie, *Prince's Thorn*, p. 236.

[112] Mackie, *Prince's Thorn*, p. 239.

[113] Cresswell, *How the Farming ... Can Be Made to Pay*, pp. 29–30.

[114] Cresswell, *Eighteen Years*, p. 235.

[115] Her son had emigrated to Texas in 1883, aged 19, with dreams of becoming a rancher. He settled permanently and eventually owned and farmed very successfully over 20,000 acres of prime cattle-rearing land.

III

Thousands of widows managed farms in the Victorian era. Usually this was a transitory period between the death of a husband and the succession of a son, a job performed with minimal fanfare, and largely invisible in the historical record. Louise Cresswell was one of these widow farmers but she was far from typical, not least because of the fact she wrote about and published her experiences of farming in the 1860s and '70s. Cresswell viewed farming as her profession, and she combined extensive reading with practical application to run a large East Anglian farm for 15 years. An energetic and capable woman, she did not consider her gender to be any impediment to farming, although she suspected that the trials and tribulations she faced – amongst them (in her view) a miscreant steward, a tyrannical landlord and his interfering agent – developed because she was a 'lady farmer' and therefore vulnerable to the machinations of men. Cresswell's account of her time at Appleton Farm is not a complete and accurate record and like other life history sources, it raises questions over motivations to write, and the selection and suppression of material. One of Cresswell's objectives was revenge and the memoir has a knowing air of scores being settled. For all its faults though it raises interesting questions about the position of women farmers and shows how difficult it was for women, even well-connected, well-heeled, self-assured ones like Cresswell, to make a success of farming in the distressed days of the late 1870s. Ultimately Cresswell's time as a farmer, like many of her contemporaries, ran aground. She succeeded, however, in leaving a dazzling and intriguing record of her endeavours.

Chapter 10

'Murmurs of Discontent': The Upland Response to the Plough Campaign, 1916–1918

Hilary Crowe

National agricultural statistics report change in the activities of thousands of individual farmers who adjust their daily round in different ways, at different times and at varying speeds, in response to events at all scales from the global to the local. Over some of these they have little or no control. The Great War was an event which limited, but did not completely eliminate, farmers' autonomy, whilst directing them down new paths. At the local level creative and proactive individuals fostered further change, adopted, adapted and applied by their peers. These developments coalesced, resulting in an almost infinite variety of agricultural activity and financial outturn as British farmers adjusted to the turbulent years of the war and the depression that followed.

Using a unique collection of the papers from West Ward District Sub-Committee of the Westmorland CWAEC (County War Agricultural Executive Committee) for the Great War,[1] this chapter examines the impact of war on the daily lives of a small group of farmers in the old county of Westmorland in the north of England. The archive provides detailed data for over 400 farms in this Ward and, most importantly, correspondence between the farming community and wartime officialdom. The West Ward as administered by the District sub-committee comprised 22 rural parishes which stretched from the fertile land of the upper Eden valley around Penrith south to the high moorlands of Shap and Crosby Ravensworth, and from Patterdale westwards towards the town of Appleby in Westmorland.

The old county of Westmorland was as homogeneous an agricultural unit as any county in England and Wales. With a total area of just under half a million acres, the county was not large. Farming was based on the rearing and fattening of sheep and cattle. Small farms predominated during the first half of the twentieth century. In 1914, the average holding was just over 70 acres and only

---

[1] Cumbria Archives (CA), Kendal Record Office (KRO), WD/BS boxes 3 and 5.

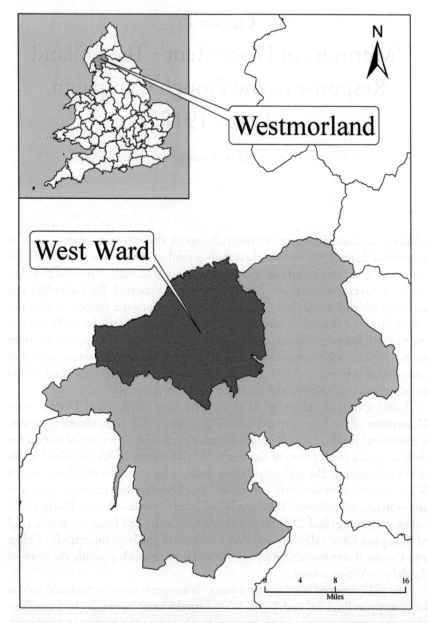

Figure 10.1   The location of the West Ward in the County of Westmorland.
Map Dr Max Satchel, Cambridge Group. This map is based on data
provided through EDINA UKBORDERS with the support of the
ESRC and JISC and uses boundary material which is copyright of
the Great Britain Historic GIS Project, Portsmouth University

22 per cent of holdings were in excess of 100 acres.[2] Farms were run using the labour of the farmer, his wife and family, supplemented as necessary with 'hired' labour, perhaps relatives or farm servants. Family farms were family units, whose members were willing to accept low cash returns and low standards of living for at least part of their family life cycles and for whom independence often made up for the limited material rewards.

However, by the early twentieth century, they were not self-sufficient 'peasant' farming units. As Donajgrodski has argued in a study of farms in nearby Swaledale, both human and animal food and household needs had to be purchased; these farmers were part of the twentieth-century world and operated within a capitalist economy, even if they did not fully embrace it. 'High farming' may not have been practised, costs were kept down by stocking at low levels to preserve cash and limit the need for hired labour, but upland farmers were not isolated from the outside world which intimately affected their daily lives.[3] 'Their culture and their operations made sound economic sense ... and produced a solid economic contribution to British farming'.[4]

In his prize essay for the *Journal of the Royal Agricultural Society of England* of 1867, Crayston Webster described farming in Westmorland in the years before the onset of the late Victorian agricultural depression. He described the 'robbing by the plough' of the Napoleonic War years which 'permanently depreciated' the land and argued that more of the land should have been kept in pasture.[5] However, he acknowledged that although Westmorland was 'admirably adapted by nature for breeding and rearing stock', due to hard winters, ample supplies of fodder crops were still required, and partial tillage with good husbandry of the soil was more productive and profitable than permanent pasture. Webster was describing the land use pattern that later set the standard for Prothero's 'back to the seventies' campaign of the Great War. Figure 10.2, comparing Webster's data for 1866 and that for June 1914 shows the effect of the late nineteenth-century depression on upland pastoral farming practice, where shortage of labour and high wages along with cheap supplies of purchased feed, resulted in an extension of grassland and a reduction in the acreage of labour intensive fodder crops.

As permanent grassland increased, so too did the number of cattle and sheep, rising by just over 35 per cent and 8 per cent respectively between 1866 and 1914.[6] Webster's computations showed that even by 1866, the financial return from grazing was 30 per cent higher than that from ploughed land.

---

[2]   *BPP*, 1914–16, XLIX pt 1, Agricultural Statistics 1914, Table 12.

[3]   A. Donajgrodksi, 'Twentieth-century rural England: A case for peasant studies?' *J. Peasant Studies* 16 (1989), p. 431.

[4]   Ibid., p. 437.

[5]   C. Webster, 'On the farming of Westmorland', *J. Royal Agricultural Society of England* 6 (1867), p. 7.

[6]   Ibid., p. 3. Data for 1914 is taken from BPP 1914–16, lxxix, Agricultural Statistics, 1914.

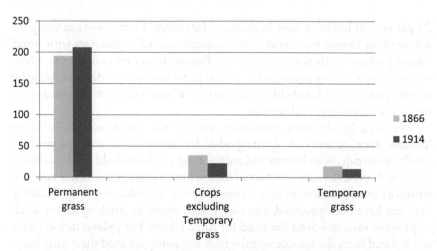

Figure 10.2   Westmorland: Comparison of land use in 1866 and 1914

Given the falls in crop prices which dominated the last quarter of the century, these adjustments to land use and production seem both rational and overdue.[7] Agriculture here in 1866 was relatively prosperous: 'so long as the tall chimneys of Yorkshire and Lancashire smoke, so long will the Westmorland farmer have a never failing demand for all his produce'.[8]

The late nineteenth-century depression was a regional experience. Upland livestock farmers were least affected; enjoying low rents, low prices for feed and limited labour costs due to reliance on family members, they benefited from sales of milk and wool which suffered least from the general deflation. Gradually, their methods of production altered; cattle were fattened for sale at an earlier age allowing for a quicker turnover in capital. With transport improvements milk came to replace the less profitable production of butter and cheese.[9] In evidence to the Royal Commission on the Agricultural Depression in 1894, Frederick Punchard, the land agent for the Underley Estate in the south of the county, stated that Westmorland had only recently suffered from depression. Farms on his estate were easily let, indeed, 'we have never been without half a dozen applicants for any farm'.[10]

This quiet, ordered and relatively prosperous world would be disrupted and changed forever by the outbreak of war in August 1914. Government direction would rob these farmers of their autonomy, force them to adopt unfamiliar

---

[7]   Webster, 'Farming of Westmorland', pp. 22–3.

[8]   Ibid., p. 16.

[9]   Jonathan Brown, *Agriculture in England: A Survey of Farming, 1870 to 1947* (Manchester, 1987), p. 45.

[10]   *BPP* 1894, xvi, Royal Commission on Agriculture, Enquiry into the Agricultural Depression, Mr Frederick Punchard, qq. 14838–9 and 14874–5.

production schedules, and disrupt the pattern of family life and labour. Many of the young men who left the fells and valleys of Westmorland did not return, and those who did came back to a changed world. The effects of government intervention and control are made visible through national, county and parish agricultural statistics which record wartime changes in livestock numbers and the 'back to the '70s' campaign to plough up the land laid to permanent grass during the agricultural depression of the late nineteenth century.[11] The minutes from just a handful of County Agricultural Committees survive, but these formal records give no voice to the individuals who had to execute a centrally determined policy vital to the nation's food supply but often unsuited to the upland environment of northern England.[12] However, the chance survival of the correspondence files from one district committee of the old county of Westmorland provides a window onto the daily life and labours of farming families facing the challenges presented by the Great War.[13] Their letters highlight the environmental and technical challenges resulting from unfamiliar production routines, and endemic labour shortages worsened by conscription. The evidence suggests that far from 'doing well out of the war', farmers faced a deterioration in the farming infrastructure which would result in costly post-war restructuring.

Using these letters and others published in the local press, this chapter will explore the tensions resulting from direction and suggest that Westmorland's successful achievement of centrally imposed production targets involved both heavy physical and psychological costs. The chapter will outline the development of agricultural policy over the course of the war considering both production targets and the control of labour and it will describe the Westmorland achievement as reported by the county statistics. Targets were met through the combined effect of numerous adaptations by individual farmers; using the farmers' own words, the chapter will then examine the environmental and technical challenges, the problems of labour shortage, and the inter-personal conflicts that lay behind the physical achievement. Finally the chapter argues that despite the successful achievement of wartime policy targets, directed production left farmers and landlords with an unwanted legacy.

---

[11] The National and County 4 June Agricultural Returns were published by The Board of Agriculture and parish summaries are available for inspection at The National Archives (TNA) under reference MAF 68.

[12] Edith H. Whetham listed the records of four surviving county committees: Bedfordshire, Huntingdonshire, Norfolk and Worcestershire, *The Agrarian History of England and Wales*, VIII, *1914–39*, p. 97. Various other archives have come to light and Peter Dewey was able to consult material from another 12 counties for his *British Agriculture in the First World War* (London, 1989).

[13] The Westmorland papers are unusual both in that they comprise the working papers of a District Committee, including correspondence from farmers, and concern farming in an upland area.

I

A continental war that would 'be over by Christmas' was not expected to strain the agricultural industry or create problems in the food supply chain. Britain was blessed with good weather in August and September 1914 and a good harvest meant war 'had not caused any appreciable losses in the crops of the year'.[14] Planning for future harvests was based on the expectation of a short war and concerns about the costs involved in adjusting production. The Food Supply sub-committee of the Committee of Imperial Defence advised relying on rising prices which would guarantee supplies as producers grasped opportunities for increased profits.[15] Farmers did respond to price changes and in 1915 the area of wheat rose by 19.5 per cent. However, this merely displaced oats, the area of which declined by 18.1 per cent.[16] The government made attempts to stockpile wheat secretly bought on foreign markets. After the policy was exposed, wheat prices remained high and the grain markets unsettled.[17] The need for a more transparent policy was evident, and the Milner Committee's interim report in July 1915 proposed the expansion of wheat output through use of a guaranteed price of 45s. per quarter. More significantly the report suggested a radical change in the relationship between government and the farming community.[18] To ensure that the structure of production was determined by government rather than by the private decisions of individual farmers, Milner proposed the establishment of War Agricultural Committees to organise the supply of labour and ensure increased production. These committees, established in 1915, were later to be given executive functions as County War Agricultural Executive Committees (CWAECs) within the Food Production Department, from January 1917.[19]

Livestock policy followed cereal crop policy. It was expected that increased arable cultivation, the increased cost of feed, and high prices for stock would lead to reduced numbers in flocks and herds. Managing the reduction was problematic: by May 1915 the *Journal of the Board of Agriculture* noted that shortages of labour and increased feeding costs 'are tempting a number of farmers to make an immediate profit at the expense of future output ... breeders are marketing their stock before it has arrived at maturity or disposing of their herds

---

[14]   T. Middleton, *Food Production in War* (Oxford, 1923), p. 103.

[15]   L. Barnett, *British Food Policy during the First World War* (London, 1985), p. 22.

[16]   MAFF, *A Century of Agricultural Statistics, 1866–1966* (London, 1968), Table 48.

[17]   Barnett, *British Food Policy*, p. 19.

[18]   P.E. Dewey, 'Farm labour in wartime: The relationship between agricultural labour supply and food production in Great Britain, 1914–18, with international comparisons', unpublished PhD thesis, University of Reading, 1978, p. 39.

[19]   Ibid., p. 41.

to an extent that is very much to be regretted'.[20] The Board sought to emphasise the importance of herd maintenance, but could do little to stop farmers taking advantage of high prices.

Military manpower requirements and higher wages elsewhere exacerbated a pre-war shortage of agricultural labour. By May 1915 the War Office sought to protect agriculture from further loss by issuing instructions to recruiters not to accept farm worker volunteers.[21] These protective measures were not always followed on the ground, so in August, the National Register for those aged 15 to 65 provided for 'starring' of essential workers who were not to volunteer or to be solicited. A final attempt to avoid conscription came with the Derby Scheme introduced in October 1915: 'starred men', including skilled agricultural workers, could attest their willingness to serve but they would pass into the reserve and return to their civilian occupation, thus protecting essential industries from the loss of skilled workers.[22]

However, conscription was unavoidable. In March 1916 starring was replaced with a list of 'certified occupations' which again included skilled agricultural workers, but as the military situation worsened, exemptions were refused to 60,000 agricultural workers with the proviso they would not be called up until January 1917 to allow for ploughing and sowing of winter crops.[23]

In the first two years of war, government was reluctant to intervene in the conduct of agriculture. The War Agricultural Committees, described by the *Mark Lane Express* as 'a very daring experiment', lacked direction from above and faced conservatism from below.[24] By 1916 livestock numbers were unchanged and the arable acreage had fallen below the pre-war average; the introduction of conscription in March, a poor harvest and a renewed German U-boat campaign made decisive intervention essential and in December 1916 the War Cabinet took steps to offer farmers a guaranteed price for cereals and to establish a Food Production Department to control agricultural production.[25]

The new president of the Board of Agriculture, the author R.G. Prothero (created Lord Ernle in 1919), inherited an industry under severe strain.[26] It was short of labour whilst being called upon to provide an increased percentage of the country's nutritional needs, as well as to supply much of the food for men and horses in the military. He described the new Food Production Policy as

---

[20] 'Notice to farmers as to the maximum production of crops and stock', *J. Board of Agriculture* May 1915, p. 182.

[21] *Journal of the Board of Agriculture*, Circular, Aug. 1915.

[22] Ibid., Circular, Dec. 1915.

[23] Ibid., Circular, Feb. 1916.

[24] Barnett, *British Food Policy*, p. 64.

[25] Dewey, 'Farm labour in wartime', p. 42.

[26] For Prothero see *ODNB*. Prothero had served the Duke of Bedford as his land agent: his *English Farming, Past and Present*, first appeared in 1912.

'the improvement and extension of arable cultivation, with spade as well as plough; decentralization, and drastic powers of compulsion which could only be justifiable or tolerable in a war emergency'.[27] The new Executive Committees of the County War Agricultural Committees were given powers under the Defence of the Realm Act (DORA) to allow them to control the agricultural production in their county. They could enter and survey land, override the terms of tenancies, issue directives for cultivation or improvement, and, if necessary, evict tenants and farm land themselves. But their resources were insufficient for the task, and by Feburary 1917 urgent demands for labour and machinery led to an extension of their jurisdiction to cover labour supply, machinery and the distribution of fertilisers and seed, to be administered through a system of district and specialist sub-committees which took over direction of production at the level of the individual field.[28]

The aim of the Food Production Policy or the 'plough up' campaign was to extend the acreage of cereals and potatoes by ploughing the land that had been laid to grass since the onset of depression in the 1870s, so providing increased food for human and animal consumption and saving vital shipping space. Targets were fixed based on the proportions of arable and grass in each county as at 1875.[29] In a memo addressed to County Executives as he took office, Ernle wrote; 'An actual addition to the land under the plough is therefore urgently needed and the Committees will fail in their duty if they do not satisfy the need'.[30] But it was January 1917 and little could be done to influence the 1917 harvest, and so the majority of the effort went into planning for the 1918 harvest in an attempt to extend the area under tillage by 3 million acres, later reduced to 2.5 million acres.[31] The committees had issued each farmer with his provisional ploughing quota for the 1918 harvest by June 1917.[32]

The Corn Production Act of 1917 provided guaranteed prices for wheat and oats, but in deference to the temperance movement, not barley. As these prices were well below the buying prices of the Ministry of Food, they were of no relevance.[33] The Act also stipulated a minimum wage for farm labourers administered by a central Wages Board supplemented by District Wage Committees. The Act gave powers to agricultural departments to regulate the cropping and stocking of land.[34] The policy for livestock followed cultivation

---

27 Lord Ernle, *The Land and its People* (London, 1923), p. 99.
28 Middleton, *Food Production in War*, p. 174.
29 J. Venn, *The Foundations of Agricultural Economics* (Cambridge, 1923), p. 157.
30 Middleton, *Food Production in War*, p. 165.
31 Ibid., p. 199.
32 The results of these three surveys for the West Ward District sub-committee of Westmorland can be found in the CA, KRO under reference WD/BS Boxes 3 and 5.
33 Whetham, *Agrarian History*, VIII, p. 95.
34 Ibid., p. 96.

policy. In September 1917 the government introduced a maximum wholesale price for meat, but unwisely on a declining scale, which led to a rush to slaughter and 'a glut of cattle and sheep in September and October, a scarcity in November, and a meat famine in December and January resulting in the hasty introduction of meat rationing'.[35] The resulting decline in livestock numbers was intensified post-war by the hard winter of 1918–19 which was exceptionally severe and resulted in a particularly high death rate for hill sheep.

In shifting the balance of agriculture away from livestock to arable production, the 'plough up' campaign increased the demand for labour, conflicting further with military needs. The extent of the labour shortage was and continues to be contentious. Ernle estimated that by the spring of 1917 'of the rural population permanently employed on the land ... 250,000 had been recruited for the Army'.[36] Murray's review of the First World War suggested that one-third of regular male workers left the land but Whetham stated that 300,000 agricultural workers in England and Wales joined the services out of the 1.25 million working in 1911.[37] Peter Dewey's revisionist work has downgraded the extent of the labour shortage; after examining both supply and demand he concluded that it was more acceptable to say that labour by the end of 1916 was deficient by about 10 per cent rather than 33 per cent, and that the labour shortage in 1917 was only 11 per cent greater than the pre-war period, falling to 9 per cent in 1918.[38] Whatever the exact position, the labour needs of a country aiming to extend its arable cultivation by several million acres was recognised by government, and the January 1917 call up was restricted by 50 per cent to 30,000 men. Further protection was given from June when it was agreed that there could be no further loss to agriculture without the consent of the CWAECs and during the next nine months farmers enjoyed a period of relative certainty about labour supply which aided the preparations for the 1918 harvest.[39] The spring offensives of March 1918 brought this period to a close, and agricultural needs were once more subordinated to the military, as the upper age limit for military service was raised to 51. In April all exemption certificates for younger men aged 18–23 were withdrawn and in May agriculture was informed it needed to yield a further 30,000 men, in addition to those released by this 'clean cut' exemption withdrawal; the individual men to meet the quota were to be selected by the County Executive Committees. The frustration of both farmers and the Board of Agriculture was expressed by Prothero:

---

[35] Edith H. Whetham, *Beef, Cattle and Sheep, 1910–1940* (University of Cambridge, Department of Land Economy, Occasional Paper no. 5, 1976), p. 17.

[36] Ernle, *The Land and its People*, p. 100.

[37] K.A.H. Murray, *The History of the Second World War: Agriculture* (London, 1955), p. 15; Whetham, *Agrarian History*, VIII, p. 72.

[38] Dewey, *British Agriculture in the First World War*, p. 140.

[39] J. Board of Agriculture, Circular, Feb. 1917.

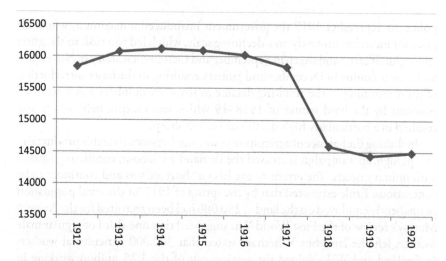

Figure 10.3   Permanent grassland acreage, England and Wales, 1912–20

the endurance of the rank and file of farmers was strained to breaking point. The Executives might be relied on to do their utmost ... but if a great mass of agricultural opinion defiantly arrayed itself against the continuance of the plough policy, coercion on a large scale would become so difficult as to be impracticable.[40]

This final withdrawal of labour forced plans for the plough up of 1919 to be adjusted; happily they were not needed.

So, in January 1917 local encouragement to arable production was replaced by a hierarchical system of direction reaching from Whitehall through county and district committees to individual farmers, who, according to Lord Prothero, 'submitted to State control ... [and] in spite of harassing difficulties they raised more human food than had been produced from the land during the previous 40 years'.[41] Control had a visible effect. Figures 10.3 and 10.4 illustrate the changes to land use in England and Wales resulting from the food production campaign.

Loss of grazing and a reduction in the production of hay, some of which was requisitioned by the army for horses, impacted on livestock but the numerical effects were delayed; slaughter weights and milk productivity declined whilst overall totals were maintained.[42] Total numbers of cattle peaked in 1917 at 6.23 million, declining slightly after the slaughter policy of 1917 to 6.2 million in 1918, but the significant decline was not evident until 1920 when only 5.55 million were

---

[40]   Ernle, *The Land and its People*, pp. 163–5.

[41]   Ibid., p. 99.

[42]   *BPP*, 1920, l, Agricultural Statistics 1919, pp. 83–4.

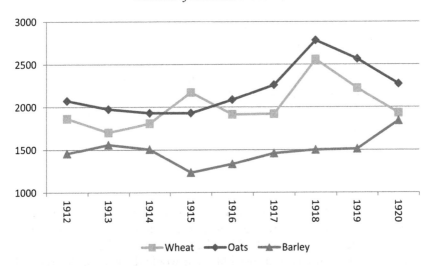

Figure 10.4   Cereal crop acreages, England and Wales, 1912–20

recorded in the annual statistics.[43] Farmers preferred to maintain their cattle herds over sheep flocks, which were more easily replaced, and Figure 10.5 shows how total sheep numbers declined from 1916 continuously down to 1920.[44]

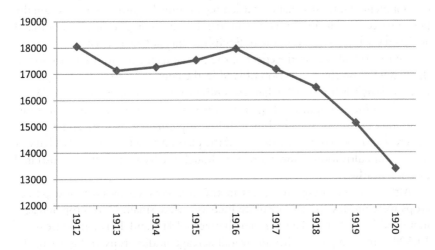

Figure 10.5   Sheep numbers, England and Wales, 1912–20

---

[43]   *A Century of Agricultural Statistics*, Table 63.
[44]   Ibid.

Government imposed a uniform production programme onto the mosaic of British soils and micro-climates. National statistics inevitably mask wide regional variations in the extent to which tillage was increased and livestock numbers altered and the local response gets lost in discussions relating to the 'national farm'. This chapter will look at the achievements of the county of Westmorland and listen to the words of those caught up in the process of implementing a production programme unsuited to the land they farmed.

II

On the eve of the Great War, rural Westmorland was a region of family farms practising mutually supportive survival strategies, both within the household and within the communities of which they were a part. The family unit was central to both economic and social life; war would disrupt and fracture this unit, adding emotional and psychological stress to the environmental and technical problems of altered production and the challenges caused by labour shortage and inadequate substitution.

In England and Wales 1.24 million acres of grassland was broken up in the year between 4 June 1917 and 4 June 1918. With the exception of Lancashire and Cheshire, which already had greater quantities under the plough due to the development of intensive market gardening, the only English county to attain the position occupied in 1875 was Westmorland. In percentage terms Westmorland achieved the highest increase for an English county at 65.4 per cent.[45]

Figure 10.6 illustrates the effect of the encouragement and then coercion of the CWAEC on the cultivation of land in the county. Land under the plough increased slightly for the 1916 harvest, unlike the position in England and Wales generally. Once compulsion began in preparation for the 1917 harvest, some temporary grass was ploughed in addition to permanent pasture and replaced by cereal and root crops. The success of the planning made for the 1918 harvest in terms of cultivation is apparent, even though the harvest itself was frustrated by poor weather.[46]

Although percentage increases in the area covered by corn and potato crops were impressive, the absolute increases were small. Corn crop acreages increased by just over 100 per cent between 1915 and 1918, an increase of 14,500 acres compared with an overall acreage under crops and grass in the

---

[45]   Venn, *Foundations of Agricultural Economics*, p. 158.

[46]   Figures are taken from the *Agricultural Statistics* published by the Board of Agriculture and the Ministry of Agriculture after 1920.

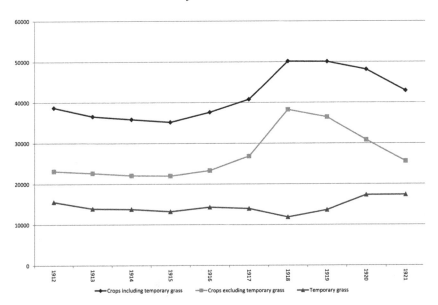

Figure 10.6   Area under cultivation, Westmorland, 1912–21 (1912=100)

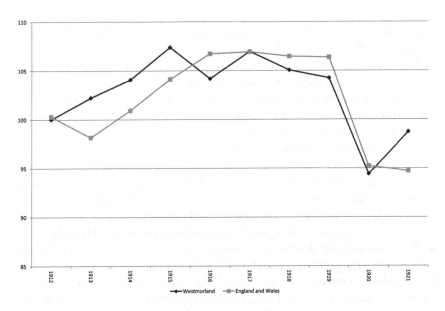

Figure 10.7   Cattle numbers, Westmorland, and England and Wales
(1912=100)

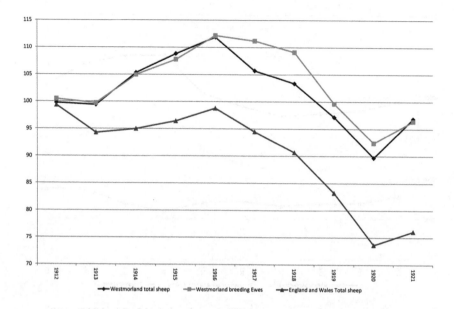

Figure 10.8   Sheep numbers, Westmorland, and England and Wales
              (1912=100)

county of nearly a quarter of a million acres. Potatoes reached a maximum
acreage of 1,953 acres in 1918.[47]

It is interesting, and also a reflection on the way national policy targeted
cereal production, that even in a county almost wholly dependent on livestock,
the local and county committees spent little if any time on livestock issues.
Apart from supplying the army with horses and hay, farmers appear to have
been left to run their livestock activities without direction. There were no local
surveys of livestock numbers, no direction on the cultivation of livestock fodder,
no slaughter programme and no attempt made to investigate the stocking of
common land or to find additional grazing. Rather there seems to have been an
undeclared ruling that if livestock could be fed they could be kept, and it was left
to the markets to regulate the sale of stores and fat stock.

Whilst shortages of feeding stuffs began to limit the national herd by 1916,
in Westmorland, the decline was delayed until 1917 when national pricing
policies led to the premature slaughter of cattle and a glut of meat in early 1918.
In 1913 sheep numbers for England and Wales were the lowest ever recorded,
recovery began in 1914[48] and continued everywhere up until 1916. With the
introduction of the food production campaign in 1917 sheep numbers in

---

47   Figures taken from the published *Agricultural Statistics*.
48   *BPP*, 1916 xxxii, Agricultural Statistics, 1915.

lowland areas fell as land came under the plough. In the uplands sheep numbers continued to rise and the increased numbers of breeding ewes resulted in larger lamb crops. Here most sheep were grazed on upland fell and common with no alternative agricultural use and outside the ambit of the plough campaign. Farmers were encouraged to make maximum use of such land, and owners asked to 'consider the use being made of their moorlands with the object of ensuring that they are stocked with as many sheep as the land can carry'. The Board of Agriculture also felt that temporarily it would be safe to pasture more sheep than were normally kept without any long-term harm resulting.[49] The winter of 1918/19 was particularly severe, resulting in a 'disquietening' reduction in the numbers of sheep, recovery from which was delayed in the uplands.[50]

The wartime production programme was unsuited to the hill farms of Westmorland and much of the rest of northern England and yet the county met its targets, however small in absolute terms, and managed to maintain viable herds and flocks. This was a great credit to the efforts of the district committees and the majority of the farmers who followed their direction. Middleton's early assessment of the achievement concluded that although no farmer lamented the passing of the Food Production Department 'they did not regret the action they had taken; for the plough policy had been justified by its results'.[51] More locally an Ambleside farmer wrote: 'Many farmers have sent their last son in response to the country's call ... now through real hard work, perseverance and determination they are just able to keep the wheels of the farm in motion'.[52] The chapter now turns to listen to some of the hundreds of individuals whose wartime activities were responsible for the Westmorland achievement.

III

Unfamiliar and unsuitable agricultural production targets presented the farmer in the uplands with environmental and technical challenges. A policy of 'cereals first' sat uncomfortably on the fellsides of Westmorland; only an optimist would have attempted a crop of oats on land lying above 900 feet. Yet the new Executive, formed in January 1917, set about their task with enthusiasm. Their first task was a rapid survey to identify badly cultivated land and assess land available for ploughing for the 1917 harvest. T.D. Shepherd, the secretary of the West Ward, received his instructions on 6 January 1917, and was to report not later than 20 January. The Little Strickland farmers' representative highlighted the difficulties:

---

[49] J. Board of Agriculture, 1916, p. 1187.

[50] BPP, 1921, lvi, Agricultural statistics, 1920.

[51] Middleton, Food Production in War, p. 292.

[52] Westmorland and Cumberland Herald (hereafter WCH), 4 Dec. 1915.

'it is not possible to reply, the area is under snow and work is so far behind'.[53] During February and March the County Executive began to coordinate supplies of seed potatoes and allocated a limited motor plough facility. The need for a more organised approach resulted in a 'Cropping Summary Form' which was distributed to farmers with more than 10 acres, requiring details of acreage, land under pasture, arable and meadow, together with comparisons between 1916 and 1917 for oats, wheat, hay, green crops and potatoes. At the same time, direction of production began with instructions to plough up being distributed in March and April 1917. The District Committee files reflect farmers' confusion and concern: lists were continually being revised and letters from frustrated farmers queried the clarity and sense of the instructions. Thomas Chambers from Tirril received two requests to plough up five acres; 'I am not sure if this is a duplicate but I do not wish to plough any'. His irritation is apparent; 'this is the third form I have filled in and returned to you'. J. Griffiths from Celleron, wrote: 'I filled in the form some time ago for Bank Head Farm. It is two years since I left The Waters'.[54]

In June, the Executive Committees received the instruction that in 1918 they were to plough the area of tillage as recorded in 1870, modified for the increase in dairy cows and the loss of land to agriculture.[55] The West Ward Committee used the Cropping Summary Form to note a provisional target for the 1918 plough quota for each farm and even small farms were allocated their acre or two, suggesting that the District were struggling to find the further 28 per cent increase in arable land allocated to them.[56] Each allocation had to be accompanied by a ploughing order to protect tenants from landlord claims for breaking established crop rotations. Many of these orders were contested by farmers, either on the basis of administrative error, lack of clarity, because the farmer objected to the field concerned or was without the equipment to carry out the order. Once the acreage allocations had been made the survey staff then had to select the most suitable grassland for ploughing and specify field numbers. Yates, secretary to the County Executive, had to exert considerable pressure on the districts:

> It is not now a question of farming on ordinary lines ... the Local Committee should clearly understand that they must not necessarily ask individual farmers to double their ploughing but must visit ... every farm and it is desirable that land

---

53 *WCH*, 4 Dec. 1915.

54 WD/BS Box 3, File from Mar. 1917.

55 In 1872 the tilled area of Westmorland was 54,335 acres which had fallen to 35,199 by 1915; 3,000 acres had been ploughed up in 1915 and 1916 and this is deducted from 75 per cent of the difference to arrive at 11,353.

56 WD/BS Box 8: Summary Cropping Forms.

that has been laid down since 1872 should be ploughed before old pasture and meadow.[57]

From September onwards notices were sent to farmers in the West Ward stipulating the number of acres of 'white crop' to be sown which generated another round of correspondence.

To the independent farmers of Westmorland, central direction of production must have seemed unnatural, eliciting an understandable and perhaps predictable response. The climate was harsh, the ground unsuitable and they lacked the equipment and technical expertise necessary. John Taylor from Gilts, Shap, a high moorland parish wrote: 'I have lived all my life near hills and never yet saw ripe corn cut here ... what is the use of ploughing a lot of land when it never gets ripe?'[58] Thomas Hudson also from Shap was asked to produce 12 acres of 'white crop':

> I beg to inform you that I have no arable land, that I am 84 years of age and have no experience of arable farming. I have no implements of husbandry necessary for the purpose nor have the necessary buildings to store crops ... I trust that your committee may see its way to withdraw its request ...'[59]

The request was not withdrawn. Many other objections came from the high-lying parishes of the West Ward. A farmer from Hardendale wrote: 'some of the land you specify is 1100 to 1200 feet above sea level. I really question the utility of it being ploughed out'.[60] The effect of ploughing on livestock was also a concern; 'my farm is high lying more for grazing, some of my arable land is "rock to top" and I have been obliged to sow it down for want of soil. I will not have room to summer all my stock at home as it is'.[61] Mrs Murray, farming near Penrith, protested 'seeing that I have only my cow pasture which is studded with trees and some meadow land which is mown annually. I think I have a strong reason for asking to be excused from ploughing'.[62]

Many of the specific fields scheduled for ploughing were thought unsuitable. A farmer from Kings Meaburn told the committee that 'the head lands around the said field is one mass of trees and not ploughable'.[63] Another draws attention to the need for fencing, 'which would be difficult and cut off access to the rest of

---

[57] WD/BS Box 3, File to May 1917, letter, 6 Aug. 1917.

[58] Idem., File from Sept. 1917, letter, 12 Sept. 1917.

[59] Idem., letter, Sept. 1917.

[60] WD/BS Box 3, File from Dec. 1917, letter, 18 Jan. 1917.

[61] WD/BS Box 3, File to May 1917, letter, 30 Mar. 1917.

[62] WD/BS Box 3, File to Dec. 1917.

[63] WD/BS Box 3, File to Jan. 1918, letter, 28 Jan. 1918.

the field. There is no land on this small farm suitable for cultivation'.[64] And yet another felt that the acres selected were not the best available:

> I am strongly convinced that an error has been made in the selection of land so far as my case is concerned. At one end of the field there is about a half acre of waste land ... then at the other end is a large hole which serves as a watering place for cattle and that means further waste ... my original offer was to plough a field called Gregor and Wise which is very good land and suitable in every way for cultivation.[65]

Despite criticism the committee was persistent. R. Armstrong was informed that 'this committee have observed that field number 9 Carleton Holmes is not fully ploughed, in particular a strip of land straight through, and they shall be glad to hear when you propose to plough it'.[66]

Requests to amend the details of ploughing orders to make things easier were common and may also have reflected an attempt on the part of farmers to exert some independence. One farmer agreed to do four acres for another and felt that '... as long as we agree I don't see anybody has any right to interfere'.[67] The farmer at Lodge Farm, Little Strickland was prepared to plough but would not grow the white crop specified.[68] J. Wright from Rosegill sounds almost triumphant:

> I object to plough Low Flatts, it is no good in these times, only labour in vain, as we should not be able to get our own seed off it, I ploughed it about 40 years ago but got nothing out of it neither corn nor straw. However it does not matter much, you have missed one field which I ploughed in addition to Wyeslack as they have always been ploughed together.[69]

Some tenants referred orders back to their landlords: 'I do not know the names of some of the fields so I have written to my landlord to give him the choice of land to be broken up'.[70] In other cases landlords attempted to intervene on behalf of tenants and attempted to have ploughing orders redistributed between them. J.C. Dent at Prospect House Bolton appealed on behalf of his tenant at Knock Hall who had been asked to plough five acres, seven miles from the homestead, which also had poor access for machinery. He had given permission to two other tenants

---

[64] WD/BS Box 3, File to Jan. 1918, letter, 8 Jan. 1918.

[65] WD/BS Box 3, File to Mar. 1918.

[66] WD/BS Box 3, File to June 1918, letter, 1 May 1918.

[67] WD/BS Box 3, File to Mar. 1918, letter, 9 Jan. 1918.

[68] WD/BS Box 3, File to Mar. 1918, letter, 22 Jan. 1918.

[69] WD/BS Box 3, File to Dec. 1917, letter, 27 Dec. 1917.

[70] WD/BS Box 3, File to Dec. 1917.

to plough 12 acres of more suitable land and sought a review of the committee's decisions; 'would it not be better to send a committee to view the whole situation as I require nothing but fair play'.[71] The allocations were not revised by the Committee. On occasion they took a very strong line. John Faulkner of Howgill, Newby ploughed field 338 instead of field 320 which had water for stock, but was told 'you will be reported to the CWAEC and liable to prosecution' if he did not comply with the order.[72] Not until after the Armistice was the pressure relaxed. Only then would the Committee 'allow a freer hand in varying the crops and so get the land back into rotation cropping. Beans will count as cereals, if any farmers choose to grow them. There can be some give and take between farms'.[73]

Added to the environmental and technical challenges was the problem of labour. Labour shortages were characteristic of Westmorland and high wages a persistent feature of pre-war agriculture. This long-standing labour shortage was exacerbated by voluntary enlistment. Conscription would then rob many family farms of both their adult sons and their hired labour. As key agricultural workers, farmers were in reserved occupations, and the assumption has often been made that farmers' sons were protected from conscription. However, on family farms in the pastoral uplands the nomination of one individual as farmer was often arbitrary. The father, often in his 60s or 70s, may have been the 'farmer', but the bulk of the work would have been done by one or more sons who perhaps better deserved the designation.[74] The Tribunal reports for the West Ward contain numerous cases of elderly 'farmers' appealing for exemption for their sons on whose labour the farm depended. 'I am 75 years of age and my wife is 70. [My son] was the only other worker and the sole manager ... the only other help on the farm was a daughter of 44 years who died in January this year'.[75] The farmer at Rectory Farm Cliburn appealed for the release of his son in training so he could plough 40 acres for corn and 15 acres for roots; 'there is only myself, 64 years of age and a young man of 18 to do all the work on the land and to attend to 40 cattle as well as the sheep'.[76]

Sometimes the farmer was the widowed mother: an appeal from Mary Rowlandson for her son Thomas to be exempted shows that farmers and their relatives were vulnerable to military conscription. She had dairy cattle and 140 sheep. 'My son is the only man on the farm and I cannot do without him'.[77] A

---

[71]   WD/BS Box 3, File to Mar. 1918, letter, 1 Feb. 1918.

[72]   WD/BS Box 3, File to Mar. 1918, letter, 14 Feb. 1918.

[73]   WD/BS Box 3, File to Dec. 1918, Letter from the Chair of the County Executive, 24 Dec. 1918.

[74]   Hilary Crowe, 'Keeping the wheels of the farm in motion: Labour shortages in the uplands during the Great War', *Rural Hist.* 19 (2008), pp. 201–16.

[75]   WD/BS Box 3, 6 Feb. 1918.

[76]   WD/BS Box 3, File to Mar. 1918.

[77]   WD/BS Box 3, File to Feb. 1917.

conscripted soldier wrote to his mother; 'they say I could get away from the army if you got someone who knows anything about it to mention the farm and how you are situated at home ... but it will have to be done quick as they move men away very soon'.[78] Mrs Hutchinson at Oaklands wrote:

> since my son left home for the army I have been without help, only a man coming occasionally for a short time after his days work at Lowther to help me in ploughing the garden which is very large. We have no servant indoors so that my daughter has more than a woman can do. The consequence is that the place is in an awful state.[79]

Farmers' sons seem to have been recruited and conscripted in considerable numbers. The military authorities on the Tribunals complained about the reluctance of farmers to give up their sons. In March 1916 the military representative took a tough line and expressed the view 'that several employers of labour had, since last November, dispensed with their hired labour with a view to getting their sons home and therefore into a safe position'. This was contrary to Lord Derby's scheme. 'A man should engage hired labour over military age ... any man who was capable of such an unpatriotic action should receive no sympathy.'[80] Married men were being released from munitions but the farmers would not engage them for fear of losing their sons.[81] The possibility of substitution left farmers' sons vulnerable to recruitment particularly when the farm was small and they undertook a wide variety of tasks, not all of which were 'skilled'. In these circumstances their exemption category was open to challenge from the military authorities who strongly encouraged farmers to take substitute workers over sons. S. Alderson appealed for his son, the only hand on a farm of 118 acres:

> Tribunal: 'Have you an objection to a substitute?'

> Applicant: 'Yes, every conceivable objection, because they know nothing about work. I will never take a substitute.'

His application was refused.[82]

Substitutes comprised soldiers, women, prisoners and children. Soldier labour was available from the Agricultural Corps of Grade C soldiers stationed

---

78 WD/BS Box 3, File to Oct. 1918.
79 WD/BS Box 3, File to Oct. 1918.
80 *WCH*, 11 Mar. 1916, p. 2.
81 *WCH*, 9 Sept. 1916, p. 2.
82 *WCH*, 2 Dec. 1916, p. 2.

at Carlisle Castle but it was not always popular. W.J. Walker from Bank Farm, Crosby requested a temporary exemption for his son:

> my farm which is 123 acres cannot possibly be carried on without him this summer. Owing to the extra ploughing he is really indispensable and cannot be replaced. I have a big hay time and harvest this summer which he has always been my greatest help, also my health is worse now and now I am very lame, have a bad foot and back and I don't know what to do and all the work looking at me.

On being offered a man from Carlisle:

> No I don't want a soldier from Carlisle they are neither use nor ornament ... I cannot do without him the state I am in. This year I have more corn than last year over 11 acres and 32 acres of hay. I can tell you about a farmers apprentice you have given exemption to and only 3 or 4 acres and one cow and a calf ... farmers in Crosby is trying all schemes they can ... you are not fair he is only 18 years old he is a skilled lad and I cannot do without him. What is the use of ploughing more if the crop will be wasted.[83]

Farmers' attitudes were criticised by the authorities: 'Last summer there were some soldiers employed on local farms but many more would have been but for the obstinate stand taken by some ... unless they got a particular soldier they would have none.'[84] Reluctance to give up a son and take on a soldier, often with limited experience, was no doubt emotional, but also in this area where family labour rarely paid, there was also an economic issue. Many farmers seem to have preferred Canon Rawnsley's suggestion: 'the success of agriculture would depend very much more than normally on the personal labour and direction of the farmer himself. He would have to go to bed later and rise earlier.' He felt for:

> the man who had worked hard and who was unable to pay for outside labour and dependent on the labour of his family but these men must also make sacrifices and the strong lass should fill the place of her brother.[85]

Unpaid female family labour, working both inside and outside the farmhouse, had always been important in the farm economy but paid women were less attractive. The Women's Committee of the CWAEC published an open letter to farmers in the local press requesting suitable training openings for women volunteers, but parish representatives were negative. Farmers were reluctant to provide training.

83　WD/BS Box 3, File to June 1918.
84　*Kendal Mercury* (hereafter *KM*), 26 May 1916, p. 7.
85　*KM*, 4 Feb. 1916, p. 7.

The representative from Lowther reported 'I have made inquiry in this parish and I do not find any farmer willing to undertake the duty at present.'[86] The Appleby District sub-committee did not report favourably on female help and 'did not hold out any hope of assistance from that quarter.'[87] A Barton farmer was only 'willing to have one or two at a time, two is as many as I could provide quiet cows to milk at one time.'[88] There is some comment from women frustrated at not being able to find work which addresses the unspoken fears of farmers:

> You admire our patriotism, our willingness and keenness to do war work but you tell us 'Keep off my land'. Women do not desire to act as aide de camps to the Military in taking men from farm service, neither do we wish to replace schoolboys ... or even soldiers but when all three have been engaged there still remain ways in which farmers are able to find work for women.[89]

Despite farmers' reluctance, the County Committee was enthusiastic: '90 per cent of farm labour could be done by women ... though the more muscular work such as filling manure carts would require men.'[90] At a meeting in April 1917 which discussed labour shortage and women workers, it was agreed that:

> farmers were reluctant to take on women, but women's labour was better than no labour at all and that was the ugly choice which would by and by be facing the farmers. There was in some quarters the extraordinary idea that farm work was degrading for women ... it might be hard and perhaps disagreeable but after all, it was nothing compared to life in the trenches.[91]

Few parts of Westmorland seem to have benefited from prisoner labour. The reason is found in the list of the requirements for use of prisoner labour: 'The Executive must be satisfied that there is sufficient agricultural work in the locality to keep at least 65 out of 75 prisoners occupied for a period of at least two months, the work to be within a radius of three miles of the depot.'[92] This was difficult to achieve in areas with small isolated upland farms and scattered parcels of land. It is unsurprising that relatively little prisoner labour was used here; the situation would have been similar in other upland areas.

---

86   CA, KRO, WD/BS Box 3, File to May 1917.
87   *KM*, 29 Oct. 1915, p. 7.
88   CA, KRO, WD/BS Box 3, File to May 1917.
89   *KM*, 11 Aug. 1916, p. 7.
90   *KM*, 19 Nov. 1915, p. 7.
91   CA, KRO, WD/BS Box 3, 30 Apr. 1917.
92   *Journal of the Board of Agriculture*, Circular Feb. 1917.

Children had always helped on family farms and the Education Committee relaxed the attendance by-laws, agreeing that 'the best thing that could be given to a boy or girl was a good education ... but at a time like this ... they must show they were not hide bound pedants and recognise the need in case of a farm where there was shortage of labour'. They asked farmers not to take advantage of the relaxation to save a few shillings a week.[93] The School Logs show that attendance was largely maintained but that school holidays were adjusted to coincide with haymaking, harvest and potato picking.[94]

The evidence for the use of substitute labour shows that upland areas had limited access to soldier and prisoner labour and showed reluctance to make use of other available substitutes, particularly women. This may have been because the shortage was not as great as the case being made for it, or more probably, that it was possible to get by and achieve what was required by the farmer working much harder himself and making more strategic use of the remaining family labour. He probably did so at the expense of farm maintenance and his capital depreciated as a result. However, he did not have to pay out significant sums as cash wages and did not have to acquire the skills required to run his business using new and unfamiliar sources of labour in place of his family. He was perhaps following the advice of the Chair of the CWAEC who reminded the farmer he 'would need to spend more time upon the farm himself, because there would be no one else to do it'.[95]

Conscription also denuded the number of blacksmiths and wheelwrights. The district committee found a 'delay in getting the necessary repairs for farm implements and machinery ... the minister of National Service should be warned not to recruit any more blacksmiths or wheelwrights for the Army'.[96] Parish representatives, usually farmers themselves were stretched. The District asked the Executive to note on 1 February 1918:

> that the members of my Committee are with one exception not men of leisure ... during the past six months they have voluntarily given much of their time in inspecting farms and selecting suitable land for the extra plough out. They now think that as the programme for 1918 has been set out they should be free to devote more time to their particular duties.[97]

It was not only manpower that was in short supply. Requisitioning also resulted in a severe shortage of horses; many farmers queried how land was to be worked

[93]   *KM*, 27 Nov. 1914, p. 7.

[94]   CA, KRO, West Ward Parish School Logs.

[95]   *WCH*, 6 May 1916, p. 6.

[96]   CA, KRO, WD/BS Box 3, File to Mar. 1918.

[97]   CA, KRO, WD/BS Box 3, File to Mar. 1918.

with just one horse. 'I do not intend working my arable land with only one horse. I intend buying a younger one to break.'[98]

So, in Westmorland the historic skilled labour shortage was exacerbated by alterations in production programmes which increased labour demand, and the loss of farmers and their sons into the military leaving wives, sisters and widows to continue to run holdings with substitute labour, or let their tenancy or land to another. No doubt there was resistance to change and frustration at loss of control, but much opposition to ploughing orders centred on the labour shortage. This may have been used as an excuse by some but it was increasingly frequently cited and particularly so in the period after March 1918. On small units with just a few workers, the loss of a son – probably the fittest man on the farm – would have made a big practical and psychological difference. The extent to which the community drew on the traditions of mutual help and support is not clear, but the Tribunals were keen to encourage such cooperation.

In December 1916 Prothero, the Minister of Agriculture, told the Executives, 'we plan to give you wide powers to enter upon, occupy and cultivate land'.[99] Landlords and influential farmers were given authority over their neighbours and tension was inevitable. Farmers were suspicious of providing information to people within their own farming circle and the request was made for 'canvassing to be undertaken by someone not living in the district concerned so that the information would not be gathered by a man's neighbours'.[100] The county Executive recognised the difficulty of the task undertaken by the Districts and Parish Representatives. The Chairman wrote: 'I am asking you to perform a somewhat delicate duty.' He thanked all who:

> undertook the very arduous task of surveying farms and interviewing farmers and also the work of additional assessment involving as I know it did many meetings lasting for many hours. I think we all realised that there would be a certain number of farmers dissatisfied about their allotted acreage and appeals would be inevitable.[101]

But the imposition of the ploughing up campaign in what some considered to be a partial fashion could turn farmer against farmer. The correspondence files of the West Ward contain letters from farmers reporting their neighbours for failures of cultivation. J. Walker of Martindale was reported for 'not

---

98   CA, KRO, WD/BS Box 3, File to May 1917.
99   *WCH*, 23 Dec. 1916, p. 3.
100 CA, KRO, WD/BS Box 3, File to Feb. 1917.
101 CA, KRO, WD/BS Box 3, File to Jan. 1918.

having cultivated his garden last year or this'.[102] Another farmer was 'quite willing to do my bit and did a great deal more this last spring than many of my neighbours ... one has 160 acres, he has five acres to plough, the other 600 acres, he has to plough 20, so why am I asked to try 25?' (He had 393 acres.)[103]

Some committee members appear to have used their position to protect their own interests, raising protests from neighbours. Thomas Lowthian wrote to the Executive Secretary contrasting his own situation with that of the Earl of Lonsdale:

> May I ask you to state a case where there is the same area ploughed lying at a high altitude namely 47.5 acres at 830 feet and rising to over 900 feet. I may say there is very great dissatisfaction being expressed about the way and manner the ploughing orders are being carried out. I consider my case a hardship, particularly so when I have sell my breeding grey-faced ewes and to reduce dairy cows considerably in the autumn. It may not have come to your notice that there is a lot of land lying much lower than my farm within 3 miles or so. One portion I may mention, Askham Hall which was stocked last summer with white heifers, served by a black bull to breed fancy blue grey cattle. May I ask you to consider what that land is making in war food supply. You might ask the Chairman of the sub-committee what interest he himself has in it. I do not know if you know that the sub-committee consists of the Lowther Estate Agent and five Lowther tenants ... I am perfectly willing to do my bit but do not see that it is fair or right when others more favourably situated are not called on to do their bit in accordance.[104]

Despite an inspection 'so that there may be no sense of injustice in the minds of the farming community of this county,' Home Farm continued to be run on pre-war lines with minimal amounts of land under the plough.[105] Here we see the effects of landownership and local personality at the lowest level of agricultural activity.

Overall the correspondence paints a picture of farmers struggling to extend their area of tillage due to the practical difficulties involved and the high cost and scarcity of labour. The dissenters were vocal, and some tensions personal. However, there were over 400 farms in the West Ward, the committee were newly engaged in their task and farmers were unaccustomed to direction; perhaps the silence of the majority reflected an understanding that some things had to change and they got on with the task in hand for 1917.

---

[102]   CA, KRO, WD/BS Box 3, File to Feb. 1917.

[103]   CA, KRO, WD/BS Box 3, File to Dec. 1917.

[104]   CA, KRO, WD/BS. Box 3, File to Mar, 1918, letter, 23 Feb. 1918.

[105]   CA, KRO, WD/BS. Box 3, File to Mar. 1918.

IV

The targets for 1918 generated more disquiet. The challenges of labour, machinery, seed and fertiliser shortage, coupled with the increasing difficulty of finding suitable land left farmers feeling frustrated. Some were simply unable to comply with direction and others were unwilling. The District Committee urged owners to take action against reluctant tenants: Mrs Hodgson, owner of a farm at Hardendale, was asked to give notice to her tenant, a Mr Potter; the land appears 'to be underfarmed and a change of tenant would appear to be desirable in the national interest'. Mrs Hodgson agreed to give Potter notice.[106] It was the Armistice which brought some relief. The Secretary of the Executive expressed this:

> it has become increasingly obvious since the signing of the Armistice ... that there is no longer the necessity to put the enormous strain upon the farmers of the county in regard to the production of cereal crops ... the committee will allow a freer hand in varying the crops and so get the land back into rotation cropping.[107]

That Westmorland met government-imposed targets, however small in absolute terms, is a credit to the efforts of the district committees and the majority of the farmers who followed their direction. But the 'farmers voice' reveals the considerable personal cost and struggle that lay behind the success. Ploughing and cultivating the extra land involved many extra hours of work with inadequate equipment and increasing labour shortages in a hostile environment. Ploughing targets were met, but broken grassland did not guarantee more calories. Crops failed or produced disappointing yields. Whilst the Chair of the Executive Committee described the 1918 harvest as without precedent 'even in the memory of the oldest men', the weather was a problem:

> it is easy to be wise after the event and there is no doubt that a policy of requiring potatoes in place of a large area under corn would have been sounder ... looking ahead my own feeling is that potatoes must play a very large part next season and should rank as equivalent to so much corn ... in Westmorland at the moment it seems tactless to talk about any increase [in corn].[108]

> Farms at high altitudes should only be required to produce what the occupier needs for consumption on his own holding with the knowledge that he cannot

---

106   CA, KRO, WD/BS Box 3, File for Feb. and Mar. 1918, letter, 11 Mar. 1918.
107   CA, KRO, WD/BS Box 3, File to Dec. 1918. Letter from Yates (Secretary), 24 Dec. 1918.
108   CA, KRO, WD/BS Box 3, File from Nov. 1918, letter from Wakefield.

buy artificial feeding stuffs [and] potatoes should be allowed to take the place of an equal area of grain at the option of the occupier.[109]

War left an altered landscape, ploughed-out grassland and reduced livestock numbers. Bad weather added to farmer's difficulties. It is usually assumed that farmers do well out of war. A combination of high prices and increased demand for home production have been assumed to deliver 'super normal' profits[110] making it 'impossible to lose money in farming just then'.[111] This farming community would have been slow to agree with that assessment. Some scepticism about protestations of poverty is healthy: but inflated cash receipts are only one side of the equation. Costs increased and the pressure for increased arable production depleted soil fertility. Shortage of grassland, fodder and feedstuffs took their toll on the quality and quantity of stock. Common land and rough grazing resources were stretched and an imbalance in the numbers of sheep and cattle detrimentally altered the composition of some grasslands. Labour and equipment shortage prevented usual routines of repair and renewal. In effect, working capital was converted into cash and this movement needed to be reversed post-war. Both landlords and tenants had to spend money on farm infrastructure, and farmers had to invest their time and expertise to re-establish production on a more sustainable basis. Some farmers were fully aware that they faced an uncertain post-war world with depreciated capital: a number left the industry. Those who stayed complained these men had 'impoverished their holdings and pocketing enough to retire upon [they have] retired to a mansion on the shores of Windermere Lake and left ... only couch grass and weeds'.[112]

V

The view that the expansion of agriculture in wartime had been at the cost of the future profitability of the industry was widely met. Comments of this sort pervade the evidence given to the Royal Commission appointed 'to enquire into the economic prospects of the Agricultural Industry' of 1919. Mr James Donaldson of the NFU stated that wartime profit was at the expense of fertility:

---

[109]   CA, KRO, WD/BS Box 3, File from Nov. 1918, resolution 19 Nov. 1918.

[110]   Dewey, *British Agriculture in the First World War*, p. 234. Super normal profits are defined by Dewey as net income after the full opportunity cost of all factors of production used in producing the output of an enterprise have been deducted from the revenue accruing from the sale of output and also an allowance for 'normal profit' has been made. Normal profit is that which is just sufficient to keep the entrepreneur engaged in business.

[111]   P.E. Dewey, 'British farming profits and government policy during the First World War', *Economic History Rev.* 37 (1984), pp. 373–90.

[112]   *WG*, 8 Jan. 1921, p. 2.

the government asked us to grow every possible acre of cereals and other products ... but we know we did it at the expense of the land and it is no use trying to disguise the fact that our land today is not in as good a condition from the ordinary farming point of view as it was prior to the war.[113]

The Essex landowner the Hon. Edward Strutt stated 'there will be a large outlay to be made by nearly every farmer to bring his land back into the state it was in 1914'.[114] Mr J. Vinter, farmer, giving evidence on his own results showed a return on capital of 13.5 per cent but he was unsure 'how much of this represents capital taken out of the fertility of the land by cross cropping and want of labour for cleaning'. He spoke of 'fictitious profits arising out of lowered fertility'.[115] The evidence given on behalf of the NFU for Scotland drew attention to the loss of manurial value during the war. 'We used up an asset during the war which will have to be put back. The good years were the result of mining stored fertility and repair should have been provided out of profits in the war years and put into reserve.[116] More locally, Henry Lord Bentinck speaking in early 1921, said that in Westmorland 'many acres of land had been ploughed during the war that never ought to have been ploughed and it would be years and years before it got back again to the same condition'.[117]

It is unclear to what extent overgrazing resulted in a decline in quality of common pasture. There is little documentation available for the commons in the post-war period: the manorial courts were ceasing to function either because they were deemed unnecessary or because abuse was so widespread that no one was willing to take action against a neighbour when he himself was breaking the rules. The long-standing rule of *levancy and couchancy*, where a commoner could not send more stock to the common than he could overwinter on the produce of his own holding, were described in some manorial documents as *'sans nombre'* and were increasingly interpreted as an unrestricted right.[118] Even before the Great War, 'the commoners of Uldale Common had to have the meaning of "unlimited" explained to them, but two "unreasonable graziers" were accused of sheltering behind their construction of unlimited'.[119]

Post-war examples of attempts to regulate common grazing are found in the files of the Hothfield Estate. In the 1920s two applications for regulation

---

113   *BPP*, 1919, viii, Evidence Donaldson, para. 11338.

114   *BPP*, 1919, viii, Evidence Strutt, para. 1327.

115   *BPP*, 1919, viii, Evidence Vintner, para. 3568.

116   Ibid., Evidence from Messrs Allison, McNicol, Stewart and Davidson, paras 14587 and 14592.

117   *WG*, 15 Jan. 1921, p. 16.

118   Eleanor A. Straughton, *Common Grazing in the Northern English Uplands* (Lampter, 2008), p. 12.

119   Ibid., pp. 217–18.

of common land were made. On Little Asby Common unlimited rights were converted to stints so 'that every farmer may be able to enjoy his just and equal rights of pasture'.[120] At Frostrow there was 'trouble with regard to the number and position of sheep on the fells' and there was a call for stinting of previously unstinted land. The manor court met to make a grazing order to prevent overstocking by appointing a shepherd to be paid for by the commoners.[121] But there were objections to regulation. James Handley had just bought a farm 'and he would not have paid as much for it if the fells had been stinted'.[122] Unusually the Kaber Parish Meeting helped with commons management by fielding representatives for the conservators of Winton and Kaber Commons and a by-law was made in 1930 to prevent those with rights on contiguous commons from letting their stock graze on Winton and Kaber.[123] The documented cases of regulation are limited but point to continuing problems with overstocking and misuse which had an effect on the quality of pasture and livestock. Improvement of pasture after wartime overgrazing was discussed widely. Farmers were warned to keep sheep numbers down and to graze them in association with cattle because 'they prefer fine grasses and if they graze in isolation the pasture becomes rough and tufted'.[124]

The clearest evidence of how future profitability had been mined in wartime comes from the backlog of maintenance needed by farms. At Julian Bower Farm, Westmorland, a report on the property of 1921 read:

> Gates and fences, drainage and spouting need repair. The front of the house needs repair and is damp. Doors into the small shed on the east of the house need repairing. Barns need new doors and the iron roof of the dutch barn should be mended. Windows in the stable need repair and the stone steps leading to the cake house are worn.

Julian Bower was in a poor state by 1921 and repair work was hampered by a shortage of labour.[125]

It was clear that farmers were increasingly anxious about the future of their industry and were reluctant to try to continue arable production at wartime levels. In 1919 the *Cumberland and Westmorland Herald* warned farmers 'that the artificial prosperity which he has enjoyed during the war is about to disappear'.[126] One farmer wrote of 'the feeling of great anxiety as to the position

---

120   CA, KRO, WD/HH/36, Regulation of Little Asby Common.
121   Straughton, *Common Grazing*, p. 155.
122   *Penrith Observer*, 28 Nov. 1922, p. 2.
123   Straughton, *Common Grazing*, p. 168.
124   *CWH*, 30 July 1921, p. 9.
125   CA, KRO, WD/HOTH Box 1, 5 Oct. 1921.
126   *CWH*, 29 Mar. 1919, p. 11.

and condition of our great national industry'.[127] So the high cash 'profits' from wartime farming were to an extent illusory. If it had been possible to construct comparative balance sheets for 1914 and 1918 which reflected both tangible and intangible assets, many farmers would have seen that wartime profits were in fact 'deferred payments' resulting from enforced neglect which needed to be reinvested to ensure the continued viability of the holding.[128] As they approached the challenges of the 1920s and 1930s farmers faced the need to reinvest and restore productivity at a time of falling prices and great uncertainty. The desire to limit risk and allow land to revert to grass was entirely rational. The 'blame' for wartime exploitation of the land might be laid on the shoulders of government but the cultivation and labour policies of the later part of the war were an essential response to wartime emergency:

> They knew that they were ... upsetting the principles of good farming for many
> years to come ... however the situation was so desperate that if it was a question of
> scrapping a system or being starved out the system would have to go.[129]

Some farmers, fully aware that they faced the uncertain post-war world with depreciated capital, got out; others stayed on, some compelled to buy their farms with borrowed money, and set about readjusting production to the post-war situation.

VI

In writing history, all levels of scale have validity, each offering a different view of the past being represented. As we pan out from the building and field, to the village, region and nation, we lose detail as we proceed but start to see patterns. The individual buildings and fields are still there, but hidden from view. However, they remain embedded in the larger image and give it a texture, warmth, personality and 'life' which is otherwise missing in generalisation. This chapter has revisited Westmorland during the Great War and examined the impact of national wartime production policy in one part of the British uplands. The chapter has listened to the voices of the farmers whose efforts allowed the county the distinction of achieving the highest percentage increase in ploughed land in England. They have told us about the environmental, technical, manpower and emotional challenges that they faced, and to a large extent

---

[127]　*CWH*, 15 Mar. 1919, p. 6.

[128]　As argued by Falconer L. Wallace before the 1919 Royal Commission on Agriculture, Minutes of evidence *BPP*, 1919, viii, 23, qq. 9030–33.

[129]　*CWH*, 1 Mar. 1919, p. 2.

overcame, in the latter years of the conflict. We hear murmurs of discontent but no revolt. Farmers wanted to have their say and assert their autonomy but this did not prevent a very high level of compliance with direction even when the effects were of questionable value.

A focus on the physical achievement and the assumed financial rewards has left the post-war legacy under explored. The wartime correspondence helps explain why the post-war situation was so hard. After 1921, tired human beings struggling with depreciated farming capital, exhausted soil, over-grazed pasture and inferior livestock faced a world of depressed prices unsupported by the government who had asked so much of them between 1914 and 1918. They needed to readjust production, invest and restore infrastructure and fashion a new method of working at a time when agriculture was left to 'the play of market forces', because 'the prospect of a future war could not justify the maintenance of agricultural production at a level which was uneconomic in a time of peace.'[130] In these difficult times many Westmorland family farms found their small size and reliance on unpaid family labour a real advantage. Their primary motive was independence ... 'the prestige of being a farmer within a closed community, the sense of continuity with the past and their pride in being independent' all constituted strong alternatives to the profit motive.[131] Their traditions of barter, exchange and community support, replaced payment in cash by payment in kind, and their 'careful' lifestyle and old habits of saving for lean years offered a prudent method of cash flow management. Enlargement of the family farm unit to include the local neighbourhood insulated the wider group from the stresses of the economic environment. As one farmer recalled:

> There wasn't much to be made; you didn't make much and you didn't spend much cause you couldn't ... But nobody grumbled. Everyone helped one another and we got by; nobody grumbled, we got by.[132]

And they did 'get by' until a new war intervened and government took control of farming once more to feed a population at war for a second time.

---

[130] Ibid., p. 165.

[131] Office of the Minister for Science, *The Scale of Enterprise in Farming* (London, 1961), p. 59.

[132] Kendal Oral History Archive Transcripts, Respondent 0113, Male, born 1930, Farmer's son from New Hutton, his father was a tenant farmer on the Underley Estate.

Chapter 11

Rex Paterson (1903–1978): Pioneer of Grassland Dairy Farming and Agricultural Innovator

John Martin[1]

Rex Paterson's career is an enigma. Unlike the vast majority of his farming contemporaries, he originated from a non-agricultural background. He embarked upon a career in dairy farming during the depressed conditions of the 1920s, when farmers were being forced to rationalise their existing enterprises and cut back on all types of expenditure in an effort to survive the collapse of agricultural prices. Even milk, the traditional mainstay of livestock farmers during periods of recession, was adversely affected by the acrimonious disputes over contract price that took place annually – before the inauguration of the Milk Marketing Board in 1933 – between dairy farmers and the large milk retailing conglomerates. Nevertheless, by the outbreak of the Second World War, Paterson had managed to develop one of Europe's largest private dairy farming enterprises, based on what were to become his trademarks: a controversial, low-cost, outdoor bail system of milk production, coupled with comprehensive and meticulous record keeping and data analysis.

At the start of the Second World War and the establishment of the state-directed food production campaign, Paterson initially took on more land, in compliance with the Hampshire War Agricultural Executive Committee (HWAEC), which was responsible for implementing the national food production programme at county level. In the wartime grading scheme, which was based on individual farm performance, Paterson was designated a Grade A farmer, with a level of output in excess of 85 per cent of potential, the highest productivity category. Nevertheless, after a controversial dispute in 1944 over his cropping plans, he was informed that the local committee would subject him to the same level of restrictions and controls as farmers of lower grades. The

[1] This chapter is largely based on Paterson's papers lodged at the Museum of English Rural Life, University of Reading, cited here as FR PAT. The research assistance of Catherine Glover is gratefully acknowledged.

official investigation that resulted from his spirited rebuttal of their allegations vindicated Paterson's claim that he was being victimised by local officials.

After the end of hostilities in 1945, Paterson played a key role in popularising more efficient systems of milk production based on grass. He firmly believed that grassland in the UK could make a substantial contribution to milk production, and his dairy farming relied almost exclusively on the use of grass and silage. This belief was backed by a comprehensive study of the problems of growing and utilising the grass crop, which resulted in his developing a unique but simple method of recording and measuring grass output on his farms. His system of cow-day recording of grassland was recognised as one of the first published examples of pasture recording in this country, and his milk graphs, which complemented his cow-day recording, enabled him to study the effect of various feeds and management techniques on milk production. He also played a key role as an innovator in agricultural mechanisation, his best-known initiative being the Paterson buckrake, a tractor-mounted machine designed to revolutionise the process of silage making. He also served with distinction as the County Chairman of the National Farmers Union and on a number of county and headquarters committees, including the Development and Education Committee. His many accolades during this period include the award of an OBE in 1964 and, in the following year, the Massey Ferguson Award for outstanding contributions to UK farming.[2]

Unlike many other pioneering farmers and individuals who were responsible for popularising the modernisation of farming, Paterson's achievements have been glossed over by agricultural historians. For example, he receives scant attention in Holderness's *British Agriculture since 1945*, while my own *Development of Modern Agriculture: British Farming since 1931* largely ignored his contribution to the modernisation of dairy farming.[3] Even in Quentin Seddon's seminal account, *The Silent Revolution*, he merits little more than a couple of paragraphs.[4]

This neglect, at least in part, reflects the fact that Paterson, instead of celebrating his own farming achievements, concentrated his endeavours on an analytical, objective evaluation of the performance of his particular style of dairy farming. His approach was in stark contrast to that espoused by other self-made farmers such as his widely acclaimed contemporary George Henderson. Both of Henderson's books, *The Farming Ladder* (which had 12 printings between 1946 and 1951) and *Farmer's Progress* (1950), exalted his progress up the farming ladder, but provided

---

[2] R. Paterson, *Milk from Grass: Rex Paterson, OBE* (Massey Ferguson Papers 2, 1965), p. 10.

[3] B.A. Holderness, *British Agriculture since 1945* (Manchester, 1985); J. Martin, *The Development of Modern Agriculture: British Farming since 1931* (Basingstoke, 2000).

[4] Q. Seddon, *The Silent Revolution* (London, 1989), pp. 35–6.

few specific details about the performance of his dairy and poultry enterprises.[5] In a similar way, Paterson's mentor, Arthur J. Hosier, who was responsible for popularising the outdoor system of bail milking, also tended in his memoirs to gloss over the financial performance of his different enterprises.[6]

This chapter seeks to reappraise Paterson's achievements by focusing on his background and early career, his contribution to dairy farming in the 1930s, the impact of the wartime food production campaign on his farms, and his post-war role as an agricultural innovator and pioneer of modern dairy farming. In particular it seeks to explain the paradox that, while his methods of food production were maligned during the Second World War, after the war he was hailed as a progressive farmer. A wide variety of national and local sources were studied, including official accounts, scientific papers, newspapers, contemporary personal accounts and Paterson's own correspondence and extensive personal records. This evaluation of Paterson's career is in part based on his extensive correspondence, which has been deposited in the archives of the Museum of English Rural Life at the University of Reading.

I

Unlike the majority of farmers in the late nineteenth and early twentieth centuries, Rex Munro Paterson came from a non-farming family. As Charles Orwin, the well-known agricultural economist, lamented, agriculture was virtually the only:

> great industry offering no chance to a salaried manager ... only as a working farmer on a smallholding, or as the possessor of a few thousand pounds of capital can a man enter the farming industry in any capacity other than that of a manual worker so that the industry is closed to all young men of brains and ambition who are looking for a chance to carve out careers for themselves.[7]

This reflected what was perceived as an almost insoluble difficulty of securing access to the necessary capital, which, for the vast majority of farmers, had been provided by 'matrimony, patrimony and parsimony'.[8]

According to this school of thought, those from a non-farming background could only acquire the necessary expertise and management skills if they could

---

5   G. Henderson, *The Farming Ladder* (1946) and *Farmer's Progress* (1950).

6   A.J. and F.H. Hosier, *Hosier's Farming System* (London, 1951), pp. 14–65.

7   C.S. Orwin, *The Future of Farming* (Oxford, 1930), p. 100.

8   This aphorism sums up the most common ways of securing access to capital. Borrowing money from strangers or from banks would have been anathema to the majority of farmers.

afford to pay the fees to become pupils of established farmers. Securing a foothold on the farming ladder and progressing upwards was even more difficult during the depressed conditions of the 1920s and 1930s, when even established farmers were forced to curtail their activities in order to survive.[9] Nevertheless, the history of a number of innovating farmers – of whom Arthur Hosier and A.G. Street are the best known – and individuals from non-farming stock such as Rex Paterson and George Henderson, demonstrate that these obstacles to advancement were not totally insurmountable.[10] Indeed, during the challenging times of the 1920s, those with non-farming backgrounds appeared to be less constrained by social conventions. As J.A. Scott pertinently noted:

> Looking back through history, we find cases where men have turned from other walks of life and, bringing with them new ideas and fresh capital have made important contributions to progress. These men have been specially valuable during periods of agricultural depression, when the hereditary farmer's capital and enterprise both tend to run low.[11]

Paterson later claimed in his unpublished biography: 'Having no true agricultural background I have never been afraid to question the reasons for commonly accepted practices.'[12] This willingness to be sceptical reflected, at least in part, his family background and upbringing. His father, Claude Dundar Paterson, was a peripatetic clergyman who, along with his mother, Elsie Verdon *née* Roe, played a key role in fostering his ambitions to become a farmer. His maternal uncle was Sir A.V. Roe, the famous aviation designer. In contrast to the vast majority of farmers who had received only a rudimentary education at their local village school, Paterson was educated at the well-known Christ's Hospital School in London, an institution which was important in developing his early professional aspiration to pursue a career in either engineering or farming. He decided to become a farmer as it offered him the opportunity to enjoy the open air.[13]

In 1918, aged 16, Paterson left school to attend Wye Agricultural College. On account of the war there was 'little being done at the College', so he left Wye after a few weeks and went to work on a farm in Kent.[14] After recognising the inherent difficulty of acquiring the necessary capital to secure a farm of his own,

---

[9]   One of the best-documented examples of this was A.G. Street (1892–1966) for whom see the biography in *ODNB*.

[10]   For details of Hosier's and Henderson's careers, see Hosier and Hosier, *Farming System*; Henderson, *Farming Ladder*; Henderson, *Farmer's Progress*.

[11]   J.A. Scott Watson, 'Mr Clyde Higgs' Dairy Farms', *J. Royal Agricultural Soc. of England* 97 (1936), p. 112.

[12]   FR PAT, SP/1, part 2, Paterson, 'From nothing to a thousand acres' (typescript, undated), p. 3.

[13]   FR PAT, SP/1, part 1, 'Introduction' (typescript, undated), pp. 3–4.

[14]   Ibid., p. 4.

he made the decision to emigrate.[15] In January 1919, 'stirred by the thought of shooting big game', he moved to Canada, where vast tracts of low-priced land were perceived to offer more opportunities for those wishing to embark on a career in farming.[16] He initially worked on a dairy farm in Nova Scotia, before moving in the spring to work on two farms in Ontario. Taking advantage of the availability of cheap fares, in August he moved to the Prairie Provinces where he worked for 10 months on a 52,000-acre cattle ranch, before gaining further experience on farms in Ontario and Saskatchewan.[17]

In June 1920 Paterson moved to Armstrong, British Columbia, where, in partnership with his cousin, Capt. Kenneth Russell Napier, he bought an 80-acre dairy farm with a retail milk round. After the worldwide fall in agricultural prices in 1921, funding the interest on the capital and taxes (which amounted to about £6 per acre annually on their 60 productive acres) meant that dairy farming was a very precarious way to make a living. However, with his milk round, he was able to save enough money to return to England in December 1924, where he thought there would be more opportunities to become a farmer in his own right.[18] Reflecting back on what he had learnt from his experience of struggling to make a living in Canada he noted:

> There was so much to be done that I got to know which foot or hand to move at which moment and in which particular direction for nearly every minute of the day, and every day of the week. It soon dawned on me that if I had done a little budgeting before starting to farm, in fact if I had never worked at all, but just sat down and done a little figuring I would be a much richer man.[19]

On his return to England, he secured a position on the farm in Kent where he had worked before emigrating. But, in April 1927, disillusioned with the attitude of his fellow workers and the complacency of his employer, he decided to leave the farm and 'seek employment that would give ... [him] more scope'; failing that, he would return to Canada.[20] Initially he accepted a job as a tractor driver on 30s. a week with 6d. an hour overtime, plus acreage money.[21] In the late autumn of that year, Paterson married Muriel Pantling and they secured the tenancy of an undercapitalised, run-down, 80-acre farm near Winchester. Rex

---

[15]   *ODNB*, 'Orwin, Charles Stewart'.

[16]   FR PAT, SP/1, 'Introduction', p. 4.

[17]   FR PAT, SP/1, part 1, 'The Development and Management of a Large Farm' (ms, undated), p. 1.

[18]   FR PAT, SP/1, Paterson, 'From nothing', p. 1.

[19]   Ibid., p. 3.

[20]   Ibid., p. 1.

[21]   A. Walsh, *The Contribution of Grass to Profitable Milk Production: An on-Farm Study Based on the Results from 34 Herds* (Rex Paterson Memorial Study, 1982), p. 4.

undertook contract work with an old Fordson tractor and supplemented their income by catching rabbits.[22] In the following year the landlord rented them another 80 acres and provided the capital for a few cows and a six-stall Hosier 'bail', or mobile milking parlour, which enabled the cows to be milked by a machine powered by a portable generator.[23]

Open-air dairy farming of this type, where the cows spent all of their time outdoors, was one of the most controversial experiments of the time.[24] Until the mid 1920s machine milking had been fraught with difficulties, not only the unreliability of the oil-fired engines which provided the power, but also the perishability of the rubber linings in the teat cups, and the need for steam-heated sterilisation after each milking. It was not until the mid 1920s that the rubber used in milking machines was of sufficient strength and durability to cope with the pressure of the vacuum and the steam used in sterilisation.[25]

Milk production in outdoor bails was adversely affected by periods of inclement weather, but this was more than compensated for by its cleanliness and low labour requirements. Bail milking virtually eliminated the need for permanent buildings in the form of cowsheds and significantly reduced the need to drive the herd to and from the fields before and after milking. It also enabled the fodder, either in the form of hay or silage, to be made and stored in the fields where it was grown, thereby dispensing with the labour and equipment needed to haul the fodder to the steading and to cart the manure back to the fields.[26] Labour productivity was also higher, as up to 60 cows could be managed by one man and a boy.[27] This was in stark contrast to conventional cowshed production, where hand-milking, and the need to cart feeding stuffs to the animals and to remove the dung, frequently required the use of several men for a herd of less than 20 cows.

The outdoor bail system of dairy farming, which had been originally developed in New Zealand, was pioneered in Britain by Frank and Joshua Hosier in Wiltshire. By the late 1920s they had five outdoor herds amounting to more than 300 non-pedigree, all-purpose cows, imported mainly from Ireland.[28] The Hosiers were particularly keen to disseminate the benefits of this system as they had a lucrative sideline in building bails to sell to other farmers. Recognising the

---

[22]   FR PAT, SP/1, part 1, 'Development and Management', p. 12.

[23]   Walsh, *Contribution*, p. 1.

[24]   G.E. Mingay, *British Friesians: An Epic of Progress* (Rickmansworth, 1982), p. 60; E.H. Whetham, *The Agrarian History of England and Wales*, VIII, *1914–1939* (Oxford, 1978), p. 269.

[25]   Mingay, *British Friesians*, p. 59.

[26]   Hosier and Hosier, *Farming System*.

[27]   FR PAT, SP/1, part 1, 'Development and management', p. 14.

[28]   Hosier and Hosier, *Farming System*, pp. 25, 32; *ODNB*, 'Hosier, Arthur Julius'. The indefatigable A.G. Street, farmer and author, in *Farming England* (London, 1937), pp. 31–2, described Hosier as the 'Wizard of Wexcombe'.

benefits of this low-cost method of milk production, Paterson rapidly became an ardent supporter of this new system of dairy farming, even though it had 'been subjected to more abuse and more slander than the most iniquitous of governments'.[29]

Despite the labour-saving advantages of machine milking it was not widely adopted. Even by the late 1930s, more than 10 years after Paterson had adopted the process, it was estimated that only 20 per cent of farmers were using milking machines.[30] The adoption of the outdoor bail system was even slower. By 1930 there were 86 farms with outdoor bails, whereas 10 years later, although there were nearly 200 farms – mainly in Wiltshire and the surrounding counties – milking in bails, this still amounted to less than two in every thousand dairy farmers.[31] Its slow uptake partly reflected the fact that bail milking was only really suited to the lighter soils of the southern counties, where relatively low levels of rainfall meant that poaching levels were not appreciable during wet weather.

In spite of the relatively low cost of purchasing a bail and milking machines, this initiative still required some initial capital investment. During the depressed conditions of the 1930s, expenditure of this kind was only contemplated by those enterprising farmers who had the vision to experiment with new methods of production. For the vast majority the low cost and ready availability of family labour encouraged the continuation of hand-milking in conventional cowsheds. As Angus Calder had noted following the 'Great Betrayal' of 1921, when the state had repealed the wartime system of guaranteed prices, farmers tended to be characterised by 'persecution mania' with 'limited perspectives' whose 'distrust of education, had tended to ignore the startling advances in agricultural science which were taking place'.[32]

Paterson left the farm near Winchester in 1929 and – with a total capital of £727, made up of £166 savings, £100 from the share of profits, and a loan of £461 from his mother – he purchased New Zealand Farm, Chute, a 396-acre, free-draining chalk downland farm in Hampshire for £4,000. It was acquired for a cash deposit of £500 with the balance to be paid three years later. The vendor, who was a cattle dealer friend of Paterson's, also agreed to supply him with £800 of cattle, to be paid off in three years at an interest rate of 1 per cent over bank rate.[33] Letting about 200 acres to tenants for the first six months, he erected a small 10ft-by-20ft hut to live in while embarking on fencing the farm, laying

---

[29] Street, *Farming England*, p. 32.

[30] Mingay, *British Friesians*, p. 60.

[31] *ODNB*, 'Hosier, Arthur Julius'.

[32] A. Calder, *The People's War: Britain, 1939–1945* (London, 1969), p. 483.

[33] Paterson, *Milk from Grass*, p. 10.

over one mile of stone road and a piped water supply more than two miles from a neighbouring farm.[34]

A second milking bail was built for him by the Hosier brothers, as a fixture in a covered yard. In 1932 the purchase of the farm was completed with a loan from the Agricultural Mortgage Corporation, while a further adjoining 300 acres was acquired on similar terms from the original cattle dealer. Shortly afterwards two other fixed bails were erected, one of which was constructed using prefabricated sections but with different feeding arrangements. Using second-hand equipment, the total cost was only about £100.[35] In 1936, having sold both farms more or less at cost, Paterson became the tenant of a 1,000-acre farm in Sussex, where he established a number of bail units.[36] In the same year he also rented two farms near Basingstoke, Hampshire, from the Earl of Portsmouth's estates and, in 1937, secured the tenancy on Hatch Warren Farm, Cliddesdon, also near Basingstoke, where he resided for the rest of his life. The acquisition of this additional land led Paterson to devote most of his time to organising and financing the growing enterprises while employing a manager.[37] This heralded a phase of rapid expansion, with more land being taken on, often at a peppercorn rent, from landlords who found it unprofitable to cultivate, given the low prices that prevailed for virtually all agricultural commodities, including milk.[38] As he explained, he had made farming pay by purchasing hay, concentrates and cattle, which other people produced at the current market price and sold at a loss, and converting it into milk which was sold at a profit.[39] Even in the case of milk, where marketing was coordinated by the newly established Milk Marketing Board, there was a growing gap between the gross price for milk (as quoted in the Official Statistics) and the actual price received by the farmer.[40] Despite the low wage levels for agricultural workers that prevailed in the interwar period, rates were still considerably higher than they had been before the First World

---

[34]   FR PAT, B, part 2, R. Paterson, 'The effect of the Supply of Capital on Food Production with Particular Reference to the effect of Excess Profit Tax'.

[35]   Paterson, *Milk from Grass*, p. 13.

[36]   Ibid., p. 10.

[37]   FR PAT, B/1, 'Is There a Place for Farming in British Agriculture?' Talk to Cambridge University Agricultural Club, 25 Feb. 1948, p. 3.

[38]   FR PAT, SP/1, part 2, p. 3. Paterson notes that, during the conditions of the 1930s, it was so difficult to find tenants for some chalkland farms that landowners were often willing to initially let them rent-free.

[39]   FR PAT, SP/1, Paterson, 'From nothing', p. 4.

[40]   P.E. Graves, 'The Trend of Milk Prices in the Eastern Counties', *Farm Economist*, July 1936, pp. 44–5.

War.[41] It was the desire to economise on the use of labour that prompted the Hosier brothers and Paterson to adopt outdoor bail milking.[42]

At a time of low-priced, imported feeding stuffs, there was little incentive to embark upon a systematic programme of grassland improvement. Indeed, given the availability of both imported and home-grown cereals at that time, it was possible and profitable to feed large quantities of concentrates to the cows.[43] Like the vast majority of other dairy farmers, however, Paterson did not attempt to improve the genetic potential of the animals through progeny testing.[44] Instead most herd replacements were imported Irish Shorthorns or Ayrshires, all of which were heifers, in order to make his limited capital go as far as possible and to avoid mastitis.[45]

Paterson focused his attention on establishing semi-independent herds looked after by a single worker, who was allowed a fair degree of autonomy in his management, and was paid bonuses according to the productivity of the herd. His farms were split into units that were big enough to be managed by one man (a sub-manager or foreman) under the control of a general manager who was responsible for a group of farms. He picked his general managers from men who had worked their way up from the bottom in farming, believing that men worked best when they were able to use their own judgement and initiative. Each farm worked independently, except for buying and selling, which had to be approved by Paterson. The records kept by each farm were analysed by Paterson and his team of office managers, who used them to foster a spirit of competition between the farms in order to make them more productive. This strategy was backed by a detailed study of the problems of growing and utilising the grass crop. Before the war he focused almost exclusively on dairy farming, growing only a small area of cereals. Those fields that were ploughed were usually reseeded directly to grass with no cover crop.[46] His adoption of this low-cost system ensured that by the outbreak of the Second World War he was farming in the region of 5,000 acres.[47]

What differentiated Paterson from other pioneering farmers of this period was that he did not see this farming system merely as a means of ensuring his economic survival in an era of depression, but as a way of establishing a farming

[41] R. McG. Carslaw and P.E. Graves, 'The Farmer's Labour Bill', *Farm Economist*, Apr. 1935, p. 203.

[42] Hosier and Hosier, *Farming System*, p. 12; FR PAT, SP/1, 'Development and Management', p. 1.

[43] R. Paterson, 'Presidential Address', *J. British Grassland Soc.* 24 (1968), p. 108.

[44] Paterson did not undertake progeny testing as he considered it more profitable to buy imported Irish heifers at £16 each than to rear his own calves to the same age at a cost he estimated as £25. According to O.B. Miller, Director of John Lewis & Co., Paterson's 'natural perceptions, his intuitive judgement may be so strong, that he tends to rely on it a little uncritically, almost in a slight mystical way'. See report, ref. JSI/MMF, in FR PAT, SP/B/1, part 1.

[45] Paterson, *Milk from Grass*, pp. 6–7.

[46] Ibid., p. 2.

[47] Ibid., p. 7.

empire.[48] By the late 1930s Paterson was an outstanding example of a progressive farmer who clearly met the criteria identified by the eminent agriculturalists Viscount Astor and B. Seebohm Rowntree, that is, 'a scientist, keeping records, always trying as far as possible to relate effect to its causes and occasionally venturing into field experiments of his own'. By this time an 'unfathomable gulf yawned between the progressive farmer and the run-of-the-road farmer, who muddled along with a rule-of-thumb wisdom inherited from his father or picked up over a glass of beer on market day'.[49]

II

Following the outbreak of the Second World War in 1939, the Ministry of Agriculture embarked upon an ambitious plan, a ploughing-up campaign designed to increase the production of arable crops, in particular wheat and potatoes. Although livestock production was deliberately curtailed by the reduction in the area of grassland and the diminution in the amount of imported feeding stuffs, the official policy was that milk production should be granted preferential treatment in terms of the allocation of fodder.[50] Translating the paper plans of Whitehall into practical policies was achieved by the War Agricultural Executive Committee (WAEC) for each county. These committees exercised a high degree of autonomy in the way they dealt with individual farmers. As the Minister of Agriculture, Reginald Dorman-Smith, claimed: 'I have given the county committees as free a hand as possible to get on with the job, as they are men with very good local knowledge, I am confident that the machinery is the best which could be adopted to carry out this great task.'[51] The Chairman of the Hampshire WAEC was Charles Chute, later Sir Charles, of the Vyne (1879–1956), landowner and farmer. Chute, along with his Vice-Chairman, Gerald Wallop (Viscount Lymington, the ninth Earl of Portsmouth), considered that landlord control was an essential prerequisite in order to ensure agrarian harmony.[52] The other Vice-Chairman was Roland

[48] FR PAT, B/1, 'Large Scale Farming', p. 3.

[49] Viscount Astor and B.S. Rowntree, *Mixed Farming and Muddled Thinking: An Analysis of Current Agricultural Policy* (London, 1946), p. 10.

[50] Milk production was deemed a priority over other types of livestock. Like other types of livestock farmers, dairy farmers were adversely affected by the wartime shortages of imported feeding stuffs, which led to a number of large dairy farmers being forced to reduce the size of their herds. The Ministry of Agriculture attempted to alleviate this decline by requiring many small farmers to take up milk production.

[51] A. Hurd, *A Farmer in Whitehall: Britain's Farming Revolution, 1939–1950, and Future Prospects* (London, 1951), p. 26.

[52] For Chute, see his obituary in *The Times*, 2 Oct. 1956 and further notices on 5 Oct. and for his attitude to landlords, his letter to *The Times* of 29 Mar. 1943.

Dudley of Linkenholt Manor, near Andover (d. 1964), a pre-war pioneer in the use of combine harvesters and crop dryers on his 1,000-acre (predominantly) arable farm.[53] He was described by his obituary as 'an eighteenth-century improving squire with twentieth-century ideas'.[54]

Even in the early stages of the war, the Ministry of Agriculture had only a vague understanding, based on the annual 4 June returns, of the condition and production of individual farms. In order to remedy this deficiency, farmers were required to complete returns every three months and to participate in the National Farm Survey, the most comprehensive survey of land ownership since Domesday Book. Farmers were graded into one of three categories based on their level of productivity: Grade A farmers were those deemed to be achieving 85 per cent or more of the holding's potential, Grade B farmers between 70 and 85 per cent, while Grade C farmers were deemed to be achieving below 70 per cent. Such a classification was clearly designed to differentiate between progressive farmers, entrepreneurial farmers who were considered capable of responding on their own accord to the wartime directives to increase output, and inefficient farmers who were deemed to be incapable of raising productivity without extensive guidance from their local WAEC. Following a lengthy inspection, Paterson was awarded a Grade A.

The war was a period of changing fortunes for Paterson. By the autumn of 1939 he had about 5,000 acres under his jurisdiction, virtually all of which was rented. Approximately 2,000 acres was derelict land covered with bushes.[55] Initially Paterson took on more land in compliance with the HWAEC,[56] taking over farms at Hatch Warren, Kingsclere, Micheldever, Stockbridge and Alresford, so that by 1942 he was farming nearly 10,000 acres. During the war, however, there was a sharp reduction in the number of milking herds on Paterson's farms. This partly reflected the difficulty of purchasing herd replacements following the cessation of cattle imports from Ireland and partly, but more importantly, the problem of finding suitable dairymen given the wartime labour shortages. The war also heralded further reorganisation of his existing dairy units as more milking bails became fixed, a shift that was primarily designed to make milking a more attractive job for land girls (Figure 11.1).[57]

The prime cause of the contraction in his dairy farming activities, however, was the state-led ploughing-up campaign. Under the direction of the HWAEC, Paterson, along with other farmers, was required to plough up specified areas

---

53   H.G. Robinson, 'A Pioneer Mechanised Farm', *Country Life*, 1 Feb. 1933, pp. 156–8.

54   Obituary in the *The Times*, 31 July 1964.

55   Paterson, *Milk from Grass*, pp. 6–7.

56   FR PAT, SP/1, part 2, p. 21.

57   FR PAT, SP/1, part 2, 9 Nov. 1943; see Hampshire RO (hereafter HRO), 15M84/E6/4/80, Correspondence file relating to the letting of Hatch Warren Farm, Cliddesden: letter from Paterson to Portsmouth's agent, F.J. Hunt, 23 Nov. 1942.

Figure 11.1   'Milking Bails at the Farm of Rex Paterson, Hatch Warren, Basingstoke, Hampshire, January 1954' (Note that concrete floor shows that this is a fixed bail.) The figure in the tie is Paterson himself. Photograph courtesy of Museum of English Rural Life, University of Reading. P FS PH1/K53441.

of pasture. As the war progressed, this was accompanied by stringent cropping directives.[58] Nationally, the campaign was intended to secure a 10 per cent reduction in the area of grassland each year. This was reflected by changes in cropping on Paterson's farms, so that by 1943 approximately half of his land was producing arable crops.[59] About 3,000 acres were rented from the Earl of Portsmouth, one of the two vice-chairmen of the HWAEC. In 1944, there was a lengthy and acrimonious dispute between Paterson and the Portsmouth Estates, about the ploughing-up of pasture and the maintenance of fences, during which complaints against Paterson were described by his solicitor as 'not only ... erroneous but trivial'.[60] This simmering conflict reflected the breakdown in trust that appears to have taken place not only between Paterson and the Portsmouth Estates but also, more importantly, between Paterson and the HWAEC.

As part of the national campaign to increase potato production, the HWAEC had instructed Paterson to plant more potatoes, but his land was ill-suited to root crops due to the poor moisture-retaining capability of the light brashy soils. Nevertheless, in spite of the low yields he achieved, in 1942 he volunteered to increase his potato acreage in response to the committee's appeals.[61] It was not until late 1943 that he applied to reduce production because of the losses incurred. This application was initially rejected but finally accepted.[62]

A full account of Paterson's wartime dealings with the Hampshire County War Executive Committee remains to be written, but on a superficial reading of the minutes and correspondence it may be seen how Paterson was something of a trial to the Executive Committee and the Number 3 sub-committee responsible for the north of the county. He took up a great deal of both committees' time. As others have described, the Executive Committee was attempting to micromanage Hampshire land use but they failed in the first instance to gain much purchase over Paterson's farming empire.[63] Paterson himself seems to have been somewhat slippery. On the question of the reduction of potato acreage, the Number 3 Committee recorded that Paterson had acted without waiting for the Executive Committee's response to his request and sent him a

---

[58] For a detailed account of the of the Ministry of Agriculture's policy of directing farmers to increase production of specific crops, see K.A.H. Murray, *Agriculture* (1955), p. 154.

[59] In Hampshire, '46,934 acres had been ploughed between 4 June 1939 and 15 May 1940, with as much as 38,000 acres ploughed voluntarily by the end of October' (B.M. Short, 'Death of a Farmer: Fortunes of War and the Strange Case of Roy Walden', *AgHR* 56, 2008, p. 191).

[60] HRO, 15M84/E6/4/80, letter from White, Nash and Brooks, Solicitors to Lamb, Brooks and Bullock, Solicitors, 11 Nov. 1944.

[61] By 1942 he was growing over 800 acres of potatoes: see Paterson, *Milk from Grass*, p. 11.

[62] His calculations indicated that it was costing £37 to grow £22 of potatoes. See FR PAT B/2, letters from Paterson to Captain Ford, Assistant Executive Officer of the HWAEC, 30 Dec. 1943, 14 Feb. 1944.

[63] Short, 'Death of a Farmer'.

letter of reprimand.[64] Paterson later claimed that he understood the Executive Committee's instructions to mean that he should grow the specified acreage of crops somewhere on his lands rather than on specified areas and it is true that in 1942 the Executive Committee was less prescriptive with him than others. In fact, it seems that Paterson's fall from grace came after the Committee had bent over backwards to meet his needs and were then disobeyed by him.

Patersons's cropping was under active discussion in the spring of 1943. On 18 March the No. 3 committee decided to visit each of his farms. Paterson submitted a proposal to the Executive Committee 'for sufficient undersowing this year to make a system of alternate husbandry' and this was approved by them. At the meeting of 6 April, the Executive Committee advised the Number 3 Committee that at their next survey, the policy to be pursued upon Plantation farm be left to Paterson; that the policy on his North Oakley farm also be left to him 'on the condition that sufficient three years leys are maintained upon the holding to provide grazing for 80 cows; and that the policy upon all other farms [in Paterson's] occupation, which are left land out for dairy farming, shall be in accordance with the needs of the said farm if maintained on a system of alternate husbandry: all long leys to be grazed in the first year'. The minutes contain a hint that the No. 3 Committee did not receive this advice well: they sought clarification on what was meant by 'alternate husbandry' and asked that they should be allowed to interpret the minute 'literally'.[65]

A report on Paterson's farms was brought to the Executive meeting on 25 May: discussion was deferred to the next meeting when Paterson was invited to attend (itself an unusual concession). On 1 June some sort of agreement was reached which Paterson was subsequently sent in writing, but he seems to have demurred at it. On 29 June it was announced that Chute and Lord Radnor would both visit the farms and it was resolved on 13 July that Paterson should be told that the committee would not treat him any differently to any other Grade 'A' farmer. Paterson remained unhappy and on 20 July the Executive saw a letter sent to Chute by Paterson and endorsed his reply.[66] It was about this time that Dudley resigned: his resignation was noted on 27 July and vote of thanks recorded on 10 August.

At this point we mighty simply notice that the Executive Committee was giving Paterson a great deal of its time and much leeway. No other farmer was being dealt with them in this way. The Number 3 Committee seem to have been less certain about what they might have regarded as favouritism and unfair

---

[64]   TNA, MAF 80/1012, 17 Feb. 1944.

[65]   TNA, MAF/80, minute 30 Mar. 1943 (3356); 6 Apr. 1943 (3271); MAF80/1012, Minutes 18 Mar, 15 Apr. 1943.

[66]   TNA, MAF 80/905, minutes 25 May 1943 (3461); 1 June (3470); 25 June (3500), 13 July (3529), 20 July (3542); /1012, 11 June (570).

access by a farmer to the County Executive whilst Dudley may have resigned either over the treatment of Paterson or the Committee's work generally – it is not quite certain which – but Paterson held that Dudley resigned on account of the Executive's treatment of him.[67]

The Number 3 Committee held a special meeting on 3 March 1944 to consider requests from Paterson to plough additional permanent pasture and grass leys. It was reported that grass had been ploughed without its permission and the Committee refused to retrospectively sanction this. But there were doubts about whether the remaining grass was sufficient to maintain Paterson's herds, and the minutes reflect an inability to grasp – or discover – exactly what Paterson was doing.[68]

In May 1944 questions were being asked whether the undersown grass ley agreed the previous year had been sown as a one-year ley or a three-year ley, Paterson having asked that the Committee's decision in this be amended, which it refused to do.[69] The Executive Committee noted that 'if in fact the land has been sown to a one year ley, the Committee take a serious view of such non-compliance with the[ir] directions and will submit the facts to the Ministry with a view to prosecution'. As Chute explained in a letter to Paterson, 'The Committee can only take a serious view of your action, and feel that they have no alternative but to submit facts to the Ministry for their consideration with a view for prosecution for disobedience to their order. Within a week, Paterson requested that Chute provide him with details of the date on which they had formally instructed him to plant a three-year ley and an explanation of why they preferred long leys to short leys.[70] By July the Ministry had ruled that it would not prosecute in this instance, but was also instructing the Committee to bring in 'detailed directions' for the whole of Paterson's lands whilst warning Paterson that future deviations would be prosecuted. The same meeting of the Executive also received a letter from the Portsmouth estates asking that their farms should be treated as separate units and cropped 'to ensure a proper balance of arable and grass acreages', that is that they wanted to unpick Paterson's integrated husbandry, perhaps with an eye to letting the farms separately after the war.[71] Consequently he was informed that he would

---

[67] J. Wentworth Day, *Harvest Adventure* (1946), p. 251; FR PAT B/2, Paterson to Col. Pollitt, 23 Aug. 1944.

[68] TNA, MAF 80/1012, minute 3 Mar. 1944.

[69] A one-year ley consisted of varieties of grasses and clover such as Italian ryegrass and red clover, which would only survive for a single year whereas a three-year ley consists of strains such as perennial ryegrass, which could survive for several years. A one-year ley in its first and only season would produce more grass than a three-year ley, which could not be so intensively grazed because of the possibly of it being poached during wet weather, affecting its longer-term productivity.

[70] Letters 17 May, 24 May 1944, FR PAT, B/2.

[71] TNA, MAF 80/909, minutes 16 May 1944 (4037); 6 June (4078); 18 July (4180).

be subject to the same restrictions and controls as those imposed on Grade B and C farmers.[72] This, according to Paterson, was 'done on a series of trumped up charges which they never investigated before passing judgement'.[73] It was the 'penalty in respect of his disobedience concerning 130 acres on which he thought the orders had been cancelled'.[74]

Paterson persuaded the press to be interested in his dispute with the HWAEC, and the press coverage together with an investigation by the NFU, helped to resolve the disagreement.[75] A substantial report by the local branch of the NFU endorsed Paterson's claims that he was being victimised by local officials.[76] It also castigated the HWAEC for pursuing a 'policy which is responsible for dispossessing quite a large number of farmers'.[77] Chute's belated attempts to challenge the findings of the report, consisting of a short letter published in the *Farmers Weekly* on 28 November 1944, were persuasively countered by A.R.L. Aylward, Chairman of the Hampshire NFU.[78] The full details of the story were reported in *Farmers Weekly*.[79] But Paterson's wartime treatment by the HWAEC, rather than being exceptional, reflects the experiences of a number of interwar progressive farmers such as George Odlum, a large progressive dairy farmer who was castigated by the Wiltshire WAEC.[80] According to R.J. Robertson Poupar, the Press Association Agricultural Correspondent, the 'uneasiness' caused by the NFU report 'appear[ed] to be almost nationwide.'[81] While *Farmers Weekly* again reported his case sympathetically,[82] it subsequently reported that the HWAEC took 'strong exception' to the way the minister's decision had been announced.[83]

---

[72]   Official Solicitor of the Ministry of Agriculture to Paterson, 11 July 1944; Paterson's reply querying the facts and asking for clarification, 13 July, FR PAT, B/2. His correspondence shows that at the same time, Paterson started to seek support in the press.

[73]   FR PAT, B/2, Paterson to Colonel Pollitt, 23 Aug. 1944.

[74]   *Evening Standard*, 14 July 1944, p. 2.

[75]   FR PAT B/2, Paterson to Colonel Pollitt, 23 Aug. 1944.

[76]   'Rex Paterson and the Hants QUACK', *FW* (hereafter *FW*), 10 Nov. 1944, p. 19.

[77]   Parliamentary Debates, 5th ser., 407, col. 2026 (House of Commons, 6 Feb. 1945).

[78]   HRO, 15M84/E6/4/80, letter from A.R.L. Aylward, chairman Hants NFU Sub-Committee, 9 Dec. 1944.

[79]   'Rex Paterson and the Hants CWAEC: Dispute Settled; Complete Vindication', *FW* 10 Nov. 1944, p. 21.

[80]   Odlum's ordeal in the rush by the Wiltshire WAEC to restructure agricultural production in their locality raised serious doubts about the impartially of the wartime system of control and administration. John Martin, 'George Odlum, the Ministry of Agriculture and "Farmer Hudson"', *AgHR* 55 (2007), pp. 229–50.

[81]   *Southern Daily Echo*, 4 Dec. 1944.

[82]   'Rex Paterson and the Hants CWAEC', p. 21.

[83]   'Settlement in Paterson Case', *FW*, 15 Dec. 1944, p. 19; 'Strong Exception to Minister's statement', *FW*, 5 Jan. 1945, p. 17.

In an adjournment debate on 6 February 1945 the MP for Southampton raised Paterson's predicament and the exercise of power by the CWAECs generally. Answering this, the Minister of Agriculture Robert Hudson, declined to discuss Paterson's case telling the Commons:

> I do not propose to go in detail into that case because I hope it has been settled and, as at present advised, I understand that Mr. Patterson has agreed with the Committee on his cropping programme, and I do not want to do or say anything that will make future relations more difficult now that this dispute has been got out of the way.[84]

Later in the debate, when reference was made to dispossessed farmers, Mr Hudson said, 'At present the person who is dispossessed has the chance of getting something else and I am satisfied from the cases I have seen that very often if the full facts came out at an enquiry, his chances of getting another farm would be very small.'[85] In a report of the Parliamentary debate in the *Daily Telegraph* on 7 February, it was made to appear that the reference to dispossessed farmers was in fact a reference to Paterson. Following a writ for libel served by Paterson, the *Daily Telegraph* accepted, in a statement to the court, that this was 'entirely erroneous' and agreed to publish a further apology, pay a sum in respect of damages and indemnify the Paterson in respect of his costs.[86]

This conflict with the Hampshire CWAEC seems to have led Paterson to rethink his priorities. He had had a long-term vision of developing a system to train and encourage young fellows with non-agricultural backgrounds like his to pursue a career in farming. This would have required considerable external support. Whilst he was able to secure the promise of financial backing for such a scheme, he 'found that the attitude of the War Committee was that they did not think it desirable that one man should be responsible for so much land and for this reason, [he] eventually abandoned many of the plans which [he] had made and changed [his] whole outlook and policy'.[87] For the same reason, in the autumn of 1943 he decided to abandon his attempt at writing his own life story:[88] as he subsequently lamented, 'Unfortunately I ran into some unnecessary trouble with the Hampshire War Agricultural Committee, which made me so bitter that I could not continue with my proposed book [for Faber and Faber].'[89]

---

[84] Parliamentary Debates, 5th ser., 407, col. 2037.

[85] Ibid., col. 2041.

[86] FR PAT, B/2, part 1, Paterson v. *Daily Telegraph*.

[87] FR PAT, SP/1, Paterson, 'From Nothing', p. 24.

[88] FR PAT, SP/B/1, part 1, letter from Humphrey Wilson, Managing Director of Crosby Lockwood and Son Ltd to Paterson, 30 Sept. 1969.

[89] FR PAT, SP/B/1, part 1, letter from Paterson to Humphrey Wilson, 2 May 1969.

III

The termination of military hostilities in 1945 initially brought little immediate change to the government's wartime policy of focusing on arable production. While the WAECs were reformed, they continued to exercise considerable authority over the way land could be farmed, particularly the commitment to tillage. Buoyed by high guaranteed prices for cereals, which were provided by the 1947 Agriculture Act, there were strong financial incentives in favour of cereal production. For those with sufficient land to exploit economies of scale, the advent of the tractor and the combine harvester meant that growing cereals was not only easier but also, for large-scale chalkland farmers, more profitable than milking cows twice a day, 365 days a year.[90] Continuing with arable farming on the wartime scale would have been feasible for Paterson who had, during the war, acquired a fleet of combine harvesters and other cultivation equipment, as well as constructing his own grain storage facilities. Unlike many of the other larger farmers who had pursued dairy farming as a means of ensuring their survival during the interwar depression, and saw no reason to return to it, Paterson decided to concentrate his efforts on milk production, grassing down the land as and when WAEC directives allowed, and re-establishing dairy herds.[91]

Conditions for livestock producers after the war were fundamentally different from those that had prevailed before 1939. The pre-war commodity surpluses and unlimited supplies of low-cost imported cereals and protein-rich seedcakes had been replaced by stringent rationing of virtually all kinds of purchased feeding stuffs. In part these shortages reflected the direct effects of the war. Agriculture everywhere, with the exception of North America, had been acutely disrupted by the conflict; food shortages prevailed across Europe and Asia, a situation which was not immediately to be resolved. Even in 1947–48, for example, world food production remained 7 per cent below pre-war levels.[92]

The difficulty of importing food was compounded by Britain's precarious financial position. The Labour government, following the termination of Lend-Lease, was heavily dependent on massive dollar loans to sustain its balance

---

[90]　See Hosier and Hosier, *Farming System*, pp. 163–201.

[91]　Paterson's strategy is discussed in FR PAT, B/1, 'Large Scale Farming'. The Hosier brothers, for example, who had pioneered outdoor milk production in the late 1920s and had, like Paterson, been required to embark upon a major ploughing-up campaign during the war, continued with arable farming after the war. See Hosier and Hosier, *Farming System*, pp. 163–200. In a similar way, A.G. Street, who had also been forced to take up outdoor bail production, decided not to re-establish the system when the war was over, A.G. Street, *Feather-Bedding* (London, 1954), p. 148. Similarly, Richard Stratton also abandoned outdoor milk production, Wiltshire and Swindon RO, 2865/1, Richard Stratton correspondence.

[92]　United States, Dept of Economic Affairs, *Salient Features of the World Economic Situation 1945–47* (New York, 1948), cited in A.S. Milward, *War, Economy and Society, 1939–1945* (1977, Penguin edn, 1987), p. 271.

of payments, which brought sterling under constant attack.[93] Under these circumstances it was essential to restrict, as far as possible, the importation of high-priced feeding stuffs that had to be paid for using scarce dollars. In 1946 the Labour government decided to introduce bread rationing, a policy which included all types of bread, flour and flour confectionery. Even during the darkest days of the Second World War, Churchill had steadfastly refused to implement such a draconian measure; it was virtually without precedent, having last been used in 1802.[94] As the embattled Chancellor of the Exchequer, Hugh Dalton, lamented, 'Never glad, confident morning again.'[95]

Faced with the difficulty of securing adequate supplies of purchased feeding stuffs, Paterson began to focus his efforts on maximising the use of his existing grassland. In 1946, experiencing difficulties in monitoring the consumption of feeding stuffs in an isolated bail herd (which was being looked after by itinerant workers as there was no cottage available to house permanent staff), he decided to reduce the use of concentrate feeding. What started out as an experiment intended to address this specific problem proved so successful that he decided to adopt it more widely. By 1953 only three of his herds continued to be fed concentrates, mainly in order to provide a benchmark to compare their performance and productivity with the rest of his herds.[96] Instead Paterson argued that the major factor influencing productivity was the ability of stockmen rather than the level of concentrated feeding stuffs that were fed to the animals.[97] His results suggested that good bulk feeds were capable of producing 560 gallons per cow in herds that were wintered outside. Following the increased availability of concentrated feeding stuffs in the late 1950s, it was decided that supplementary feeding should be reintroduced, but this was restricted to 8–10 cwt of a mineralised barley supplement per cow.[98]

His early experiments, prompted by his overwhelming need to ensure that milk production was as profitable as possible, led to Paterson to become an untiring champion of the idea that grass could make a substantial contribution to milk production. He was one of the earliest farmer members of the British Grassland Society (BGS), which had been established in 1945. He also developed the Milk Graph, which enabled the stockman to understand the milk-stimulating effects of grass and other feeds. Based on observations on a large number of herds, it was possible to develop a formula that would indicate milk production at any particular

---

[93] For an authoritative account, see A.K. Cairncross, *Years of Recovery: British Economic Policy, 1945–51* (London, 1985), ch. 6.

[94] R.J. Hammond, *Food: Studies in Administration and Control* (London, 1962), pp. 703–18.

[95] H. Dalton, *High Tide and After: Memoirs, 1945–60* (London, 1962), p. 269.

[96] T. Wannop Williams, 'Cows and Acres: The Story of Rex Paterson', *Agriculture* 70 (1964), p. 270.

[97] Paterson, *Milk from Grass*, p. 62.

[98] Wannop Williams, 'Cows and Acres', p. 273.

time. This 'potential' milk yield could then be plotted against the 'actual' milk yield to observe the effects of different feeds and feeding methods on production, as well as the relationship with current management and feeding.[99] One of the main advantages of these graphs was the confidence they provided when the decline in milk yield was no greater than forecast.

Grass, Paterson postulated, could not only provide the main source of feed in the summer but also, more controversially, if conserved as silage, it could be used as the main source of bulk feed for the winter. His ideas were completely at odds with those of other dairy experts, such as the well-known Bobby Boutflower, Principal of the Royal Agricultural College at Cirencester, who was one of the leading proponents of using high-energy concentrated feeding stuffs to maximise production per animal.[100] Followers of Boutflourism, as it became known, tended by implication to dismiss grass and fodder such as hay and silage derived from it, as being of low feed value.[101] According to their approach, the key to profitability was to maximise milk production per cow.[102] This was based on the premise that 4lb of concentrates would produce an extra gallon of milk. Conversely, Paterson's feeding policy was based on the belief that a high stocking rate rather than yield per cow was the key to profitability. Paterson's experiments indicated that between 11 and 14lbs of concentrated feeding stuffs were required to produce a gallon of milk. These results led to fundamentally different approaches to feeding policy, and to milk production in general.

Paterson's philosophy was based on his scientific approach to evaluating the performance of his cows. In order to measure the productivity of his pastures he developed a unique but simple system of cow-day recording of grassland which was recognised as one of the first published examples of its type in this country; the accompanying milk graphs enabled him to study the effect of various feeds and management techniques on milk production. The most important records were the weekly milk sheet and the grazing record. From these Paterson concluded that each seed mixture had a characteristic yield that varied little

---

[99]   R. Paterson, 'How They Feed and How They Milk, I', *FW*, 6 Jan. 1950, pp. 38–9; idem, 'How They Feed and How They Milk, II', *FW*, 13 Jan. 1950, pp. 48–9.

[100]   An idea of Boutflower's long-term legacy can be gleaned from J.G.S. and Frances Donaldson's *Farming in Britain Today* (London, 1972), p. 174, in which they note, 'Probably the most important and certainly the most colourful pioneer in the field of nutrition was the late Professor Boutflower. For better or worse, the Boutflower system has left a lasting mark on the UK dairy industry'.

[101]   Seddon, *Silent Revolution*, pp. 35–6. For an account of Boutflower's early work in pioneering the feeding of cake, see A. Court, *Seedtime to Harvest: A Farmers Life* (Bradford on Avon, 1987), p. 45. The post-war expansion in the supply of cake partly reflected the fact that some of its protein content was a byproduct of imported oilseeds, which were crushed to extract the oil to make margarine and soap.

[102]   Another leading exponent of this view was Kenneth Russell who was also a member of staff at the Royal Agricultural College, Cirencester. See K. Russell, *Making Money from Cows* (Ipswich, 1949) and *The Principles of Dairy Farming* (Ipswich, 1953).

from one year to the next and was not significantly affected if part of the crop was cut and conserved as silage.[103]

Paterson also noted that one of the main weaknesses of the existing systems of grassland recording was 'an almost complete failure to isolate and make any attempt to record the production from grass which is conserved as hay or silage'.[104] In particular he embarked upon an ambitious plan to undertake a meticulous study of the problems of growing and utilising grass silage. In stark contrast to many of his farming contemporaries in the late 1940s and the 1950s, he was a staunch proponent of the merits of silage. More importantly he considered that the greatest economic success could be obtained from self-feeding high-quality silage from low-cost clamps which, to save labour, had been constructed in the fields adjacent to where the milking bails were located (Figure 11.2). A pioneering approach of this kind, however, encountered considerable opposition from the farming community.

Many farmers considered silage making to be a costly and laborious way of spoiling good grass. Widespread reluctance to making silage resulted partly from the cumbersome methods that had been propagated by commercial interests, who wanted to sell concrete silos, cutter-blowers, earth scoops, and various acids and chemicals. It was perceived as a complicated and uncertain practice: during warm, dry summers it was thought to offer few advantages over traditional haymaking, which made good use of the existing labour force and facilities on the majority of pastoral farms.[105] As Mark Riley's account of upland farming in the Peak District has revealed, haymaking, in spite of its uncertain outcome, required less technical proficiency and could be undertaken without the need for additional labour. Moreover, it was a communal activity that helped to unite the whole family.[106]

Paterson played a key role in pioneering a new, more scientific approach to grassland farming which focused on evaluating the productivity of the sward rather than merely considering its superficial appearance, while the actual output of livestock products from grassland was still well below its true potential. In 1958 he acted as host to the first series of National Grassland Demonstrations held at Hatch Warren Farm, where attendances were up to 15,000 visitors per day. He also gave several papers at meetings of the British Grassland Society. Many members recall taking part in 'Paterson Seminars' at Summer Meetings,

---

[103] FR PAT,/B/1, part 1, R. Paterson, 'What We Have Learnt from Pasture Recording', talk given to the BBC, 8 Nov. 1951.

[104] Paterson, 'Presidential Address', p. 115.

[105] R.J. Hammond, *Food and Agriculture, 1939–45. Aspects of Wartime Control* (Stanford, 1954), p. 72.

[106] M. Riley, '"Silage for Self-Sufficiency"? The Wartime Promotion of Silage and its Use in the Peak District', in B. Short, C. Watkins and J. Martin (eds), *The Front Line of Freedom: British Farming in the Second World War* (Agricultural History Review Supp. Ser. 4, 2007), p. 85.

Figure 11.2   'Rex Paterson with a Silage Pit at Hatch Warren, Basingstoke, Hampshire, July 1957'. Photograph courtesy of Museum of English Rural Life, University of Reading. P FS PH1/K68606

and it was these small intimate discussions and exchanges of ideas on grassland management that he valued most; here his personal philosophy and theories acted as a stimulus to many grassland research and advisory workers, and also to farmers.

In 1964 Paterson received the approval of the BGS, following its two-year study of grassland recording methods. His long-term involvement with the Society led to his election as president in 1967. His presidential address was considerably longer than those of his predecessors, focusing on the statistical analysis of the performance of the dairy sector. His plea was for the country's grassland research centres not only to undertake basic research but also to provide 'practical information to assist the enthusiastic grassland farmer in this country'.[107] His meticulous record keeping enabled him to identify a link between potash application and the incidence of hypomagnesia commonly

---

107   Paterson, 'Presidential Address', p. 108–9.

known as 'staggers' – and to reduce its incidence in his own herds – before scientists had confirmed the connection.[108]

IV

One of the salient features of Paterson's system of farming was the emphasis on reducing costs by using machines to eliminate, as far as possible, labour-intensive tasks. In spite of the advantages derived from building the silage clamps in the fields where the grass was grown, there still remained the technical challenge of devising a low-cost, efficient way of moving the cut grass to the clamp. Traditionally this had entailed using mechanical elevator loaders, which picked the grass from the swath, depositing it on the trailer. This was very labour-intensive, imposing immense strain on the work force, as they strove to complete silage making at the optimum time, particularly in wet seasons. This was especially true for Paterson's outdoor system of milk production, which had only a very small permanent staff, consisting mainly of cowmen who would only be available to assist with silage making during the middle part of the day when they were not milking.

Paterson's early interest in engineering proved an invaluable asset. His initial development entailed using ex-War Department vehicles, to the rear of which he fitted home-made buckrakes. These vehicles, rather like those that Hosier had developed before the outbreak of the Second World War, used winches to raise the loaded buckrake for transport to the silage pit. The advent of the Ferguson tractor, with its hydraulic three-point linkage, prompted Paterson to design a rear-mounted buckrake for use with the new tractors (Figure 11.3).[109] It revolutionised the labour-intensive task of moving cut grass.[110] Paterson calculated that, using the buckrake, it was economical to collect and transport cut grass up to a distance of about 600 yards. More importantly it fitted in well with the concept of a single tractor driver both cutting the grass in the field and then carting it to the clamp so that it could be levelled and compressed by the dairyman between milkings.[111]

Following its initial introduction, the buckrake was modified on several occasions to make it even more robust and versatile.[112] It was 'acclaimed

---

[108]   P.A. Naylor, 'Multiple Dairy Herds', *Agriculture*, 75 (1968), p. 480.

[109]   L.T.C. Rolt, *Waterloo Ironworks: A History of Taskers of Andover, 1809–1968* (Newton Abbot, 1969), p. 218; R. Paterson, 'Fertilizer Distribution: Problems of Corrosion Prevention on the Farm', *Proc. International Fertilizer Soc.* 32 (1955), pp. 1–33.

[110]   'The Paterson Earth Scoop and the Latest Buck Rake for the Ferguson', *Farm Implement and Machinery Review*, 1 Apr. 1949, p. 1301.

[111]   Paterson, *Milk from Grass*, p. 50.

[112]   'Paterson Earth Scoop', p. 1301.

Figure 11.3   Paterson Buck Rake with Haycock Transported by Tractor, 1951. Photograph courtesy of Museum of English Rural Life, University of Reading. P FW PH2 H34 1

internationally as a major contribution to the development of silage making on dairy farms'.[113] By 1953, the peak year for production, its manufacturer, Taskers of Andover, had made more than 7,500 Paterson–Taskers Buckrakes.[114] As Table 11.1 shows, making silage with a mower and buckrake reduced the amount of labour required per acre by more that 50 per cent. The task could be completed more quickly and was less dependent on the vagaries of the weather, resulting in enhanced productivity. Table 11.1 also shows that, while further improvements in productivity were later achieved by the development of forage harvesters to cut the grass and transport it back to the clamp, the buckrake still played an important role in positioning the grass in the silage clamp. By 1970 over 50,000 of these buckrakes had been manufactured for sale in the UK and abroad.[115] Subsequent modifications involved a specially modified railway sleeper being attached to the frame, enabling it to be used as a tractor-mounted concrete scraper.[116]

---

113   C. Crichton, 'Rex Paterson, an Appreciation', *Grass and Forage Science* 34 (1979), p. 239.

114   Rolt, *Waterloo Ironworks*, p. 219.

115   FR PAT, SP/B/1, part 1, Dr D.H. Lloyd, recommendation of Rex Paterson for OBE.

116   *Farm Implement and Machinery Review*, 1 Apr. 1960, p. 1743.

Table 11.1   Man and tractors: Hours per acre expended in conserving grass

Year	Method	Hours per acre	
		Man	Tractor
1946	Haymaking in the field in stacks	12.6	3.7
1950	Making silage with mower and buckrake	5.6	3.8
1959	Making silage with forage harvester and buckrake	3.6	2.3
1964	Making silage with forage harvester to larger stacks and with better equipment	2.0	2.0

Source: R. Paterson, *Milk from Grass: Rex Paterson, OBE*, The Massey Ferguson Papers, No 2, p. 25.

Faced with the need to spread large quantities of artificial fertiliser, Paterson also developed a large-capacity, trailed fertiliser spreader, enabling the constant speed of a hydraulic motor to spread fertiliser, metered by a chain driving a land wheel. This was subsequently fitted with an axle-mounted hydraulic shovel, which enabled the machine to refill its 25-cwt hopper in three minutes from bulk supplies, an innovation which was awarded silver medal at the RASE show in 1965.[117] This became a popular and valuable piece of equipment for the handling and distribution of fertiliser on many larger farms. More than 3,000 of these Taskers–Paterson Fertispreads had been manufactured by the 1970s.

Paterson's lesser-known innovations included an earth scoop fitted to the three-point linkage of Fordson, Major and Nuffield tractors, which was used to excavate trenches for silage, and for covering the silage after it had been placed in the trench or clamp.[118] It was fitted with a 'Paterson' grain shutter, which could virtually double its bulk-holding capacity and prevent the material from falling out, permitting the speedy transport of grain and other types of feeding stuffs.[119] This was also accompanied by the development of a Taskers–Paterson grader blade, which could be fitted to the base of the earth scoop. Its numerous uses included shaping road surfaces as well as levelling banks and ditches.[120] Paterson's contribution to agricultural engineering resulted in his becoming a Companion

[117]   Rolt, *Waterloo Ironworks*, p. 220.

[118]   'Paterson Earth Scoop', p. 1300.

[119]   *Farm Implement and Machinery Review* (1 Apr. 1950), p. 1690.

[120]   Ibid.

of the Institute of Agricultural Engineering, a position 'reserved for those who, not normally practising agricultural engineers, have rendered important services to the institution'.[121]

V

Paterson's decentralised approach to managing his units was, in part, a pragmatic response to the way his business had grown in the pre-war period and been reconfigured during the war. The appointment of a working manager in 1937 had been accompanied by the employment of permanent office staff whose work was not simply confined to accounting, but also involved the collection of data relating to the performance of his enterprises. This had enabled the central office to record details of all the cows that had calved or dried off, the type of feeds being used, and the fields the animals were using.[122] Thus they were able to obtain a continuous record of all the factors that influenced yields, making it possible to compare deviations between actual and potential yields.[123] It allowed Paterson to identify appropriate incentives to ensure high levels of output without 'the need for excessive drive or for too detailed control of the individual'.[124]

Unlike many of his contemporaries, who attempted to establish a close-knit, autocratic organisational structure where all activities followed a definite routine and the aim was ascertain how big a centrally controlled unit could be, Paterson focused his efforts on investigating how small a unit could be to operate economically. Initially he developed self-contained units in the region of 1,000 acres, which were under the control of a manager who, although he was expected to follow the general policy, was allowed freedom to use his own initiative regarding the detail. By the late 1940s, Paterson was pursuing a policy of selecting individuals – from his own workforce, or even from outside the agricultural sector – who had the ability to use their initiative and operate with as little supervision as possible.[125]

This decentralised system of control was accompanied by a shift to the use of contract work for the head bailsman, and for workers under the control of the farm managers. Paterson developed a payments system that encouraged employees to accept as much responsibility as possible for a reasonable basic wage, allowing them the opportunity to increase earnings by bonus payments.

---

[121]   FR PAT, SP/B/1, part 1, Dr D.H. Lloyd, recommendation of Rex Paterson for OBE.

[122]   Paterson, 'How They Feed ... , I', pp. 38–9, 'How They Feed ... , II', pp. 48–9.

[123]   R. Paterson, 'The Milk Stimulating Value of Grass and its Influence on Animal Health', *J. British Grassland Soc.* 11 (1956), p. 95.

[124]   Paterson, 'Is There a Place?', p. 4.

[125]   Ibid., p. 4.

This applied to tasks such as ploughing, cultivating, drilling and even harvesting. The aim of this approach was to focus attention on productivity as a means of making the work more interesting and to encourage the workforce to adopt the methods most likely to give the best results.[126] He created good conditions for working and living by allowing individual workers to determine their hours of work, and by encouraging them to use their initiative within the framework of a general policy.[127]

Paterson, probably more than any other farmer of his era, believed that one of the main influences on milk yields was the ability of the stockman; the way to enhance performance was by isolating stockmen and their units, to give them the opportunity to demonstrate their ability to look after the cows. Their success in this sphere could then be evaluated by a detailed statistical analysis of the herd's performance in comparison to different herds. Throughout his career he remained a staunch advocate of having multiple dairy herds, each one run by its own herdsman. The number of cows in each herd and labour productivity continued to increase.

Paterson did not take any particular interest in the breeding of livestock, and it was not until 1947 that he embarked upon a programme to eradicate tuberculosis, a task that was successfully completed in the following three years. After the Second World War he had begun to rear his own replacements while continuing to buy in Ayrshires. Initially, some of the Shorthorns were sired with Friesian bulls and some with Jerseys. Later, cows of all three dairy breeds were bred to their breed of bull, with Galloway or Aberdeen Angus bulls being used on the heifers in order to facilitate easier calving.[128] Artificial insemination was employed in most herds, with bulls used mainly on heifers. His analysis indicated that the problem of ensuring that cows were got in calf was associated with standards of management rather than infertility.[129]

Paterson's most novel and formidable contribution to the transformation of farming, however, was his pioneering scientific approach to grassland management for dairying. His extensive agricultural business and meticulous record keeping enabled him to carry out research on a scale comparable with contemporary research institutions. Indeed he essentially provided an important bridge between research and the farming community, putting technical knowledge into practice to enable more efficient grassland production.[130]

By 1965, Paterson's 10 farms in Hampshire – organised into six separate groups within a 20-mile radius of Hatch Warren, where the central office was

---

[126]   Ibid., p. 5.

[127]   Paterson, *Milk from Grass*, p. 25.

[128]   Ibid., p. 29.

[129]   Ibid., p. 39.

[130]   Paterson, 'How They Feed … , I', pp. 38–9; 'How They Feed … , II', pp. 48–9.

located – extended to nearly 7,000 acres, most of which were rented. Livestock numbers amounted to 2,310 dairy cows in 35 herds; 1,707 dairy replacements of all ages; 36 beef cows in one herd; and 157 young beef animals. In addition 1,473 acres were devoted to grain, mostly barley.[131]

In addition Paterson had purchased four farms in Carmarthenshire and four in Pembrokeshire, where the climate was more amenable to grass production. Amounting to just over 1,900 acres, of which nearly 1,500 was clean land, these predominantly dairy units were managed by his eldest son, John. Not only was average herd size larger than in Hampshire, but also two-thirds of the cows were housed in outdoor cow cubicles, and in the northern group of farms, which had 465 cows, two of the five milking parlours were seven-a-side herringbones equipped with bulk milk tanks.[132]

By this stage, Paterson's typical sub-herd had in the region of 75 cows on 100 acres of grassland, which received 250–300 units of nitrogen per acre, with the animals being paddock-grazed. Previously these sub-herds had comprised about 65 cows, which had been allocated 120 acres receiving 50 units of nitrogen per acre. The cows were milked in open-backed parlours capable of achieving outputs comparable with the newly developed herringbone parlours.[133]

While multiple herd organisation, where the animals lived outside, offered the advantages of a relatively low-cost system and ease of management, by the mid 1960s the system was attracting few adherents.[134] This not only reflected the impact of the abnormally bad winter of 1963, but also the growing impression that it was associated with cows 'roughing up' outdoor silage heaps in wet weather, shack-like buildings, low yields and high wastage.[135] Dairy farmers who considered themselves to be progressive were, by this time, experimenting with the labour-saving possibilities of new types of cow handling equipment and management based on housing animals in large barns with cow cubicles during the winter, and milking in newly developed herringbone or even rotary parlours.[136] Zero grazing, which involved cutting the grass and carting it to

---

[131] Paterson, *Milk from Grass*, pp. 6–7.

[132] FR PAT, B/3, J.H. Paterson, 'Suggestions for a Change in the Financing of the Farming of three Welsh Farms', 29 June 1971, p. 1.

[133] Naylor, 'Multiple Dairy Herds', p. 479.

[134] Ibid., p. 481.

[135] Ibid.

[136] Paterson recognised that 'although based on long experience, the Company's approach could be criticized for apparent lack of sophistication compared with many other dairying enterprises'. See FR PAT, B/3, J.H. Paterson, Report attached to 'Suggestions for a change', p. 5. For a more detailed analysis of the adoption of subsequent developments in the design of milking parlours, see O. Grant, *The Diffusion of the Herringbone Parlour: A Case Study in the History of Agricultural Technology* (University of Oxford, Discussion Papers in Economic and Social History, 27, 1978).

the yarded animals even during the summer months, was also regarded as one possible way of managing large herds of dairy cows.

The post-war period saw Paterson become nationally and internationally renowned as a leading pioneer of grassland dairy farming. As one of earliest farmers to join the BGS and a keen supporter of Local Grassland Societies, he rapidly became a popular speaker at meetings throughout the UK, imparting information not only about his own farms, but also the wealth of knowledge on grassland management and utilisation he had gained from visits to many countries, and from his prodigious absorption of articles, learned papers and reports on grassland and milk production. Hatch Warren Farm was a magnet for visitors from many countries and every farming discipline, eager to see and hear about a method of dairy farming that became known as the unconventional 'Paterson System'. An analysis of the visitors' book between 1952 and 1970 reveals that he received visitors from 35 countries.[137]

Paterson was recognised and honoured by the agriculture profession in many ways. He was made a Companion of the Institute of Agricultural Engineering in 1958 and in 1964 he served as Chairman of the Oxford Farming Conference, the same year that his services to agriculture were formally recognised with the award of an OBE.[138] In 1965 he was awarded the Massey Ferguson Award for services to United Kingdom Agriculture. Then in 1967–68 he held office as president of the BGS and, in his presidential Address to the Society, appealed for practical and coordinated research between farmers, research workers, economists and policy makers to assess the future technical possibilities for grassland in the UK, believing as he did that grass could make a major contribution to animal production. He also served with distinction as the County Chairman of the National Farmers Union, as well as on a number of county and headquarters committees, including the Development and Education Committee. In 1970 he became one of the first to receive the Fellowship of the Royal Agricultural Society. He died in 1978.

VI

Paterson was truly an outstanding agriculturalist who, throughout his long career, demonstrated an outstanding ability to adjust to radically changing market conditions. During the depressed conditions of the 1930s, with very limited resources, he managed to establish himself as one of Europe's most successful

---

[137] For a detailed analysis of the number of visitors, see FR PAT, B/1, Dr D.H. Lloyd, Department of Agriculture, University of Reading, 'Rex Paterson OBE, Hatch Warren, Cliddesden, Basingstoke, Draft proposal for the award of an honorary doctorate from the University of Reading, 30. Jan. 1970'.

[138] FR PAT, SP/B/1, part 1, correspondence relating to Paterson's OBE.

milk producers; during the wartime period of state-directed food production he reorganised his farming system; and after the war he again became one of Britain's largest dairy farmers.

These practical achievements could almost be described as incidental to the many contributions Paterson made to the transformation of dairy farming. He was a leading pioneer of low-cost milk production based on the use of open-air bails, popularising the idea that grassland in the UK could make a substantial contribution to milk production. His dairy farming relied almost exclusively on the use of grass and grass silage. This was backed by a thorough study of the problems of growing and utilising the grass crop; he developed unique but simple methods of recording and measuring grass output on his farms. His system of cow-day recording of grassland was recognised as one of the first published examples of pasture recording in this country, and the milk graphs that complemented this enabled him to study the effects of various feed and management techniques on milk production. An early interest in engineering proved invaluable in his development of machinery and equipment for farming. The Paterson–Tasker Buckrake was acclaimed internationally as a major contribution to the development of silage making on dairy farms. Paterson will be remembered for his pioneering, innovative, simple, but very thoughtful approach to farming as a business, and as one of the leading architects of the modern revolution in dairy farming.

Chapter 12

Compost in Caledonia: The Work of Robert L. Stuart, Organic Pioneer

Philip Conford[1]

We live at a time when the organic movement is likely to be represented in the national press by fawning articles on 'The World's Most Glamorous Farmer', model and actress Liz Hurley, whose chief claim to fame is once having worn a dress full of safety-pins but who now 'farms' organically in the Cotswolds.[2] A distinctly less 'glamorous' figure, Robert Stuart, would be of little relevance to the celebrity-driven priorities of today's Soil Association; but he is a far more interesting and significant one when seen in the context of the organic movement's history. Before looking at what his archival materials tell us, we can briefly survey the course of his life.

---

[1]   In the summer of 2005, I was contacted by Mick Stuart in response to a call I had put out asking whether any long-term members of the organic movement might be able to help me with my research into the movement's history. Mick Stuart, then approaching his eightieth birthday, still held a substantial collection of material belonging to his father, Lieutenant-Commander Robert L. Stuart, a Soil Association stalwart who had died in 1980. This material was mine if I wanted it, and if I was prepared to make the trip to the Inner Hebridean island of Islay to collect it. Not having visited Scotland since 1979 I required no further prompting: I hired an estate car, travelled up from the south coast of England and spent a couple of days sorting through the many boxes of papers, journals, index-books and farming publications which Robert Stuart had left behind. During my visit I was able to record two interviews: one with Mick Stuart himself, and the other with Christopher Badenoch, whom Mick had also invited to his home in Port Ellen that week. Christopher is a land-use ecologist and the son of Robert Stuart's close associate Dr A.G. Badenoch. Given the restrictions on space, some material had to be sacrificed, but I was able to take back home about 18 boxes' worth, which I then sorted more systematically. Stuart's papers will in due course be lodged with the Museum of English Rural Life at the University of Reading. The author is most grateful to Robert Stuart's sons Mick and Malcolm Stuart, and his daughter, Mrs Heda Borton, for providing information about their father's life; and to Christopher Badenoch for providing information about his father's life and sharing memories of childhood visits to Robert Stuart's holding.

[2]   'Muck and Class: Elizabeth Hurley, the World's Most Glamorous Farmer', by Jane Gordon, *Daily Mail*, 1 Nov. 2009.

I

Robert Laurence Stuart was born in Edinburgh in 1900 to George Malcolm and Elizabeth Stuart. George was a lawyer of considerable standing, but Robert did not – at first – follow him into this profession. Aged 12, he joined the Royal Navy and trained at Dartmouth; in 1916 he became a midshipman, serving in HMS *Valiant*, and was present that year at the Battle of Jutland. By the end of the war he had been promoted to sub-lieutenant, but his naval career suffered a prolonged hiatus from 1922 to 1939 as a result of the so-called 'Geddes Axe' (public spending cuts imposed by a committee of businessmen chaired by former coalition minister Sir Eric Geddes). He was retired with the rank of lieutenant-commander, but enjoyed a pension for the rest of his life. He then went to Assam to manage a tea plantation, moving after two years or so to the Nilgiri Hills in Southern India, where he ran the Rob Roy tea estate. In 1924 he married Barbara Milward and his first son Moncrieff (Mick) was born the following year. 1927 saw the birth of a second son, Malcolm, and Stuart's return to Britain; in 1930 his daughter Heda was born. Stuart now followed his father into the legal profession and qualified as a Writer to the Signet in 1936. In 1939 he was recalled to the Royal Navy to command the initial training camp for Royal Navy seamen at Howstrake Camp on the Isle of Man, and later became first lieutenant of HMS *Valkyrie*, a radar training establishment on the sea-front in Douglas. The navy then made use of his legal expertise by appointing him its legal adviser for Scotland; he worked from an office in Edinburgh and, he subsequently recalled, spent most of his time sorting out the matrimonial problems of Wrens.[3]

Illness was to change the course of his life. In the late 1940s he spent a good deal of time in hospital suffering from tuberculosis; the treatment was prolonged and he was invalided out of the Royal Navy. Wishing to escape urban life, and forced to consider issues of illness and health, Stuart sold his house in Edinburgh and rented a property called Hopes, a fine Georgian manor house in the Lammermuir Hills near Gifford in East Lothian. Hopes had a large but neglected garden, which he set about restoring through sheet composting, a technique in which moist, rich farmyard manure is kept under cover for two or three months, then spread over pasture and worked in by disc or tiller. Mixed with the roots of the previous pasture, this forms a shallow layer of compost with nutrients readily available for the following crop. (The method was successfully used on a wide scale by Louis Bromfield on his land at Malabar Farm, Ohio.) In opting for this method, Stuart was drawing on his experiences 20 years earlier in India, where the rains would cause serious soil erosion. According to Mick Stuart, he was unaware of Albert Howard's work at that period and had

---

[3]   Interview with Mick Stuart, Port Ellen, 5 Oct. 2005.

Figure 12.1   Hopes Compost Club. Photograph, Stuart Papers

developed his own methods of combating erosion. These included inter-planting with green crops; reduction of hoeing in favour of hand weeding, and terracing with stone, with banks of tea-prunings and with a kind of cold compost made by running liquid manure from the cowshed on to layers of vegetable matter and covering it with earth.[4] Stuart adopted the same principle of the 'organic surface' in reclaiming the two acres at Hopes, disturbing the topsoil as little as possible, and mulching with compost. He tackled the plot section by section; he added poultry and then a piggery, and before long Hopes became a centre for the production of organic (or 'humus-grown' as it was termed at that time) food.

Stuart was actively involved in the organic movement by 1948; that year saw the first meeting of the Scottish Soil and Health Group, which he founded with his friends the physician Dr A.G. Badenoch and the radiographer Dr Angus Campbell. The Group can be seen as a Scottish response to the founding of the Soil Association in 1946. Eve Balfour, the leading spirit in the Soil Association's establishment, was a neighbour of Stuart in the sense that her family lived at Whittingehame, by Haddington, and when she was staying with them she regularly visited Hopes. Agricultural botanist Sir Albert Howard, the chief inspirer of the Soil Association (though he did not join it) died in October 1947, and the Scottish Soil and Health Group approached his widow Louise to see if they could take over his journal *Soil and Health* (formerly Dr Lionel Picton's *News-Letter on Compost*). She granted their request and, re-cast as *Health and the Soil*, it became the Group's equivalent of the Soil Association's

---

[4]   *The Soil Association* [the journal of the Soil Association], Apr. 1974, p. 15.

journal *Mother Earth*. Louise Howard took an active interest in the Society's work and often visited Stuart at Hopes.

In 1949, Stuart turned Hopes over for use as a licensed and residential Compost Club: this was his first foray into the world of catering, another profession at which he would prove accomplished (Figure 12.1). We shall consider its activities in more detail below, but should note here that the Club's primary purpose was to provide compost-grown food, uncontaminated by chemicals, and that it was a form of experiment to investigate whether there was a relationship, as the organic movement considered likely, between diet and health: specifically, whether organically grown produce might help to improve health. From 1950 onwards Stuart expanded his activities, composting the whole of the sludge at the sewage works at nearby Gifford for most of the decade by using farm wastes and slaughterhouse refuse. From 1953 he operated a service hiring out a composting team and their machinery.

After nearly 20 years at Hopes, Stuart moved to Maines House at Chirnside, near the English border, and established it as the Chirnside Countryhouse Hotel, serving the guests organic home-grown produce. Such were his skills that in 1976 he won an AA award for providing the Best Breakfast in Britain. Maines House was also the venue, during the 1960s and '70s, for several Soil Association conference weeks, which drew together many leading figures of the organic movement and occasionally some of its opponents. Stuart died in 1980. Stuart's three children involved themselves in the organic movement in various ways. Mick and Malcolm worked with him on the farm composting scheme and helped him prepare a special one-off issue of *Health and the Soil* for the Royal Highland Show in 1955 (the journal had folded in 1951). Malcolm worked full-time for his father during the 1950s, while Mick farmed nearby. In the early 1960s, Malcolm went out to farm in Rhodesia; later that decade, Mick became a lecturer on agriculture in the Borders Region and helped his father organise the Soil Association Weeks. Heda trained as a physiotherapist and developed an interest in natural childbirth; she became a close friend of Dr Innes Pearse, co-founder of the Pioneer Health Centre in Peckham, South London and one of the key figures in the development of the British organic movement, towards the end of the latter's life.

In this chapter, I supplement the material from Robert Stuart's archive with information provided by his children and by Christopher Badenoch; and further material drawn from Soil Association publications. Together, these sources provide a portrait of someone whose decades of commitment to the organic cause mark him out as a practical exponent of its principles. We shall focus on the following areas of his activities: the Scottish Soil and Health Group and *Health and the Soil*; the Hopes Compost Club and the farm composting service; Chirnside Soil Association Weeks; and, as a coda, the success of his Countryhouse Hotel.

II

Stuart's archive includes a complete run of *Health and the Soil*. Its first issue appeared in summer 1948 and the final issue of its continuous run, with Dr Campbell as editor, was dated summer/autumn 1951. The Special Highland Show Number referred to above appeared in 1955 and was evidently intended to be the first of a revived series under Stuart's editorship, though in fact it remained a one-off. The final issue of Howard's *Soil and Health* was a memorial number in spring 1948 and, that same spring, on 13 February, Lady Howard spoke at an informal dinner held at the Scotia Hotel, Edinburgh, about the work of her late husband and the need to carry it on. *Health and the Soil* described this occasion as 'in effect, the inaugural meeting of the Group', whose membership then 'widened, on almost Rotarian lines'. It had been Howard's wish that the journal's title should die with him, 'but it was believed to be in accordance with his wishes that the work should go on'. *Health and the Soil* was started in the summer of 1948 with Lady Howard's full approval, and its sponsors and editorial panel began to be known as the Edinburgh Group. Further organisation was then thought desirable, and in November 1948 a new association, the Scottish Soil and Health Movement, came into being. Its objects were threefold:

> To demonstrate the connection between the health of mankind and the health of the living soil. To collate and publicize information on the cultivation and preparation of foodstuffs by natural methods, particularly by the use of compost. To encourage and sustain any action to increase the supply of fresh and satisfying food to the community.

By the winter of 1950 it had renamed itself the Scottish Soil and Health Society.[5]

Like its previous incarnation as *Soil and Health*, the journal was published quarterly. Its contents were 'influenced' by the Edinburgh Group, whose members included doctors, vets, farmers, millers, housewives and others who favoured 'a return to more natural methods of producing food'. *Health and the Soil* described itself as 'devoted to the interests of soil, plant, animal and man, with particular reference to organic husbandry'. It would work 'in close cooperation with the Albert Howard Foundation of Organic Husbandry' and would 'appreciate association and interchange of views with other groups of like interests'.[6]

---

[5]   On the group's development and changes of name, see *Health and the Soil*, winter 1948, p. 5; spring 1949, p. 12; summer 1949, p. 5; winter 1950, p. 44.

[6]   *Health and the Soil*, summer 1948, quotations from pp. 5, 4, 5, 1 respectively. The Albert Howard Foundation of Organic Husbandry was established by Lady Howard and some of her late husband's disciples after his death. Its most notable supporter was the Somerset farmer, herbalist, author and journalist F. Newman Turner. The Foundation merged with the Soil Association in 1953.

Health and the Soil did not significantly differ in its stance and contents from either *Soil and Health* or the Soil Association journal *Mother Earth*, nor were its contributors exclusively Scottish. Its first three issues, for instance, dealt with familiar organicist topics (soil humus; municipal composting; the treatment of flour with agene; nutrition and dental decay; the role of agriculture in the national economy, and the need for a holistic philosophy of nature) and featured various figures important in the history of the organic movement. Among them were F.C. King, head gardener at Levens Hall near Kendal; J.C. Wylie, the County Engineer for Dumfries and a pioneer of municipal composting; agricultural scientist Dr Hugh Martin-Leake; dental scientist E. Brodie Carpenter; and Dr J.W. Scharff, former Chief Officer of Health at Singapore and a leading spirit in the Soil Association's very active Middlesex Group. The journal's editorial board was fortunate in having Sir Albert Howard's personal assistant Miss Ellinor Kirkham to assist its work and supervise the journal's printing and production.

Among the papers relating to *Health and the Soil* I found an address book which would appear to have belonged to Dr Angus Campbell. Robert Stuart's name and address are in it, so it is reasonable to conclude that it was not his, while the address on the front endpapers, 48 Manor Place, Edinburgh, was Campbell's home and the location of his X-ray surgery, as well as the journal's registered office. The names it contains indicate the range of the owner's contacts in the organic movement. Among them are the Sydney-based Organic Farming and Gardening Society; Allinson's Bakery; Dr Norman Burman, a biologist at the Metropolitan Water Board; Roy Bridger, a crofter in north-west Scotland; G.C. Dymond, a chemist at the Darnell Sugar Estates in Natal; the biodynamic farmer Deryck Duffy; the *Guild Gardener*, a pro-organic horticultural magazine edited by Lady Seton; the Society of Herbalists; the French organic society L'Homme et le Sol; Dr John Kerr, colleague of the late Dr Lionel Picton and a Soil Association founder member; Land and Home Publications, run by L.B. Powell and the Earl of Portsmouth; Captain J.M. Moubray, a farmer and disciple of Sir Albert Howard in Rhodesia; Helen Murray, the Soil Association's Scottish Representative; the journal *Rural Economy*, published by the Rural Reconstruction Association and edited by Jorian Jenks, who also edited *Mother Earth*; the organic farmer and author Friend Sykes, one of the three founders (along with Eve Balfour and Dr George Scott Williamson) of the Soil Association; Newman Turner; J.P.J. van Vuren, South African exponent of municipal composting; Maurice Wood, the biodynamic farmer and miller; the market gardener Roy Wilson, and Leonard Wickenden, the American writer on contaminated foodstuffs.[7]

---

[7] Land and Home Publications published work by many leading organicists of the post-war decade, and Powell contributed to the Soil Association's newsletter *Span* during the late 1960s and early 1970s, and to *The Ecologist*. Moubray was a vigorous opponent of chemical fertilisers who successfully applied organic methods to fruit-growing. Scott Williamson was, with Dr Innes Pearse, founder of the Pioneer Health Centre in South London, a noteworthy experiment in social medicine. J. P. J. Van Vuren

There was clearly nothing narrowly provincial about the outlook of the Scottish Soil and Health Society: an impression which is confirmed by a collection of letters, written between 1948 and 1952, to and from subscribers. What is striking is the interest that the Society aroused in distant lands. In Madras, the editors of a journal called *The Antiseptic* subscribed; in Pennsylvania, the editors of *Biological Abstracts*; in New York, the Devin-Adair publishing company; in South Africa, a librarian at the University of Witwatersrand, Johannesburg; in Israel, Roma Zur of Haifa and a Mr S.P. Guttfeld; in India, the Plant Protection Adviser to the national government; in Northern Rhodesia, the Senga Agricultural Training School; in Southern Rhodesia, the Natural Resources Board; in California, the Essene School of Life; also in the USA, the United Farmers of Illinois; in Lausanne, the monthly journal *Voilà ... Votre Santé*; and in New Zealand, Compost Limited of Dunedin. Of especial interest for historians of the organic movement are two letters from Dr G.T. Wrench in Karachi: Wrench was the author of the influential organicist text *The Wheel of Health* (1938) and of studies on land reform. In the second of these letters, Wrench thanked the secretary Miss Whitelaw for sending him four issues of the journal, but appeared not to have been over-impressed by them: 'I shall not want any more copies; there are so many of these papers coming to me already'.[8]

British subscribers included various organic notables: John S. Blackburn, of Ben Rhydding, Yorkshire, who in 1949 put together a handbook of writings on *Organic Husbandry* containing information on all the pro-organic organisations of that time which is now of considerable value to historians; Dr Norman Burman of the Metropolitan Water Board, who regretted having to cancel his subscription partly for financial reasons and partly because, like Wrench, he had too many such journals to read; Lord Douglas of Barloch, the former Labour MP who had helped establish the Soil Association as a legal entity; E.C. Gordon England, a noted test pilot, aviation engineer, motor designer and businessman who was on the Soil Association Council from 1951 to 1956; P.H. Hainsworth, an organic market gardener in Pembrokeshire and author of *Agriculture: A New Approach* (1954); the Institute of Public Cleansing; Dugald Semple, who attached a flyer advertising his latest book *What to Eat* and proclaiming him 'the famous food expert'; and Miss W.M. Holmes, an Honorary Secretary of the Soil Association's Middlesex Group.

There also exists a sheaf of letters written after the closure of *Health and the Soil* in 1951, in which subscribers wonder why they have not received either

---

wrote *Soil Fertility and Sewage* (London, 1949). Roy Wilson's Fenland smallholding had been one of the showpieces of organic husbandry in the 1930s. Leonard Wickenden wrote one of the earliest attacks on the use of chemical methods of food production, *Our Daily Poison* (New York, 1956).

[8]   The Essene School of Life was founded by Professor Edmond Szekely, who encouraged the work of the noted herbalist Juliette de Bairacli Levy, a close associate of Newman Turner. Wrench to Miss Whitelaw, 25 Mar. 1950.

their copies of the journal or some notification of why it had failed to appear. From these we might draw the conclusion that people were far more long-suffering then than they would be today: John Colville of Salisbury, Rhodesia, had sent Dr Campbell a cheque in July 1954, nearly three years after the final issue of 1951, and received no response until January 1955. More significantly for agricultural historians, we find letters from the Ministry of Agriculture of the Gold Coast, from Baltimore, from Jersey, from the Canadian Department of Agriculture's library in Ottawa, from the Rev. O. Barry in Ceylon, and from the Yorkshire organic farmer Sir Robert Milnes-Coates. This correspondence suggests that there was a worldwide interest in the problems which the early organic movement addressed, and it gives a tantalising glimpse of what might be termed the 'organic network' of the post-war decade. And some rather forlorn typescripts of articles submitted to the journal 'on spec' have survived, which, despite being accompanied by stamped, addressed envelopes, were never either accepted or returned. Those that are dated are from the autumn of 1952, despite the non-appearance of any issues of the journal since the previous autumn. All of them are about either compost and manure, or earthworms.

Subscribers disappointed to learn that *Health and the Soil* had closed down would have been encouraged by the appearance of the 1955 Highland Show number. Robert Stuart took over as editor and apologised for the journal 'having gone to sleep for over three years'; but it was now waking 'like a giant refreshed'. The Special Issue contained a foreword by Lord Sempill, the former air ace, 'fellow-traveller of the Right' and founder member of the Soil Association, plus articles by Jorian Jenks, Louise Howard and Brodie Carpenter. A typed, duplicated 'Note to past subscribers' begged forgiveness and offered them compensation consisting of either return of money or credit, membership of Hopes Compost Club, or a free copy of the 1955 journal and credit on account for subsequent issues. Alas, there were no subsequent issues: financial obstacles proved too great to surmount, and *Health and the Soil* went to sleep again, this time for good.[9]

Many of the activities of the Scottish Soil and Health Society are summarised in the journal. To take 1950 as an example: in January it held a Brains Trust in the Central Hall at Tollcross in Edinburgh, the speakers including the Society's President Professor Henry Dryerre, a noted physiologist, and J.C. Wylie; the following month Mr Ferguson of Haughley in Suffolk spoke about the work being carried out there on the Soil Association's experimental farms. In April, the Society held a public meeting at which the chief speaker was James Bruce, senior horticultural adviser at the Edinburgh and East of Scotland College of Agriculture. At another public meeting the following month, Eve Balfour

---

    [9] *Health and the Soil*, Special Highland Show Number 1955, p. 6. On Sempill, see Richard Griffiths, *Patriotism Perverted* (London, 1998), pp. 144–5.

spoke on Haughley and showed the new Soil Association film 'The cycle of life'. Afternoon visits were in order during the summer: Dr Campbell's farm at Eddleston in Peeblesshire was one venue and Hopes another. At the former, Society members saw the Ayrshire pedigree stock judged, while at Robert Stuart's estate they were treated to a display of composting followed by a strawberry tea with home-produced wholemeal bread. When autumn returned, Campbell talked about his visits to organic holdings in Argyll and Perthshire, and Badenoch spoke on nutrition.

Little material relating to the running of the Society is to be found among Stuart's papers, but a typed notice about a general meeting to be held on 21 September 1955 indicates that the principal matter under consideration was the Society's future, 'with particular reference to its relationship with the Hopes Compost Club'. Another typed notice, dating from 1952, indicates the closeness of the link between the two bodies, referring to a visit to Hopes by Louise Howard as an opportunity for the Scottish Soil and Health Society to promote its aims and objects. Society members were invited to assist at similar gatherings the following year.

III

We can now turn to examine what Stuart's papers tell us about the activities of his Compost Club and its relationship to the Scottish Soil and Health Society. A substantial amount of material relating to the Hopes Compost Club exists, including a handwritten draft of the original Club Rules, drawn up in 1949. The Club's primary object was 'to maintain and promote interest in Compost Gardening', and among the means of achieving that object were visits to farms, gardens and smallholdings which employed organic methods; collecting and publishing relevant information; establishing a library; installing recreational facilities, and holding social functions. Paragraphs 10 and 11 deal with membership, which was by invitation from the Council only, the possibility of invitation being 'confined to members, of 18 years or over, of the "Soil and Health Movement", members of the Albert Howard Foundation, the Soil Association of Great Britain, and all kindred Societies and Associations at home and overseas and to all resident at Hopes, past, present and future'. Another typed sheet, undated, but from some years later, says that the Club was formed so that members of the Scottish Soil and Health Society could have 'a country headquarters with a garden where composting was carried out regularly and where demonstrations could be held'. Stuart had found the work and expense beyond his unaided capacity, so a guest house was established: with an increasing number of visitors, entertaining had to become a business. Hopes also became a centre of nutritional experiment, as the doctors in the Scottish Soil and Health

Society began to see it as a place to which they could send their patients, in order to observe the effects of organically grown food.

Various lists of Hopes Compost Club members survive, though, unfortunately, most are undated. They show that Stuart's enterprise attracted a wide range of support. One such list indicates that the Club had, at some point, around 650 members; while these were predominantly from Scotland, some were from London, Kent, Liverpool and Cornwall. There were overseas members too, including one in Alaska.

In April 1954, Helen Murray celebrated Stuart's work in the Soil Association journal *Mother Earth*;[10] by then, as we shall see shortly, he had expanded into sewage composting and was running a farm composting and machinery hire service. Periodically, he produced a duplicated Hopes Compost Club newsletter. A complete run of them does not survive among his papers, but the one for October 1955 is of particular interest as it marks the final stages of the Scottish Soil and Health Society. In September, the Society had met to discuss its own future, given that meetings were no longer well attended. It was felt that the time for a society existing chiefly to hold meetings was past, and 'that the purposes of the Society would be better carried out by an organization such as Hopes Compost Club', which, with its guest house, library and licence could cater for members and give practical demonstrations and teaching. So the Society used its remaining funds to subsidise the provision of transport to Hopes, 23 miles from Edinburgh, on Club days during the summer, and Robert Stuart's home and holding became the main centre for promoting the organic cause in southern Scotland. The Club's July 1955 newsletter had reported that the Club's stand at the Highland Show in June brought in 80 new members, many of whom had since visited Hopes.

Other newsletters indicate that the Hopes Compost Club continued during the remainder of Stuart's time at Gifford and survived the move to Chirnside in 1964. From these, we can gain some idea of the Club's activities. In the mid 1950s, the Club was offering demonstrations of compost-making at the Gifford Sewage Works and of farm composting at Fenton Barns, a few miles north of Hopes. Anyone wishing to have tuition in practical composting was welcome to spend some time at Hopes. Lady Howard and Dr Norman Burman had visited, and the Club was promoting Maurice Wood's 'Huby' mill for stone-ground flour, and the seed catalogue produced by Kathleen Hunter of Truro, which offered herbs and rare vegetables.

Stuart contributed frequently to newspaper correspondence columns, as the many cuttings in his archive testify, and a 1956 Club newsletter urged members to use the press as a means of influencing officials. If Club members wanted 'a return to more traditional farming', there needed to be 'agitation by

---

10   *Mother Earth*, Apr. 1954, pp. 21–7.

the consumer'. Stuart wrote that he had had various conversations with those in agricultural authority, and that they showed no inclination to disturb the status quo. In 1951, a correspondence in *The Scotsman* about artificial fertilisers and ill-health had lasted for two months, but articles on Hopes in *The Scotsman* and the *Edinburgh Evening News* in 1956 had not been taken advantage of as a means of further discussion of modern farming methods. In *The Scotsman*, an anonymous column called 'A Scotsman's Log' gave an account of a visit to Hopes, describing it as not just a social club, but as a place whose aim was 'to foster a kind of moral and practical philosophy of the soil'. Stuart it summed up as 'a practical kind of idealist' who did 'not care much for cranks' but believed in the effectiveness of consumer protest against the poor quality of conventionally produced food. Farmers who used his composting service were enthusiastic about his pioneering work.[11]

The newsletters were very sporadic: secretarial help was difficult to find for such a remote spot as Hopes, and by 1961 Stuart was seriously considering a move to somewhere more convenient. The April newsletter that year was evidently the first for a long time: in the period since the previous one, electricity had reached the valley where the house stood, making life easier and more pleasant. Stuart, a 'strictly practical' farmer, valued such amenities and was dismissive of those who were 'starry-eyed but bright nowhere else'.[12] He was keen to find competent catering help and, with the re-equipping of the farm composting service, offered a vacancy for a keen young agricultural mechanic. The Club's activities were cryptically described as 'somewhat specialised', but it appeared that some of its medical members had tried to establish a feeding trial, approaching a charitable society whose Research Panel felt that the proposal would not count as valid research in the present-day medical sense. Nevertheless, the Club put out a leaflet recommending Hopes as a place where a diet of organically grown food, free of additives, preservatives, hydrogenated fats and all the paraphernalia of the expanding industrial food industry, might benefit those suffering from allergies or from a lack of well-being with no obvious physical cause. The leaflet emphasised that it did not make 'extravagant claims of cures ... nothing more than has been claimed for good food and good air down the ages'. The April 1961 newsletter mentioned another of Stuart's projects: a wholefood shop in Gifford, providing fare grown by Mick Stuart.[13]

---

[11] Strictly speaking, the correspondence on artificial manures and ill-health began at the end of January 1951 and continued through to 7 Mar. 1951. Stuart, Badenoch and Lady Howard all contributed; the cuttings are in Stuart's archive. *The Scotsman*, 8 May 1956.

[12] Hopes Compost Club newsletter, no. 8, dated 6 Apr. 1961.

[13] In the mid-1960s Mick Stuart worked for the Soil Association's Wholefood shop in Baker Street for a time as assistant manager, but disliked London life and returned to Scotland to teach farming.

A typed list of members dated 1961 indicates that membership was around 560 in that year and was by no means confined to Scotland. Names of interest to historians of the organic movement include the laird John Drummond; Edwin Evetts, who ran a well-known biodynamic herb nursery; Lord Glentanar; Dr Hugh Martin-Leake; Helen Murray; Dr J. W. Scharff, and Miss Kathleen Talbot of the Village Produce Association.[14] There was a fair sprinkling of naval officers, doctors and aristocrats, but the bare list of names provides minimal information about most members' backgrounds.

The last newsletter produced at Hopes, of which a typed draft exists, deals with the forthcoming move to Maines House, Chirnside, at Easter 1964. Some carbons of letters written to Club committee members in May that year suggest that Stuart had been finding it difficult to bring the committee together. Just one newsletter from Chirnside exists among Stuart's papers. Dated 12 May 1965, it consists of one sheet of paper which advertises vegetables for sale and offers a few tons of organic Record potatoes produced by a local farmer-member. These were available owing to a miscalculation of its requirements by the Wholefood shop in London (an enterprise which the Soil Association had established in Baker Street in 1960). We shall look at Stuart's activities at Chirnside later in the chapter.

IV

We saw above that the anonymous *Scotsman* reporter who visited Hopes in 1956 categorised Robert Stuart as 'a practical kind of idealist', and his practical approach was well demonstrated by his interest in composting – both farm-scale and municipal – and in agricultural machinery (Figure 12.2). The holding at Hopes was about two hectares, of which just under half was a walled garden, intensively cultivated. The rest was shrubbery, garden cottages, outbuildings and rough grazing for the cow. Stuart kept beehives along the edge of a wood (the honey being, by all accounts, particularly delicious). Labour was provided by Stuart himself, his sons Mick and Malcolm, summer-time volunteers – perhaps two or three – and 'hangers on' like Christopher Badenoch, to use his own phrase.

Helen Murray described Stuart's success with composting in the April 1954 issue of *Mother Earth*. He kept the cow, pigs and poultry housed separately at the top of the sloping garden and undertook continuous composting of their manure, both liquid and solid, with garden wastes and straw. Stuart developed

---

[14]   Drummond was author of *Charter for the Soil* (London, 1944) and *Inheritance of Dreams* (London, 1945). Lord Glentanar was an Aberdeenshire landowner with a particular interest in biodynamic cultivation. Kathleen Talbot contributed to H.J. Massingham's symposium *The Small Farmer* (London, 1947).

Figure 12.2   Robert Stuart in 1974, Measuring the Temperature of one of his
Composting Heaps. Photograph taken from *The Soil Association*
[the journal of the Soil Association] 2(4), Apr. 1984, © Soil
Association and reproduced with permission

a 'no-dig' approach to growing potatoes, planting them through a two-inch
organic surface and replacing earthing-up by another earthworm-rich application
of compost, kept in place with light wooden battens. Murray reported that the
health of the crops was generally good, and that the fruit bushes, after three
somewhat barren years, had responded spectacularly to the build-up of compost,
restored to health from degenerate stock. Stuart kept the composts separate,
partly to ensure that, if there were problems with one, only a small area of the
holding would be affected; and partly for experimental purposes, to see what
effects different animal activators and vegetable ingredients had on the growing
crops. He was of course aware that the results of such trials would hardly provide

evidence to convince advocates of chemical methods, and wanted research stations and agricultural colleges to follow, and greatly expand upon, his lead. It was also important to try to refute the suggestion that composting was uneconomic, and to convince people that conservation of organic wastes was an urgent need. With the agreement of the East Lothian local authority, Stuart established a municipal composting scheme in Gifford, a village of about 700 inhabitants served by sewage tanks. He undertook the experiment at his own expense as a commercial enterprise.[15]

An account of this project was included in a *Memorandum on the use of wastes in Agriculture and Horticulture*, presented in the autumn of 1952 to the Advisory Panel on Waste Materials of the Ministry of Materials by the Soil Association in conjunction with the Albert Howard Foundation of Organic Husbandry. Stuart left behind a typed draft of this document, which also included information on composting schemes in Dumfries, Jersey, Leatherhead, Nantwich and Nuneaton. The section on the Gifford scheme listed the materials composted as 'any type of vegetable waste, straw, chaff, weeds, and roadside wastes [and] sewage from the Gifford sewage tank'. The machines required were a three-ton Bedford lorry, a Land Rover, a John Deere forage chopper and blower, a side-rake, a sewage pump, an auto-sifter, a mixer-elevator on a Fordson tractor, and a Ransome tractor fitted out as a miniature bull-dozer. The farmer (or in the case of roadside wastes, East Lothian Council) would cut and collect the wastes; Stuart's work began with raking up the material and chopping it. The blower would then convey it into the lorry. A detailed account of the actual composting process followed, and there are, elsewhere in Stuart's archive, various photographs of the work being undertaken. Some of these are also reproduced on a DVD which Mick Stuart made, entitled *Hopes Farm Composting*. As they are shown, he asks rhetorically why, if such a project of turning wastes into fertility was technically feasible in the early 1950s, it should not be feasible on a much larger scale in the early twenty-first century. On a small scale, the scheme was a success, arousing local approval; the account of it tells us that the County Architect believed it made a valuable contribution to amenity services.

In planning the scheme, Stuart enlisted the support of the Balfour family, and a carbon copy of a letter dated 24 October 1950 from the Earl of Balfour to Major Sir G. Broun-Lindsay, Vice-Lieutenant of East Lothian, has survived, in which the Earl asks Broun-Lindsay to talk to Stuart about 'the possibility of using some of the sludge disposed of by the East Lothian County Council'.

---

[15]   Murray's article is in *Mother Earth*, Apr. 1954, pp. 21–7. An article in the *Haddingtonshire Courier*, 3 Sept. 1954, p. 5, gave an account of Stuart's demonstration of farm-scale composting on David Ogilvy's farm at Winton Hill. Eve Balfour was present on that occasion.

Figure 12.3   Compost-making on Lord Balfour's farm. Photograph, Stuart papers

Balfour described Stuart as 'a most interesting man', a view which Broun-Lindsay seems to have come to share, given that the scheme went ahead.[16]

For just under 10 years, until around early 1959, Stuart ran his farm composting enterprise, and composted the whole of Gifford's sludge for seven or eight of those years. Stuart's method involved creating a layer of approximately six to eight inches of crop residues and weeds, followed by a considerably thinner layer of lawn mowings and any organic material to be disposed of. The materials would be moistened continually by spraying. To activate the heap, animal dung, sewage sludge, pigeon loft droppings and slaughterhouse waste would be added. A sprinkling of good soil provided soil organisms, and, finally, a very sparse sprinkling of ground rock limestone was applied in order to prevent acidity. These layers were repeated until the heap reached the desired height, which on a farm was likely to be about five feet. The heaps might extend 100 yards and would reach temperatures which produced abundant steam (Figure 12.3). Heaps were turned when the temperature dropped to 70 degrees and were then allowed to re-heat. Stuart never varied this recipe, the art of which was to blend

---

[16]   By 1956, Stuart was corresponding with Lady Broun-Lindsay about the possibility of bartering Hopes compost for the droppings in her pigeon-loft (letter, 19 Apr. 1956).

materials in order to achieve a balance between air and moisture and encourage proliferation of living organisms.

Hopes compost was used by Sir David Ogilvy on his Pencaitland Estate; by the engineers Stuart Turner Ltd. of Henley-on-Thames for their bowling green; by agricultural contractors R. Wyllie and Sons of Haddington; by the Duchess of Hamilton (for whose estate Stuart undertook the building of a compost heap, using a machine called a Dungle-dozer); by Green Park Market Gardens of North Berwick; by A.W. Reynolds, a London dentist; by Church of Scotland clergy, and by many other businesses, estates and private individuals. Local consignments might be delivered by Stuart's sons, while consignments sent by rail sometimes suffered delays or disappearance, necessitating time spent on chasing them up. A substantial sheaf of correspondence relating to the business gives an idea of the work he and his sons put into it, and of his pride in it. In a letter dated 17 November 1952 to a Mrs Pass, who ran a vegetarian guest house in Dunbar, he wrote without any false modesty: 'My compost is as good as any you will buy anywhere – approved by Sir William Slater of the Agricultural Research Council, the Department of Agriculture and Health, and specially recommended by the Howard Foundation of Organic Husbandry'. A Mr J. Grieve of Edinburgh wrote in a letter of 28 May 1956 that the growth in his garden had improved considerably since Hopes compost had been applied the previous year.

From composting the sludge provided by the Gifford works, Stuart expanded into contract composting and hiring out farm machinery. His archive contains many booklets and advertising leaflets, demonstrating that he took a thorough interest in how advances in agricultural technology might serve the purposes of organic farming. For the composting at Gifford he had assembled 'ingenious machinery' which, however, could not be continuously used there. By providing a composting service for neighbouring farmers he could try to correct 'the local impression that composting meant sewage compost and demonstrate that the very best compost of all could be produced on the farms themselves at reasonable cost'.[17] Surviving correspondence between Stuart and Rupert Chalmers Watson at Fenton Barns gives some idea of what providing this service actually involved. In addition to Mick and Malcolm Stuart, this work involved a mechanic and driver, and, from the mid 1950s, a qualified motor engineer.

The relationship with Chalmers Watson is particularly interesting, and some background is necessary in order to demonstrate this. Chalmers Watson was the first subscriber to *Health and the Soil*,[18] which is hardly surprising when one considers his parental background. His father, Dr Douglas Chalmers Watson (1870–1946) and his mother Alexandra (known as Mona, 1873–1936) were

---

[17]   *Mother Earth*, Jan. 1961, p. 541.

[18]   *Health and the Soil*, summer 1948, p. 5.

noted physicians: Mona was the first woman to be awarded an MD at Edinburgh University. Douglas had been a consulting physician at the Edinburgh Royal Infirmary, where Mona was a manager. Among many achievements, Mona had helped to establish the Queen Mary Nursing Home and been physician at the Edinburgh Hospital for Women and Children. With her husband she co-edited the *Encyclopaedia Medica*, and they collaborated on a book with the very 'organic' title of *Food and Feeding in Health and Disease* (1910). Douglas Chalmers Watson also wrote on agriculture and in later life was interested in Sir Albert Howard's ideas on the relationship between humus farming and health. He inherited the Fenton Barns estate in 1923, and this provided an opportunity for Mona to work towards producing germ-free milk from the dairy herd, a cause dear to her heart since the days when she had studied tuberculosis. She developed stock-breeding techniques and improved management, creating a tuberculin-tested herd whose certified milk became an important source of supply for Edinburgh. According to her (perhaps biased) brother Auckland Geddes, by the early 1950s Fenton Barns was 'one of the show features of Scottish agriculture'.[19]

Rupert Chalmers Watson and his brother were partners in D.C. Watson and Sons, a firm which dealt in pedigree Ayrshire cattle, TT milk, seed grain, seed potatoes and poultry. It seems that Watson first expressed interest in Stuart's composting service in the autumn of 1953: Stuart suggested that Watson should visit Hopes to see the machinery in action and that Malcolm Stuart and his team should visit Fenton Barns for a week's trial in the local conditions. Offering what was apparently a reduced fee, Stuart would charge £5 a day for a service which included: two 'expert composters', an assistant and any of his machines, plus 4s. an hour for use of the chopper-blower and Dungle-dozer. 'A day' was eight hours (eight and a half less half an hour for lunch), including half an hour each way for travelling time. The trial went ahead and, although Watson's response is missing, the results appear to have been somewhat problematic. Stuart made a financial loss and there were various 'teething troubles' – perhaps caused by trying to make compost on a concrete base – but he considered the experiment worth continuing, estimating that it would be possible to make 1,000 tons of compost in 1954. By May 1954 Watson had decided that he could not, for financial reasons, take up an accelerated rate of composting; but Stuart tried to convince him that no farmer could afford to let 'organic matter run to irreclaimable waste'. Stuart's motives were not purely commercial. He considered the midden at Fenton Barns 'as near the ideal for large-scale composting as we are likely to find on any farm', and he regretted the sheer waste of compostable material. He also

---

[19]   Auckland Geddes, *The Forging of a Family* (London, 1952), p. 261. There is an irony in the fact that one of Alexandra Chalmers Watson's other brothers, Eric, was the wielder of the 'Axe' which put a premature end to Robert Stuart's naval career.

hoped to appeal to the 'great and generous' side of Chalmers Watson's nature: the kitchen garden of a local sanatorium was crying out for compost, because the doctors there wanted to grow health-promoting vegetables for the patients, and Hopes was unable to provide the amounts required. Stuart concluded his efforts at persuasion with the assurance that he would keep his charges as low as possible.[20]

Exactly what happened, the surviving letters do not reveal; but the relationship continued, with both Chalmers Watson and his brother as members of the Hopes Compost Club, making use of Stuart's composting service and, as letters from the winter of 1955–56 demonstrate, helping him gain recognition for farm composting. In one of these letters, we learn that Stuart was working at a loss, and there is a certain grievance implicit in one of the reasons he adduces for this, namely, that his workers, not being fully self-sufficient in machinery, had 'to await the farmer's pleasure'. Stuart was struggling to keep the service going, and asked Chalmers Watson to use his influence to help achieve this end by committing to writing three things which he had told Stuart orally: that use of Hopes compost had led to an increase in both the health and yield of the crops grown with it; that it would be feasible to make more than double the amount of compost, given more equipment; and that Watson and Sons would be happy to employ the Hopes composting service to convert all their residues and manures, up to a certain cost. Chalmers Watson obliged, and a carbon copy of his statement is to be found with the other correspondence between him and Stuart. Watson began by saying that, after nearly four years of using the Hopes composting service, he was confident that Stuart's pioneering efforts would 'prove in the long run to be of inestimable value to the agricultural community' and that 'endless opportunities [we]re opening up'. Stuart's methods greatly improved the farmyard manure, and the resulting material in turn improved the soil. Yields of both potatoes and grain had increased. Watson commented that unskilled farm staff tended to regard compost-making as unnecessary, and that it was essential for the process to be undertaken by a specialist organisation. The chief problem had been that Stuart's equipment was inadequate to make the quantities of compost required. Watson's concluding comments suggest that, while appreciating the benefits of compost, he was not fully committed to the organic approach. 'I hope and believe', he wrote, 'that, as the Hopes Compost Service develops, you will find an increasing demand, and before long it will be regarded as important to make really first-class compost on the general farm as it is to order one's complete fertilisers from the manure merchant'. Stuart replied

---

[20]   Robert Stuart to Chalmers Watson, 16 Oct. 1953, 19 Jan. 1954, 15 May 1954.

by return of post to express his gratitude for Watson's endorsement. We do not know how Stuart used it.[21]

A year later, the two men were still discussing how to increase the amount of composting carried out at Fenton Barns. The issue hinged on whether Stuart would be able to find sufficient equipment and manpower to ensure that Watson's workers would not need to be involved: Stuart's tasks would be to assemble the materials, to make the compost, and to spread it, for which he required volunteers who would undertake the manual work, particularly sorting and tidying materials, removing bricks, bolts, stones and other hazards. Stuart hoped to be able to undertake all this in 1957. He concluded one letter by rather mysteriously referring to reports which Watson might have heard about his 'leanings to the left in agriculture'. He had tried very hard to gain financial aid from the right, but as it was not forthcoming he was soliciting help from wherever he might get it. Watson sympathised with his pragmatic attitude. Whom Stuart had approached, this correspondence does not reveal, and no later letters in this correspondence survive.[22]

Some correspondence from the mid 1950s between Stuart and C.D. Wilson, General Secretary of the Soil Association, suggests that a number of Stuart's problems with composting were created by a member of the Association's Advisory Panel. This was Deryck Duffy, who, as a biodynamic farmer, opposed the use of sewage in composting. Stuart objected to Duffy being on the Advisory Panel, finding him 'quite a thorn in my flesh'. He publicly connected his own composting with the work of the Soil Association, but Duffy, a Lothian representative of the Association, refused Stuart's offer to put him in touch with organic growers, apparently telling him that 'he would rather eat vegetables grown with artificials than those grown on [Stuart's] compost'. When Stuart offered Duffy farm compost with no sewage in it at all, Duffy rejected this too, saying: '[W]e do not consider *anything you* make to be compost' [emphasis in Stuart's letter]. According to Wilson, most Soil Association members considered the biodynamic attitude to municipal compost unreasonable. Stuart pointed out the contradiction involved in his own compost at Fenton Barns being linked with the Soil Association's name, when the Association's local representative repudiated what he was making. A pencil annotation on the carbon copy of this letter indicates that Wilson gave no answer and made no further reference to this matter.[23]

Although Stuart often joked about 'living in Hopes', his hopes of the composting service proving viable were not realised. In a letter to Dr Hugh

---

[21]   Robert Stuart to Chalmers Watson, 11 Jan., 27 Jan. 1956; Chalmers Watson to Stuart, 10 Feb. 1956.

[22]   Robert Stuart to Chalmers Watson, 6 Feb.; Watson to Stuart, 11 Feb. 1957.

[23]   Robert Stuart to C.D. Wilson, 8 Feb.; Wilson to Stuart, 11 Mar.; Stuart to Wilson, 19 Mar. 1955.

Martin-Leake, dated 6 October 1959, he described the business as 'languishing'; he had come frustratingly close to the point where it could have snowballed, but he lacked 'another man and another £5000'. The final newsletter he produced at Hopes, shortly before the move to Chirnside in 1964, indicates that he was still looking to expand his activities: the extensive stabling at the new property would provide a base for the service where all the machinery could be kept and maintained under cover. Among the equipment, he now had a Jabelmann shredder-loader, a much-improved machine whose use had been demonstrated in Northumberland.

V

By the time he moved to Maines House at Chirnside, Stuart was in his mid 60s, but he had no intention of resigning from the organic cause. Maines House was ripe for demolition when he bought it, and its transformation into an attractive country house required months of hard work. Commanding a view over the Whiteadder and Tweed Valleys towards the Cheviot Hills, the house stood in 56 acres of land, and, from these, Stuart and his staff set about providing the food which the hotel guests enjoyed. We shall return later to his success as a hotelier. The guests included those who attended the annual Soil Association Weeks, conferences which Stuart organised and held in the spring. A good deal of material on these conferences has survived, including many reel-to-reel tape recordings of the talks given and the discussions which followed them. Stuart was organising his first Soil Association conference within two years of having moved to Maines House, and one can see its genesis in the programme drafted out in biro on sheets of graph paper sellotaped together and in the list of names on the back of a brown envelope. Various pieces of correspondence show that in March 1966 Stuart was in touch with members and non-members of the Soil Association, drumming up support: he wrote to local farmers, to the Horticultural Adviser at the East of Scotland College of Agriculture, to the Public Analysts' Laboratory at Newcastle-upon-Tyne, to the Wholefood shop in York, to Lawrence and Cherry Hills of the Henry Doubleday Research Association, and to Major Sedley Sweeny, who ran a hill farm near Brecon and undertook large-scale composting as a means of land reclamation.[24]

The duplicated letter and application form which Stuart sent out on 30 March 1966 did not give very much notice, as the Soil Association Week was scheduled for 12–19 April; but visitors were free to attend for as many days as they chose. Douglas Campbell, the research-director of the Association's

---

[24] I have had the material on the tapes copied to disc – 41 of them in all. On Sweeny, see *Mother Earth*, Apr. 1964, pp. 109–16.

farms at Haughley, would be present for some of the week, as would Robert Waller, editor of the Association's journal. On offer during the week were visits to a fully organic farm, discussions with some non-organic Borders farmers and agricultural officials, and a showing of a BBC television film about the Shropshire farm of the Association's vice-president Sam Mayall.

Stuart really began to get into his stride the following year. Much correspondence relating to the Soil Association Week of May 1967 survives, as do advertising leaflets and the duplicated programme of events. One should bear in mind that Stuart was still keeping his composting service going, as well as running a hotel and restaurant for which he produced the food. On top of all this, he organised a conference week which included the following: a visit to the organic farm of Brigadier A.H.C. Swinton; a farm walk accompanied by the Agricultural Adviser for Berwickshire; a visit to the East of Scotland College of Agriculture to study its growing trials; discussions with Campbell, Waller, the City Analyst for Edinburgh and the local Medical Officer of Health; a day's visit to Abbey St Bathans to see its farm, woodlands and organic garden; a film on deep-freezing ('of particular interest to farmers' wives'); films on gardening; a visit to the Edinburgh municipal composting works; a picnic lunch at Winton Castle, courtesy of Sir David and Lady Ogilvy; and an illustrated talk by Eve Balfour on the Haughley Experiment.

The 1968 Week was on a similar scale: it offered a 'marathon programme', as the *Berwickshire News* described it; and Stuart continued to organise and oversee such programmes every year through to 1977. His archive shows that the weeks were advertised in several Borders newspapers and that he ensured they were reported in detail; the tapes show that for a least a couple of years (1972 and 1973) he gained radio publicity as well. There is some interesting correspondence with representatives of the opposing side, whom Stuart tried to persuade to take part in debates. For instance, Alan Yeo of British Petroleum, which in 1970 was developing yeasts on selected hydrocarbon types from petroleum, to be marketed as an animal-feed supplement, rather sniffily rejected an invitation. Stuart's report of the 1969 Soil Association Week indicated to Yeo that 'the general tone of the meeting' was inappropriate to discussion of BP's product. Much more amiable was John Hawthorn, Professor of Food Science at Strathclyde University, who had argued the case for additives during the 1969 Week and requested the opportunity to argue against them in 1970; he told Stuart how much his wife had enjoyed the visit to Chirnside.[25]

More ambitiously, Stuart was keen to attract royal visitors to Chirnside. An exchange of letters with the Soil Association's General Secretary Brigadier A.W. (Bill) Vickers in the spring of 1971 indicates that Vickers met the Queen

---

[25] *Berwickshire News*, 21 May 1968. Alan Yeo to Robert Stuart, 27 Mar. 1970. John Hawthorn to Robert Stuart, 2 Feb. 1970.

Mother, who, Stuart wrote, 'was always very keen on compost and wholefood'. In 1955, she had visited the Soil Association stand at the Highland Show. He wanted Vickers to persuade her to visit Chirnside during the Soil Association Week, as he was sure she would enjoy both the food and the opportunity to participate in discussions on nutrition and health. Other correspondence is at a more humble level: for instance, the Scottish Office of the Royal Society for the Protection of Birds demanded the return of a folding display that Stuart had borrowed for his 1974 conference and had still not returned two months later.[26] There is also correspondence with prominent Soil Association figures such as Dr Norman Burman, Sam Mayall, and the Buckinghamshire farmer and miller Hugh Coates.

The many tape-recorded talks and discussions enable us not just to hear the voices of various important figures from the 1960s and '70s, but to form an impression of the organic movement's tone and atmosphere at that time. Among the speakers preserved on tape are Robert Waller; David Stickland, Waller's successor as editor of the Soil Association journal and founder of the successful marketing concern Organic Farmers and Growers; Dr Bernard Stonehouse of Bradford University, an environmentalist and Antarctic explorer; A. Harry Walters, a microbiologist, Chairman of the UK Section of the Institute of Food Technology and author of *The Living Rocks: An Introduction to Biophilosophy* (1967); Professor R. Lindsay Robb, an agricultural scientist of world renown; Mrs Dinah Williams, a noted dairy farmer in mid Wales; Sir Robert Milnes-Coates, a Yorkshire landowner who was on the Soil Association Council from the early 1960s to the late 1970s; Hugh Coates; the surgeon Laurence Knights; Arthur Hollins, Shropshire dairy farmer and marketer of organic yogurt; Dr Walter Yellowlees, a GP in Perthshire; and the nutritionist Professor Curtis Shears. Speakers at Chirnside conferences who are not preserved on the tapes include environmentalist and journalist Peter Bunyard; the scientist Dr Anthony Deavin, who himself ran a number of successful courses on biological husbandry at Ewell Technical College, Surrey, during the 1970s; nutritionists Barbara Latto and Margaret Brady; market gardener and apostle of cloche cultivation J.L.H. Chase; and, in 1977, Kenneth Barlow and Innes Pearse, doctors whose commitment to the organic movement went back to the pre-war days of the Pioneer Health Centre. Stuart's daughter Mrs Heda Borton, by then a close companion to Pearse, was also present. Pearse died the following year.

It is coincidental, yet somehow symbolic, that the Chirnside conferences came to an end at the time when a new generation of activists (which I have elsewhere dubbed 'the Seventies Generation')[27] was beginning to make its presence felt in

---

[26] Robert Stuart to Bill Vickers, 23 Apr., 21 May 1971. John F. Hunt to Stuart, 4 July 1974.

[27] Philip Conford, '"Somewhere Quite Different": The seventies generation of organic activists and their context', *Rural Hist.* 19 (2008), pp. 217–34.

the Soil Association. We know that these activists tended to regard the older generation with impatience, and, on the whole, as an obstacle to the progress of the organic movement and therefore requiring to be removed from positions of influence. Listening to the tapes of the Chirnside talks and discussions, one can to some extent understand why this was: a certain preciosity in the voices of various speakers; a strain of lament about the decadence of contemporary society; the suggestion that a diet of organically grown food might ensure less frequent strikes among the nation's troublesome workforce; a sense, despite the occasional presence of those who put a contrary view, that it was all a preaching to the converted; and, in general, a leisurely philosophical tone, with no great sense of urgency.

While there is truth in this, we know from Robert Stuart's surviving correspondence that he tried hard to involve people who were not sympathisers with the organic approach, and one could argue that the range of topics which an average Soil Association Week covered indicates a breadth of approach lacking among the more commercially minded members of the Seventies Generation. The organic philosophy has always been about much more than merely the sale of humus-grown produce: a topic which in any case featured among Stuart's concerns, given that he was a practical horticulturist and businessman who knew how hard it was to survive financially. The Soil Association Weeks were also significant in the prominence they gave to scientific topics and speakers – like Dr Anthony Deavin, Professor Lindsay Robb and Harry Walters – with scientific qualifications. What impresses the listener (or this listener, at any rate) is the seriousness of the discussions, the sense that the speakers were in fact still open to debate, and the depth of knowledge and experience represented on these occasions. One cannot accuse those present of being indifferent to the outside world: a conference is, after all, a time for withdrawing in order to think, and a willingness to explore issues in depth should not be mistaken for lethargy.

VI

In 1976, Chirnside Countryhouse Hotel achieved national fame when it won the Automobile Association's award for providing the Best Breakfast in Britain. One sometimes hears enthusiasts for organically grown food claim its superiority on grounds of taste: a very subjective standard of judgement, but one that Robert Stuart succeeded in justifying to the satisfaction of the AA. Stuart provided his visitors with compost-grown vegetables and fruit, fresh salads, meat from pigs and poultry, free-range eggs, cows' and goats' milk, honey from beehives and home-baked wholemeal bread. In a letter to Mary Langman, who ran the Soil Association's Wholefood shop, Stuart said that Chirnside's proximity to the port of Eyemouth meant that fresh herring could be on the breakfast table the morning after it had been caught.[28]

The hotel was pictured in a full-page feature about the 1967 Soil Association Week, in the *Scottish Daily Mail*, along with advertisements for Allinson's wholemeal bread and the Edinburgh wholefood restaurant Henderson's Salad Table. Two years later, the magazine *Border Life* informed its readers that the hotel was included in both the AA and RAC handbooks, and also in Raymond Postgate's *Good Food Guide*. Stuart was keen to point out that he was fighting a battle on two fronts: against the present orthodox methods of food production on the one hand and 'cranks at the other end of the scale'. Four years later, Jack Gibson, a journalist for *Scotland's Magazine*, organ of the Scottish Tourist Board, was an enthusiast, reporting that 'the taste buds never had it so good'.[29]

An undated advertising leaflet among Stuart's papers claims Chirnside as 'The Original Wholefood Hotel', serving, as far as possible, unrefined, fresh food, prepared with the least possible loss of nutriments and grown on 'soil that is fertile and biologically vital' (an interesting reference to the oft-criticised 'vitalist' strain in organicist thought). In pencil, on the back of a dinner menu, Stuart quoted a definition of 'vital' as 'of, concerned with or essential to, organic life'. This undated menu, conventional in form and content, offered cream of spinach soup, iced melon or fresh grapefruit as a starter, followed by a choice of salads (17s. 6d.), creamed haddock (£1 2s. 0d.), roast lamb or grilled steak (£1 4s. 0d.), with potatoes, peas and leeks; a selection of sweets or fresh fruit; biscuits and cheese, and, for a mere 3s. 6d. coffee with fresh cream.

Stuart's award for Chirnside's breakfasts involved him in an appearance on Scottish television. A videotape of the interview survived and has been transferred to DVD by Mick Stuart. It shows his father ill-at-ease in the garish studio and old-fashioned in his serious, rather hesitant replies; clearly he had not realised the obligation on him to provide 'soundbites'. Stuart was in no doubt that changes in agriculture had adversely affected food quality, but he came across as nostalgic rather than as angry about it. A few years later, the organic farmers Patrick Holden and Peter Segger were interviewed for Radio 4's 'On Your Farm', and the difference in tone – forward-looking, and aggressive towards the food industry – was very marked. There is a distinct poignancy about the way in which, as the closing credits roll, Stuart is sidelined by a group of other studio guests among whom can be seen the future 'national treasure', Sir Bruce Forsyth.

---

[28] Robert Stuart to Mary Langman, 29 Mar. 1967.

[29] *Scottish Daily Mail*, 2 May 1967, p. 8. *Border Life*, Nov. 1969 (photocopy with no page number). Gibson's article was reprinted in the *The Soil Association* [journal], April 1974, p. 12; some of it was lifted word for word from Helen Murray's article of 20 years earlier (see n. 15 above).

VII

At the beginning of his DVD on his father's life and work, Mick Stuart recalls that 'The Commander', shortly before his death, said to him: 'Mick, I have failed'. Mick Stuart replied: 'You will never know how much you have achieved'. This was early in 1980, when the organic movement was still very much on the fringes of public awareness. Over the next 10 years, the activists who had joined the movement in the 1970s would help propel organic produce into supermarkets and collaborate with government on establishing national standards for organic foodstuffs; organics, as they would come to be known, moved from margin to mainstream. Or so the myth would have us believe: in fact organic farming remains marginal in the UK in comparison with mainstream conventional agriculture.[30] And while the Seventies Generation prided itself on challenging the wealthy and aristocratic figures who, it was claimed, dominated the Soil Association, one cannot help but notice that the rich, famous and aristocratic have reasserted their dominance. Zac Goldsmith, Peter Melchett, television 'celebrity' Donna Air, the Marchioness of Worcester, Hugh Fearnley-Whittingstall and the Prince of Wales – to say nothing of Liz Hurley – are among the most prominent public faces of the organic movement, with the enthusiastic endorsement of dominant elements in the Soil Association. So Robert Stuart's connections with the Scottish aristocracy, and his keenness to involve members of the Royal Family in his activities, do not greatly differentiate him from various of his successors.

What, then, can we conclude from this survey of Commander Stuart's archive? First, we can agree with the correspondent with an indecipherable signature, who, writing from Liss in Hampshire in 1967, praised Stuart's 'dogged persistence and faith', qualities which are plainly evident in his papers. He was enormously dedicated, committing himself to the organic cause for nearly 40 years with no likelihood of, or interest in, achieving celebrity for himself. The account given above, of his many activities, establishes this beyond doubt, even though the surviving correspondence can be but a fragment of all he wrote.

Secondly, we learn that he was indeed a 'practical idealist': someone with much experience of the world, a sharp mind and a gift for organisation, and displaying a disciplined approach to all he undertook. One imagines that he would have been impatient with the Seventies Generation and their 'counter-culture' ideas. Stuart wanted to convince farmers, with their interest in the balance sheet, that organic farming was an economically viable proposition: hence his dislike of the 'cranks' whose presence in the organic movement would have risked alienating

---

[30] According to the *Farmers Guardian* of 10 Apr. 2009, p. 6, only 3.9 per cent of the UK's land area was being farmed organically in 2008. Lawrence Woodward, director for many years of the Organic Research Centre at Elm Farm near Newbury and a leading member of the Seventies Generation, doubts whether the organic movement has been successful, and, in fact, doubts if the organic movement even exists in any meaningful sense. Interview, 28 July 2006.

them. And thirdly, Stuart's archive offers intriguing glimpses of the organic movement's early years, the links that existed between some of its leading figures, and of internal disagreements between its different branches. We see that there was a worldwide interest in the issues that the movement was addressing, but we also gain some sense of the difficulties it faced. So much material relating to the organic movement has been lost that anything that survives takes on a greater value than would otherwise have been the case. We shall never have anything like the whole picture, but collections such as Robert Stuart's provide valuable clues as to what it might have been like.

Index

Der Verlag weist ausdrücklich darauf hin, dass im Text enthaltene
externe Links vom Verlag nur bis zum Zeitpunkt der Buchveröffentlichung
eingesehen werden konnten. Auf spätere Veränderungen hat der Verlag
keinerlei Einfluss. Eine Haftung des Verlags ist daher ausgeschlossen.